MELANESIAN RELIGION

MELANESIAN
RELIGION
G. W. Trompf

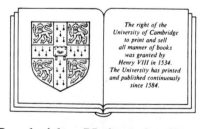

*The right of the
University of Cambridge
to print and sell
all manner of books
was granted by
Henry VIII in 1534.
The University has printed
and published continuously
since 1584.*

Cambridge University Press
Cambridge
New York   Port Chester   Melbourne   Sydney

Published by the Press Syndicate of the University of Cambridge

The Pitt Building, Trumpington Street, Cambridge CB2 1RP, UK
40 West 20th Street, New York, NY 10011, USA
10 Stamford Road, Oakleigh, Melbourne 3166, Australia

© Cambridge University Press 1991
First published 1991

Printed in Hong Kong by Colorcraft

National Library of Australia cataloguing-in-publication data:

Trompf, G. W.
  Melanesian religion.
  Includes index.
  ISBN 0 521 38306 4.
  1. Melanesia — Religion. 2. Christianity
  — Melanesia — History. 3. Cargo movement.
  I. Title.
299.92

British Library cataloguing-in-publication data:

Trompf, G. W. (Garry W.)
  Melanesian religion.
  1. Melanesia. Religion
  I. Title
  291'.0993
  ISBN 0-521-38306-4

Library of Congress cataloguing-in-publication data:

Trompf, G. W.
  Melanesian religion.
  Includes bibliographical references and index.
  1. Melanesia — Religion. I. Title.
BL2620. M4T76 1990 299'.92 90–2291
ISBN 0–521–38306–4

CONTENTS

PLATES

Plates are located following page 132

Wahgi spirit stones
(Photographed by the author, at Fatima Museum, central highlands, New Guinea)

Vlisso, god of war and hunting, from the Yuat River, Sepik River region, New Guinea
(Plate from *Oceanic Art: masks and sculptures from New Guinea* © Unesco 1968. Reproduced with the permission of Unesco)

Roviana war god, from New Georgia, western Solomons
(Photo courtesy of Bishop David Pratt)

Abelam *haus tambaran* ('spirit house'), from the east Sepik River region, New Guinea
(Photo courtesy of Antony Forge)

View of a Melanesian 'temple', in the Biak-Numfor region, west New Guinea (now Irian Jaya), taken from a nineteenth century Dutch lithograph

Interior of an Elema *eravo*, from the Papuan Gulf area, in which the *gope* boards are visible
(Photo by Frank Hurley, from the Australian Museum Collection, negative V.4784)

Asmat shield, from the south coast of west New Guinea (now Irian Jaya)
(Photo by Robert Mitton, courtesy of George and Lil Mitton)

Fuyughe war clubs, with pineapple-shaped carved stone heads, from the Papuan highlands
(Photo by the author)

Silas Eto, the Christian Fellowship Church prophet, in his ceremonial robes, at Madou, New Georgia, western Solomons
(Photo by the author)

John Teosin, the Hehela leader, in front of his house on Buka Island, off Bougainville, New Guinea
(Photo by the author)

MAPS AND TABLES

For Sharon, Carolyn, Sasha, and Leilani
toujours les tropiques!

PREFACE

This is the first introductory monograph specifically devoted to Melanesian religions. Hans Nevermann and others have surveyed Oceanic religions more generally, John Parratt has written of Papuan traditional beliefs and rituals more particularly, and there exist a number of edited symposia (those of Peter Lawrence and Mervyn Meggitt, Norman Habel, Ennio Mantovani, and others) which present case studies from a variety of Melanesian quarters. Most of these limit their focus to indigenous 'pre-contact' or 'pre-Christian' religious life, as do a few works on single themes documented from a wide range of Melanesian cultures. In this study, by contrast, I attempt to encompass both primal traditions and more recent adjustments in the one synoptic study. Fortunately there already exist useful introductory books on the planting of Christian missions and on the emergence of the so-called 'cargo cults'. It thus seems high time to reflect on Melanesian religious activity as a whole, assessing the persistence of time-inured values, explaining the relative willingness to adopt or accept radical change, and making more sense of the journey from archaic warrior cultures to modern black theology.

To achieve this, I have drawn together materials which I have previously published in journals or presented as conference papers. I give thanks, and grateful acknowledgement, to Sione Latukefu, Normal Habel and the editors of *Religious Traditions*, *Oceania*, *Point* and *Mission Review* for their kind permission to republish articles in revised form. In the case of the chapter on Dreams (in Part 1), I am thankful to Remi Dembari for being able to include his hitherto unpublished researches (undertaken when he was my student at the University of Papua New Guinea), and also to Father Theo Aerts, MSC, for permission to use our co-authored article on the Catholic Missions (in Part 2).

The book falls into two halves: the first covers the traditional scene and the second, changing Melanesia. The reader will be conducted in the first half from simpler, less methodologically sophisticated surveys to chapters in which more difficult theoretical and analytical problems are raised. These first five chapters contain certain observations which look ahead to the second half of the book; while the materials on changing Melanesia, in the second half, although intelligible as an independent cluster, can best be understood in the light of traditional factors. Again, this second half deepens analytically as the chapters proceed, from some rather basic historical accounts of the Christian missions to more complex assessments of indigenous responses to Christianity and colonialism. A greater variety of mission histories could have been treated, admittedly, and a more straightforward account given of the different types of cargo cultism, but that would have been to enlarge the book beyond acceptable bounds, and also to duplicate what is still readily available in my other writings and edited collections.

Readers should also appreciate at the outset that this book keeps the technicalities of anthropological analysis to a minimum. To reckon with the significance of the intricacies of kinship systems and totemic relationships, or the fine details as to the social recipients and economic distribution of ceremonial exchanges or even, for that matter, demographic details as to the size of settlements, cultic participation or engagement in war and trade, the reader is advised to consult individual ethnographers or anthropological works concentrated on these matters: all this simply cannot be provided within the scope of a general textbook. The whole subject of this book is so broad and complex that it has hardly been possible to consider all the relevant cultures, movements and sectional histories in any exhaustive way. It stands as an introductory work, dependent rather more on processes of judicious selection and thematic analysis than on encyclopaedic coverage. So many additional details and points of interest will have to await other publications.

The ethnographic information in the following pages derives mainly from Papua New Guinea, where most scholarly research on Melanesia has been undertaken. Other quarters, however, have certainly not been neglected. I have tried to strike a balance between illustrating religious life from as wide a range of the region's societies as possible and the need to provide readers with a necessary sense of continuity. To secure the latter, I keep returning throughout the book to a select number of cultures. The selection process has been largely determined by my own fieldwork in a variety of coastal, highland and island contexts in Papua New Guinea and in the western Solomon Islands. Suffice it to say that virtually all the societies referred to in the following pages are stateless and segmented into tribes, clans or lineages. At the time they became known to the outside world, they all occupied relatively small territories, whether landlocked valleys, islands, coastal swamp and plain, or hinterland hills. The small-scale nature of these societies made for relative egalitarianism (though various chiefdoms and more hierarchical arrangements are to be found), and for some variety in social structures and marriage patterns (matrilinearity not being uncommon, and both endogamy and polyandry occasionally present).

Of the scholars who have been especially encouraging in the production of this work I name the late Peter Lawrence of the University of Sydney, Ennio Mantovani of the Melanesian Institute and Noel King of the University of California (whose book *African Cosmos* is laid out along fairly similar lines to my own). I pay homage to my former colleagues at the University of Papua New Guinea, especially Carl Loeliger and Willington Jojoga, for many consultations over the years. I must also thank Stuart Lawrence for suggesting this production, Margaret Gilet for committing it so carefully and patiently to disk, Peter Johnson for the maps, Roderic Campbell for his perfectionism as editor, and both Lucy Davey and Irene Rolles for their computer skills right at the end of the process. As always, too, not a sentence could have been written, or would have been worth writing, without Bobbie's loving support.

Garry W. Trompf
University of Sydney

PART

1

THE
OLD TIME

MAP 1

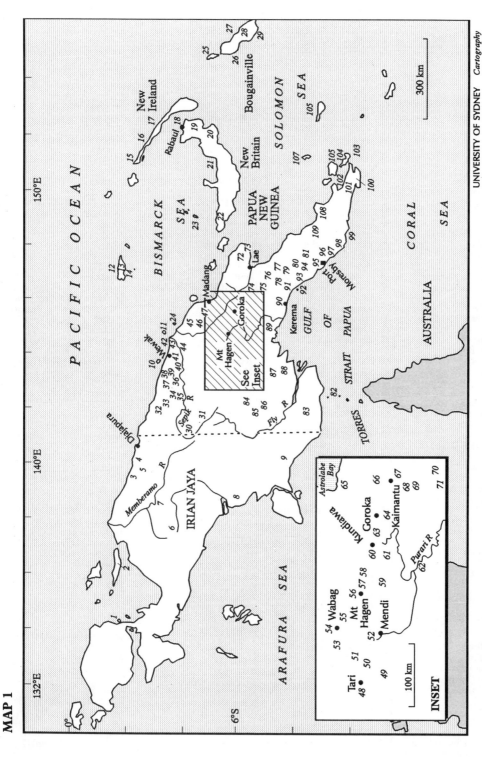

LOCATION OF TRADITIONAL MELANESIAN CULTURES: NEW GUINEA MAINLAND AND OUTLYING ISLANDS

The cultures are those cited in this book. They are shown by number and can be identified by referring to the key on the following page.

UNIVERSITY OF SYDNEY Cartography

KEY TO MAPS

NOTE: This key lists the Melanesian cultures in numerical order as used on Maps 1 and 2, and then in alphabetical order (also showing the relevant map location).

Melanesian Cultures: by number

1	Biak-Numfor	60	Chimbu
2	Yapen	61	Siane
3	Nimboran	62	Daribi
4	Sentani	63	Asaro-Gururumba
5	Kume	64	Bena Bena
6	Kapauka	65	Ngaing
7	Dani groups	66	Taiora
8	Asmat	67	Kamano
9	Marind-Anim	68	Kogu
10	Kairuru	69	Fore (Okapa)
11	Wogeo	70	Baruya
12	Manus	71	Sambia
13	Usiai	72	Hube (and Huon)
14	Matangkor/Baluan		groups
15	Lemakot	73	Yabim (Finschhafen)
16	Nalik	74	Atzera
17	Madak	75	Menya
18	Tolai	76	Mumeng
19	Baining-Sulka	77	Zia (including Seragi)
20	Mengen	78	Kunimaipa
21	Lakalai	79	Tauade (Goilala)
22	Sengseng	80	Fuyughe (Mafulu)
23	Unea (Bali Vitu)	81	Koiari
24	Manam	82	Torres Strait
25	Halia (Buka)	83	Roku
26	Kiriaka	84	Kaluli
27	Torau	85	Samo
28	Nasioi	86	Etoro
29	Siwai	87	Erave
30	Telefomin groups	88	Gogodala
31	Baktaman	89	Purari
32	Wape (Lumi)	90	Elema
33	Gnau	91	Toaripi-Moripi
34	Wam (Dreikikir)	92	Roro
35	Avatip	93	Mekeo
36	Kwoma	94	Kuni
37	Yuat	95	Motu
38	Arapesh groups	96	Rigo
39	Abelam	97	Balawaia
40	Iatmül	98	Hula-Aroma-Velerupu
41	Yangoru-Negrie	99	Mailu
42	Murik Lakes	100	Suau-Kwato
43	Buna	101	Daga
44	Angoram	102	Wedau
45	Tangu	103	Massim
46	Begesin	104	Rogeia (including
47	Garia		Normanby)
48	Huli	105	Dobu
49	Wiru	106	Muju (Woodlark)
50	Wola	107	Trobriand
51	Nipa	108	Maisin
52	Mendi	109	Orokaiva (including
53	Ipili Enga		Jaua, Tainyandawari,
54	Mae Enga		Binandere)
55	Kyaka Enga	110	Choiseul
56	Melpa (including	111	Roviana
	Tumbuka)	112	Toabaita
57	Nii	113	Kwaio
58	Wahgi*	114	Guadalcanal
59	Kiripia	115	San Cristobal
		116	Banks
		117	Espiritu Santo groups
		118	Malekula groups
		119	South Pentecost
		120	Tanna
		121	Houailou
		122	La Foa
		123	Fiji(an) groups

* The Wahgi are referred to, in the literature, as 'Mid-Wahgi', 'Middle Wahgi' and 'Wahgi'. In this work the term 'Wahgi' has been used consistently to refer to these groups.

Melanesian Cultures: reference list

Abelam (39)
Angoram (44)
Arapesh groups (38)
Asaro-Gururumba (63)
Asmat (8)
Atzera (74)
Avatip (35)
Baining-Sulka (19)
Baktaman (31)
Balawaia (97)
Banks (116)
Baruya (70)
Begesin (46)
Bena Bena (64)
Biak-Numfor (1)
Buna (43)
Chimbu (60)
Choiseul (110)
Daga (101)
Dani groups (7)
Daribi (62)
Dobu (105)
Elema (90)
Enga
  Ipili (53)
  Kyaka (55)
  Mae (54)
Erave (87)
Espiritu Santo groups (117)
Etoro (86)
Fiji(an) groups (123)
Fore (Okapa) (69)
Fuyughe (including Mafulu)
  (80)
Garia (47)
Gnau (33)
Gogodala (88)
Guadalcanal (114)
Halia (Buka) (25)
Houailou (121)
Hube (and Huon) groups
  (72)
Hula-Aroma-Velerupu (98)
Huli (48)
Iatmül (40)
Kairuru (10)
Kaluli (84)
Kamano (67)
Kapauka (6)
Kiriaka (26)
Kiripia (59)
Kogu (68)
Koiari (81)
Kume (5)
Kuni (94)
Kunimaipa (78)
Kwaio (113)
Kwoma (36)
La Foa (122)
Lakalai (21)
Lemakot (15)
Madak (17)
Mailu (99)
Maisin (108)
Malekula groups (118)
Manam (24)
Manus (12)

Marind-Anim (9)
Massim (103)
Matangkor/Baluan (14)
Mekeo (93)
Melpa (including Tumbuka)
  (56)
Mendi (52)
Mengen (20)
Menya (75)
Motu (95)
Muju (Woodlark) (106)
Mumeng (76)
Murik Lakes (42)
Nalik (16)
Nasioi (28)
Ngaing (65)
Nii (57)
Nimboran (3)
Nipa (51)
Orokaiva (including Jaua,
  Tainyandawari, Binandere)
  (109)
Purari (89)
Rigo (96)
Rogeia (including
  Normanby) (104)
Roku (83)
Roro (92)
Roviana (111)
Sambia (71)
Samo (85)
San Cristobal (115)
Sengseng (22)
Sentani (4)
Siane (61)
Siwai (29)
South Pentecost (119)
Taiora (66)
Tangu (45)
Tanna (120)
Tauade (Goilala) (79)
Telefomin groups (30)
Toabaita (112)
Toaripi-Moripi (91)
Tolai (18)
Torau (27)
Torres Strait (82)
Trobriand (107)
Unea (Bali Vitu) (23)
Usiai (13)
Wahgi (58)
Wam (Dreikikir) (34)
Wape (Lumi) (32)
Wedau (102)
Wiru (49)
Wogeo (11)
Wola (50)
Yabim (Finschhafen) (73)
Yangoru-Negrie (41)
Yapen (2)
Yuat (37)
Zia (including Seragi) (77)

MAP 2

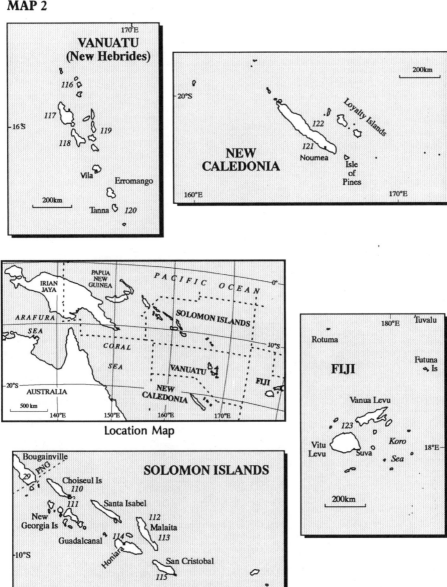

LOCATION OF TRADITIONAL MELANESIAN CULTURES: THE SOLOMONS, VANUATU, FIJI, NEW CALEDONIA
The cultures are those cited in this book. They are shown by number and can be identified by referring to the key on the page opposite.

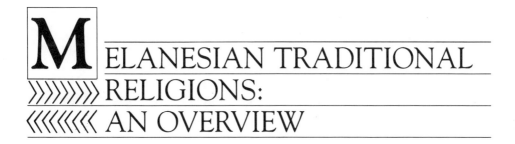MELANESIAN TRADITIONAL RELIGIONS: AN OVERVIEW

Who *were* the savages?

Thomas Henry Huxley (1825–1895) was possibly the first great European intellectual to meet Melanesians at close hand. On his way to fame as a natural scientist, he was appointed a ship's assistant surgeon and took off on 'an exploring expedition to New Guinea' under Captain Owen Stanley (from 1846). On their eventual arrival at that mysterious land, however, he had to be patient for action. Coming up on deck each day to gaze at the distant jungles of Papua from the safety of the 28-gun frigate, the *Rattlesnake*, he found himself more than often exasperated. The heat (for which Europeans were usually overdressed) was unbearable enough, but much more so was Captain Stanley's stubborn refusal to send a landing-party ashore, so paranoiacally suspicious was he that the 'savages' would stage an attack. What Huxley could see of the local people at a distance made him more interested in them than in the flora and fauna so important for his researches as a young biologist; yet, it was not until mid-August 1849 that he felt he had genuinely encountered the so-called 'savages'.

After 'symbols of friendship' were exchanged with the inhabitants of 'Brumer' (properly Bonarua) Island — and Huxley found their signals quite 'ludicrous' — an individual was allowed on board to be presented, just to make it awkward for the fellow, among the anchor chains. His face blackened, and in contrast to a necklace of white cowries (the string of which he had placed between his teeth) this 'great wag', as Huxley called him, put on a show by beating off a drum roll on a tin can. He danced and was enthusiastic about it, so much so that Huxley, evidently forgetting the man's unmanageable position and reading into this behaviour all the old London stories about the trances of blackmen, noted in his diary that 'the wag was like to go out of his senses, prancing about on his unstable foundation'.[1] Further encounters with the islanders of the Louisiade Archipelago were to come as the ship's journey progressed, at least two episodes being not so pleasant as black hosts and white foreigners were brought close to blows. On one occasion a 'portly member' of the ship's gun room was cut off by the locals, and 'only saved his life by parting with all his clothes as presents to them, and keeping them amused by an impromptu dance in a state of nature under the broiling sun', until a relief party stopped what seemed like an ironical 'payback' for the unpaid, uncomfortable performance of the 'wag on chains'.[2]

More's the pity that reciprocities were limited to an exchange of iron axe-heads for some foodstuffs, water and goodwill, and that Huxley could not persuade his fellow voyagers on one occasion that they were being invited to a feast. 'To my mind', he wrote, 'the killing [of] a pig among these people is considered a great occasion, a sort of grand feast in their church.'[3] This quaint reflection combines a touch of paternalism with a characteristic lunge at the Christian church he had rejected back home. As a teenager his faith had been cruelly tested through witnessing the dissection of a corpse. Yet, though by the time of the cruise he was something of an 'agnostic' (it is he who has been credited with inventing the term), there is, as he left that primal and mysterious Papua, a nice touch of residual paganism in the mind of the young biologist who found religion too much of 'one wild whirl'. 'We are fairly off', he spills out in his diary for 8 January 1850, 'blessed by all the Gods therefore. Today finished eight months since we have been in harbour — I mean of course in a civilized place.'[4]

Most of the earlier impressions that Europeans gained of Melanesia's religions are locked away in this scenario. The themes of ritualized greeting, dancing, states of possession, simple trading, feasting along with a readiness to retaliate, and savagely — all went back to the drawing-rooms of Britain (and in fact, together with the reputation for cannibalism, all were in rougher forms already there). Huxley doubtless reported on his experiences to his friend, Herbert Spencer, an early sociologist, whose attention was also drawn to a published account of the voyage by John MacGillivray. Thus, Spencer could confidently write of the 'New Guinea people' in 1874 (at the time when the London Missionary Society was beginning its work along the Papuan coast) that any one of them was more than likely to welcome you with the same standard salutation. 'Touch the nose with the forefinger and thumb of one hand, and pinch the skin on each side of the navel with the other; repeating at the same time "*maga suga*"'.[5]

The whole representation in the writings of these two Englishmen is, of course, polemically evolutionary, both scholars being the chief advocates for the Darwinian cause during the last four decades of the nineteenth century. Social Darwinists proposed that, in the overall history of mankind's social forms, including religion, there was a procession from lower, elementary, primitive forms to higher, complex, civilized manifestations, following the general law of progress. Put briefly, Spencer's position makes the point nicely: all religion begins with the worship of ancestors; ancestors, in the course of time and in select cultures, become elevated into the gods of such pantheons found in ancient Rome and modern India; belief in one supreme being is a later development. Even monotheism, according to Spencer, moved out of cruder, more concrete approaches (the warrior's god of the Old Testament and Islam) to more subtle and abstract religions (Christianity). Protestantism improved on Catholicism, furthermore, by purging Christianity of images and magical associations; but best of all, and most civilized, was a position beyond that, one which left all outward expressions of worship and ritual behind, and simply conceded that an unknown force governed all — the great unknowable behind the law of evolution. For Spencer, then, the lowest was savage, and the highest had to be civilized, agnostic and (one justifiably suspects) English.[6]

Huxley's experiences in southern seas, it appears, influenced Spencer's formulation of this 'ghost theory of religion' (that all religion began with ancestor veneration). Significantly, Huxley was embraced by an Aboriginal chief at Cape York who took him as 'the returning spirit of his dead brother'. Even if Spencer might have later conceded there was some evidence of belief in a supreme being among New Guinea people, it never suited the theoretical preconceptions he had settled on by the late 1850s that nothing profound could come out of Melanesia, so full he deemed it to be of 'rude superstitions'.[7] The religions of civilized and primitive were thus presumed to be poles apart, and this presumption unfortunately left its heavy imprint on subsequent popular views of the 'Oceanic tribes'.

Had either one of these British researchers possessed the opportunity to return to Bonarua Island, however, they would surely have found their snap judgements and aphorisms sorely tested. The islanders there actively honoured a supreme being and great Dweller-in-the-Sky under the name Yabwahine. He was:

> the god of plants, land, seas and all creation. They believed that he saw all human beings and could punish anyone doing evil to others. They also believed that there were spiritual worlds, where the spirit of the dead person would go . . . However, they strongly believed in the pay-back system for wrong-doing while on earth and that Yabwahine also punished the wrongdoer . . . in the human . . . and in the spiritual world.[8]

This 'primal monotheism', as later theorists would have called it, at least shared certain points of principle (though perhaps not detail) in common with the Old Testament tradition and popular forms of western Christianity. As controller of crops, trees and animals, Yabwahine was understood to have imposed special laws (not to waste life while hunting, but to kill selectively; to clean the coconut tree after climbing it; to clean the gardens, and so on). Admittedly, the Bonarua emphasis was on the fear of requital if tabus were not kept, rather than on a god of love as found in the New Testament (or on an uninvolved unknowable for agnostics); yet, who would deny the role of fear among most Christians as they reckon with consequences of 'breaking the rules'? In any case, if Spencer considered conceptions of deity to be more profound when a divine agent was deemed to be less personal and to be high above mere mortals, he could have found such ideas — had he ever had the gumption to leave England — in various quarters of Melanesia. Aitawe, for instance, was held to be the One without whom the (Mae) Enga universe could not be sustained (central New Guinea highlands); the Ngaing Parambik (hinterland Rai Coast, Madang), who first 'put' the natural environment — 'land, rivers, wild animals, birds and plants (including totems), and even war gods' — was somehow remote and elevated beyond all else, 'all pervasive' and 'without fixed sanctuary'.[9] There are other cases besides and, although such monotheistic-looking themes form but one part of a very complex religious scene, there is more than enough to call the lie to early cultural imperialists who have written off Melanesians (and so-called 'negrito' peoples in general) as among 'the lowest races' of humanity.

Today, over a century after these early Darwinian exercises in misunderstanding, we know better, hopefully. Melanesia has been revealed as the home of about one-third of mankind's languages, and that means — considering how languages are so crucial in defining discrete cultures — just as many religions. It is now eminently clear that accurate generalizations about Melanesian traditional religions are very difficult to make; it is also becoming more palpable that anyone wishing to assess these religions has first to gauge the effect of over one hundred years of prejudice and ethnocentricities on one's estimates. There has been a long voyage of consciousness from the time when it was acceptable to write in the official *British New Guinea Annual Report* that certain Melanesians were 'more ape-like than any human beings seen', and were 'cannibals from sheer love of human flesh' or of 'common desires', to the present situation in which there is just enough conscience and knowledge to brand such remarks 'racist'.[10] It is a journey unfortunately still not over, and there is reason to be exasperated that there are still many who are simply too frightened of losing something of their own authority and self-esteem to reckon all peoples as worthy of respect and all of them as possessing certain profound insights, however strange to foreigners, about life and reality.

En route to the present, the rattlesnake of history has not only sloughed its skin but loudly rattled its tail across Melanesia. Change in attitudes to the beliefs and practices of indigenous cultures, borne out through a complex interaction between intruders and those intruded upon, colonizers and colonized, has taken shape within the wider context of imperialism. There are lots of ironies in this history: Germans, who did not trust the 'lying, thieving natives' bought great parcels of land from them for the unjust prices of mere beads; Europeans and Japanese, who looked down on so-called savages, found themselves on the Melanesian islands engaging in forms of warfare far more horrific than tribal fighting, sometimes exposing their dishonour to the locals by desperate acts (such as the looting of the bombed-out Burns Philp's bulk store in Moresby in 1942). Overall, it is remarkable how so many Melanesians were able to adjust to very rapid shifts of the post-war era — along the path from the Stone to the Jet Age — and often coped better than the curiously motley bunch of colonials bringing the changes (or even better than the intellectuals who, coming in and out of universities and 'the field', wrote so much about 'the strain' of it all).

The missionaries were part of this saga-like voyage. They were different for having stayed very much longer among Melanesian peoples than most of the foreigners and, as I have recently written elsewhere,[11] despite their reputation for paternalism, those who brought the Christian message had to come to terms with the values and resilient properties of traditional religions. It was mostly through the missionaries' written observations and their role as informants that accurate, more sympathetic accounts were given, and that Melanesians were encouraged to write about their own cultures. I say this with qualifications: even the best of the old missionaries wanted to eliminate what they considered the worst in the old traditions. A few might have believed the south seas housed some lost tribes of Israel and harboured traditions like the 'books of the Old Testament',[12] but most saw the horrors of heathenism, not the vestiges of veracity. Even today, moreover, there is a definite conflict of approaches between 'conservative' and 'open-ended' styles of missiology; the conservatives still play the old tune of bringing the Light of the Gospel into a dark, savage and unevangelized arena ruled by Satan, and to this day can write in mid-Victorian terms of 'highland dandies adorned with parrot wings' (shades of Huxley's 'great wag'!).[13] The pressures of prejudice can still be found, then, even among those whose hearts are boundless with good intentions.

The Melanesians themselves have often experienced difficulties, having to come to terms with the problem of a great new Truth which seems to drive holes in so much of what they have held sacrosanct in the past. I have met many who were under the impression (conveyed by certain missionaries) that their people did not ever possess anything fine enough to be called a 'religion'; I can remember how various young nationals at the University of Papua New Guinea expressed their astonishment that courses in Religious Studies (sponsored by the Melanesian Council of Churches) took in traditional Melanesian religions, not just Christianity (and other well-known faiths). Thus, the inhabitants of the 'Last Unknown' have often been made to feel that 'nothing good comes out of their Nazareths', and it is probably only in recent years, after various piecemeal attempts at cultural revival (by way of art and dancing) that the real issues have begun to be exposed. In any case, the Melanesians themselves have long been victims of their own prejudices, and each group found it difficult to accept as intelligible, let alone true, the beliefs of another. 'Sheer superstition!' shouted an adamant Fuyughe prophet as he stole a sacred pig-tusk out of a Seragi sanctuary (in the Papuan highlands); and (to take a New Guinea islands case) who among the Tolais took a Baining belief seriously when the Bainings themselves were reckoned sub-human?[14] A few

Melanesians, as with the Polynesians before them, became Christian missionaries themselves at the 'frontiers', and they were just as ready as many a white
to advise the elimination of practices which they found utterly alien to their
new-found faith.

   One fact remains certain, however. The 'pre-pacified', 'pre-missionized'
inhabitants of Papua New Guinea and the Solomon Islands were not the
ignoble savages outsiders have often made them out to be (although there is no
need to re-ennoble them through a compensatory romanticism either). Those
foreigners, too — who, by some providential paradox, created the conditions
for Melanesians to see themselves as whole blocks of territories (rather than as
small tribal groups) and form the newest nations on earth — were, themselves, only rarely untainted with barbarism, greed and discourtesy. And,
from syphilitic castaways and ruthless blackbirders to certain insensitive
administrators and exploitative multi-nationalists, much non-Melanesian
'savagery' abounds. One might also say that Melanesia was exposed to the
world when it was 'closing time' for Western civilization, to use Norman O.
Brown's phrase[15] — when the old imperialisms were scrambling for remain-
ders before going out of business. For Melanesians, when they greeted and
pinched their navels before the 'whiteman', it was 'opening time'; yet, after a
century in which the old proud inquisitiveness has mingled with lack of
confidence, or a sense of inferiority, much business is left to be done.

Major themes in Melanesian religions

If the Melanesian religious tapestry is so variegated that generalization is
risky, there is still a sufficient number of recurrent motifs or themes begging
for analysis, and a good deal of ignorance and misconception to counter by
disclaimers. This chapter is intended to be a general, introductory account of
traditional religions; it concentrates on major features and, for sheer manageability, mainly draws on examples from Papua New Guinea and the
Solomons. In this way the reader will be prepared for more in-depth chapters
on themes in traditional Melanesian religious life which are of most interest to
modern students.

Deities and spirits

There is no uniform pattern of belief about 'spirit-beings' in Melanesia. The
number of such powers in the host of traditional cosmoi vary from the many to
the one. When Ralph Bulmer lived among the Kyaka Enga in the New Guinea
highlands, for instance, thorough anthropologist as he was, he uncovered as
many as ten classes of spirits including a (recently imported) fertility goddess,
'nature demons', 'sky beings', a female 'forest spirit', 'cannibal ogres', 'minor
native spirits' and the dead both recent and long since departed. When
Maraga Momo, the Motuan pastor, found himself sent as the first missionary

to Roku in the wet Trans-Fly region of Papua as late as 1952, the people there informed him they only knew one great spirit (apart from their sky-dwelling ancestors) — the Originator and cosmic Serpent, Kampel — and, although he gave birth to a son ('the heavenly rainmaker') and other beings, these could all be prayed to as the one 'Primordial' (*Gainjan*) now in the sky.[16]

If some peoples possess the sense of a transcendent being in terms of their cosmos (as in this last case or that of the Mae Enga), others personified the moving objects in the sky — the sun and moon (as with brother Ni and sister Hana, deities important for fertility among the Huli (central highlands, Papua), and the Morning Star — all of whom often make their appearance in mythologies in human guise, even being encountered by mortals. If some differentiated 'place-spirits' (pidgin: *masalai* etc.) from 'gods', and treated the place-spirits as being less important for being dangerous powers located in specific areas, others could talk of these same sorts of powers as welcome 'Protectors' of recognizable mountains. So, among the Fuyughe of the Papuan highlands, for instance, each cluster of hamlets could expect its *sila* (or mountain spirit) to look after that tribal area below its gaze, and scare off enemy trespassers who might think of a surprise attack. If some, however, so found 'divinity in nature' — in Jari, for instance, who urinated of old to open up the Sepik river system; or Karaperamun, the spirit of Tanna Island's volcano (southern Vanuatu) — others worshipped deities to extend their arms in war. I think of Koukoinamb, 'the Power behind the Stone', a raised mortar which had been ground and rounded by some long forgotten generation, yet which the Wahgi (New Guinea highlands) took to be placed by an occult strength demanding pig sacrifices to bring fertility and victory in war (see plate 1). And there were other formidable tribal defenders: from Vlisso, the snub-nosed Sepik god of war and hunting (see plate 2), to the terrifying ear-ringed idols of New Georgia, Western Solomons (see plate 3).[17]

Such variety should make us wary of assuming any uniformity in the conceptualization of spirit-powers and their attitudes. Veritable polytheistic pantheons are virtually absent; yet, sometimes the gods appear fully-fledged, with powers and creativity impressive enough for any missionary to use the name of one of these gods as the vernacular equivalent of the supreme being (if not then, perhaps, the terms 'high- or sky-god').[18] In other instances there seems a much less clear distinction between deities and the dead. We learn from traditions about Vlisso, the Sepik (or more accurately Yuat) River god just mentioned, that he was once a great man who slayed many people, and, after his suicide, received sacrifices of appeasement. If that is an apparently clear example of euhemerism (or of humans being deified in the course of time), elsewhere we simply find conceptual fluidity. 'What is a *vui*?', the well-known Dr Codrington asked a Banks Islander (Vanuatu), and the answer (translated): 'It lives, thinks, has more intelligence than a man; knows things which are secret without seeing; is supernaturally powerful with *mana* [spirit effect], has no form to be seen; has no soul, because itself is like a soul.'[19]

And we will be disappointed if we seek many better attempts at definitions, because formal, doctrinal instructions into the nature and attributes of the spirit-powers have been rare in Melanesia: one 'feels into' one's cosmos and its inhabitants through an organic process, with paradigmatic moments of disclosure into cultural secrets at initiations, until one knows what to *do*, rather than possess speculative knowledge for its own sake. It is far more important to learn whether the deities are supportive or harmful, and need offerings of the confident or apotropaisms of the nervous, and whether they are ethically neutral or like the retributive Yabwahine and the Huli Datagaliwabe, whom 'one man described . . . as a giant . . . with legs astride', looking 'down upon all' and punishing 'lying, stealing, adultery, murder, incest, breaches of exogamy and . . . [of] taboos'.[20]

Differing classes and hierarchies of spirit-powers in Melanesia certainly present us with a forest of complexity, yet Herbert Spencer and his supporters were not completely without warranty when they sensed the special role of ancestors or the departed for south-west Pacific religions. That the dead can take a prominent place in religion, however, need not be a clue to primitivity. Just because the Indo-Europeans have shown (distastefully?) little interest in their ancestors does not mean they are higher on the ladder of progress. The Chinese and the Japanese, for example, have achieved their so-called 'high civilizations' while paying very dutiful respect to their forebears. Whatever comparisons are worth, however, one theme which tends to bind Melanesian religions into a common whole is an endemic concern to preserve good or untroubled relations with the departed.

There is a perennial (rather too European-style) question asked in this connection: did Melanesians *worship* or *venerate* the dead? Or, put another way, did they sacrifice, offer prayers and perform other rituals before them as if they were gods? One can see the question itself is already loaded, and its answers are very vulnerable to subjectivity; and I suspect it has become an important question, ironically, because the resilience of Melanesian traditional religions has shown itself in this very concern for those who pass to the next life. The bearers of Christianity worked towards displacing the old notions of deity by the new; there seemed to Melanesians more leg-room to continue paying deference to the dead (especially considering masses were said for them in Catholic areas), and certainly nothing in basic Christian teaching enjoined their neglect. But the picture, nevertheless, remains highly complex.

It is no longer clear that some of the more sophisticated generalizations about Melanesian concerns for the departed can stand the test of time. In 1965, for example, Peter Lawrence and Mervyn Meggitt drew a working distinction between seaboard and highland religions 'on the basis of their beliefs about the dead'. Most highlanders, they observed, make 'a sharp division between the recent and more remote dead', while the seaboard peoples simply concentrate on the recently departed; the two scholars concluded that seaboard confidence in the unquestioned support of their dead makes for more distinctly 'religious' societies, while highland fear of ghosts engenders a certain secular flavour, or less dependence on the more-than-human. This loose dichotomy has already been questioned, and Peter Lawrence himself, before his recent death, accepted the need for a revision. Are there not coastal and island Melanesians who have been fearful of ghosts — certainly of ones not related to them? (Ann Chowning, to take one critic, directs us to the Lakalai and the advice they took to avoid danger and apply nettle leaves to strangers suspected of a ghostly status.) And a new look at highland intellectual and religious life, after the over-emphasis of anthropologists on social structures, shows how impossible it is to prove that highlanders are less 'religious-minded' than others. Nervousness about ghosts, of course, can make for a distinctive approach to religion — through warding off adverse influences, or apotropaism — but that could make people more, not less concerned about the spirit-world. The distinction between remote and recent dead, moreover, can be important in some cognitive and ritual contexts but may melt away in others. In the giant Wahgi pig-kills, for instance, and thus in what is surely the greatest expression of that culture's religious life, a preliminary sacrifice of pigs is made to the *kipenbang* (= 'red spirits' = '[more distant] ancestors') on the first of the festival's three major days. Yet, it is all the *kipe* (ancestors), as collectively conceived by the Wahgi, who are to witness (and be both pleased and honoured at) the most spectacular proceedings to follow.[21]

Far more significant than the status of the dead in time or memory, to go further, are the cultural repertoires that guide how one relates to the dead when appropriate to do so, or when their presence is attested in particular situations. Among many others, Trobrianders leave food for the dead outside their houses after feasts, not expecting it to be difficult for them to come such a long way from the westward isle of Tuma to pay a visit. The Mafulu (or eastern Fuyughe), by contrast, who hold that the great majority who have died rise to the mountains and do not interfere with humans thereafter, used to bar their doors against ghosts at night, because those among the dead whose bodies had not been disposed of properly were believed dangerous, especially after sundown. Since the Roro (coastal Papua) held that anyone dying a quick, unexpected death (by ambush, crocodile, for instance) became a wandering ghost in the bush, there was good reason to avoid straying from the village nocturnally and much discussion in the morning as to the meaning of noises through the dark hours. Among these people, then, some dead were feared, others revered. When it came to requesting aid, moreover, a Roro might call upon the dead, whether remote or near, most appropriate to the present need. Bishop Navarre overheard a Roro man's 'prayer' for a good fishing catch in 1889 (a quite inappropriate one according to the image proposed by Lawrence and Meggitt for a seaborderer): the names of long-famous ancestor fishermen were first run off, then a few names of the more recently departed, including a woman, with a final inclusion of the requester's own name. Pleas which the Roro might put to their dead, others might put to a god (as at Murik Lakes, Sepik coast); so, variations in attitudes and ways of dealing with the deceased keep on eluding safe generalization, and are complicated by the variables of individualism and innovation in cases where the prescriptions of tradition are not hidebound. A point often strangely missed, too, is that one's own dead and the dead of one's enemies are almost invariably sharply distinguished, and the latter always thought ill-disposed.[22]

On rare occasions one can find instances of the apparent treatment of the dead as gods, and so handled worshipfully. The stern Sir Ghost who 'administers an impersonal government' from the Manus house-rafters may be one such case (New Guinea islands), though he eventually gets thrown peremptorily into the sea and replaced by another when, on the death of the family head, his job is done. The most common outlook across the region, however, places the dead as if they are still part of, even if much freer and more powerful in comparison to, the community of the living. Those released from this life take their natures with them for good or ill, and are rarely thrust out of the cosmos or the network of social relationships they leave behind. Occasionally (too occasionally for the neo-euhemerist Spencer!), they may metamorphose into deities (the prominent Lakalai 'sib ancestor' Sumua became a volcano god, evidently); commonly some event or movement in the environment (such as fire-flies, birds, fungi, speckled sunlight) or the very locations where their corpses have been deposited, will betoken their presence.[23]

All this only goes to confirm, unfortunately, that themes or a selection of phenomena cannot be effectively studied in isolation — that no adequate account of Melanesia's beliefs about the spirit world, indeed, could ever be given without also considering the cosmologies and mythologies of the region (an exercise inevitably drawing in still more extra-human agencies than we have so far discussed) or without a whole range of social facts also being assessed.

Cosmologies and mythologies

Lawrence and Meggitt have contended that Melanesian cosmoi generally have two main parts: on the one hand, there is the 'natural environment' with 'its economic resources . . . and human inhabitants'; on the other, there is the 'non-empirical realm' of 'spirit-beings' and impersonal 'occult forces'. It is characteristic of Melanesian world-views, according to Lawrence and Meggitt, that these two parts are not strongly demarcated (as in the West), however, and the perspective is lateral rather than vertical. The Mae and Kyaka Enga certainly believe in the existence of sky people — these beings, nonetheless, occupy 'a physical replica of this earth above, and as for most spirit-beings in most societies, they are assumed to live somewhere on the earth'.[24]

This overview, however much in need of refinement, helps to remind us that each Melanesian cosmos was not vast. People had a fair degree of intimacy with their own cosmos; it was only when they undertook inter-territorial trade ventures (by sea or land) or were engaged in attack or flight on foreign soil that that sense of intimacy diminished (at least so far as the adult males were concerned). The world was bounded, and only its inner core or confines really counted and was secure. The Huli will assure you that the sun rises up quickly from the region of the Enga (in the east), and goes to sleep just as rapidly in the direction of Lake Kopiago (to the west). It does not shine directly over Mount Bosavi to the south or the Porgera in the north, it passes directly over the Huli, who inhabit 'the best part of the earth'. In the main valley occupied by Wahgi tribes the movement of clouds is traditionally understood to result from the ancestors pushing them backwards and for-wards across the sky, the dead being disposed of on the high peaks in former times. The position of the moon is important in deciding whether the timing of a giant pig-kill is propitious, but the reckoning is based on where the rising moon lines up on the mountain tops (from very loosely defined points of observation); it is thus worked out in relation to a very circumscribed universe. Where interest in the heavenly bodies was more highly developed than this (such as with the memorized location of stars for navigational purposes among the Biak Islanders of west New Guinea, or Irian Jaya), it was still very much formulated in terms of highly localized cosmoi.[25]

Such limits on the world are likely to have a bearing on beliefs about the exploits of culture-heroes (sometimes called special 'creative' or *dema* deities) as well as about so-called 'totems'. As Theo Aerts has ably argued, there is a need to classify myths and views about these special agencies with care; but here (while nonetheless referring readers to his interesting analysis) I will make my own working generalizations. According to various Melanesian traditions, beings (of human form and qualities but with supra-human powers and abilities) were abroad in the land during primordial time, bestowing on a given group's ancestors 'the skills of warfare, food production and other technologies', and even establishing certain features of the environment. These figures then went away, or died, although there can be consensus expectation that they may return or be re-contacted. Totems, on the other hand, or specific species of objects in the cosmos on which clans (or other specific groups defined by blood ties or activity) place sacred meaning or tabus to identify themselves, are usually already a visible part of the 'known order'. In either case, however, mythic wanderers and totems appear as primary components of an ordained pattern of things, which normally carries the quality of having always been there since humans began. It is usually up to humans to discover or have disclosed to them what is already there.[26]

I have used the term 'cosmologies' here to denote pictures of the world in spatial terms, and with regard to this term one asks whether a people believe there are realms above and below the known earth (notions of an order of life underground are quite common in Melanesia),[27] and which parts of the preconceived cosmos are populated by which agencies, human or otherwise. 'Mythologies' I take to be narratives which sacralize the accepted cosmos, showing in memorable form and suggestive phrase how various parts of the world came into being or, better still as a generalization, how everything came to be as it now is. Perhaps there is room to draw a line between tale and myth, for certain Melanesians themselves (the Lakalai, for example) distinguish between entertaining anecdotes (such as 'how the pig got its flat nose, why the wallaby has short forelegs') from stories which were held to be true and vital for the group. However funny, fictitious or even lewd and outrageous, the varieties of narrative nevertheless carry confirmation of what is culturally expected — endowing life and its different aspects with deeper meaning or assurances; and, when used innovatively (a dream being transformed into a new myth, for example), they usually build on rather than break with traditional world-views.[28]

Some myths manage to intimate the limitations of the cosmos, the creation of its present form, and the implications its character has for humanity, all in one and the same breath. For a long time I have felt this to be true of a myth belonging to the Zia-speaking Seragi, a hunter-and-gatherer group from the Papuan highlands now without identity as a result of having been ordered to settle with lower lying villages by the colonial administration. 'About five generations ago at Dubiti', it begins (and the time-depth of traditional Melanesian myths is characteristically limited), a snake was captured after it had stolen sugar cane in the gardens. The adults hung it in a net bag, however, while they went for firewood, leaving only the children in the hamlet. The serpent then turned into a proud, dancing warrior, who warned the children that, once the catch was cooked, a great catastrophe would occur, so that they should persuade their parents to flee to the mountains. Only one family heeded the warning, however, and when the snake was cut and placed in the (earthen) oven, 'there was a huge thunderous landslide' which carried the hamlet and surrounding land away 'into the Ilamba and Beuva rivers, destroying all the people with it'. The story about the primal serpent (and here is a motif found among many cultures) seems to bear both aetiological and sacralizing properties. It taught the Seragi about the unchallengeable nature of things, and it gave cosmic (if also implicitly tragic) significance to their fragile, forest-bound existence without a sedentary village life.[29]

Myths, in my estimation, are absolutely necessary for human society, offering security fundamental for social health. Often denigrated by westerners as 'fairy tale' and 'false history', myth has been misunderstood by those failing to appreciate that the conveying of truth may require more than one type of expression. Melanesia's mythologies, moreover, as well as its world-pictures, reflect its people's remarkable affinity with the environment, which was rarely over-exploited for its natural resources and this partly on account of preconceptions about preternatural forces found in it.[30] Admittedly, fear was an important component in this environmental consciousness, with talk of

sprites and ogres, of spirits in awesome and eerie places, manifesting themselves in stagnant water, whirlpools, birds of omen, reptiles in unusual
contexts, great fish, snails, luminescent fungus, dead trees and so forth. Yet
this prevalent sense of a preternatural life in select environmental features (an
awareness which has been popularly and wrongly called 'animism', as if all
nature were endowed with 'soul') usually squared with experiences and
common sense. Mosquito-ridden stagnant pools and sickness do have a
connection, for example, even if secularized westerners do not see spiritual
forces behind either; and injunctions to women and children not to wander
near isolated, allegedly spirit-laden places, nor go out at night, at least resulted
in saving lives from being lost in ambush.

Reference to danger from human attack can hardly stop with an allusion;
one of the distinctive features of Melanesian world-pictures is that the cosmos
is peopled by enemies, and often fringed by the 'otherness' of groups with
different tongues and customs. Mythology, too, along with other oral literature, has been found replete with associations of warrior exploits, and no
account of Melanesian religion can be adequate without considering social
strife, instability and the means of holding them in check.

Revenge, reciprocity and the explanation of significant events

It has been a perverse tendency of some modern analytical scholarship to
consider war and economics as if they are distinct from religion. The task of a
much needed multi-disciplinary investigation is to reconsider how they have
all been integrally related; in particular, traditional Melanesian societies
virtually cry out for a more adequate, synthetic understanding. Taking up this
theme, I will be suggesting (in chapter 3) that one sensible alternative
approach is to interpret motives for revenge and exchange (or 'negative and
positive reciprocity' in Marshall Sahlins's terms)[31] as reflections of consensus
rationality, or modes of thinking and problem-solving, which in turn interrelate with the way a given group explains trouble, sickness and death in its
midst.

A society has recourse to a range of reasons for sanctioning retaliation
against enemies or punishment on its own members, and reasons for such
requitals are normally discussed in group situations long before they are
enacted. The same pre-establishment of norms underlies material subsistence;
precedent and long experience are vital for deciding trading partner relationships and other bonds of trade and economic organization. The vicissitudes of
war and exchange are the most obvious features of change in the life of any
society, especially those of smaller scale, with adjustments having to be made,
or a new turn of events to be met with an appropriate response, when someone
dies or falls sick or is unable to meet his or her obligations. The heart-beat of
Melanesian religions, I estimate, lies in that constant round of give-and-take
— or of payback, both vengeful and conciliatory — from which has been

generated great warriorhood, the excitement of ceremonial exchange, the anxiety felt during funerary and healing rituals, and the most prolonged intra-group discussions over why events turned out as they did.

Retribution against enemies took a variety of forms: the more formal array of plumed warriors lined up against each other; the unexpected ambush; the employment of a sorcerer to effect a special vendetta; the refusal to invite a clan to a grand presentation of food and valuables, and so forth. This is a side to life which appears to represent the very opposite to the teachings of love and peace borne by Christian missionaries; for this reason, it can be used to malign Melanesian traditional ways as wretched and uninspiring. Sensitivity concerning radical cultural differences is required here. Defensive retorts on the old order's behalf, with the comparative claims that warriors armed with clubs and spears look innocuous beside the sophisticated weaponry of most so-called Christian nations, can threaten a balanced discussion as well. It is preferable to acknowledge in the first instance past realities for what they were: that tribal religion and violence against enemies were integral, and that the highly valued pursuit of manliness and the sense of fulfilling obligations conditioned warriors as they killed, took heads or even ate enemy flesh 'on behalf of' their people.

> The muscular vigour, the armed skill in face of beast and track of prey, the brilliant flashes of energy as the spear-shafts are hurled quivering into the air against the enemy, the exhilaration of victory itself, as well as the precarious exploit to retrieve one's dying clansman from the field in the moment of defeat, are all close to this primal anthem of life.[32]

Thus, the pre-contact atmosphere of 'military uncertainty' — with small-scale, separated 'revenge wars' being played out across the whole region — demands an effort at reconstruction. It was in those pre-contact days when the Iatmül lit pyres each night along the banks of the Sepik River, for the better spotting of hostile raiders; and when Dani warriors sat tense in their 20 ft (6 m) watchtowers, looking out for intruders within range of their gardens and women in the spacious Baliem Valley (of Irian Jaya).[33]

Success in war, furthermore, or in the working out of conflicts with enemies, was closely bound up with Melanesian notions of well-being, prosperity and group vitality. If anything distinguishes Melanesian religions from most, it is their apparent emphasis on the material results of rituals and of relationships with the more-than-human. Blessing is far less inward peace of the soul (as with western Christianity) or bodily health (so common a theme in black and equatorial Africa) than abundance in pigs or other foodstuffs and valuables. Group wealth is taken as a reflection of good relationships between humans and the spirit order, and in many cases as the possession of procedural skills or knowledge (commonly and dubiously termed 'magic') which make for successful hunting, fishing, gardening, and so on.[34]

Wealth, however, even if obtained by individuals or families, has not generally been hoarded in traditional Melanesia, since prestige has depended upon generosity rather than exclusive possession. He who has much to give, on the other hand, will put others in his debt and thus acquire more power, because others will borrow from him to fulfil their transactional obligations. When it comes to exchanges or presentations of wealth involving whole groups, such men will have emerged as leaders ('bigman' or *bikman*) or will show that they are indeed worthy to be chiefs (in chieftain societies), because they have contributed the most. Certain great festivities, in fact — such as the *Bugla Yungga* (or giant pig-kill among the Chimbu) or the *kras* (great decked displays of bananas among the Atzera of the Markam plains) — are nothing less than gracious offerings of food to invitee tribes, who are expected to be overawed by the hosts' might and riches, and who each feel pressure to enact their own 'justifications of existence' in the future. These moments of gratuitous generosity, indeed, along with other procedures, could act as opportunities for peace (and the fresh alliances and marriages which went with it), so that it is palpably false to imagine Melanesians were incapable of escaping from the horrors of 'internecine strife'.

It is in the gains and losses of inter-group conflict, and in the endless round of exchange at varying levels, that Melanesians learn and pass on a sense of equivalences, and it is in calculating the price which ought to be exacted in revenge, or in assessing the current 'state of play' in a network of reciprocal obligations, that more *obviously* religious elements come into view.[35] Melanesians have usually explained their successes or failures in terms of a 'retributive logic'; that is, each culture has its repertory of reasons to explain why a death may have occurred, why sickness has struck, why one family or person is more prosperous than others, why trouble has arisen between two parties, and the like.

Much of traditional communal intellectual life was devoted to explaining such events of the time and, thus, in laying the groundwork for wise decision-making. Since there is need for guidance as to how one 'reads' the relationship between actions, events and group explanations in such a variety of cultures, chapter 3 has been devoted to this subject. With the explanatory side to the 'logic of retribution' we uncover the most reflective side to Melanesian religions — their philosophic aspect, one could say. Here one must be on the look-out for attempts at classification (the catalogue of medicinal herbs and disease types among the coastal Papuan Motu, for instance, is remarkable); or for the manner in which myths may function as 'ultimate explanations' (as to why humans are mortal, for instance, or have one way of life rather than another, as in the Seragi story). What also becomes important here are the clever or gnomic sayings, proverbs, metaphors, parabolic expressions, rhetorical devices, pointed anecdotes, and the traditions about previous migrations, about exploits, about memorable inventions, about prophecies, and so on — all of which have their places in the multiple bodies of Melanesian wisdom so sadly neglected by most missionaries and anthropologists alike. All these contributed to the given and prevailing set of values which was the proud possession of each culture — ethics, religion and the exertions of economics and war, thus, being utterly inseparable.

Ritual life, religious specialization and the capacity for change

We have already touched on ceremonies, particularly those expressive of reciprocity, and much more could be written about these and the various forms of traditional ritual activity throughout Melanesia. To reduce the astounding complexity to generalization is hazardous, yet at least we know that most societies could avail themselves of rites ranging from those involving the whole group or broad 'security circle' (as Peter Lawrence terms it) to those performed by single persons with the knowledge of special spells. In some instances, large group festivals were performed only very rarely and each individual might expect to help organize and enact them once in his or her own lifetime. Such was the case with the *Hevehe* among the Elema of the Papuan Gulf, a dramatic moment returning in macro-cycles spanning as much as twenty-five years. When the time was ripe, long, thin *Hevehe* masks were secretly constructed in the cathedral-like *eravo* structure, with representations of creatures important for different 'totem groups' painted on their surfaces. The ceremony proper began on a moonless night with the electrifying sound of shell-trumpets, drums and bullroarers, when novices to be initiated into the mystery of the *Hevehe* cult were taken to join the noisy dancers. The novices were later to re-emerge from the *eravo* in bright yellow bark-cloth, heralding the appearance of those who would wear the *Hevehe* masks. These mask-bearers act as spirit-powers connected with both the bush and the sea. After large quantities of pigs were slaughtered, the masks were summarily burnt, with the admonition 'Go back to your homes in the bush; we have fed you!' (as if to the bush spirits), and their charred remnants then cast into the sea.

  The different components of the whole cycle being complex and subtle in relationship, and the designs and procedures being carefully preserved by a non-literate tradition, the *Hevehe* 'ritual well illustrates the artistic and dramatic heights of which Papuan peoples were capable'.[36] But the richness does not stop short at one such spectacle, and even within Elema culture there is much more one could relate besides. The *Hevehe*, interestingly, was more specifically an act of 'cultic initiation' marking the entrance of select warriors into a male cult, and thus distinct from most of the renowned pig-killing or exchange ceremonies of the Papua New Guinea highlands (which also only occur after long intervals, yet in which initiation plays a lesser part). The *Hevehe* is also distinguishable from many other forms of sacrifice traditionally found in the region (some of which are further discussed in chapter 3) and from what we may term 'classic' rites of passage. 'Rites of passage', as van

Gennep called them, are those rituals marking the transition from one stage of life to another, following the human life-cycle from birth to death. In most Melanesian societies initiating the young into manhood and womanhood involved collective activity with a good deal of anxiety on the part of novices (young males facing such ordeals as circumcision, flaying, stinging, hunger and dehydration, all usually in enforced seclusion) and of parents and guardians (who were deeply concerned to see their progeny through the transition).

Some societies have cultivated further stages of initiation, with more ordeals or more disclosures of truth (as among the Malekulan groups of Vanuatu, or the Yangoru-Negrie and the Baktaman near the opposite reaches of the Sepik River); others are more consistent in responding to biological changes (such as feasts in honour of males with their first grey hairs, among the eastern Fuyughe, for example). Interest lies in the cultic procedures of special initiatory societies or 'clubs', the secrecy surrounding them, the requirements for passing from one grade to another, and the implications they have for relations between the sexes. With male secret societies (such as the famous *Dukduk* and *Iniet* among the Tolai of east New Britain), women and children were strictly excluded, and those of them bent on learning any of the cultic secrets courted death. A lesser number of female initiatory groups existed (as with the cult of Jari, Murik Lakes), and male fear of sexual contamination together with women's access to special spirit power kept these female groups intact against male interference in what were, otherwise, male-dominated societies. Apropos secret societies and sexuality, there has been a renewed spate of research into cultic homosexuality in traditional Melanesia, especially into sodomic rites for passing on warrior virility, as was first brought to wider attention by Jan van Baal's work on the Marind-Anim (south Irian Jaya) in the 1960s.[37]

As for funerary rites, one cannot afford to underestimate their importance both for the people themselves (who, unlike most Westerners, brought death out into the open) and for a balanced assessment of Melanesian religions. It is easy to give Melanesia a bad press by concentrating on the horrific and cadaverous side to burial or disposal practices, virtually all of which have now been left aside in favour of 'Christian norms'. Mourning Motuan widows, for instance, were expected to lie down next to the putrefying bodies of their deceased husbands, and the odour from the shallow graves near or under houses was meant to stir villagers into revenge against the enemies held responsible for the deaths. Among the Okapa or Fore (eastern New Guinea highlands), endocannibalism was practised over the corpses of warriors, the disease *kuru* being passed on to the wives who ate the infected brains of their husbands. And cadavers were flayed by magicians of the Hube (Huon Peninsula), in a daemonizing act to prepare for vengeance on enemies. Certainly, there have been many unprepossessing features of mortuary practice, even for Melanesians themselves.[38] The event of a death, nonetheless, evoked strange and special reactions precisely because it cut across the existing fabric of life, calling for reshuffling, adjustment, as well as remorse and recrimination. Not only did it affect social relations and productivity in societies constantly concerned with group survival, but dying was itself a profoundly religious event and meant crossing to a spirit-order very real and powerful to 'primal consciousness'.

Furthermore, no general account of Melanesian religions would be adequate without recognizing the significance of different social structures, or 'patterns of belonging', so crucial for group and individual identity, and especially without acknowledging the role of 'sacral kingship' or 'religious specialization'. Against popular impressions, it is simply not justifiable to tuck Melanesian social organization away on a lower rung of the evolutionary scale or as betokening something less than religion — as if Polynesia, for example, had its distinct hierarchical structures (with monarchs, chiefs, priests and other functionaries) and thus 'religion', while Melanesia spawned acephalous (even if more egalitarian) societies and thus mere 'magic'. It is too often forgotten that there is a fair sprinkling of chieftainship societies in Melanesia — mainly, though not exclusively on her coastlines — and we can now better appreciate how so-called 'secular' leadership in its various forms could be endowed with more-than-human authority.[39] It is also worth remembering that one of the forgotten 'greats' in the history of social theory about religion, namely A. M. Hocart, began his work *Kingship* with an account of Fiji's paramount chieftaincy, albeit a phenomenon on the very eastern edges of Melanesia's wide zone; and of all societies in Papua Malinowski chose to study the one with the most impressive paramount chieftaincy.[40]

Religious specializations, what is more, have been in very many cases hereditary and more 'institutionalized' than first met the eyes of earlier observers. It is not inappropriate to describe as priests, for instance, the custodians of the *Gebeanda* caves sacred to all Huli, where sacrifices were made to the superior one within, and the same term applies to the so-called *gapar* at Murik Lakes, whose special task it was to line up the sacred battle clubs before combat and thus 'bring into operation' the war god, Kakar. Some societies possessed castes or families of cultic specialists (on Melanesia's fringes the *Zagoga* priesthood of the Torres Strait and the *bete* sacrificers of Fiji were impressive among them), while in others individuals were specially, if temporarily, sacralized for important priestly-looking roles. The tabued man (*mapilie*) of the Wahgi, who watches over the ceremonial grounds and keeps up communication with 'the fighting dead' between one great pig-kill and another, eventually determining who should be invited to the great feast or not, and whether the pigs, crops, lineages and even (as we have already seen) the position of the moon are *kar* (good, right) for the occasion. There have been other types of tabued persons, with rather different functions. The famous *helaga tauna* (or holy man) among the western Motu, for one, was publicly elected to prepare and sponsor the building of the large *lagatoi* craft to sail to the Gulf for trade. He was tabued from certain foods and from sexual intercourse during the whole procedure, and on the voyage itself could not look upon the sea until arrival at the trading point and then home. He would meditate on the success of the journey in a dark enclosure on the vessel, speaking to the spirits of the sea, or of the sharks, not to impede his fellows' progress.[41]

Melanesia has also witnessed its fair share of prophets, shamans, sages, visionaries, healers, diviners, over and above figures one may describe as 'workers of black or white magic'. Problems will always arise, of course, as to the applicability of English or other foreign words to cover phenomena of religious specialization in any given cultural complex. Such problems occur because scholars have sometimes been too eager to see a universal presence of certain leadership types on the one hand, and yet also because more than one recognizable type of religious expression can manifest in any functionary's career or activity on the other. Thus, there is a real temptation these days to use popular terminology — describing, for instance, any psychopomp who is found bringing the living in contact with the spirit order as a 'shaman' — or else to apply such epithets as 'magician' or 'prophet' to figures who are known for quite an array of duties or achievements.[42] Common sense should lead scholar and student alike into gauging the relative appropriateness of one or other appellation, and deciding whether any of them should be coupled for the sake of clarity or specificity. The word 'prophet', for instance, is best employed when the personage in view is most known for oracular utterances, or for outstanding verbalized claims and premonitions as a spokesperson of the divine.[43] To refer to 'shamanism' in Melanesia we should surely require of specialists that they enter ritually into an altered state of consciousness and understand themselves to undertake a spirit journey on behalf of their clientele's welfare, and not just be any kind of healer, or diviner by dream, and so on.[44] By the same token one should be prepared to combine terms — into prophet-diviner or prophet-leader, let us say, or shaman-priest — if it means that, thereby, the complex roles of the figures are more accurately characterized. Another factor regarding specialists concerns the degree to which they are institutionalized. Are their 'functions' temporary (as can easily be the case with prophets, who can arise to meet pressing but transitory situations), or are they permanent? Are such specialists a feared and liminal, if necessary, part of the social landscape (as with many sorcerers)? or are these specialists, despite even their fearsome aspects, accepted in the group as critical for survival (like many others sorcerers, who can work harm against enemies and malefactors yet heal members of their own security circle with counter-sorcery)?

Leadership, and the experiences which might lead one to lay claims to it, were of obvious consequence for the resilience and adaptability of Melanesian societies. It is quite inadmissible, indeed, to pass off primal cultures as 'static' and susceptible only to the most limited changes. As my own and others' oral historical investigations have revealed, basic alterations in ritual usage are now known to have been accepted by whole tribes — such changes occurring independently of white contact or else with only the vaguest knowledge of the 'white phenomenon' on the horizon. Such shifts in practice, as well as of belief and outlook, needed to be vouchsafed by contact with extra-mundane dimensions. Dreams, visions, numinous encounters and other special occurrences, then, were of determinative importance for taking a group in new directions — to embark on trading expeditions, such as the Motuan *Hiri* (allegedly begun after well-known Edai Siabo saw the spirit-world), or to orient life afresh around a particular item of food (as with the Taro cults among the Papuan Orokaiva). So-called 'cargo cults', in fact, are adjustments in the face of intrusions and rapid change, which reflect the time-honoured indigenous reliance on spirit-sanctioned attempts at innovation and new departure, since such movements usually issue out of dreams, visions, spirit-possession, supernatural intervention, the revelation of mythic truths, or the divulging of a great secret. For significant changes of direction the role of individual leaders and purveyors of spiritual insight was fundamental.[45]

Sacred space and creative artistry

In passing we have touched on matters to do with the mastery of materials in artistic creation — in physical representations of the gods, masks, architecture, and various other sacralized objects. The most significant work done in the field of artistic activity, or skilled craftsmanship, always involved some quest for the acquisition of ('magico'-) spiritual power (with the welfare of one's own 'security circle' in mind), and was therefore not a secular business. The present-day tourist trade, of course, creates the impression that the optimal concern of the creator was for decorativeness, beautiful design and even entertainment. But, for all artefacts, the inspiration usually came from traditional responses to the spirit order, passed down by generations of skilled specialists who only allowed for spontaneity and deviation from age-old expressions in very limited ways. Museum holdings of Oceanic 'primitive art' around the world also convey false impressions by isolating individual oddments from their original context — from their eerie corner in the cult house, let us say, or from use as sacral or practicable objects. Our imagination can be taxed, then, in restoring art to its pre-contact place in the maintenance of a thousand-and-one tribal identities.

Various regions are famous for distinctive achievements. In architecture few Melanesian cultures can match the great cathedral-like structures of the middle Sepik and the eastern Gulf. Relative inaccessibility, cultural resilience and greater mission tolerance have allowed various Sepik *haus tambaran* (spirit houses) to be kept intact (see plate 4); but even the ruins of the equally impressive edifices of the Papuan coast are very hard to find today (see plates 5 and 6). In both kinds of 'temple', effigies representing the ancestors and other spirit powers were carefully arranged. Prominent in the spirit houses of

Middle Angoram, to illustrate, were placed the stylized effigies of each deceased male of the clan(s), cautiously carved to represent their continuing presence among the living. In the comparative structure built by the Ilahita Arapesh, most noticeable were the paraphernalia of the vengeful deity Nggwal, the fearful monitor of external warfare and internal tabu-breakage alike.[46] In the 30–40 foot (9–12 m) high Elema *eravos* the most striking internal features were the decorated *gope* boards — long elliptical discs representing the ancestors (see plate 6); in the great *ufu* houses of the Mekeo (further east in hinterland Papua) the most striking features were, rather, the objects of chiefly power, including finely decorated lime-gourds.[47]

Remembering the themes introduced so far, we can see how Melanesian artistry almost invariably arose out of religious preoccupations. Because sculptures, effigies and representations of the spirits were made as renewals of decayed or destroyed prototypes, the creator's kinsfolk would be expected to respond to them in caution, fear, and in the making of offerings and sacrifices, as they had been doing previously. In many cases a sculpture was conceived to be a special locus of a spirit's power (as with the Roviana figure in plate 3); in other instances symbols, such as discs denoting the sun, were indicators of gods and sacred places — as on the façade of spirit houses among the Mendi (southern central highlands, Papua).[48] Because Melanesians were recurrently at war, moreover, almost all cultures manifest some concern for a skilfully constructed artifice of warrior exploit — as with the arresting designs of the great Asmat shields (south Irian Jaya), for example, or the painstakingly carved stone heads of Fuyughe pineapple war-clubs (see plates 7–8).[49] Because Melanesians held feasts, some peoples put a great deal of artistic energy into the ceremonial grounds themselves, or the platforms dominating them (as with Huon Gulf cultures, or the Rigo of Papua); while others concentrated on the manufacture of masks to be disclosed in the ceremonies, or the skilful application of body paint, or the arrangement of precious feathers into head-dresses.[50] Again, because certain groups put to sea in trading canoes (Trobriands), or undertook raiding expeditions in war canoes (Gogodala, west of the Papuan Gulf), the time invested in carving parts of their vessels reflected the seriousness with which they viewed these undertakings.[51]

Thus, we are certainly not dealing in Melanesia with 'art for art's sake' or even with simple spontaneity, as Raymond Firth rightly reminds us. Further-more, however susceptible some of the exaggerated breasts and genitalia of certain effigies might be to a Freudian analysis, what traditional art has been produced over the last century or so has not resulted from 'instinctive impulses' or the 'crude unconscious' of 'savages', but from fixed rules of the game — including spells and invocations — all very consciously adhered to within lineages.[52] So critical has been the transference of skills from one specialist to another, moreover, that the language and lore used could actually suggest a transformation of one person into another, as with those responsible for carving the *lagimu* and *tabuya* prows on the Trobriands.[53]

The art–religion connection, indeed, abounds everywhere in so many different forms. The fine mask-work, for which Sepik River and middle New Ireland cultures are famed, was virtually without exception for veneration and ceremony; the most delicately carved wooden bowls among the Manus were to hold the skulls of the 'Sir [or Head-of-the-Family] Ghost' in the rafters at the entries of houses; the beautiful initiatory tattoos on Motuan women or the bravely borne female scarifications among the Kume (northern Irian Jaya) are mainly about socio-religious identity; the polished and carefully arranged stone structures for which Unea (or Bali) Island (in the Bismarck Sea) is noted were for recurrent family sacrifices; the artificial islands engineered off the shores of Malaita (in the Solomons) were to hold spirit-shrines; while even the great rope-bridges of the Enga highlanders were boundary-markers, and therefore as much delineators of the cosmos as they were a means of access to neighbouring clans.[54]

Far from being independent of religion, such works were the very expressions of it, and even the left-overs of previous creators — such as the megaliths of Malekula (in Vanuatu) — could become especially hallowed by subsequent generations as key focal-points of ritual.[55] In all this we are not to forget the relation of specific creations to distinctive forms of ritual or sacral tasks: feathers and masks to dances; perforated bamboo pipes for local tobacco-smoking to collaborative meetings (as among the Fuyughe); decorated flutes, pipes and drums to the act of voicing the spirits.[56] Of course, many of the individual arts, whether connected with ceremony or exchange, make for fascinating study in their own right — pottery among the Motu, for example; tapa cloth manufacture by the Maisin; iron forging in north-west Irian Jaya (consequent upon Islam's easternmost expansion)[57] — and nowhere is this truer than in the case of dance and music.

Dance itself was a 'religious statement', particularly at highpoints of ceremonial life. It typically evoked myth, closeness to the animals and birds of the cosmos, love-magic and generative power, and mutuality or the handling of tensions between groups (with the by now famous compensatory *gisaro* dancers among the Kaluli of the Mount Bosavi area, on the other hand, spectator reaction was often to burn the grass skirt of a good performer who had shamed them into contemplating their own past hostilities).[58] Dancing, of course, also had its own created or well tended paraphernalia — along with body paints and the head-dresses, the most startling costuming sometimes, and always some musical instrument(s). Even the least durable but nonetheless carefully constructed musical object could be the most sacred, as with the bull-roarers of many Huon Gulf cultures in New Guinea. Strangely incorporating in symbolic form many of the themes we have been pursuing, the 'genuine' and indeed most fragile bull-roarer can only be whirled a few times at the height of important ceremonies in some of these cultures. As the voice of the ancestors, its temporary and successful application by a bigman will bring peace and security to his tribe, but its breakage spells utter disaster.[59] An impressive comment on the delicate matter of preserving right relationships in small-scale, survivalist societies!

Praeparatio evangelica

It makes sense to conclude this introductory survey by asking what bearing all this information has on today's rapidly changing and 'Christianizing' Melanesia. In what senses were traditional religions a 'preparation for the coming of the Gospel' to the region? Any (would-be or relatively) objective observer should perhaps only go so far as to note how fertile the ground has been for a transition to Christianity over the last hundred years, although believers will want to speak freely of God's hand behind the quite extraordinary transformations in modern Melanesia. Remaining within the constraints of history and other related academic disciplines, at least one can affirm how much in Melanesian tradition chimed in with, or seemed to foreshadow, the teachings and practices of the new religious order (whatever the differences in mission proclamation and programmes might have been).

To begin with, virtually all Melanesian religions are 'theistic' (or deal with gods of some kind). Among them, moreover, although it may not do justice to the variations in saying so, one finds temples, shrines and sacred space; myths and beliefs, held firmly enough to serve as dogma; sacrifices and offerings; ethical and kinship rules consolidating each group into a vital, supportive unity; leaders and initiates with spiritual power; as well as access to another realm through revelation and types of religious experience: all these being analogous to the phenomena of the new faith. The preamble to the Constitution of Papua New Guinea appropriately acknowledges the worthy traditions which are her unique inheritance, even while thus employing a preparedness to put aside what is considered bad. If the steady Christianization has been such, however, that many Melanesians have been led to denigrate the distinctly religious face of these traditions as paling into insignificance before the bright light of the new faith, let it be recognized from this book once and for all that Melanesia did and does possess *genuine* religions. They may be small and seem vulnerable, but they are to be taken seriously; for, there is indeed about them a resilient, primordial strength, and an Old Testament quality of sternness matched by a Sarah-like patience, which makes Melanesia the worthy Mother of new children, who have now embarked on a new journey.

As with the voyage of the *Rattlesnake*, there has already been and will be much tragi-comedy, but if the adventure itself is to be noble, and in any case well-nigh irresistible, there will be no arrival at a safe harbour unless the many places from which the adventurers have set out are studied with conscientiousness.[60] The first priority in this present work, in any case, is to arrive at an accurate and representative assessment of Melanesia's primal foundations, and to gauge the significance of the 'Old Time' for the New.

NOTES

Chapter 1 derives from material originally contributed to S. Latukefu (ed.), *The Christian Missions and Development in Papua New Guinea and the Solomon Islands*.

1 T. H. Huxley, Diary of the voyage of H.M.S. Rattlesnake 1846–50 (unpublished MS collection, Mitchell Library, Sydney, B1079), 17 August 1849; cf. J. MacGillivray, *Narrative of the voyage of H.M.S. Rattlesnake*, London, 1852, vol. 1, pp.257–58. On the mounting of the whole expedition, see L. Huxley, *Life and letters of Thomas Henry Huxley*, London, 1908, vol. 1, ch. 2 (and p.36 for the very first quotation above).

2 ibid., vol. 1, pp.60–62; cf. MacGillivray, *Narrative*, pp.269–300, etc.

3 T. H. Huxley, Diary, 20 August 1849.

4 ibid., 8 January 1850; cf. W. Irvine, *Apes, angels and Victorians*, New York, 1959, pp.11–12.

5 Spencer, *The data of sociology* (ed. G. Duncan), London, 1874, table, col. 11 (s.v. ceremonial: laws of intercourse), and p.24; cf. MacGillivray, *Narrative*, vol. 1, p.258. For the initiation of the friendship between Spencer and Huxley in 1852, see Spencer, *An autobiography*, London, 1904, vol. 1, p.402.

6 G. W. Trompf, The origins of the comparative study of religions (master's thesis, Monash University, Melbourne 1965), pp.129–71. There are various parallels between Spencer's views and those held by Edward Tylor, the first English Professor of Anthropology, and also later by James George Frazer, cf. Trompf, *In search of origins*, New York and New Delhi, 1989, chs 1 and 3.

7 cf. L. Huxley, *Life*, vol. 1, p.61; Spencer, *Principles of sociology*, London, 1885–96 edn, vol. 1, esp. sects 73–96. In the history of social-scientific reflection on Papua, the turning-point was not to come until 1888; cf. A. Hingston-Quiggin, *Haddon the headhunter*, Cambridge, 1942, pp.42 et seq.

8 Iaro Lasaro, 'History of Bonarua Island', in *Oral History* 3/7 (1975), p.172. Names for such a high deity cognate with Yabwahine are found in neighbouring cultures, e.g. Dobu, Rogeia and Normanby Islands, Suau. Lasaro's use of the phrase 'spiritual world' seems to reflect mission influence, and would better read 'land of the dead or spirits'.

9 cf. R. Freund, R. Hett and K. Reko, 'The Enga concept of God', in *Exploring Enga Culture* (ed. P. Brennan), Wapenamanda, 1970, pp.141–66; P. Lawrence, *Road belong Cargo*, Melbourne and Manchester, 1964, p.16.

10 cf. *BNG Annual Report*, 1899–1900, p.98; 1902–3, p.14. On the ever-present dangers of racism, esp. A. Montagu, *Man's most dangerous myth*, Cleveland and New York, 1965 edn.

11 Trompf, 'Missiology and anthropology: a viable relationship?', *Oceania*, 55/2 (1984), pp.148–153.

12 A phrase taken from R. Langdon, *The lost caravel*, Sydney, 1975, ch. 13; cf., e.g., D. MacDonald, *The Asiatic origin of Oceanic languages*, Melbourne, 1894, MacDonald's work being critically examined by A. Capell, 'Semites in the Pacific?' in *Essays in honour of E. C. B. MacLaurin on his sixtieth birthday* (eds A. D. Crown and E. Stockton), Sydney, n.d. [1970s], pp.146ff.

13 The quotation comes from a Church of Christ booklet *Walking in yesterday*, *Papua New Guinea*, Port Moresby (?), 1979, p.1; cf. ch. 10 below.

14 See Trompf, '"Bilalaf"', in *Prophets of Melanesia* (ed. Trompf), Port Moresby, 1977, p.40; P. Sack, *Land between two laws*, Canberra, 1973, esp. pp.12–13, 142.

15 Brown, *Closing time*, New York, 1973.

16 Bulmer, 'The Kyaka of the Western Highlands', in *Gods, ghosts and men in Melanesia* (eds P. Lawrence and M. Meggitt), Melbourne, 1965, p.136; E. Thomas, 'Religion among the Trans Fly people of the Western Province', in *Melanesian and Judaeo-Christian religious traditions* (ed. Trompf), Port Moresby, 1975, bk 3, pt C(1), pp.22–23 (as well as unpublished interviews with pastor Maraga Momo, 1976); cf. F. E. Williams, *Papuans of the Trans-Fly*, Oxford, 1936, pp.318–29.

17 Relevant ethnographic references are too many to list here, although writings on cultures immediately specified are documented in subsequent notes. For a useful introductory survey of types of gods and spirits in Melanesian world-views, see T. Aerts, 'Melanesian gods', *Annales aequatoria* I (1980), pp.357–42; cf. also n.26 below.

18 More research is required on the various principles used by missionaries in adopting (or modifying) such near-equivalents; cf. ibid., pp.357ff.

19 K. Laumann, 'Vlisso, der Kriegs- und Jagdgott am unteren Yuat River, Neuguinea', in *Anthropos* 47 (1952), pp.898–902, 904, 907 (Sepik); R. H. Codrington, *The Melanesians*, Oxford, 1891, p.123; cf. p.124 (Banks). For problems comparable to those raised by Codrington in Maurice Leenhardt's account of New Caledonian material, see his *Do Kamo* (trans. B. M. Gulati), Chicago and London, 1979, pp.27ff. on the Houailou. For the ongoing debate about *mana*, see R. Keesing, 'Rethinking *Mana*', *Journal of anthropological research*, 40 (1984), pp.137–156.

20 So R. M. Glasse, 'The Huli of the Southern Highlands', in Lawrence and Meggitt, *Gods*, p.34.

21 See Lawrence and Meggitt, 'Introduction', in *Gods*, pp.19, 22; cf. A. Chowning, 'Lakalai religion and world view and the concept of "seaboard religion"', in Trompf, *Mel. and Judaeo-Christ. relig. trads*, bk 1, p.84, cf. pp.75–77, 95; Trompf, Fieldnotes, 1973.

22 See esp. Trompf, 'Man facing death and after-life in Melanesia', in *Powers, plumes and piglets*, (ed. N. Habel), Adelaide, 1979, pp.132–33 (also ch. 2 below); cf. Mgr Navarre, Notes et journal [June 1888–July 1889] (handwritten MS, Yule Island Catholic Mission).

23 Esp. R. F. Fortune, *Manus religion*, Lincoln, 1934, esp. pp.7–8; Chowning, 'Lakalai religion', pp.87–88; cf. C. A. Valentine, 'The Lakalai of New Britain', in Lawrence and Meggitt, *Gods*, pp.184–85.

24 Lawrence and Meggitt, *Gods*, pp.7, 9. For comparable material in non-highland contexts, e.g., S. J. Harrison, 'Stealing people's names'; social structure, cosmology and politics in a Sepik River Village (doctoral dissert., Australian National University (ANU), Canberra 1982), p.84.

25 B. Gayalu, Traditional religion among the Huli: the *Tege* (unpublished MS, University of Papua New Guinea, Port Moresby 1976), pp.2–3 (by kind permission) (for Huli); Trompf, Fieldnotes, 1973 (for Wahgi); J. G. Geissler, Een kort overzigt van het land en volk op de Noord-Oost-Kust van Nieuw Guinea (unpublished handwritten MS, Archives of the Hendrik Kraemer Institut, Oegstgeest, Doreh 1857), pp.42–50 (for Biak).

26 See e.g. Lawrence, *Road*, pp.21–24; Trompf, '"Bilalaf"', pp.27–28 (whence the quotation); cf. esp. Aerts, 'Melanesian gods', *Bikmaus* 4/2 (1983), pp.4–18. On '*dema* deities', J. van Baal, *Dema: description and analysis of Marind-Anim culture* (Koningklijk Instituut voor Taal- Land- en Volkenkunde Trans. Ser. 9), The Hague, 1966; E. Schwimmer, *Exchange in the social structure of the Orokaiva*, Sydney, n.d., esp. ch. 4; W. Flannery, 'Appreciating Melanesian myths', in Habel, *Powers*, pp.164–71; D. Whiteman, 'Melanesian religions: an overview', in Mantovani (ed.), *An Introduction to Melanesian religions* (Point Ser. 6), Goroka, 1984, p.106. For 'creative deities' and the distribution of mythology, ritual and related skills, e.g. C. A. Schmitz, *Historische Probleme in Nordost-Neuguinea (Huon-Halbingel)*, Wiesbaden, 1960, pp.319–38 (Manup and Kilibob complex in the Madang and Morobe districts); E. C. Brower, 'A Malagan to cover the grave'; funerary ceremonies in Mandak (doctoral dissert., University of Queensland, Brisbane 1980), pp.160, 166–67.

27 cf. R. Wagner, *Habu: the innovation of meaning in Daribi religion*, Chicago and London, 1972; R. Lacey, 'A glimpse of the Enga world view' in Trompf, *Mel. and Judaeo-Christ. relig. trads*, bk 1, pp.42–48 etc. These views are not common, however, among inhabitants of smaller islands!

28 Chowning, 'Lakalai Religion', p.81 (whence the quotation); cf., e.g., K. A. McElhanon, *Legends from Papua New Guinea*, Ukarumpa, 1974; R. M. Berndt, *Excess and restraint*, Chicago, 1962, etc.

29 cf. Trompf, '"Bilalaf"', pp.41–44. Here I foreshadow an article called 'Myth and meaning in Melanesia', submitted to *Man*.

30 For background, e.g., J. Winslow (ed.), *The Melanesian environment*, Canberra, 1977; W. C. Clarke, *Place and people: an ecology of a New Guinea People*, Berkeley, 1971. See also F. J. P. Poole, 'Melanesian Religions: mythic themes' in M. Eliade et al, *The Encyclopedia of Religion*, New York, 1987, vol. 9, esp. p.362.

31 cf. Sahlins, 'On the sociology of primitive exchange' (ASA Monographs I), New York, 1965, pp.139–236.

32 Trompf, 'Salvation in primal religion', in *The Idea of Salvation* (eds D. Dockrill and G. Tanner) (*Prudentia*, special issue 1989), p.209.

33 Oral Testimony (hereafter OT or OTs): Cherubim Dambui, 1985 (Iatmül), K. Heider, *Grand valley Dani* (Case studies in cultural anthropology), New York, 1979, p.100 (Dani).

34 Trompf, 'Salvation', pp.207–09 and cf. p.225, n.3.

35 'Obviously' here for the benefit of Westerners; considering traditional Melanesian societies, it is in fact virtually impossible to separate culture in general (or any facet of life) from religion. For background to the above paragraphs, esp. Trompf, *Payback: the logic of retribution in Melanesian religions* (forthcoming), ch. 1, sect. B.

36 J. Parratt, *Papua belief and ritual*, New York, 1976, p.55 (whence the quotation), cf. pp.52–55; F. E. Williams, *The drama of Orokolo*, Oxford, 1940.

37 cf. A. B. Deacon, *Malekula* (ed. C. M. Wedgwood), London, 1934 (Malekula); P. Gesch, *Initiative and Initiation* (Studia Instituti Anthropos 33), St Augustin, 1985, ch. 14 (Yangoru-Negrie); F. Barth, *Ritual and knowledge among the Baktaman of New Guinea*, Oslo and New Haven, 1975, pt 2 (Baktaman); Trompf, '"Bilalaf"', pp.25–27 (Fuyughe); M. ToBung, An essay on Tolai culture (unpublished typescript, Holy Spirit Seminary, Bomana 1977), pp.8ff (Tolai); M. Tamoane, 'Kamoai of Darapap and the legend of Jari', in Trompf, *Prophets*, ch. 4 (Murik Lakes). cf. M. Allen, *Male cults and secret initiations*, Melbourne, 1967; G. Herdt (ed.), *Rituals of manhood: male initiation in Papua New Guinea*, Berkeley, 1982; (general); van Baal, *Dema*, esp. pp.147ff; G. Herdt (ed.), *Ritualized homosexuality in Melanesia*, Berkeley, 1984 (cultic homosexuality). Note also I. Hogbin, *The island of menstruating men*, Scranton and London, 1970 (Wogeo, Sepik Islands).

38 For the Motu case, see the letters of the Rarotongan pastor Piri to Rev. W. Gill, 1878 and 1880 (unpubl. trans. by M. Crocombe) (New Guinea Collection, University of Papua New Guinea [hereafter UPNG]). cf. Lindenbaum, *Kuru sorcery* (Explorations in world ethnography), Palo Alto, 1979 (Fore); H. Gerber, 'Die Realität des "Unwirklichen". Zur Funktion der Magie in der Religion', in *Theologische Beiträge aus Papua Neuguinea* (ed. H. Bürkle), (Erlanger Taschenbucher Band 43), Neuendettelsau, 1978, pp.61–64 (Hube).

39 In this respect older works have a renewed importance, esp. Codrington (*Melanesians*, pp.46–60); C. G. Seligmann (*The Melanesians of British New Guinea*, Cambridge, 1910, pp.21, 28, 337, 701–18); B. Blackwood (*Both sides of Buka Passage*, Oxford, 1935). We await work by W. Standish on a reappraisal of Chimbu bigman leadership, with recognition of the succession factor and religious functions. cf. also M. Godelier, *La production des grands hommes*, Paris, 1982 on the Baruya. On the tendency to over-state the Melanesian-Polynesian dichotomy, e.g., R. Firth, *Human types*, London, 1956 edn, esp. ch. 6.

40 Oxford, 1927, ch. 1; cf. Malinowski, *Argonauts of the western Pacific*, New York, 1961 edn, passim.

41 Esp. B. Gayalu, 'The Gebeanda: a Sacred Cave Ritual', in Habel, *Powers*, pp.20–23, cf. p.9 (Huli); M. Tamoane, 'Kamoai of Darapap' (Murik Lakes); D. Passi, 'From pagan to Christian priesthood', in Trompf (ed.), *The Gospel is not Western*, Maryknoll, 1987, pp.45, 47–48 (Torres Strait); Hocart, *The Northern States of Fiji* (Royal Anthropological Society Occasional Paper 11), London, 1952, p.178 (Fiji); J. Guilliam, 'Some religious aspects of the *Hiri*', in T. Dutton (ed.), *The Hiri in history* (Australian National University Pacific Research Monograph 8), Canberra, and Miami, 1982, pp.35–63 (Motu).

42 The problem of looseness is already present in the influential works of Mircea Eliade, in *Shamanism: archaic technique of ecstasy* (trans. W. R. Trask) (Bollingen Ser. 76), Princeton, 1972, esp. ch. 10, and of Max Weber, in *The sociology of religion* (trans. E. Fischoff), Boston, 1963, chs 1 and 6 on magicians and prophetism.

43 Trompf, 'Introduction' to *Prophets*, pp.8–9.

44 Following Å. Hultkrantz, 'A definition of shamanism', *Temenos* 9 (1973), pp.25–37. Here I also foreshadow my article 'Shamanism in Melanesia?' prepared for *Temenos*.

45 Esp. W. Jojoga Opeba, Taro or Cargo? (honours dissert., UPNG, Port Moresby 1976); cf. his 'Melanesian cult movements as traditional religious and ritual responses to change', in Trompf (ed.), *Gospel not Western*, pp.49–66. Also M. Stephen, 'The innovative role of altered states of consciousness in traditional Melanesian religion', *Oceania*, 50/1 (1979), pp.3–22; cf. R. Lacey, 'Journeys and transformations', in *Cargo cults and millenarian movements* (ed. Trompf), (Religion and society ser.), Berlin, 1990, ch. 4. On the persistence of the 'static' approach in anthropological writings, see esp. R. Brunton, 'Misconstrued order in Melanesian religion', *Man*, 15/1 (1980), pp.112–28, an article which has recently

called forth the reproaches of D. Jorgensen in the same journal. cf. also Trompf, 'Oral sources and the study of religious history in Papua New Guinea', in *Oral Tradition in Melanesia* (eds Lacey and D. Denoon), Port Moresby, 1981, pp.153ff.

46 OTs: Hermen Leny and Daniel Guren 1981 (Middle Angoram); D. Tuzin, esp. *The voice of the Tambaran*, Berkeley, 1980, pp.48ff (Ilahita Arapesh). cf. on Abelam *haus tambaran*, A. Forge, 'Style and Meaning in Sepik Art' in Forge (ed.), *Primitive Art and Society*, London and New York, 1973, ch. 10.

47 See esp. ch. 2, n.25 (Elema); OT: Faupugu Oaeke, *lopia* at Veipa'a, 1974 (Mekeo).

48 Trompf, Fieldnotes, 1976 (see also ch. 5 below) (Mendi); cf. also Schmitz, *Oceanic art; myth, man and image in the South Seas* (trans. G. Guterman), New York [1969], colour plate 1, for a Sentani sun disc (north-east Irian Jaya).

49 For the varieties of Asmat design, esp. H. C. van Renselaar, *Kunst van Asmat; Zuidwest Nieuw Guinea* (Konigklijk Instituut voor de Tropen 121; afdeling culturele en physische antropologie 55), Amsterdam, n.d. [1950s], plates 43b–51; cf. Schmitz, *Oceanic Art*, pp.83ff.

50 Schmitz, *Tanz- und Kultplatz in Melanesien als Versammlungsort und mimischer Schauplatz* (die Schaubühne 46), Emsdetten, 1955 (Huon); J. Specht and J. Fields (eds), *Frank Hurley in Papua; photographs of the 1920–1923 expeditions*, Bathurst, 1984, plate V4431, p.27 (platform Motuan but also Rigo style); see n.47 on the Elema (for masks); A. and M. Strathern, *Self-decoration in Mount Hagen*, London, 1971 (Melpa body paint); M. O'Hanlin, *Reading the Skin: adornment, display and society among the Wahgi*, London 1989 ch. 4 (Wahgi feather decoration).

51 U. Beier, 'The position of the artist in traditional society' (mimeograph, UPNG, Port Moresby 1976), pp.8–11 (Trobriand canoe prows); A. L. Crawford, 'Artistic revival among the Gogodala' (*Institute of PNG Studies discussion paper 14*), Port Moresby, 1976 (Gogodala canoes; with caution).

52 cf. Firth, *Art and life in New Guinea*, London and New York, 1979, pp.30–31. Sigmund Freud, in this light, can surely be ranked among the 'savage-mongers' (cf. ch. 5 below).

53 cf. the repeated song-spell 'you are transformed into me'; G. M. G. Scoditti, 'The use of metaphor in Kitawa culture', *Oceania*, 54/1 (1984), pp.52–53.

54 On masks, e.g., Brower, 'Malagan'; on Manus bowls, Fortune, *Manus Religion*, p.229; on tattoos, etc., e.g., S. Chauvet, *Les arts indigènes en Nouvelle Guinée*, Paris, 1930, plates 52, 54; on Bali, Trompf, Fieldnotes, 1984–85; on Malaita, W. G. Ivens, *The island builders of the Pacific*, London, 1930; on Enga, e.g., A. Ruhan, Enga bridges (unpublished mimeograph, UPNG, Port Moresby 1974).

55 cf. J. Layard, *Stone men of Malekula*, London, 1942.

56 On pipes, e.g., Trompf, '"Bilalaf"', pp.36ff; concerning music, note, e.g., how Wahgi and Chimbu voicing of the spirits through the playing of the sacred flutes is crucial for the commencement of their pig-kill festivals. Overall, cf. also Chauvet, *Les arts*; M. Leenhardt, *Folk art of Oceania* (trans. M. Heron), Paris and New York, 1950.

57 Motuan clay pots were taken to the Gulf on *Hiri* expeditions, cf. Dutton (ed.), *Hiri*; the Maisin, who dominated *tapa* manufacture and design, are east of the Orokaivan cultures (Papua); on iron forging, esp. F. C. Kamma and S. Kooyman, *Romawa forja; child of the fire*, Leiden, 1973.

58 More generally, see P. Spencer (ed.), *Society and the dance*, Cambridge, 1985, esp. chs 1 and 4 (cf. also n.48 above); on *gisaro*, in particular, B. Schieffelin, *The Burning of the dancers and the loneliness of the sorrowful*, New York, 1976, pp.21ff.

59 See esp. L. Biró and J. Jankó, *Beschreibender Catalog der ethnographischen Sammlung Ludwig Biros aus Deutsch Neuguinea (Berlinhafen)*, Budapest, 1899, p.514; cf. also T. Bodrogi, *Art in north-east New Guinea*, Budapest, 1961, p.73.

60 For longer term missiological background, note the Dominican Fr Diego Durán's comments (in 1581) on the folly of attempting Christian conversion with efforts at a total, forced elimination of previous beliefs *Historia de las Indias de Nueva España* (ed. J. F. Ramírez), Mexico City, 1951 edn, vol. 2, p.71.

DEATH AND THE AFTER-LIFE IN TRADITIONAL BELIEF AND PRACTICE

It is a common viewpoint that religion is essentially an affirmation of personal post-mortem survival or continued existence in some form beyond the grave. While this view lends itself to reductionism — for religion, as we have already seen, has many constituents — there can be little doubt that death and the after-life have been central preoccupations in virtually every traditional culture across the globe. Melanesia's religious scene is no exception to this general pattern. In this chapter the response to death will be taken up as the first of four thematic approaches to the region's varied traditions. Ethnological analysis and the exploration of methodological issues, however, are not pressing concerns at this stage; a general survey is offered once more, although in this case with only one major aspect of religious life in mind.

The materials shall be structured around the human *life cycle*. This is partly for the better management of a complicated array of beliefs and phenomena, but more so because the complex emotional responses, sentiments, mental associations and intricate reasonings of *homo religiosus* will be in less danger of losing their pristine vitality and becoming disembodied data or mere curiosities of custom. In order to avoid viewing traditional Melanesia in a vacuum, moreover, something will be made of the neo-Marxist, if rather arbitrary, distinction between the traditional, the transitional and the modern, so as to account for important shifts in religious expression during post-contact times.

The ancient Chinese philosopher Hui Shih once said that 'man begins to die from his birth',[1] and this is an appropriate comment on the subsistence, survivalist cultures of Melanesia. It is appropriate not only because of what appears to be a very high infant mortality rate in pre-contact Melanesia but because young people were expected to fulfil adult tasks of food production and childbearing as early as possible and because, too, an individual's life had a good chance of being cut short — by a spear, or through sickness, or by something so terrible as the crocodile.

Reflecting on pre-contact or 'traditional' Melanesian societies, then, one has to appreciate how death was an ever-present reality, and how much more intensely so than for those of us who have the time and security to read this book, and who put off all thought of dying (and its implications) as long as possible. We are therefore dealing with the problem of describing and empathizing with a consciousness or a species of awareness — and one whose depths are only glimpsed rarely, at moments when symbols are grasped, for example, or when occasional articulations of religious feeling are made and understood. In Melanesian society, then, death itself was not generally objectified — it was not the object of speculation, in the way that it often is in western culture. Death was, far more commonly, an event in one's environment which induced *action*, usually a set pattern of actions, and virtually automatic responses. There is no better illustration of this than Melanesians wailing, which to an outsider may seem contrived and artificial, but which is in fact a natural, inbred — even if sometimes gameful — response.

Growth

Since this chapter is structured around the human life cycle, let us begin with Melanesian children. Young boys and girls were confronted with death from the first: it was common and occurred in the open, not behind hospital walls. Corpses were on public display, not in mortuaries. Humanity's mortality was not only a public spectacle, it was mimicked in the war games of children, and was also explained to the young in story and myth. Explanations as to why people must experience death are obviously fascinating and important. They are also highly varied. To illustrate the mood and intonations we might expect from mythic aetiologies of death, though, I will fasten on an interesting myth told among the Daribi (Chimbu Province, central highlands of Papua New Guinea).

> At a place called Sawo-Hwiau where the Pio river joins the Tua, two women were making sago. At noon Sau arrived [he is a kind of cult hero] and the woman with pendulous breasts heard the call of a *kaueri* bird; she wanted to go and see what the bird had sighted, but instead the girl with upright breasts went. She saw Sau sitting in the sun; he had white hair. He told her to look for lice in his hair. She stood behind him and searched through his hair; as she did so, he had an erection, and his penis went behind him and entered the woman's vagina. She cried out and ran away; Sau was shamed *and to get even he cursed mankind with fighting and with death.* Sau's skin was getting old, and to get rid of it he sloughed it off; the *gura* snakes, sago grubs and eels took it. Man, for his part, received the *clay of mourning* [or lamentation], body shields, arrows, etc., whereas the snakes settled down to a quiet existence.[2]

Here humanity loses immortality; it is banished from an Eden of uninhibited sexual prowess, and has to bear the burden of life's termination. A snake, that 'most subtle beast of the field', lives a quiet existence; men and women, on the other hand, have to relate to each other in a restrained (and to that extent more troublesome) way,[3] and men must fight and die on the field of battle.

Mortality or the human condition, then, is something of a blight. Yet, if we may reflect on this myth still further, this condition has its generative aspects as well; for, children arise from the 'social' mediation between men and women, and it is by war that the group defends its very existence and takes vengeance. Death, moreover, is not the end; no 'traditional' Melanesian, I suspect, would have said that! Nothing is more endemic to 'archaic' or 'primal' consciousness than that life is stronger than death, that audacity, courage, vitality, strength, power, breath, soul-substance, spirit, will forever replace lifelessness. The universe is alive with all these energies, the signals of ultimate survival: the noise in the dark, the cry of a bird, the howl of dogs, fire-flies, surfacing fish, snails, the silence of sacred stones, the evocative designs on a *gope* board, the atmosphere of the cemetery — the world is alive with the manifestations of immortality. Each Melanesian child came to feel and interact with this environment because others felt and related to it that way; the children came to sense all this in their bones, not by reflection nor by being schooled in the objectification of phenomena.

Let us move to a further stage in the life cycle, however, to initiation. When its moment arrived, initiation was much more an emotional than an intellectual experience. In those coastal and island societies in which initiation ceremonies were both colourful and highly significant, moreover, one could be forced to deal with death by literally coming face to face with the dead — that is, by meeting the ancestors, in the form of skulls, or carved representations, or other emblems.[4] When young Melanesians entered the community, it was a community of both the living and the dead — of men, women and *ancestors*. For most Melanesian societies the ancestors or dead relatives were an integral, supportive part of the whole company of souls, so that ordinary humans were dependent on their aid, their more-than-human power and, at the very least, on their contentment. In some cases, initiation itself was a form of ritual 'death', the passing from one order into another (more decidedly onerous) one through temporary contact with that spiritual realm in which ancestors move and have their being. Such a ritual death is vividly enacted by groups such as the Wam in the eastern Torricelli Mountains (Sepik). When the initiates enter the cult house or *haus tambaran*, the first in line falls to the ground as if dead, and the others behind crawl in over him. Once they are all inside, they disappear from public sight for three months; in a special sense they die in their seclusion until, after having been fed carefully by the elders, they return as proud, healthy warriors for the final and colourful ceremony. It is intriguing that participants in these events, including even the initiators, have not been found to reflect on the symbolism involved with any exercise of the intellect; they just *do* it, and it is simply part of their time-honoured 'eco-system' (in other words, their symbiotic relationship with the environment).[5]

Acme

But we have already come to the subject of young adulthood. When Melanesian man was recognized for his manhood and woman for her womanhood,
they were not only expected to cope with the passing away of their own
relatives and others, but to face the real possibility of their own deaths as well
— the man as a warrior, the woman as a childbearer.

The motives for engaging in a fight form a complex subject in itself (and
will be dealt with in chapter 3); what we are interested in here is how the
warrior thinks about the possibility of death when he joins his fellows with his
weapons. In the absence of helpful evidence, much is left to our creative
imagination. I once talked with a highland warrior who claimed to have killed
or wounded over twenty enemies before the Middle Wahgi Valley was
'pacified' in 1947. He was unhappy to talk about any of his personal fears; the
very articulation of them would be an act of weakness. It is unfortunate, if
only to be expected, furthermore, that Melanesia as yet lacks its Sholokhov to
relate what it might feel like in the heat of battle.[6] However, Wauru Degoba,
in his story 'The Night Warrior', has written quite arrestingly of such matters.
Dawagaima, his people's chief, lies wounded, isolated at night in enemy
country:

> [He] was waiting and thinking. He thought of his three wives, he thought of his
> far distant country. How would he get home again? He listened to the night
> birds calling. 'They are warning me,' he thought. The moon was right on his
> forehead; no warning noise came to him. 'If I do not take my revenge, will I be
> the great father of the warriors of Kaigunua?'[7]

Here we have a hint of the doubting moment, but it is only a hint. For
Melanesians fear was often considered a disease, a real sickness, which could
mean death. One might almost be tempted to say, in searching for a
comparative emphasis, that if ancient Greeks and Romans made much of
death on the battleground as bringing proud remembrance among the living,
and a direct passage to the choicest things offered by the other world,[8] most
Melanesians would tend to first think of such an end as failure. A warrior's
prime object in fighting was to get his skull, his man; a warrior who remained
alive to die older would be most honoured. To die in battle, was not,
admittedly, the death of a useless fellow, and for most groups a dead warrior
would inherit a choice dwelling place among the spirits; falling to an enemy
weapon could, however, often be one way of falling under suspicion — that
one had deserved a sorry fate, perhaps, or that one's magical or individual
powers had not been up to the test. Certainly, the warrior was expected to
drive death from his mind, to fight for his life with utter — some might say,
brutish — fearlessness. Those who fought, moreover, sometimes refused to
sleep in the reclining position of death. The Motuan warriors of Tubusereia, it
is reported, slept sitting up, never sure when an invasion might come.[9]

A woman, for her part, was expected to face the possibility of death in childbearing, and yet avoid it like a warrior was supposed to avoid a spear. There were ways by which women comforted each other before the moment of ordeal — the worst pangs experienced by humans who are not wounded. In the Murik Lakes area on the Sepik coast, for instance, a long story is recounted about the goddess Jari, a story very much cherished by those initiated into the female cult. It is said that Jari left her first husband and travelled along the Sepik coast in an easterly direction, creating rivers with a broken paddle and her own urine. At the first village she visited, however, she came upon a group of women surrounding a very expectant mother. 'What are you doing?' she asked. 'We are going to cut the mother open to save the baby.' 'Don't do that!' Jari exclaimed, 'fetch me some *mangas* bark and a coconut bowl full of water.' When these were brought, she rubbed the woman's waist with both the water and bark juices. After the woman had delivered successfully, Jari then passed on the magical formulae for childbirth. 'Thank goodness you came!' shouted the villagers, 'we have lost many a good woman that way!' And so Jari went further along the coast to other villages and the same incident was repeated numerous times.[10] From Manam Island to near Wewak, at least during the first thirty years of this century, most women relied on Jari for uncomplicated deliveries, secure in the realization that an old order of things, when childbirth meant inevitable death, had passed away. And the naming of a new-born child in Melanesia, incidentally, often affirmed new life in the face of death, since a child was commonly named after a grandparent. The birth marks the beginning of a new cycle; for, the grandparents will soon leave the land of the living, or will deal kindly with namesakes once they have departed to the spirit-world.[11]

There is more to observe about adulthood, or better still, the prime of life. In the 'normal course of events' Melanesians had to face death in the form of malevolent forces and sickness. The world was more often than not inhabited by evil spirits and not just beneficent ones. Kelfene is such a spirit for the Lumi or Wape people (south of the Torricelli Mountains, Sepik hinterland).

> He lives in all pools of water, lakes, rivers and creeks, not being bound to any one particular place. Kelfene, on smelling a menstruating woman as she approaches a pool of water, causes the woman to have a large haemorrhage, following which the pool of water gushes up, enveloping and killing her. Just nothing can be done for the hapless victim. The only safe places for menstruating women are in their villages. All women are terrified of this spirit.

Children, while in the bush, must neither complain of being hungry nor ask to eat; 'if they do, there is the probability that Kelfene will come and kill them all, especially if they are near water'.[12]

Women and children often had the fear of death instilled into them with such beliefs, even if one can quickly perceive in the above case how the instilling of such fears was a means of social control — albeit a very male-dominated one — to prevent wandering by unclean (and therefore highly dangerous) females, and to put children in their place. But it is not unusual for male adults to be afraid of encountering a deadly force. This was a fearfulness distinct from that despicable fear towards one's enemy or prey. It was a sense of awe, uncertainty, obligation, and sometimes plain terror in the face of unknown powers.[13] It is a sobering thought that the extraordinary lifestyle of many southern Koiari of Papua, with their houses built high in the trees, was determined by fear of Vata, a deadly spirit.[14] And ghosts, as well as place spirits or other supernaturals, could be encountered by the Melanesians. As already noted in passing, the Lakalai of West New Britain are among those who fear meeting a ghost, especially a 'man from the bush', who is a spirit in human form. Ann Chowning writes of these people:

> Even daylight encounters near the village may be dangerous especially if they end in sexual intercourse. There are a few clues to the non-human nature of these shape-shifters, and a man who is suspicious will apply the tests of asking the person to name a common object or spreading nettle leaves for the woman to lie on.[15]

Sickness, as is well attested in literature, was often ascribed to the supernaturals, to malevolent spirits or to displeased dead relatives, especially those relatives cross for being disposed of at the funeral in an improper or careless manner. Infirmity, too, could be the work of a sorcerer, who could control inimical forces or who could work the magical techniques necessary for creating harm or murder. Melanesians had various ways of dealing with the possibility of death arising out of sickness. The most common practice was to consult the person who would either know what had happened or was going to happen. The manner of diagnosing certain death varies from culture to culture. A Wahgi magician, for example, may choose to pierce a series of sweet potatoes with a sharp stick, posing a series of alternatives before each prod, and deciding on the answers by the softness or toughness of a given potato.[16]

A Roro diviner — usually female — will first fast from meat; then she prays quickly over the sick body and, after passing a banana leaf around the person's face, will sleep with the leaf under her head. The dead relatives who are trying their hardest to take the person's spirit away with them are expected to explain the whole matter to her.[17] Specialists such as this diviner would tell if the ailment were fatal or not — though whether they would also prescribe the cure depended on the social structure and the nature of its specializations. The judgement of death was taken with the utmost seriousness. Even today, a person without any recourse against sorcery (or against sickness supposedly brought by a malevolent spirit) will surely die, so real to people are the powers of destruction which overshadow their existence.[18]

The perils of Melanesian life were real in other ways, too: famine and epidemics had to be contended with, for instance, and there were also the dangers faced by those who dared to brave the sea along the coasts. We must not forget that when the western Motu or the Elema set out on their long *Hiri* expeditions in impressive trading canoes, they realized that 'their bones and flesh could well become the manure of a distant land or meat for the sharks', and it is worth reporting that the *Hiri* traders found security for the journey by making an offering to Kaeva Kuku, a female deity shared by both trading groups. They certainly needed that security; we know that in 1876, for example, 177 *Hiri* traders were massacred by enemies as they were plying their way along the Papuan coast.[19]

Decay

Now that the life cycle we are considering has passed its acme, we come to old age. To be an elder in Melanesian societies — and I think mainly of males — was usually to be in a privileged, responsible position. Having survived this far, having made sure that one's own skull was not displayed on an enemy's rack, and having in some cases undergone further initiations into the deeper mysteries of the cult, an elder often found himself in more sheltered, more secure circumstances. But in his life's journey, he was now closer to the ancestors, and that realization was firmly embedded in his consciousness by the way younger people related to him, and sought his advice on matters of ritual, lore and custom.[20] Some societies went so far as to celebrate the onset of old age. Among the eastern Fuyughe, for instance, the major feasts conform to stages in man's life. First comes the initiation ceremony; then, eventually, two important festivities take place — one to celebrate with those men who have their first grey hairs (*anukevadad*), followed by one to salute those elders with loosening teeth (*usiadad*) — before the last feast of all, the funeral to honour the recent dead. These particular ceremonies were usually for groups of males, and they also provided the opportunity for making peace and new alliances, since visitors from other Fuyughe-speaking areas were invited to attend. The elders being honoured usually sat back in the men's house or *emu*, while the young danced through both day and night.[21] The approach of death, in various cultures, suggested to the aged that they must settle certain obligations or put things in order. A Manus Islander, for example, might have lived long enough to have had the privilege of actually *seeing* his daughter-in-law, and to have completed the payments for his son's wife. According to Margaret Mead:

> This is one of the few situations which the Manus feel as romantic, the adventure of looking upon the face of a loved son's wife. 'Should I die,' says an old man, 'and never see the wife whom I have purchased for my son?' So the old father, tottering towards death, beyond the age when disrespect could lurk in his glance, is allowed to make a feast for his daughter-in-law. After thus publicly

showing his respect for her, the taboo is removed forever and father, son and daughter-in-law live as one household.[22]

More's the pity, however, that because Manus life was so exacting such a situation seldom occurred. Melanesians, in general, were only too aware of how many people died before they could open their eyes, grow a beard, breast-feed a child, let alone see old age.[23]

Disposal of the dead

It is fairly safe to generalize that death is taken by Melanesians as the most important event in any person's career. For those of us who prefer to relegate death to an hour's funeral service, or to 'let the dead bury the dead', we would be as astounded as Malinowski was to discover 'the immense social and economic upheaval which occurs after each death,' as he puts it, and which 'is one of the most salient features of the culture of these natives'.[24] Malinowski's statement can be applied to Melanesia generally, not just to Trobriand Island societies. What is very difficult to generalize about, however, is the manner in which funerals are conducted, the way corpses are disposed of, and the various attitudes people have toward the recent dead. At this point there is the real danger of selecting those examples which are most unusual and interesting, and thus not necessarily representative: one could have a field-day with the horrific and cadaverous — and not just by talking about cannibalism or bloated bodies floating down highland rivers.[25]

Women often bore the brunt of male-dominated tradition in those contexts in which death was an expected outcome. The Lemakot widows of north New Ireland, for instance, would be strangled and then thrown on the cremation pyres of their departed husbands in a Melanesian version of *suttee*, though they could avoid such a hideous fate if they were still suckling a child; elsewhere, relatively more females committed suicide over unrequited love or unfaithfulness (as among the Roro).[26] Even dead women, especially in societies where they are expected to have no ancestral significance, could be given a 'raw deal'. Among the Wahgi, some women were literally thrown face downwards into the grave, to lessen the likelihood of their ghostly vengefulness — especially against husbands who took another wife.[27]

Very common in Melanesia was the raised wooden burial platform rather than the pyre or the pit. The corpse was exposed in the open air to facilitate its putrefaction, so that the skull could be preserved, or a bone hung *in memoriam* around a mourner's neck. In some areas the hands and the feet were treated and dried for pendants (as within the Purari watershed), and techniques of uncased mummification have been found, unevenly distributed, from the Torres Strait to Yapen Island (Irian Jaya).[28] This feature of Melanesian culture was bound to be destroyed by the colonials; when that did occur, interestingly it was more often representatives of the colonial administrations than of the missionaries who were responsible. The government officials could not put up with the odour of decaying flesh and the dripping pits — and besides, it was unhealthy! Some of these officials at least made it their business to describe burial customs, though, or make sketches. C. A. W. Monckton has bequeathed us with an impressive line drawing of an eastern Fuyughe burial platform (1906), and the presence of infant bones in an adjacent tray probably indicates that it was the burial shrine for a mother and child.[29] Among the Fuyughe the platforms were raised high (about 11.5 ft or 3.5 m) because the spirit of a dead person was expected to depart to the heights of Mount Albert Edward, the spirit being likely to remain around as a nuisance if the procedure for disposal of the body was not properly followed.[30]

Because of the relative egalitarianism of Melanesian societies, only rarely does one come across any outstanding funerary grandeur. Missionaries sketched an elaborately carved tomb for a chief in the Biak-Numfor area (north-west Irian Jaya) during the middle of the last century: an unusual phenomenon. Perhaps the fascinating earthworks to which I led a small 1985 expedition in the Rigo area (hinterland Papua) are grand tumulus burial sites of bygone chiefs, thus representing a disposal pattern quite different from the immediate pre-contact custom of inserting bones into cliff clefts. Yet only archaeology — and in this case upon a sacred site of some sensitivity — will tell.[31]

Returning to more typical situations, it is generally true that the manner of treating the recent dead is symbolically, though not necessarily consciously, related to assumptions about the dead person's immediate and future whereabouts. By piecing together a mass of oral historical information, for example, it can be established that, around 1860, all the ten-and-a-half 'clans' on the northern side of the Middle Wahgi Valley buried their dead high on the mountainsides in fenced enclosures and under sacred trees. The dead were reckoned to inhabit the highest terrain. By 1930, however, following the continued presence of an eleventh, immigrant Chimbu group from the east, the Wahgi peoples were burying their dead in quite a different fashion and in different places: bodies were being placed under little houses in large cemeteries adjacent to long *sing sing* (or ceremonial) grounds. The departed were expected to inhabit these houses, receiving food from their live kin. They dwelt there together, waiting for the community of the living to perform the *Kongar* ceremony — a ceremony of such colour and spectacle that it made their previous customs pale into insignificance.

The Wahgi *Kongar* ceremony was a great pig-killing festival, which has its counterparts in the Chimbu, among the Melpa, the Mendi and other groups in the central highlands of New Guinea. In focussing on the *Kongar*, we pass, rather unobtrusively — and perhaps too quickly — from talk about the funerals of individuals, to periodic ceremonies which involve *the collective dead*, the whole group of those clan members who have died in recent times or over the last few generations. Every part of the *Kongar* ceremony must be carried out in correct order — otherwise, as its custodians will aver, the ancestors will bring disaster on the clan by their displeasure.[32] The ancestors are involved in the decision as to when the ceremony should be performed. The functionary most important in arriving at this decision — the *mapilie* or tabued man (who we earlier thought could fit the category of 'priest') — has the onerous task of keeping up contact with the 'spirits of the fighting dead' from one *Kongar* to another so that their displeasure is not incurred by inviting the wrong people. When the day of the festival arrives, dancing warriors burst into the long *sing sing* ground, with armed men pushing back the crowds and displaying their might and their beauty. But it is not only the visitors who see and marvel; so do the company of dead relatives. The scene is acted out before the community of living people *and* spirits. In the very centre of the activities, where the women sit chanting their entrancing song, the ancestors are provided with a tiny grandstand, a Melanesian 'doll's house' (or *bolimgar*), with pig-jaws strewn around it to satisfy their appetites and surrounded by the vigour of the dance, for their delight. The clan ancestors will determine the fertility of the clan for another cycle: it is they who — impressed by the dance and the song, by the mass killing of hundreds of pigs on the following day, and by the clan's generosity — will fatten the pigs for the next long period, bless the soil for yams and the wombs for children. Without the living dead, the community as a whole would die; with them it will undergo rebirth.[33]

It would divert us from our present task to exhaustively detail the extraordinary diversity of mortuary rites, feasts and processions, careful accounts of the various precautions taken in handling the corpse, of self-decorations for mourning, or of the way food is exchanged after a death, and so forth. In any case, there is no substitute for witnessing a funeral, the experience of collective sorrow, or the hearing of a lament, with one's own senses. A film so sensitively produced as *Dead Birds* (on the Dani of the Baliem Valley, Irian Jaya) will bring such matters to life for those who are too far off to know Melanesia at first hand.[34] Although there is no doubt that one gains many insights by observing or reflecting on the symbols, rituals and the external phenomena of funerals and related ceremonies, more important still are the articulated beliefs concerning death and after-life, and explanations given as to what happens to a person who has died. This complex subject usually demands patient dialogue and empathy, as well as linguistic skill, and will be treated more fully in the next chapter.

Access to the dead

As we have already seen, many groups believed (and still do) that the dead are never far away. Some who believe this affirm that the dead can be called upon for help; others, however, are fearful of their anger. Many believe, admittedly, that the dead dwell together in some far-off place, although their departure there may not be immediate (a 'ghostly' stage preceding habitation with the 'spirits'), and in any case their super-human power allows them to return for food or communication at a moment's notice or when they choose. Integrally related to the question of a dead person's whereabouts, though, is the question as to *why* the person died. In advance of my lengthier discussion of these matters in the next chapter, one simple illustration will suffice to clarify the issues.

According to the eastern Toaripi (coastal Papua), every individual death was the result of sorcery. Irrespective of the kind of death, moreover, every Toaripi spirit eventually crossed the ocean to the land of the setting sun (quite Polynesian, you might say). But the soul did not journey to its far-off place immediately; it waited in the bush to disclose to its living relatives the one(s) who performed the sorcery. The bereaved family would remain in their house quietly for several days after the funeral. At night one of them would get up and proceed into the bush, looking for the ghost or any sign which would indicate the person (or, in some cases, the group) responsible for the sorcery. If one of the family failed to make contact, others would try until there was an appropriate encounter. As with Motuans, the eastern Toaripi believe that people are 'blind', so that they cannot see the spirits, whereas the spirits can see everything. Whether, like the Motuans, they used to eat certain leaves to remove their blindness, remains uncertain.[35] Once contact has been made, the spirit would be free, and the family would either take revenge or else precautionary measures for the future, depending on whether the dead person was young or old. The logic involved here has further implications, as we shall see later.

Heavens

What about rewards and punishments in the after-life, and what kinds of mental pictures do Melanesians have of those places eventually reached by the dead? Again there is a diversity of opinion, and some explanations for the spirits' whereabouts are not tied to any conception of a moral order in the universe. A Roro (of coastal Papua), for example, would have told you that some spirits have the joy of proceeding to a safe haven (near Cape Possession at the far western limits of their territory), and this is because they had died a 'normal' kind of death or one in relatively pleasant, unexceptional circumstances. As for those who had met a hideous fate — such as being speared in the back or devoured by a crocodile — they were doomed to a protracted, if not permanent existence in the bush.[36] A Motuan, on the other hand, would probably have told you what certain Motuans told the famous missionary, James Chalmers, in 1880.

> At Port Moresby the natives say that the spirit as soon as it leaves the body proceeds to Elema [the Gulf] where the dead person forever dwells in the midst of food and betel nuts and spends the days and nights in endless enjoyment, eating, chewing . . . and dancing. Most *worthless fellows*, [however], are sent

back to Poava and Udia, small islands near Boera, there to remain until the goddess (Kaeva Kuku) sees fit to send them.[37]

Not bad eschatology? And note how it differs from the Roro model. One's fate depended on one's moral virtues, not simply on historical contingency. But, as we shall see, explanations did vary from group to group.

Now it is time to treat of the journey into the other world or order, which in itself was typically conceived to be a form of rebirth. The dead person had to be made comfortable for this journey: pots and utensils were commonly laid beside the corpse to prevent loneliness and despair; food was prepared for the dead who sets off (as much as for the living who remain behind to wish the dead person well). As for the images of the other world, they also vary considerably. In the earliest known systematic ethnographic study of a Melanesian people — by the neglected Italian savant, Pier Ambrogio Curti, writing in 1861 — we find described the extraordinary journey of the Woodlark or Muju Islander's soul as it heads towards its beautiful goal.

> When one dies, the soul, the islanders say, travels to *Tum*, a brutish paradise which they imagine to be a place of delight situated on an island to the west of Woodlark . . . The journey is carried out on the back of the great serpent *Motetutau*. He who does not freely stand on the serpent and falls into the sea is changed into a fish or shell; but whoever stands firm finds at the entrance of *Tum* an inexorable old woman, who has the task of not allowing further anyone who does not carry two lines of tattooing on his arm, and whoever does not have this distinctive mark is rejected and thrown into the sea. Once having entered *Tum*, one enjoys all material pleasures, and has copious supplies of everything; one lives, one dies again and yet revives, as does the drunken alcoholic who kills his reason with liquor, yet after a dream receives it back again.[38]

For the highlander Daribi, by comparison, the road to the place of the dead was the Tua River, which ran to a lake they had never seen, somewhere in the west. There, the dead supposedly live in caves.[39]

It was all very well these spirits taking off, however, but the living often considered it was vital for some part of the old body, or some effigy or emblem, to remain behind. Bones of the dead were frequently worn as personal adornments and reminders among Melanesians. The skull of the departed could be particularly treasured. The skull of a dead chief among the Roviana people of the western Solomons, for instance, was highly prized as a source of *mana* (spirit effect).[40] In the Papuan Gulf, by comparison, the western Elema would be meticulous in arranging the skulls of dead foes on a rack above the *gope* boards representing the family ancestors, who still remained ravenous in their desire for enemy flesh.[41] Among the Iatmül on the Sepik River, by contrast, an effigy of a recently dead man was propped up by a complex of poles, while the real body was transported miles off to a place where the earth was not soggy.[42] All such practices, it may be argued, indicate that there was regenerative power in each death: the group or ordinary mortals received some of that power. After the point at which the dead was severed from its companions, its 'soul' (or sometimes two 'souls'[43]) finds the proper resting place. Then, some time later, when the mourning was absolute, when love was mingled with fear, the bereaved men and women could return to their normal affairs and live again.

Return

A crucial question might now be asked: were the dead expected to return? Such a query, of course, can be quite misleading. For most Melanesians, ghosts or ancestors were quite capable of making their presence felt among the living whenever they chose. The real question is this: did Melanesians expect the dead to be reborn in any tangible form on this earth? There are, to be sure, a few instances of belief in the transmigration of souls — roughly parallel to the Hindu notion of *samsara*. A. W. Murray, in fact, believed that he detected such a belief among the Motuans — at least in 1874. Although the soul was supposed to remain 'for an indefinite time at Erema', he reports, 'it returns to the place from whence it came and becomes the occupant of some other body'.[44] Murray was only an amateur at anthropology and his conclusions remain questionable; yet, the fact remains that beliefs about reincarnation are scattered throughout Melanesia, and have been analyzed in more recent literature.[45] At a Bena Bena village in the eastern New Guinea highlands, I vividly remember, an old woman wept before me for half an hour, believing that one of my little daughters was the reborn soul of a child she had lost years before. A more important issue in the study of Melanesian religion, however, concerns myths or beliefs about the return of the dead collectively, not just in individual reincarnations. At last we have reached that highly interesting aspect of Melanesian religious life — the so-called cargo cults.

In his important book *The Trumpet Shall Sound*, Peter Worsley has ably argued that most of those cult movements of the twentieth century which expected the coming of European cargo, also expected the ancestors to come as the bearers of that cargo.[46] So-called cargo cultists, as we shall see (in chapter 8), usually supposed that the ancestors, so crucial for the economic security of the group, were in fact the real manufacturers of the new, marvellous items handled by the intrusive Europeans. The dead were the ones who could bring to the living a complete transformation of the (albeit localized) cosmic order. It was through reflecting on these Melanesian beliefs in the collective return of the dead that the famous Romanian scholar Mircea Eliade was induced to write of cargo cultism as belief in the coming of cosmic regeneration or rebirth.[47] I will take issue with some of Eliade's arguments in a later chapter, yet a few pertinent comments about these matters will not go astray at this point.

Let it be clear that too little fieldwork has been done to demonstrate how and if cult movements expecting the return of the dead were affected by *longstanding*, traditional beliefs about such a return. It may well be that in most cases the startling new circumstances brought about by 'the whiteman phenomenon' *produced* and *diffused* such beliefs. Since there has been little or no detailed investigation of this particular issue, I can only report my own findings. In 1973, for example, I started to plot the intellectual biography of an impressive prophet figure among the eastern Fuyughe of the Papuan highlands, who was Ona Asi or Bilalaf. What emerged from the bits and pieces of evidence intrigued me greatly. In the 1920s, for instance, when the missionaries were settling in, the prophet's beliefs about the dead were much the same as those held by everybody else in Fuyughe country. The dead, having been properly placed on raised high platforms, were expected to rise to Mount Albert Edward, and never to bother the living any more. The important spiritual powers which the eastern Fuyughe often sought to appropriate were *not* the ancestors, but the *sila*, protector place-spirits, which guarded each cluster of hamlets, and which could even be called up in séances.[48] By the 1930s, however, the prophet Ona Asi began to hold séances with the *dead*, and in his meetings he sought to make contact with 'the other side', as they do in the spiritualist churches of the West. What was the object of these séances? One of them was to find out who enemy sorcerers and murderers were. Another, most interestingly, was to bring wealth and *susum* or 'goods' (very generally conceived) to his people. In 1942 the prophet was arrested as a troublemaker, and was detained on Yule Island, on the coast. There, among other things, he came into contact with ideas about how the ancestors would return bringing European cargo. These were ideas, incidentally, held by certain Roro and Mekeo people on the coast who had set their hopes on a young prophetess by the name of Filo, and a young black priest by the name of Louis Vangeke. To cut a long story short, however, the prophet had returned to his home country by 1945; and what do we find him preaching in the early 1950s? That the ancestors — collectively — will return.[49] Here in one lifetime, then, we have a shift in ideas, which represents an adjustment to changing circumstances.

This, admittedly, is only one example, and we shall have to wait for a discussion of other cases. Reflecting not only on these brief points, however, but on all the evidence at our disposal, a working conclusion presents itself: that the remarkable circumstances and changes of the twentieth century *demanded an eschatology from the Melanesian*. Melanesian groups may have had incipient beliefs about the end of the known order, but they *needed* the myth of the returning dead — they needed the Christian doctrine of resurrection, the Last Judgement, and related notions, because, in their own special way, the events, the drastic changes they faced, *were* eschatological; for, these changes drew to a rounded conclusion the hard, relentless order of lithic (or stone age) existence which had lasted for thousands of years.[50] The Melanesian had to cope with a brand new world, and if some chose the baptism or the new birth offered by the churches, others (as we shall see in chapter 8) were baptized by the fire of the so-called 'Vailala Madness'.[51]

Now we are left with emergent 'modern' Melanesia, the infant colossus issuing from the womb of an ancient mother, youthful unities arising from time-honoured diversities. Despite modernization, however, today's Melanesian will have to go on facing the ancient, inexorable fact of death. Christianity, which is now the most powerful religious force in the region, may whittle away 'the worship of the dead', as some people choose to call it.[52] But, far from destroying the importance of the funeral, or the tribute to the departed, or the strong sense of a community between the living and the dead, or anticipations of life beyond death and beyond history, Christianity will in the end, I think, reinforce these things, and so foster what is already on the way — a distinctly Melanesian brand of the Christian faith, a distinctly Melanesian way of facing death and the resurrection. The forces of secularism are on their way as well, however slowly, and one day some Melanesian may be brave enough to leave his body for medical research!

NOTES

Chapter 2 is a revised version of material that originally appeared in N. Habel (ed.), *Powers, Plumes and Piglets.*

1 Or, 'The creature born is the creator dying'; see J. Needham, *Time and Eastern Man* (Henry Myers Lecture 1964), London, 1965, p.2.

2 See Wagner, *Habu*, p.30 (with slight modifications and emphasis added); cf. Wagner, *The curse of Souw; principles of Daribi clan definition and alliance in New Guinea*, Chicago, 1967.

3 The Freudians might say 'more repressed way', see H. Marcuse, *Eros and civilization*, New York, 1962, pp.15ff, N. O. Brown, *Life against death*, New York, 1959, esp. ch. 2. On Wagner's interpretations, *Habu*, pp.30–37.

4 e.g., A. M. Kiki, *Kiki: ten thousand years in a lifetime*, Melbourne, 1968, ch. 3, for an account of a personal experience. In general see M. R. Allen, *Male cults*, and by contrast M. Eliade, *Birth and rebirth* (trans. W. R. Trask), London, 1958, ch. 2.

5 On eastern Torricelli Mountain groups in the Dreikikir area, see B. L. Allen, Information flow and innovation diffusion in the East Sepik District, Papua New Guinea (doctoral dissert., ANU, Canberra 1976), pp.44–45, with pers. comm. on the symbolism.

6 M. Sholokhov, *And Quiet Flows the Don* (trans. S. Garry), Harmondsworth, 1967, pt 2, chs 2–3.

7 (Pacific Writers Series) (ed. U. Beier), Brisbane, 1971, p.4.

8 See Herodotus, *Historiae* 1.31; Thucydides, *Historiae* 11.34ff; Livy, *Ab Urbe Condita*, 11.10, etc.

9 Oral Testimony (OT): Sibona Kopi, 1976. It is interesting to note that the Motu dead were buried in a reclining position, whereas in other cultures — the Dugum Dani of the Baliem Valley, Irian Jaya, for example — the corpse was placed in a sitting position, whether for cremation or deposition.

10 M. Tamoane, 'Kamoai of Darapap', in Trompf (ed.), *Prophets*, pp.187ff (*mangas* is a species of *Hibiscus*).

11 Again, Bryant Allen insists that such naming among eastern Torricelli Mountain groups is quite unconscious and not the result of policy or ideology. In other cases, by contrast, the custom of tabuing the name of the dead (within the clan) applies. cf. van Baal, *Dema*, pp.135f. etc.

12 D. E. McGregor, Spirit-magic beliefs and concepts of the Wape People in relation to the effective communication of the Christian message (mimeographed discussion paper, Anguganak Conference, Lumi 1965), p.5. Lumi is inland from Aitape.

13 The two senses of fear may be compared to the Hebraic distinction between fear of danger and 'the fear of Yahweh', see e.g., Psalms 23:4, 22:23.

14 So, W. G. Lawes, Diary: Visit to Villages in the Interior (unpublished report dated Dec. 1876, Mitchell Library, Sydney, microfilms item 33, A3923–1, LMS). The Koiari live inland from Port Moresby.

15 'Lakalai Religion and World View', in Trompf (ed.), *Mel. and Judaeo-Christ. relig. trads*, bk 1, p.84.

16 OTs: Peter Kuiwan and Kulne Aipe, Sanglap clan, 1975.

17 M. Ume, Woman Diviners among the Roro (handwritten MS, UPNG, Port Moresby 1974), pp.1–2; OT: Louise Aitsi, 1976. For the idea that a person's spirit travels on its way towards the place of the dead during sickness, see also Wagner, *Habu*, pp.112–13.

18 By contrast, a healer who has decided the patient will live usually refused to face the person's death on principle, so implicit is the acceptance of the sources of supernatural power. Chalmers comments on the great chagrin of two Motuan 'medicine men' (= *babalau*) who failed to revive a child, Diary; trip to the West (unpublished report dated 20 June 1884), p.7 (Mitchell Library microf. item 33, cf. n.14).

19 See Chalmers, Diary; Trip to Papuan Gulf (report dated 2 Jan. 1880), p.11, cf. p.19 (Mitchell Lib. microf. 13); Chalmers and W. Gill, *Work and adventures in New Guinea*, London, 1885, p.305.

20 On the Houailou of north-eastern New Caledonia, for instance, the aged are considered to have more and more *bao* (the character of spirits) and less and less of ordinary humanness; see M. Leenhardt, *Do Kamo: la personne et le mythe dans le monde mélanesien*, Paris, 1971, pp.81–83. Among the Orokaiva of Papua it is understood that men ought to prepare themselves in life to become helpful spirits, cf. W. Jojoga Opeba, Taro or Cargo?, p.31.

21 Trompf, '"Bilalaf"', in Trompf (ed.), *Prophets*, ch. 1.

22 *Growing up in New Guinea*, Harmondsworth, 1942, p.86.

23 For a relevant demographic assessment, D. A. M. Lea and L. H. Lewis, 'Masculinity in Papua New Guinea', in L. A. Kosinki and J. W. Webb (eds), *Population at microscale*, Hamilton (NZ), 1976, p.73 and the literature cited there.

24 *Argonauts of the western Pacific*, p.490. It is rare for a snap burial to occur in Melanesia. B. J. Allen happened to witness one in the Dreikikir area; a man was put out of the way quickly because in his bodily infirmity during life he had been largely useless to the subsistence of the group (pers. comm. 1976). cf. also van Baal, *Dema*, pp.771f.

25 See F. Hurley, *Pearls and savages*, New York, 1924, plate 11; I. Willis, An epic journey (honours subthesis, UPNG, Port Moresby 1969), p.80.

26 T. Bodrogi, 'Malangans of North New Ireland; L. Biró's unpublished notes', in *Acta ethnographica* (Hungarian Academy of Science), 16 (1967), pp.63ff. cf. J. L. Whittaker et al., *Documents and readings in New Guinea history; prehistory to 1889*, Brisbane, 1975, pp.107ff. (Lemakot); OT: Louise Aitsi, etc. 1974 (Roro), and for the males by contrast, J. G. Frazer, *The golden bough*, London, 1911, vol. 1, p.213 and the literature cited there.

27 M. Reay, 'Politics, development and Women in the Rural Highlands', *Journal of the Administrative College of Papua New Guinea*, 5 (1975), p.4.

28 For Purari pendants (from Udi village), see items A946, 44–45 and A847 in the Macleay Museum, University of Sydney. For mummification, G. L. Petty, 'The Macleay Museum mummy from Torres Strait; a postscript to Elliot Smith and the diffusion controversy', *Man*, 4 (New Ser.) (1969), pp.24ff; cf. C. E. Joel, 'The Case of the Macleay mummy', *The new diffusionist*, 2 (1971), pp.73ff.

29 Monckton in Commonwealth of Australia, *British New Guinea, Annual Report (BNGAR)*, 1906, plate 2, following p.93. On the health policies of officials or patrol officers (the *kiaps*), e.g., Ioma Patrol Reports, 11 Oct. 1912, pp.4, 7 (National Archives of Papua New Guinea, G91, file 228) for one of my own areas of interest. B. L. Allen and A. Strathern both reported on similar approaches by these officials in the Dreikikir and Western Highlands areas respectively (pers. comms 1976).

30 P. Fastré, Moeurs et coutoumes fouyoughèses (unpublished MS, Popole 1937), pp.164–65, 170.

31 S. Chauvet, *Les arts indigènes en Nouvelle Guinée*, plate 22 (tomb at Doreh Bay, Irian Jaya); Trompf, The Tumulus Expedition (unpublished file [1985]), University of Sydney.

32 OT: Munil of Bolba Village, Nov. 1973.

33 See L. J. Luzbetak, 'The socio-religious significance of a New Guinea pig festival', *Anthropological quarterly*, New Ser. 11 (1954), pp.60ff, 102ff.

34 cf. also R. Gardner and K. Heider, *Gardens of war*, Harmondsworth, 1974. For musical recordings of events, too, note *Papua New Guinea: Manus, Bougainville* (ed. Beier, prod. C. Duvelle), Port Moresby, 1974, Side B, Track 5.

35 On the eastern Toaripi, V. Koroti, Explanations for Trouble, Sickness and Death among the Toaripi, with special reference to Lese Oalai and nearby villages (handwritten MS, UPNG, Port Moresby, 1974), pp.2–3; cf. H. Brown, Social and Political Change among the Eastern Elema (Dip. Anthrop. thesis, London School of Economics, London, 1956), ch. 8, and C. Siaoa, The *Sevese* and *Harisu* Ceremonies among the Elema (handwritten MS, UPNG, Port Moresby, 1976), pp.3–5. On the Motuans I rely heavily on the oral testimony of Sibona Kopi, 1976. The relevant Motu plant is called *api api sioha* (and for reference to Kopi's written work, ch. 4, n.124 below).

36 Even death in battle was ascribed to sorcery — the superior magic of the enemy. cf., however, Brown, Elema, p.92.

37 Chalmers, Trip to the Papuan Gulf, p.19. Both Rev. Sir Percy Chatterton (translator of the Bible into Pure Motu) and my former colleague, Nigel Oram, warned me that the Motuans told Chalmers what they wanted him to hear on this issue, but the special details in Chalmer's report and my own subsequent investigations (especially with the elders of Lealea village, 1977) persuade me otherwise.

38 Unpublished trans. by D. Affleck of Curti: 'The Island of Muju or Woodlark', *Politechnico*, 14 (1862), pp.38–39 (by kind permission of translator).

39 Wagner, *Habu*, p.112 (the Daribi ghosts were animated through a need for water).

40 See E. Tuza, The Rise of Eto; an historical perspective (honours subthesis, UPNG, Port Moresby, 1974), pp.14–19.

41 Hurley, *Pearls*, p.225.

42 See G. Bateson, *Naven*, Stanford, 1958, ch. 11, and plate XXa.

43 On this question esp. F. Jachmann (now Tomasetti), *Seelen- und Totenvorstellungen bei drei Bevölkerungsgruppen in Neuguinea* (Arbeiten aus dem Seminar für Völkerkunde der J. W. Goethe-Universität), Wiesbaden, 1969, pp.166ff and passim.

44 A. W. Murray, Diary; second voyage to Port Moresby, 1874, p.10 (handwritten MS, Mitchell Lib. microf. item 13).

45 On uncertainties in connection with early mission reports, see above n.37. For beliefs about reincarnation among the Siane, Kyaka Enga, Iatmül, Trobriands and South Pentecost Island people, see P. Lawrence and M. J. Meggitt (eds), 'Introduction' to *Gods*, p.11, and the literature cited there. For the emergence of such beliefs as 'modern' phenomena, see M. Mead, *New lives for old*, New York, 1961, pp.287–88.

46 London, 1970 edn, esp. Map 1.

47 *The two and the one* (trans. J. M. Cohen), New York, 1965, ch. 3.

48 Fastré, Moeurs, p.186.

49 Trompf, '"Bilalaf"', for the above account in detail, and cf. ch. 6 below. Note also ch. 8, n. 48.

50 cf. Trompf, 'The Future of Macro-Historical Ideas', *Soundings*, 72 (1979), p.70.

51 This is the pre-war term for cargo cultism, and see Worsley, *Trumpet shall sound*, ch. 4.

52 See L. J. Luzbetak, 'The worship of the dead in Middle Wahgi (New Guinea)', *Anthropos*, 51 (1956), pp.81ff.

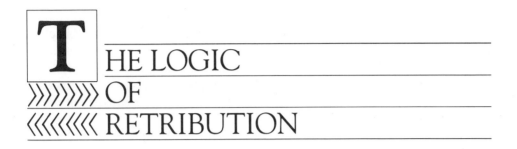

CHAPTER 3

THE LOGIC OF RETRIBUTION

This chapter concerns some of the more remarkable features of Melanesian life: the taking of 'indiscriminate' revenge (or payback killing), prestigious acts of generosity without guarantee of comparable returns; and the intricate modes of explaining significant events in human affairs, such as prosperity and disaster, well-being and sickness, life and death. These features, as already intimated in the preceding chapters, are integrally related in most Melanesian world-views. It is as well to examine them in depth at an early stage because neither the pre-contact nor still more complicated post-contact religious scene can ever be understood without an adequate grasp of them. In reflecting on these features, a more analytical approach to traditional phenomena will be developed.

As I have shown in other cross-cultural studies, collectively held views of revenge, reciprocity and the explanation of significant events are components of a discrete logical framework of ideas.[1] By the 'logic of retribution', or 'retributive logic', to put a name on this framework, we simply mean the way people think or reason about rewards and punishments. Human thinking, admittedly, is bound up with action, yet this chapter will concentrate on forms of logic or logical explanation, putting priority on the way people understand their own or others' actions, and on their manner of explicating the world, with less attention to external behaviour and realities. That Melanesians interpret affairs in terms of requital or basic principles of retribution is evident enough from published research on their belief-systems, but the notions involved have not been studied in their interrelationship, and too little has been written about the general area of investigation for retributive logic to have been appreciated as an important trans-cultural phenomenon.

I have already set out a substantial theoretical prolegomenon, to this topic in another place,[2] and a repetition of it, or a discussion of how it has commenced to be taken up by Melanesianists,[3] is not appropriate here. For present purposes it is enough to state that 'retributive logic', as we have termed it, is reflected in three modes, which shall be dealt with in turn. The first is negative and covers all those efforts, from tribal warfare to personal vindictiveness (between single competitors, spouses, and so on), to get back at the source of resentment in an appropriately antagonistic way. Even punishments by legal sanction and consensus generally fall under this category. The second, however, is positive and has to do with peaceful recompenses (especially in mending alliances), payments made in the give and take of socio-economic exchanges, as well as sacrifices (whether to spirit powers or on behalf of other humans). The ancient Roman understanding of *'retributio'* (retribution), after all, incorporates such a concessive, redistributive meaning alongside the stern implication of revenge, recrimination and merited penalty. The third mode is explanatory, and this is the intellectual process — crucial in the understanding of Melanesian traditions — by which people explain events in terms of blessing and trouble, praise and blame, reward and punishment.

Revenge and negative payback

To kill one's enemies, whether by stealth or in battle, was a favoured pastime of many Melanesians (or at least of men, who proved by their prowess that they were not women).[4] It is not wise to make exaggerated claims; perhaps the widespread *pebek* (payback) killings which have been documented (mostly from the time of contact), were the outcome of vicious wars erupting in the wake of pre-contact epidemics. Diseases spread from the earliest, coastal interaction between newcomers and indigenous populations, and their inflictions would normally have been ascribed to enemy sorcery.[5] Be that as it may, killing was part of the game of Melanesian life, and to do it well added to a man's reputation. It appears that for many males, indeed, payback killing 'was a very good kind of sport', as the Tolai writer Paulias Matane once put it,[6] and as has been so vividly illustrated by the romping, supple Baliem Valley fighters of the Peabody Museum documentary film *Dead Birds*. But pressures were there to play the 'sport' seriously; otherwise it could cost you your life.

Bena Bena payback runners

Payback killing, however, was never enacted for its own sake; it was a powerful expression and integral part of tribal religious life. For a preliminary exemplification one can do no better than consider the extraordinary phenomenon of 'payback running' among the Bena Bena (eastern central highlands, New Guinea, and to the east of the present-day township of Goroka). Such running bears as much interest for the study of approaches to death and the after-life, surveyed in the previous chapter, as it does for the analysis of retributive principles and action. An elderly lady named Aubo, who consented to be interviewed in 1973 about the leading part she played in such a process, disclosed its essentials with some arresting and specific details. Aubo had in fact married her step-son Piaruka, following the death of her first husband. When Piaruka subsequently fell ill, she was debarred from seeing him; then, as she returned from her gardens one afternoon in July, she was informed he had died. Her husband's relatives began gathering at the hamlet Kalagefagheai for the lamentations. Aubo slept with them, but early the next day, as she described it, a special wind (*bunemeha'a*) entered her body and she began to shiver. Her dead husband had taken control of her. It was not the first time she had been seized this way, for when her real seven-year-old son, Ethaphuthapa, had died of suspected poisoning, the wind came in full force. So she was not frightened, but she was not herself. Friends of her own age secured a special bark called *yahuba*, and a young man, biting it, spat its juices on her back as she was trembling. In an instant she began running and everybody ran after her.

It was the implicit belief that as the man's death had been effected by an enemy sorcerer, his spirit would eventually find its way to the culprit's hamlet. On many occasions the runners, after much meandering, would 'arrive' somewhere, a place marked as the scene where an indiscriminate pay-back killing would occur when the time was opportune. On many occasions, though, a runner would run in a circuitous, but apparently directionless way, up hill down dale, until the group was exhausted. Then, although the runner might have more energy, the others would perform a curious act to stop the whole thing; they would pass across the runner's shadow, whereupon the running would stop and the spirit be released. Aubo told me that, in her case, Piaruka's spirit gave her very great strength and yet drove her through the bush in a most haphazard way. At one point she sank down in a place where she believed enemy sorcerers hid and smoked, all her impulse to move being momentarily lost. But she knew her husband's power was still in her, and when more bark-juice was splattered on her back, she was away again. This forty-year-old woman was already some 6 miles (9.6 km) from her home, sprinting along the highlands highway with a sizeable crowd behind her, when the police moved in, and her shadow was crossed in the ensuing mêlée. Aubo told me how important her possession had been for the continuance of traditional ways. In former days, she claimed, a dead person's spirit could seize any adult member of the clan, but nowadays only relatives are incited. 'My kinsfolk knew and believed that the spirit would enter into me!' she cried, for Piaruka had once said he would go inside a friendly relative. Now his spirit had been unhappily released without his killers being identified.[7]

The Bena Bena are strangely uninterested in the final condition and influence of the ancestors. Nevertheless, the crucial rite of passage from this life to the spirit order almost always demanded knowledge of the enemy responsible (or in the case of death by sickness at least the *attempt* to gain such knowledge), so that steps towards revenge or war could either then be taken or, if totally unwise, not taken. It is tempting to see the Bena Bena payback system as a paradigmatic if controlled rage against the universe when the human's awful mortality has been unmasked. Death seems to elicit from them a primal burst of energy, which satisfies the pressure to rebel against death itself, and the desperate need to *blame*. One hesitates to make too much of this approach when most literature on tribal wars and payback ambushes has placed emphasis on survivalist and economic elements.[8] The student of religion is bound to ask questions, however, about the integral relationship between consensus beliefs and those overt patterns of behaviour which Westerners tend to compartmentalize, too often arbitrarily, as 'socio-economic' or 'secular'. Although researchers have considered wars in various Melanesian contexts, explanations for the occurrence of wars have either been too broad (land, survival, the maintenance of an overall equilibrium) or too narrow (a man from A killed someone from B, therefore B waged war with A), and the traditionally conceived notions of pretexts for war have been neglected.

L. L. Langness, whose work on fighting among the Bena Bena must stand among the most sophisticated analyses of tensions within highlands society, still tends to by-pass traditional, local reasons for warfare, and apart from recognizing the Bena Bena principle 'survive or be struck down', proceeds to search for a theoretical model intended to do justice to the whole structure of Bena Bena society as well as comparative ethnography.[9] Perhaps it is excusable for a social scientist to avoid the apparently warped conceptual frameworks of warrior Melanesians themselves, but the reasoning of the indigenous mind itself is obviously of fundamental importance for under-standing tribal war. Although it may never explain tribal war either in any complete sense or at a higher level of sociological abstraction, it unfolds the 'consistency-logic'[10] on which a people base their actions. What the members of a human group believe to be true will at least render their own and others' deeds intelligible to themselves, and hopefully reveal to the observer that there are avowed reasons for killing which fit into a total world-view.

The Bena Bena, for example, believe virtually every sickness bringing death is the end-product of sorcery, of a *nalissalobo* (sorcerer). War does not stop short when warriors leave the field of battle, but is continued under cover by sorcerers who manipulate coastal shells to kill their victims. Even a wounded warrior who dies sometime after battle is understood to have been sorcerized; an enemy can sneak in close to his hamlet after dark, hear his groaning and allow a sorcerer to 'catch' his utterances, using them to worsen the damaged part.[11] Moreover, although there were many open clashes in the past, the ambush of the individual was just as common and as great a source of hostility (so that given sporadic ambush killings, as many as five near Ketarobo during the Christmas period of 1976, it can hardly be said that tribal fighting has been eliminated from Bena Bena society).[12] Key enemies got to be known and marked out as targets for encounter. Yet, in ambushing, it was preferable to take the life of a foolish, rather useless specimen (nowadays a drunkard), not only because it was safer but also because those who came to find the speared body of a good (kins)man (*hetafobo*) would devour his corpse instead of burying it, and so gain extraordinary strength for payback. Thus, it is impossible to account for Bena Bena warfare without comprehending Bena Bena religion, and without grasping the logic of retribution, which encapsulates deep feelings of fear and hatred before the obstacles of life, meets the ever-pressing need to find and blame the causal agencies of death and sickness, and legitimizes the urge to act on feelings and interpretations corporately, channelling the response towards an outside force threatening the whole group.

It is hard to assert that Bena Bena payback logic is typical for Melanesia. In some respects it may be, but there is no emphasis on pleasing the ancestors — as we saw among the coastal peoples of the Western Gulf for example, who carefully ranked the skulls of those taken in raids above the *gope* symbols of their ancestors. Neither is there a conception of power being transferred to the group or specialist through feasting on the flesh of an enemy — as among the Marind-Anim of Irian Jaya.[13] A motif common to most Melanesian payback thinking, namely the fear of the dead if revenge is not taken,[14] is only very weakly represented in the Bena Bena case. Neither in that case does there seem to have been any frenzied gloating over the successful kill, as found, for instance, among the Dugum Dani (Irian Jaya highlands) nor conceptualization of the degrees of revenge, such as the distinction between killing and throwing a body into a river to destroy its soul (as among the Baktaman, New Guinea highlands).[15] Whatever the differences, however, we are dealing with comparable patterns of thought, and I have yet to find a Melanesian world-view without consensus reasons for taking revenge.

Along with blood vengeance the most common pretexts for war are the theft of land and pigs, and the abduction of women. Among the stock of reasons, though, the notion that numbers should be kept down and a population equilibrium maintained finds no place; for, only in more recent years have certain peoples been able to comprehend their own acts as parts of an eco-system. Among the Kamano (New Guinea highlands), for example, clansmen buried their dead in shallow hillside graves close to water-courses, so that sickness resulted from drinking the water lower down; sorcery was suspected and killing (with a new burial!) the worst outcome of all. In the last few years the young and educated have been trying to depict all this as a vicious cycle and to convince the people that they are victims of their own insanitary habits.[16] Before that the Kamano were all interpreters of a 'different world'.

Outer-directed sorcery

Sorcery, it will have become obvious, is an important Melanesian payback technique. As the Bena Bena case already suggests, sorcery can be inextricably bound up with actions of war and can serve as an explanation of disaster.

Among the Wahgi we find the connections in a still more complex form, especially because they distinguish between war magic and sorcery proper.

When an open engagement is pending, a war magician (*obokunjeyi*) plants a special piece of wood (called *ond kisan*) to mark a line across the middle of the battlefield. During the battle he surreptitiously makes a whistling noise whenever a warrior from either side crosses the line (it sounds like the makings of a football game!); unless the fighter concerned knows procedures for counter-magic, he will surely die, for the other tribe's (war) sorcery will make him immediately vulnerable or eventually 'find' him. In the past every Wahgi clan had an *obokunjeyi* come with its men to the field; he carried some magical red wood (*ond kunambang*) acquired from the Jimi Valley or neighbouring Chimbu area and, by guarding the wood in a small *bilum* (net-bag) under his arm-pit, as well as by uttering appropriate spells, he would give his band the power to kill. Such a man lived close to a house reserved for weapons and *ond kunambang*, and it was tabu for him to eat with others, his meals being left by his wife some distance away.[17] War magic, however, is distinct from *kum* (a term used of both sorcery and witchcraft among the Wahgi), and *kum* becomes involved in the fight scene only under special circumstances. If there have been a number of deaths by sickness, efforts are made to identify the sorcerer (who may 'dance around in the night'), and to locate the *kum* material he deposits. *Kum* objects, if found, should be wrapped up by the leader of the men's house in *tanget* leaves or hair until a day of war. On that day it should be placed near a *mumu* cooking-pit and the warriors' spears poked into it. When the pig is killed for cooking, there is a cry in unison that a relative of the sorcerer is to be killed in the clash; after the meal has been eaten, the warriors withdraw their spears and utter the war cry. In the subsequent onslaught another man on the opposing side is also marked as the associate of the sorcery — a man who, ofttimes other than the relative to be killed, is taken to be dangerous owing to his strength. This is done because it is also believed that *kum*, if brought to the fight ground, can effectively weaken the strongest man without him realizing it, making him a slow, easy target.[18]

In most Melanesian cultures, however, sorcery is an insidious cause of sickness rather than a tool in the hand of a lively combatant. Among the Wahgi, again, those fatal sicknesses deemed to be the results of sorcery are normally taken to derive from acts performed by the spouse's kin. Thus, if a widow returns to her family of origin in another tribe, this will allegedly indicate the origins of the sorcery, and the spirit of the departed will seek out his murderer and then, in turn, cause sickness among his wife's relatives.[19] This, then, is the equivalent to the Bena Bena payback run, but here it is left to the woman to decide if she will return to her people, and left to the spirit itself to requite: the outward details differ but the way of thinking is the same. In the Wahgi case, however, *kum* has only been a pretext for war when its traces have been discovered; in any case territorial conditions usually prevented a tribe from fighting with any but its nearer neighbours, so room had to be created for some spirits to take their own revenge. Whoever the avenger is, though, payback remained just and necessary. Even for the Wahgi, its failure to actualize was jarring and unnerving. Their outlook justified inaction in many sorcery cases. But, unlike the Bena Bena, the feelings of their ancestors dominated their consciousness immediately following a death, and enough trouble understood to be brought on them by an unavenged spirit could impel them into a *pebek* raid.

Inner-directed sorcery

Sorcery, as distinct from straightforward payback killing, was in most cases consciously directed at specific individuals not just anyone who happened to get in its 'line of fire'. One should appreciate, however, that the quite prevalent fear and awareness of sorcery in Melanesia today is in a special sense a modern development, and one of the unfortunate side-effects of colonial and mission pacification. Traditionally, payback activity and sorcery were pre-dominantly outer-directed, against enemies; for, one's own group could not hope to survive if faced with a traitor within. Upon pacification, however, there has been a recognized (but not necessarily real) increase in the amount of inner-directed payback and sorcery; hence, sickness and deaths now get blamed on people near-at-hand rather than farther away, or on strangers who are temporarily hosted and paid to satisfy some vindictive person in one's own village. Idiosyncratic individuals are soon branded as sorcerers; despite the attempt to impose Western law, they could be killed if found in the act (Tangu, coastal New Guinea), or forced by social pressure to live away from the village (eastern Toaripi, coastal Papua).[20] Or else every family in a village came to buttress itself with some knowledge of sorcery and counter-magic, for the purposes of balancing power and safeguarding one's interests (certain Roro villages, coastal Papua).[21]

There can be little doubt, however, that inner-directed sorcery did exist in pre-contact times, even if to a lesser extent. Men of power, such as the chiefs of Buka (*tsnunono*), could become the prime objects of sorcery, and from near at hand as much as anywhere, so that their female kinsfolk wept for them at their installation.[22] Competition between bigmen could easily lead to antagonism and thus sorcery, while a person wronged or put down by a powerful figure found sorcery rather than open revenge-killing the safer recourse. Such *pebek* sorcery can be neatly illustrated from among the Nipa and the Mendi (central highlands, Papua), by the procedure known as *hultem* or *hultrem*. Disclosing the source of his grievances to his close kinsmen, a man performing *hultem* will build a small house on stilts in the bush and take up into it a specially selected red or brown pig. While the kinsmen wait below the pig must be killed without emitting a squeal, and then thrown below, blood flying everywhere. When the beast is ready for cooking, its heart is extracted and placed in a small reinforced bag containing a live rat or bird, which is to nibble at the heart. To complete *hultem*, the aggrieved man fires an arrow with great force in the direction of his adversary.[23] Here 'sympathetic magic', as J. G. Frazer termed it, is the vehicle of retribution, with ritual specialists only acting as advisors in the working out of this bitter personal rivalry.

In most Melanesian societies, by comparison, individuals or parties have access to the power of revenge sorcery provided by *man bilong poison*, or perhaps purchasable from foreigners. In various settings the paid sorcerer emerges as a clear-cut equivalent to the 'hired killer' of the West; even while being expected to murmur spells, his task was not uncommonly the mixing of poison, which is secretly added to the victim's food or offered as a pretence of hospitality. Whatever the shades of difference, the resort to sorcery invariably signalizes an unrequited resentment, a reaction to an imbalance, which demands rectification and is blamed on an offender. A problem for present-day researchers, though — if they perhaps had hopes of recovering the 'purely traditional' in any given society (!) — is that of discovering whether the amount of actual or feared sorcery *within* each clan or tribe has substantially increased since the 'time of peace' brought by missionaries or colonial administration, as opposed to that earlier time when inter-group hostilities pressed each social unit into a stricter loyalty.

Whether under pre- or post-contact circumstances, however, a common hatred of sorcery has not detracted from the fact, most often noted of coastal Papuan societies, that certain people are thought to deserve sorcery. Individuals can provoke it through arrogant attitudes, or by acquiring too much power and prestige in societies which jealously guard relative solidarity and equality.[24] In some cases, what is more, as among the Mekeo (hinterland Papua), the sorcerer was the instrument of chiefs in executing their covert punishments upon miscreants and unwanted persons within their own settlements.[25] Not that the Mekeo have for this reason escaped an increase in inner-directed sorcery after pacification, because the influence of the sorcerers increased while that of the chiefs and war magicians diminished under the colonial jurisdiction. But all this brings us to the complicated subject of variations of payback — as 'legal penalty', personal redress, parental and custodial discipline, and related matters.

Variations of payback

If there had been offence within the war unit, or even within the compass of long-inured alliances, what happened would naturally depend on the perceived grievousness of the fault. A Trobriand Islander who had not been paid the debt due from a trading partner is just as likely as not to try harm-dealing magic on the delinquent.[26] As for common complaints — over uneven exchanges, overbearing behaviour, and so on — if the parties are equal or relations not so strained to breaking-point, there may be procedures to bring out anger into the open. Sharp threats across the village may produce a recognizable compromise (as among the Tangu). Or else the parties may engage in a mock fight, as with an aggrieved Huli, who will carry learnt curses and imprecations to his antagonist and challenge him to take a joint oath. If the adversary agrees, each party slaps the face of the other with pork, exclaiming 'If I lie may my eyes be blinded, my hearing fail, my skin become dry and my penis fall off'.[27] In these ways individual or family redress could be secured, without appealing to consensus or chiefly legal sanctions, but satisfying the urge to requite injury nonetheless.

Thus, the various acts of retaliation within families and clans, and the range of possible actions — from murder to healthy quarrel — correspond to an understanding of the degrees of revenge or of the social contexts in which different types of actions are appropriate. As Fredrik Barth has put it, of the Baktaman in particular, 'killing is not only banned but solemnly declared to be inconceivable within the primary community'.[28] To kill clansmen, with or without premeditation, normally brought a sense of sorrow and guilt; to kill a relative of one's wife in battle was considered a painful necessity, whereas to kill an enemy always brought a sense of relief and exhilaration, even if one had to guard against the menace of the dead man's vengeful spirit.

In considering less violent, along with the more drastic forms of payback or punishment, attention should be drawn to a host of related thoughts and behaviour patterns. We can think first of different kinds of social custodianship: parental control, the imposition of initiatory ordeals, and community discipline. The use of extremely strict methods of child-rearing, with the infliction of corporal punishment, obviously relates to the Melanesians' traditional readiness to take physical revenge. I remember a young Roro girl being thrown overboard for crying in a stranded canoe — a lesson she never forgot! Young initiates face endurance tests during which elders take apparent delight in mockery or in making the going very hard, as with rites of entry into the Tolai secret society *Iniet* or *Dukduk* (New Britain), let us say, or the interesting Kiriaka wig cult (west Bougainville). The punitive sadism which could be involved in these situations is no better illustrated than by the Wahgi (and thus highland) practice of pushing male initiates closer and closer to a fire in the men's house until they virtually de-hydrate.[29] This kind of custodianship, independent of distinctly legal decisions, can include 'social ostracism', and sometimes pressure to remove pollution.

Such a rebel as Jim Baitel's fictional character, Tali, who flouts his ancestral ways (having intercourse with his cousin-sister, for instance), may carry the stigma of his act indefinitely, if his parents refuse to compensate those wronged.[30] Or perhaps a noted individual will be exploited politically for some ritual misdemeanour. I remember one Aitsi, an influential Roro, who, because his leg had accidentally brushed a dead corpse, was forced by the elders to eat a special diet of water and moist food for more than the customary length of time.

These retributions of a more custodial kind also entail the typical

Melanesian role of husband as would-be lord (even owner) over his spouse(s). The need to manhandle women to secure their compliance in family and clan tasks was widely assumed. But payback syndromes in male–female relations assume wider than disciplinary implications, because women had their own techniques of getting back at unworthy menfolk. Central highland Melpa women suffering under ill-treatment in marriage could walk over the top of food or people in their anger (playing on the fear of dropping polluting menstrual blood), and in other cases re-enliven their loyalties toward their old (ofttimes enemy) clan of origin.[31] Kogu males (central highlands), who believe their 'strength is maintained' both 'by fighting and by erotic adventure', might have enjoyed inducing pain in women as they copulate; Sengseng females (New Britain) willingly intimidate their menfolk, by playing on their horror of menstrual 'pollutions'.[32]

Most critical of all the retaliations used within tribal or clan units, however, were those with more recognizably legal punitions or sanctions. In these instances elders, chiefs, fight leaders, or other social authorities made judgements (the severer side of which can hardly be seen any longer because jurisdiction has passed to the new governments).[33] The breaking of the stricter tabus brought swift and violent punishment. Death was the punishment in most societies for female adulterers, and, almost always, for females who learnt the secrets or gazed on the hidden activities of the male cult. Warriors who disobeyed leaders' commands, by initiating war ahead of due time with a maverick assault, for instance, were clubbed on the head three times in traditional Kapauka society (Irian Jaya).[34] Leopold Pospisil, who has written about the Kapauka, has done more than any other scholar to rehabilitate our sense of legal retribution in traditional Melanesia, with his listing of as many as 117 punishable offences.[35]

There are other variations on the theme of retaliatory payback. Revenge upon objects and animals as against humans, for instance, is a special subject in its own right, which we can just illustrate with a couple of examples. Father J. Tschauder once recalled how a beautifully decorated Buna warrior, when he tripped on a stone and fell in the mud (near Marienburg, Sepik), turned on the rock with a prolonged burst of kicks and curses. When a child is hurt through contact with an object among the Murik Lakes people (Sepik), the object itself is first touched by the parent and so controlled or disciplined.[36] To the Wahgi, if a rat or lizard is killed near a sorcerized person, this marks the elimination of the *sanguma*, the sorcerer's creature which has temporarily wandered away from its human prey.[37]

All this scattered material is worth bundling together if only to provide signposts to a whole area of psycho-religious study which merits detailed analysis and far more attention than it has so far received. And all these traditional ways of retaliatory payback have their modern urban analogues in the practices of backbiting, favouritism and theft, in vandalism, rape and 'neo-Ludditism', in the way some women pulverize their promiscuous husbands' cars, let alone in the regionally-oriented payback murders of crowded shops and dark alley-ways. But it is high-time to summarize.

Overall, despite the varying outflows of emotional energy, complexes of retributive thought and action are identifiable systems which can be checked out because people give reasons for their acts of revenge and punishment — reasons that hang together as an intelligible logic of retribution. Not all the members of a small-scale society will comprehend the consensus logic in its inherited complexity — for, that would require specialization or higher degree initiation — but group consciousness is determined by the general range of possibilities covered in the system. As Barth has ably shown, admittedly, Melanesian conceptual frameworks (or, in my terms, the accepted logic of retribution) may often inhibit appreciation of 'Man [with a distinct capital M] as a social and moral person' wherever he is found.[38] The point (dare I say, function?) of most traditional retributive logic, however, is to confirm the need to destroy the ostensibly or potentially destructive. A person operating within this framework cannot stop to reflect on the worth of an enemy or 'barbarian', because the enemy embodies destructive power and may even represent something 'other-than-a-person' when compared with one's own kind. When it comes to attacking the enemy or punishing a patent evildoer, the forces of life, as a total vision of survival and continuity, achieve their highest degree of objectivity, for the whole group is of one accord. Even enemies have taken joint payback action if some established inviolate code of fight-ethic is broken; if, for example, a Mekeo chief who sought to stop war between two clans had his lime-pot knocked from his hands, the warrior responsible would be beaten to death by someone from either party.[39] When it is a matter of sorcery *within* the community, then the group may sense the danger of self-destruction. Some communities were able to contain sorcery as a useful means of private or familial vindication, as a necessary evil or fringe development; in others, however, sorcery was conceived by consensus as a dreadful force of Death which was 'outside the system', was under the management of abnormal individuals and required elimination by violent means.

Jealousy, resentment, ferocity, lust for power or cruelty, however, are not private affairs: these, when channelled together for the value and continuance of the community, become affirmations of survival (in a more than mere economic sense), of 'Life against Death'.[40] And anything beyond the ken or unknown to the living — such as some secret misdemeanour or undetected trespass — will be handled by the dead or some unseen power as part of a wider (and usually lateral) social framework. In understanding life this way, primal humanity is no more nor less innately savage than moderns; nor is it psychically more open to the realms of the unconscious, nor less rational, nor in a state of half-awakened consciousness: it is just that its premises and frames of reference are noticeably different from those current in the 'internationalized' urban cultures of today. On the arrival of the expatriate intruders, in fact, the Melanesian sense of appropriate revenge was to fuel the fire of rebellions and other assaults. When conventional weaponry could not stem the tide against guns, more subtle means of reprisal were to be applied — in the deliberate non-cooperation of the 'cargo cults', and eventually in political parties opposed to foreign domination.

Reciprocities

Payback, as negative thought and action, does not exhaust the scope of retributive logic and its practical implications. Melanesians concede and reward as well as avenge and punish, and we would do well to look at this other side of the coin. The material continues to be complicated and unmanageable; yet, case studies and pertinent examples will at least expose the crucial issues, which this time concern the reciprocal principles of exchange and generosity, as well as sacrificial acts both in one's own and others' interests. Be warned, though, that the coin of retributive logic can be flipped from one face to the other more easily than we might have imagined, so that punishments (such as those brought upon a child) may be rewards in the long term, while rewards (as in sumptuous presentations of food — among the Massim of Papua, for example) may be signs of aggression or of the desire to be *magister*, to take a position of power.[41] A cautious game of interpretation is required.

Peacemaking

Peacemaking presents a good starting-point. It is significant that one side in a war often presses for peace because they have been the decisive victors, thus making the enemy (who long for vengeance, or a 'just balance') feel all the more intimidated. This was clearly the reason behind a peace-making ceremony I witnessed near Kup (mid-December 1976), involving the Kumai (a Wahgi tribe) and Endugla (a Chimbu tribe) tribes on the edges of Wahgi country. The Kumai had the advantage, so they announced the day when they kept their own peace feast, and it culminated in a mock display of belligerence before the wrapping up of weapons in the men's house. On the following morning both sides were to face each other, holding stones in their hands and pledging not to fight, planting *tanget* as a reminder of peace, and eating much pork together. But the Endugla, for their part, did not keep the preliminary feast, and they had no intention of appearing on the day of reconciliation because they had just lost three good men.

Whatever the circumstances, peacemaking demands some effort to do something which benefits the other side, not just oneself. The loser, however, finds it hardest to make the sacrifice. Logically the loser must never forget his task of avenging; yet logically, too, if one has more than requited the enemy, it is time to cease hostilities. In prehistoric times there were, doubtless, instances of unrestrained expansionism.[42] The Bena Bena, for example, occupy a vast territory. They appear to have forced the Asaro groups into the upper Goroka Valley, and the limits of their spread are probably best reflected in the famous dance and myth of the mud men (which celebrates how one group of fleeing Asaro tribesmen fell into light-coloured mud and arose as fearsome ghosts). But in documented and immediate pre-contact times, the group which over-excelled as victor was ready to make concessions or compensations. Peace may have meant consolidation, but it did give time for the losers to forge new alliances and gain redress. To win too many times, also, could spawn feelings of self-recrimination. Jojoga Opeba has recently shown how, among the Orokaiva (Papua) at least, ideology militates against aggrandizement — guilt feelings about the expansion of one's own group having led to migrations of contrition. Complete peace, as well, could allow the victor to dictate a peace policy which entailed intermarriage with the losers, a settlement that might, at times, achieve only partial success, as in the case of Ikaroa Raepa, the Papuan 'Ned Kelly'. Raepa made a marriage peace with the Moripi after carving out a large territory for the western Mekeo but at the same time, in so doing, set the stage for the reversal to come after his death, when his own descendants were driven out.[43] When it was achieved, then, victory was considered for its consequences — whether the enemy's hostility was more intense, whether too much prestige had accrued from constant success, or whether the opportunity was there to be magnanimous and to enhance one's standing outside the strictly military context. The assessment of one's position lies within the ambit of retributive logic, and must certainly be considered an aspect of Melanesian religious life, since it involves ethical decisions and because intentions to make war or peace are expressed ritually.

By now it can be more easily seen how the issues of war and peace are bound up with the reciprocities of trade and gift-giving. As with sorcery, principles of exchange and presentation between potentially hostile communities should be distinguished from those applying within the tribe or clan, and each sphere shall be considered in turn. We shall, however, concentrate on matters which are of obvious ethico-religious significance, and deal with them selectively. Types of compensation procedure, for example, which seem to fit between peace-making rites and the hosting of great feasts, will have to be left for another place.[44] So, here, let us begin with some of those extraordinary acts of magnanimity we find in various pig kills or grand food ceremonies, where, superficially at any rate, visitors are rewarded by their hosts without apparent limitation and without guarantee of repayment.

The great feasts

At the spectacular Wahgi *Kongar*, or at its Chimbu counterpart the *Bugla Yungga*, guests have very rarely brought gifts to the ceremonial grounds. It is for the hosts (a given tribe whose clans enact the rites simultaneously in different *sing sing* compounds), to do the giving. When the pigs are killed in hundreds on the last of three crucial days, virtually all of the meat is carried away by the visitors. But this magnanimity is preceded on the second day by a fantastic demonstration of the host tribe's vitality — by its richly decorated dancing warriors, and by a pandemonium-like burst of tribal ferocity. These actions are reminders that the hosts are exceptionally dangerous and best to be kept as friends. Thus, we begin to perceive that the generosity is not unconditional; its association with the hosts' aggressiveness puts their guests in debt. The very sumptuousness of it all will inevitably 'wound' the visitors, who must ask themselves whether they can possibly emulate the celebrants or do better; and the exhibition of power will 'prove' to the hosts' ancestors, who are understood to witness and participate, that their tribe is flourishing and desires continual Life.[45] And not anyone was invited to a *Kongar*: consistent enemies were consciously excluded, in contrast to allies and those wooed as such, or tribes expected to return the invitation in their own good time. But in the moment of truth, when the beaten pigs squeal one by one, and the taste of freshly cooked pork is on one's lips, all this is nothing more nor less than a spontaneous gift, the reward received from seven long years of others' labours. It is like the black Australian's totem, regenerated by its soul-mates every year, but eaten only by the other tribes, who seem to have done much less to keep it alive.

Edward Schieffelin once observed to me that the great Melanesian ceremonies were 'modes of philosophic reflection', acted out rather than written in books.[46] It is extremely difficult to prove, but the *Kongar* seems to elevate thinking about giving and receiving to a plane beyond the routine trade and exchange of everyday life, just as the aristocratic, highly ritualized *kula* surpasses the humdrum *grimwali* (or day-to-day exchange) in the mind of the Trobriand Islander.[47] As Marcel Mauss rightly judged, Melanesian 'social life is a constant give-and-take';[48] so, one would expect to find societies in which the excitement of exchange is gathered up to a point of culmination (as with the Mae Enga *Te(e)* or Melpa *Moka*). In the *Te* cycle, for example, which involves a long network of pig exchanges across the large Enga territory, the high-point (known as *te pingi*) is a ceremony of 'prestige-seeking', when men line up all the grown pigs they then own, and those they have been able to borrow, to contest for 'bigmanship'.[49] In such a case, there is the prospect of generosity through a future repayment of debt (as pork); yet, in those various societies in which extravagant giving rather than exchange marks the high-point, we can more readily detect the holding of values which transcend the worth of material objects or bargaining techniques, even though these values may be best symbolized in material prosperity. In some cases such values may amount to being just a recognition of honour or magnanimity, or perhaps of the magical powers which enable gift-giving to be carried on; yet, in the *Kongar* and comparable occasions of one-sided generosity found elsewhere (such as the western Fuyughe *gab* in the Papuan highlands, the Atzera *kras* on the Morobe plains), one finds an incipient theology of grace. In the Wahgi case, certainly, the great pig-kill has not been nor ever will be possible without the ancestors, who are part of the community, so that what is given away marks the fruits and benefits of the spirits as much as it does of the living.

General exchange and obligations

If we are unable to cover all aspects of outer-directed giving, we can at least briefly consider some of the more important related issues — the general run of reciprocal interchanges within one's own group and along friendlier trade-lines with others (often forged through marriage links), as well as reciprocity between spirit beings and venerator. Concerning the first issue, few need reminding of the intricate complexity of reciprocal relations within a Melanesian society. People grow up learning how to behave towards close relatives and those from whom to expect the choicest gifts; they learn which are the pleasantest families or groups with whom to make untroubled exchanges of food and goods. They learn the subtleties of giving — not to repay with exactly the same amount, for example, but a little more or less.[50] They learn to assess equivalence, or to gauge whether somebody has been given an inadequate amount at a feast, whether somebody is too greedy or has failed to meet his obligations. They learn to interpret pointed hints, or repeated rumour and gossip.

In this kind of atmosphere Melanesians have social pressures upon them to be relatively egalitarian, and to make sacrifices for the community and its survival. They also find that they are rewarded for their contributions; the accumulation of personal wealth is not condemned provided the rich man is generous with his possessions, and by generosity such a man can enhance his prestige enormously. In reality the chief, *bikman*, wealthy manager or influential specialist are symbolic representatives of the group, thus being embodiments of transcending values or allegedly endowed with more-than-human power. Even in the homogeneous small-scale societies of Melanesia, it is necessary for somebody to have this authority for the granting of patronage and reward as well as for punishment, for the organization of ceremony and maintenance of peace, as well as for the master-strokes of vendetta.

Sacrifices and dealings with the spirit order

The capacity of human authority to dispense rewards and punishments has its analogue in the more mysterious, over-arching dispensations of the spirit order. In Melanesia it was not expedient to effect a negative paying back against deities or the ancestors for their alleged uncooperativeness or hostility; nor can one become like a great Jain yogi, 'whom even the gods fear'.[51] Admittedly, occasionally we hear of ancestral spirits being set aside, even contemptuously, once their job is done (as with the Sir Ghost on Manus who gets replaced upon the death of each family head[52]); there are also various instances when individual spirit agencies have been set aside and are no longer recognized as being significant. The gods and ancestors of complete outsiders, furthermore, were sometimes treated with scorn rather than fear, or as objects of 'mere superstition';[53] on the other hand, the sanctuaries in one's own language area were treated with great respect, their despoliation, if considered at all, being done *in extremis*.[54]

The spirits, for their part, have the freedom to bring harm as well as benison, although it has been the concern in every known Melanesian religion to placate forces which potentially threaten and induce rewards from those accepting negotiation. Obviously, in most Pacific world-views there are demonic powers which have no other intent but to kill those who cross their path. Usually these include nature- or place-spirits, though malicious or vengeful ghosts — those persons spiteful in life or dishonoured at death — may be ranked among them. But sacrifices or acts of worship were mainly performed before those spirit powers which were capable of bringing weal to the group (and thus probably woe to its enemies). Invariably the principle of approach was one of *do ut des* ('I give in order to be given to') — to a being not adored for its own sake but satisfied in the expectation of receiving some gift. As for any malevolent power, pork or an offering might be left in a suitable place to avert harm or divert its attention. The belief in so-called magic or the magical effect of ritual is usually so tightly woven into these distinctly religious procedures that it is often inexcusable to treat it as a separate category, when it simply amounts to the recognition of a supernatural transaction or to a worshipful technique of persuasion.[55]

What we would readily identify as sacrifices are important activities in which the spirits are cajoled or manipulated, and in which the offering or dedicating of victims reflects assumptions about give-and-take between humans and other-than-human agencies. More analysis is required about the range of relevant phenomena here, and the 'principles' thought to be in operation. At odd times we come across the building of sacrificial altars, somewhat comparable to Middle-Eastern models, with a priesthood and special holocausts to the gods included (as among the Toabaita, north Malaita, Solomons).[56] Equally, as a variant of sacrifice — albeit less impressive — on many occasions small offerings of food will be made, perhaps left out for the departed to partake after each meal (as among the Trobrianders and Orokaiva).[57] As for the great pig-kills and huge prestations of food discussed above, questions need to be carefully asked about the senses in which these are sacrifices also, because they are carried out in the presence of the spirits, presuming their great interest and following their pre-ordained procedures. Considering indigenous vocabularies as well, personal sacrifice — to save a kinsman from the field of battle, for instance — may have to be included in this analysis for particular cultures.[58]

By way of conclusion, we need to recall the changes brought to patterns of reciprocity through colonization. Money, of course, is having its effects. It takes the sting out of losing a warrior if you can be compensated with thousands of kina in cash;[59] if inflation makes the pig-kill too expensive, then the visitors can be asked to buy their pork at the ceremony.[60] It is now harder for a young Motuan nephew to enter his uncle's house and take what he wants in traditional style, for his hands might fall on a costly stereogram. Still, the competitive drive to give generously persists in the new monetarized world: when a bride-price well exceeds the local government council's statutory limitation, for example; or when the Motu of Hanuabada (Port Moresby) give over 75 000 Kina as a love-sacrifice to God on the great fund-raising day called *Bobo*, for the United Church (in 1976).[61] Finally, and en route to modernity, as it were, there are also 'cargo cult' dreams of a perfect reciprocity to consider: the projection of a time flooded with the new style of goods, which would decisively alleviate the faltering of traditional exchange patterns under the pressure of the colonial impact, and which was often thought to be possible only by the immense sacrifice of destroying crops and livestock in anticipation of a welcome transformation.

But the progress of our discussion has brought us at last to the third 'face' of the logic of retribution.

Explanations for significant events

Crises brought on by trouble, sickness and death represent the most significant events or situations in any society, along with the moments of salvation constituting their opposites. Such events, especially those threatening survival, required explanation (as the basis for practical problem-solving), and it is in the various ways Melanesians accounted for them in terms of rewards and punishments that we find the most complex, most noticeably intellectualized manifestations of retributive logic. It is in explicating these events that Melanesians developed a science, an ordering of thought which prepared them for change and induced them to action. To attempt to identify the science with magic would be utterly superficial, arbitrarily confining a society's ideas about cause and effect to a narrow sphere, and also confusing science with technology. This framework of knowledge is certainly different from the naturalistic or mechanistic outlook which now dominates in the West, but we should not over-exaggerate the dissimilarities. Certainly, Melanesians usually asked '*who*' caused the situation rather than 'what', but reference to purposive, personal agencies still has its appropriate place in Western causal thinking and, given their different premises, Melanesians have still worked out day-to-day problems as logically (or with the usual mixture of logic and intuition) as Westerners are supposed to do. Even notions equivalent to 'natural' or 'accidental', often claimed to be absent from

Melanesian thought, do make their appearance if we probe hard enough. A Bena Bena does not think twice about the death of an old man or woman — it is 'natural' (*uyailoto*); a Wahgi sees no significance in a slight bruise or stubbing of the toe — they are 'accidental' or 'unlucky' (*olom erlim*: literally, 'it just happened').

Thus, that old distinction between pre-logical and (modern) logical thought — one which keeps on coming back in modern guises — is quite obfuscating, and detracts from our common humanity.[62] In this final part of our discussion, however, we are confronted with logical intricacies to which one could never do credit. When faced with very special or exceptional circumstances, for instance, primal peoples have means of subtly adapting their frames of reference to meet the case; the new situation will often — as indeed with many superficially normal cases — only be fully intelligible when the whole story of 'what happened' has been told in a certain way, with particular nuances and emphases intimated. Is it so different in the West? In order to communicate something in detail of this more highly reflective dimension of retributive logic, I shall concentrate on one culture, namely the Wahgi (which has received a good deal of my attention already): I will treat in turn interpretations of trouble, sickness, death, and then their general opposite, 'blessing'.

Trouble

'Trouble' (*trabel, wari*) is an all too imprecise expression to cover a whole range of difficulties — from conflict between two individuals (relatives, husband and wife) to patent social disasters (famine, war ravage, volcanic eruptions, and so on) which usually bring sickness and death. 'Trouble' is unfortunately a category to cover loose ends, but it is usefully included if only to introduce the other two states — sickness and death — and to incorporate situations not involving these two. A Wahgi example, dealing with séances, will expose the issues.

The prime purpose of séances among these people is to resolve familial conflicts. A female specialist (*golmolk*) is a medium for spirit contact, with different dead relatives audibly whistling through her once the darkness comes and the fire is extinguished, when the attitude of waiting unifies the participants. One memorable séance was precipitated by the sickness of a baby girl (in the Zagoga tribe, 1976); yet, the child's condition was shown in the *golmolkia* (séance) to be connected with a quarrel. It was all very complex, and in recounting the explanation that emerged out of this 'contact with the other side', it should be remembered that this case reflects certain new social problems brought about through contact.

It all started some time before the sick child was born, when A (who was her grandfather) went on a visit to another tribe. While A was away, he left two kinsmen, B and C, in charge of his twin sons, D (who was the sick child's father) and E.

Now, at this time D's wife had recently had a son and the payment for the boy was due. (This is a payment made to the wife's kinsfolk when the child is formally named, somewhat similar to a bride-price, but considerably less.) As arrangements for this celebration were being discussed, C became very angry with D. The reasons for this anger had to do with the nature of the extended family relationship that now arose because B and C had been entrusted with D and E.

Because of this relationship, D and E were expected to behave like elder sons and help B's son and C's son. C, however, felt that they were favouring B's son and doing nothing for his own son. D and E had, in fact, just helped B's son to build a house. And now the celebrations for the payment of the child were being discussed in the hamlet where B and his son lived.

Therefore, C was furious, and all the more so because there were signs of a departure from tradition at the celebration (there was to be beer-drinking). So, C boycotted the celebration. And D was deeply disturbed by the fact that C hadn't appeared at the naming of his child.

Now, a year after these events, D's second child, the baby girl, was sick.

After the whistling of five identifiable relatives during the séance, the *golmolk* made it plain that D and C should come together to confess their resentments, which in turn had made C's dead relatives cross enough to harm the child. Thus, a sickness had been explained, but also a family quarrel was brought out into the open. Reconciliation was the prescription for the infant's recovery. The need was answered by killing one pig in the bush (*kipe kong*), in the presence of the interested ancestors, and the subsequent distribution of pork among the parties concerned. (As a postscript, though, it should be mentioned that the late arrival of a reconciliatory truck-load of beer led to a midnight brawl, which marred the tradition and re-enlivened the conflict.)

In this instance trouble did not arise without the involvement of the ancestors, who perforce form part of its explication. When analyzing explanations for disasters befalling whole groups, then, it is to be expected that the ascription of spirit powers with destructive tendencies will be all the more apparent. Thus, for the Mae Enga, great loss — successive military defeats, a rise in the death rate of pigs, as well as widespread disease or noticeable loss of human life — will constitute good reasons for a cultic propitiation of the ancestors under the full moon (and, often, near the 'eggs of the sun' or sacred clan stones).[63] Such a rare ceremony marks the very opposite to the Wahgi *Kongar* as the celebration of ancestral blessing, though the basic logical principles behind each ritual process are the same. The recognition of sickness and death in the one contrasts with the elation over fecundity, well-being and life in the other. Relations within the community of people and spirits demand urgent repair in the one case, so that an admission of the spirits' justifiable *pebek* against the people leads to the propitiatory rite. With the *Kongar*, relations must be in order, the pigs fat, the moon right, the hosts generally well, the central pole of the last *bolim* fertility house recovered, and the ritual procedures correctly followed for the ancestors' rewards to be celebrated.

Otherwise, there arises the danger 'of no fertility in the time ahead'.[64] Countless illustrations of parallel thinking in Melanesia could be added.

Sickness

Sickness is a special type of trouble yet one possible prelude to death; whether it is associated with trouble or death depends on the kind of ailment. A wound sustained in war and one subsequently bringing death was usually attributed to sorcery, as we saw with the Bena Bena. A healed wound, or a salvation in the sense of being hit defectively or in a less vulnerable part of the body, will most often be reckoned the work of a protective dead relative, who also assists the healer. One young Wahgi man (B's son referred to earlier) was told through a séance that he was saved from a fatal 'accident' because his dead sister watched over him. As he bled, moreover, the same rite of *minmanui* was performed for him as for a wounded warrior. A chicken was killed so that his soul (*minman*) could smell animal rather than human blood and be enticed back into his body. A feast of meat is always a symbol of reward and reconciliation for these people, and the ancestors' intervention crucial for salvation. Admittedly, the warriors used to ascribe their general victory over enemies to the ancestors as a collective group or to 'the power behind the[ir] sacred stones'; but saving someone wounded or seriously hurt was left to those close to him, including the ancestral nurses.

Injury incurred between family members, however, such as between husband and wife, tends to give rise to a greater variety of explanations and rationalizations. Such an act could be blamed on any one of a number of dead relatives who incited the anger; or perhaps group consensus would have it that it was the injurer (especially if that person is disliked) who was clearly culpable. Among the Wahgi, though, injuries to close relatives which looked like bringing death could be blamed not on the physically violent person but on one of the angry departed, so that a magician (*kunjeyi*) would be consulted.[65] On the other hand, many Melanesians would not think twice about small injuries (such as cuts, stubbed toes and the like) unless the context was significant — if they happened, for example, in the jungle of place-spirits and non-human tricksters.

Sicknesses are classified in different ways from society to society. In some, as has been recently shown of the Motu, the medical tradition is so rich that, depending on their nature and danger, causal explanations vary and diagnosis becomes a veritable art. Not that explanatory simplicity signals cultural inferiority, since any society's tendency to complexify one area of thought as against another has to do with the 'ecology' of the religion as a whole. Certain groups — scattered as wide apart as the eastern Toaripi of coastal Papua, the highlands Bena Bena, and the cultures of the Torricelli Mountains (in the Sepik region) — hold all fatal sicknesses to be the work of sorcerers and the spirit forces they conjure up; yet, among these peoples the art of sorcery identification, for example, or group reflection on the dead person's life and his associates, is far from simple. Among the Wahgi, the magicians share a code of medical knowledge which connects certain states of sickness with at least fourteen harmful place-spirits (*kangekes*). It is assumed that the ancestors are basically friendly, though the recent departed are the more easily offended if not shown enough respect while they feature strongly in group memory. In every case the final reason for sickness concerns a spirit agency, and pig(s) of appeasement would require to be killed (and payment made to the magician).[66]

Even nowadays natural causation is considered unsatisfactory. One magician admitted to me that a patient could take pills to stop the work of *kane bang*, a red spirit he identified with the whites' malaria, yet only as a supplement to his own prescriptions. Curing was not just a matter of bodily change; it was also total change to the better, and it was driving out a malignant oppressor. As we shall see in the next chapter, this is an approach which can be paralleled right across the Melanesian zone.

Death

Death evokes a variety of profound responses. In terms of retributive logic, these can be divided into three general areas of focus in indigenous thinking: general explanations for humanity's mortality, explanations of specific deaths, and beliefs about the condition of the dead.

Who gets the blame for mortality in general varies across Melanesia. To bring disparate mythological material together, however, let me at least venture the judgement that the blame is usually assigned to humans themselves, even though death more often than not becomes a reality through some higher power paying back mankind. Thus, according to the Erave (north-west Gulf), a sky being bestowed the gift of immortality on the snake because men and women had not been patient enough to help him in his predicament of being suspended between sky and earth.[67] Humanity pays for its neglect. Death as a consequence of the first sexual intercourse is the meaning of the Genesis-like Wahgi myth about the first two people, Taimel Dam and Taimel Mam, who could wish for any food to come to them without exertion, until their sexual union brought labour, difficulty and disease. No punishing spirit is mentioned in this myth. Of the two it is woman who is most responsible, for she accused Taimel Dam of laziness and wanted 'to do hard work' (which, in parabolic language, means sexual intercourse, and also childbirth).[68] Admittedly, in a sprinkling of other myths, it can be culture heroes who are held responsible (as in the Daribi story of Sau discussed previously). Whatever the variations, though, the imputing of blame and the acknowledgement of death as either appropriate or unfortunate retribution is widespread — and in virtually all primal mythologies, not just those of Melanesia.

Specific deaths, like particular sicknesses, are almost always the effects of negative payback — sorcery, the enemy (usually with his sorcery), the vengeful dead, disturbed *masalai* (place-spirits), or a wrathful person driven by a power beyond himself. To qualify this slightly, it should be remembered that many cultures have no interest in exploring the rationale behind the death of outsiders or enemies. If some happen to be captured or taken into the group, their death at the hands of capturers or temporary hosts will not need interpretation.[69] Both dying and disease, however, are certainly not always considered the result of unfair, unfortunate or undeserved retribution. To reiterate, a person is practically inviting sorcery by offending someone, and along the Papuan coast, for example, most people would not strive to kill the effective witch or sorcerer because, however much hated sorcery is, it is an accepted recourse and part of the system, and one attacks its bearers at one's peril. Again, a death can be seen to result from a person's mistakes: a failure to keep tabus (for which, of course, transgressors may be killed by their own people), the breaking of social ties, wandering foolishly in dangerous places or across battle lines, and the like, may be identified as the *as tru* (pidgin: 'real cause'). People will discuss likely causes of a death for days, and it is normally very important for a group to arrive at a satisfactory conclusion embodying the consensus view.

The persuasive power of this kind of thinking is amply illustrated by explanations of death in more distinctly modern Melanesian contexts. The Wahgi continue to account for the passing of their own village folk in traditional terms, referring to *kangekes, gonjipkipe* (ancestors) and *kum* (sorcery). A significant death which concerns them as a whole people or as part of the nation, however, evokes talk of God. For many of them it was God who punished the Wahgi returning officer who died with his family in an air crash en route to Mendi in 1972, because he had (allegedly) manipulated the elections. There are many comparable explanations indicating the survival power of retributive logic. I recall how a young Asaro senior high school student argued that the 1977 typhoid epidemic in Asaroka High School (central New Guinea highlands) was due to the decline in Christian belief among the pupils. Again, a tragic case comes to mind of a young university student who died of bone cancer in 1973. He had come to believe in science rather than God. Science could not help him in the end and he eventually returned to the village to die, smothered by a host of rumours as to the 'real reasons'. His fellow Velerupu villagers had to make up their minds, and the consensus (not inappropriate) view has stuck — that he had been contaminated by the 'whiteman' and his ways. This particular explanation had the capacity to please all uniformly, while among the same people, those reflecting on others' deaths can oscillate between consensus traditional and consensus Christian explanations, holding these to be equally true of the same cases.[70] I present these interpretations not because I believe the Melanesians' conclusions to be far-fetched, but above all to elicit an important bridge of continuity between Melanesian and popular (non-Augustinian!) Christian retributive logic.[71] This Melanesian retributive logic is a cross-cultural phenomenon, and it is palpably unwarranted to characterize its articulation among tribal peoples as 'pre-logical', when the same kind of thinking is so readily evinced in the intellectual traditions of the apparently 'civilized'.

As for Melanesian beliefs about the after-life, we have already begun exploring them in the last chapter, making the distinction between those people who conceive rewards and punishments to be dispensed in the next world and those with alternative models. Here I will simply make a few new points focussing on retributive logic. There are only a few Melanesian belief-systems with ideas of both a 'heaven' and a 'hell'. The Erave, for instance, held that all warriors who died on the battle-field, and women who devoted their lives supporting them, would proceed after death to live in a (heavenly) red place with the sky people. Those who died in any other fashion, as well as uncooperative wives, were doomed to an earthy brown hell, where they forever felt estranged.[72] Such a clear-cut parallel with Christian conceptions, despite being thought out in terms of a military ethic, is a rare find. A rough comparison may, perhaps, be drawn between Erave and Huli notions since the Huli, although having very hazy ideas about the ultimate destiny of most people, insist that the ghosts of slain warriors go to Dalugeli, 'a celestial resting place' worthy of their valour.[73] But as usual traditional pictures will vary enormously, perhaps because in most cases they are primarily meant to validate the known order of the living, and are not conscious exercises in metaphysics.[74] Sometimes the retributive implications are strong, in other cases they are not. Many of the Chimbu buried recognizably wicked people away from the ancestral places;[75] but among the neighbouring Wahgi all dead persons will find themselves in much the same situation, even though it is recognized that they carry their personality characteristics (some of which are inimical) with them. Members of other societies talk of each person having two souls, the wild one returning to the bush and the preferable one, reflecting one's better side, proceeding to the spirit world;[76] still others have notions of reincarnation, but which are not, upon inspection, tied in with any doctrine of *karma*.[77] The logic of retribution, then, has not always been taken with vigour and clarity to the bitter end, a sign that its greatest potency lay in the maintenance of order and custom among the living. Perhaps that can teach the Christian to put greater value on this life instead of over-contemplating the other-wordly haven, while the Christians, for their part, are offering a unified vision which challenges Melanesian parochialism.

Blessing

No account of the explanatory side to Melanesian retributive logic would be complete without considering the 'security', 'health' and 'life' of communities as perceived rewards of good relationships between human and human, between humans and the spirits. Overall, it is useful to appeal to the Anglo-

Saxon concept of 'blessing', or total 'well-being' to cover these fruits of success in affairs. The swelling of the tubers in the soil, the fattening of the pigs, the healthy pregnancies of women, the maintenance of numbers and morale among the warriors — all these are not merely signs of human (let alone 'natural') skill, but signifiers of an effective, ongoing interaction between the tribe and various powers of the cosmos. They are very opposites to negative requital, or to 'the bad' which follows from neglect and wrongdoing. They constitute 'salvation' in which tangible and physical results are inseparable from a more spiritual sense of worthwhileness.[78]

As we can already anticipate, the introduction of new goods to Melanesia — a whole range of items far and above the imaginings of men and women in Stone Age cultures — naturally created a focus of attention on the material 'blessings' of the whites. The coming of the Cargo — as looked to in the so-called 'cargo cults' — can also present itself as blessing and salvation for those falling into powerlessness under the colonial order. The Cargo signifies the regaining of lost esteem upon colonial intrusion and the access to items which will at the very least limit white superiority. In typical Melanesian fashion, Cargo integrates the physical and non-empirical into a total salvation.[79] This is an integration which, as we shall later see, is constantly reappearing in the life of the Christian churches, as they become increasingly responsive to village concerns and indigenous intellectual activity.

NOTES

The material in chapter 3 is based on a paper given at a conference on 'Traditional Melanesian Religion', given at a Melanesian Institute colloquium at Goroka (1978).

1 *The idea of historical recurrence in Western thought*, Berkeley, Los Angeles and London (1979), vol. 1, ch. 2, sect. B, pt. 2; ch. 3, sect. B; ch. 4, sect. G; ch. 5, sect. B, pt 2; 'Notions of Historical Recurrence in Classical Hebrew Historiography', in *Studies in the historical books of the Old Testament* (ed. J. A. Emerton), (*Supplements to Vetus Testamentum 30*), Leiden, 1979, pp.219–29; 'The logic of retribution in Eusebius of Caesarea', in *History and Historians of Late Antiquity* (eds A. Emmett and B. Croke), Oxford, New York, Sydney, 1983, pp.132ff; etc.

2 'Retributive Logic in Melanesian Belief', in Trompf (ed.), *Mel. and Judaeo-Christ. relig. trads*, Bk. 3, pt. C, opt. 1, pp.77ff; and Trompf, *Payback*.

3 e.g. T. Ahrens, *Unterwegs nach der verlorenen Heimat* (Erlanger Monographien aus Mission und Ökumene 4), Erlangen, 1986, esp. p.37.

4 In rare cases only did women also participate in fighting, e.g. Orokaiva women bore arms for warriors, removed spears from their shields, and even used staves to block weapons from falling on the wounded. cf. J. Waiko, Problems of method in Melanesian history (unpublished public lecture, UPNG, Port Moresby, 17 December 1985).

5 cf., e.g., K. Burridge, *Mambu; a Melanesian millennium*, Oxford, 1960, pp.122–23.

6 *Aimbe; the challenger*, Port Moresby, 1974, p.5. For useful preliminary reading, e.g., M. J. Meggitt, *Blood is their argument: warfare among the Mae Enga tribesmen of the New Guinea highlands* (Explorations in World Ethnography), Palo Alto, 1977; A. Ploeg, *Government in Wanggulam* (Verhandelingen van het Koningklijk Instituut voor Taal-, Land- en Volkenkunde 57), The Hague, 1969, pp.161ff (fringe Dani), etc.

7 OT: Aubo of Sitokalehai, 1973.

8 e.g. R. Fortune, 'Arapesh warfare', *American anthropologist*, New Ser. 41, (1939), p.24;
   A. P. Elkin, 'Delays exchange in the Wabag Sub-District, Central Highlands of New
   Guinea, with notes on the social organization', *Oceania* 12 (1953), p.170; R. M. Glasse,
   'Revenge and redress among the Huli; a preliminary account', *Mankind* 5 (1959), p.274;
   R. A. Rappaport, *Pigs for the ancestors*, New Haven, 1967, ch. 6; A. P. Vayda, 'Phases of
   the process of war and peace among the Marings of New Guinea', *Oceania* 42 (1971), pp.1ff.
9 Bena Bena social structure (doctoral thesis, University of Washington, Seattle 1964),
   pp.142ff.
10 cf. W. R. Boyce Gibson, *The problem of logic*, London, 1921, p.1.
11 OT: Flotime Rasinakafa (*bikman* of the Kapogunagabo tribe), 1976.
12 OT: Umakive Futrepa (and others), 1976.
13 van Baal, *Dema*, p.746; cf. D. Richardson, *Peace child*, Glendale, 1974, p.38 (on compa-
    rable notions of power transference among the Sawai).
14 cf. C. A. Schmitz, 'Zum Problem des Kannibalismus im nördlichen Neuguinea', *Paideuma*,
    6 (1958), pp.381ff.
15 K. Heider, *Grand Valley Dani* (Case Studies in Cultural Anthropology), New York, 1979,
    pp.102–03; F. Barth, *Ritual and Knowledge among the Baktaman of New Guinea*, p.149.
16 OT: Suluba Wabadaba and others (at Tirokave School), 1977.
17 OT: Peter Kuiwan, Clitus Tongil, 1975.
18 OT: Boma Kai, Kumai tribe, near the scene of battle a mile from Kup, 1976.
19 OTs: Peter Kuiwan, Klitus Tongil, Karap Stek, 1975.
20 K. Burridge, 'Tangu, Northern Madang District', in Lawrence and Meggitt (eds), *Gods*,
    pp.235f; Trompf and V. Koroti, Fieldnotes (Gulf), 1974. For parallel developments further
    afield in Melanesia, see E. Métais, *La sorcellerie canaque actuelle: les 'tueurs d'âmes' dans un
    tribu de Nouvelle-Calédonie* (Publication de la Société des Océanistes 20), Paris, 1967, on La
    Foa (western New Caledonian outliers).
21 Trompf and L. Aitsi, Fieldnotes (Coastal Central), 1973–74.
22 OT: Sahun Dash, 1977; cf. also R. Parkinson, 'Zur Ethnographie der nordwest-
    lichen Salomo Inseln', in *Abhandlungen und Berichtes des Königliches Zoologisches und
    anthropologisch-ethnographisches Museum*, 7 (1899), pp.10–15.
23 OT: Pus Dus, 1978.
24 I rely especially on my fieldwork with V. Koroti, L. Aitsi, S. Kopi, S. Varagi, L. Pilu, and
    on J. Kadiba for my general assessment of central coastal Papua here.
25 See M. Stephen, 'Sorcery, magic and the Mekeo world view', in Habel, *Powers*, pp.149ff.
26 OT: Seti Entonia, 1976.
27 R. M. Glasse, 'The Huli of the Southern Highlands', in Lawrence and Meggitt (eds), *Gods*,
    p.40 (and for the Tangu, see Burridge, *Mambu*, pp.83–107).
28 *Ritual*, p.145.
29 M. ToBung, An essay on Tolai culture, (typescript, Holy Spirit Seminary, Bomana 1977),
    pp.8ff; M. Roberts, The Kiriaka wig cult (handwritten MS, Holy Spirit Seminary, Bomana
    1977); OT: J. Kai, 1976.
30 J. Baitel, 'Tali', in *Three short novels from Papua New Guinea* (ed. M. Greicus), Auckland,
    1976, pp.108ff.
31 M. Strathern, *Women in between*, London, 1972, pp.166, 183.
32 R. M. Berndt, *Excess and restraint*, Chicago, 1962, pp.150 and ff. (Kogu); A. Chowning,
    Women in traditional Melanesian societies (unpublished lecture, Women's Conference,
    Sirinumu Dam, Sogeri, April 1972) (Sengseng).
33 cf. esp. A. L. Epstein (ed.), *Contention and dispute*, Canberra, 1974.
34 L. Pospisil, *The Kapauka Papuans and their law* (Yale University publications in anthropo-
    logy 54), New Haven, 1958, p.237.
35 ibid., pp.144–247.
36 OT: J. Tschauder, 1976; M. Tamoane, 1977.
37 OT: Amin Opai, 1972.
38 *Ritual*, p.153.
39 Trompf and E. Hau'Ofa, 'Mekeo Chiefs and Disputing Villagers', *Journal of the Polynesian
    Society* 83 (1974), p.234 (the Mekeo being near-coastal Papuans).

40 To allude to the title of Norman O. Brown's important book, New York, 1967.

41 cf. M. Young, *Fighting with Food*, Cambridge, 1971, pp.228ff., 256f.

42 Langness, Bena Bena Social Structure, pp.132, 142ff., as background; and my own fieldnotes among the Bena Bena and Asaro 1977.

43 Willington Jojoga Opeba, 'Migration history of the Sebaga-Andere, Binandere and Jaua tribes of the Northern Province — a religious and philosophical approach', in D. Denoon and R. Lacey (eds), *Oral tradition in Melanesia*, ch. 4 (Orokaiva); Trompf, '"Ikaroa Raepa" of Keharo, Western Mekeo — Conqueror and Peace-Maker', *Oral History*, 5/7 (1977), pp.32ff. (Mekeo and Moripi, the latter a group closely related to the Toaripi).

44 See *Payback*, ch. 1, sect. B2. Note also R. Scaglion (ed.), *Homicide compensation in Papua New Guinea: problems and prospects* (Law Reform Commission of Papua New Guinea monograph 1) Port Moresby 1981; yet cf. D. K. Feil, *The Evolution of Highland Papua New Guinea Societies*, Cambridge, 1987, pp.80ff.

45 In capitalizing Life here I take my queue from E. Mantovani, 'A fundamental Melanesian Religion', *Point* 1 (1977), pp.154–65.

46 cf. also Schieffelin's *The Burning of the Dancers and the Loneliness of the Sorrowful*, Brisbane, 1977 edn (on the Kaluli, Southern Central Highlands of Papua).

47 Malinowski, *Argonauts*, pp.95, 189ff., 473.

48 *The Gift* (trans. I. Cunnison), New York, 1967, p.27.

49 R. Lacey, The Holders of the Way (unpublished typescript, UPNG, Port Moresby 1973); Feil, *Ways of exchange: the Enga Tee of Papua New Guinea*, Brisbane, 1984, esp. pp.38–40; A. Strathern, *The Rope of Moka*, Cambridge, 1971; cf. P. G. Rubel and A. Rosman, *Your Own Pigs You May Not Eat*, Chicago, 1978; Trompf, *Payback*, ch. 1, sect. B for more detailing than can be afforded here.

50 A practice found, for example, throughout Manus (New Guinea islands), OT: Polonou Pokawin, 1974. There are debt repayments in some cultures, however, such as the Engan *yano*, in which near exactness is expected; see Feil, *Ways of exchange*, p.39.

51 cf. N. Smart, *The religious experience of mankind*, London, 1977, p.103.

52 Fortune, *Manus religion*, pp.1, 165. I thank Michele Stephen for reminding me of this case.

53 See Trompf, '"Bilalaf"', p.24.

54 e.g. Barth, *Ritual*, p.149.

55 For background, Trompf, 'Salvation and primal religion', in Dockrill and Tanner (eds), *Idea of salvation*, p.211.

56 Esp. P. B. Indulusia, 'Viewing His sacrifice through Melanesian eyes' (B.Th. thesis, Christian Leaders Training College, Banz 1979), passim; cf. for a nearby culture, R. Keesing, *Kwaio Religion*, 1984, ch. 9.

57 OTs: Seti Entonia, 1976; Jojoga Opeba, 1983.

58 For deeper analysis, Trompf, *Payback*, ch. 1, B 3ii.

59 The Taiora (central highlands, New Guinea) are a group better known for exploiting this fact. OT: Thomas Vogasung (Kainantu Court House), 1977.

60 As did the Nii in April, 1977. Pers. comm., Ross Weymouth.

61 cf. V. Gadiki, Offering; an approach to practical theology (handwritten MS, UPNG, Port Moresby 1976), p.16.

62 Against L. Lévy-Bruhl, *La mentalité primitive*, Paris, 1921 (although he qualified his views at the end of his career), yet cf. P. Pertierra, 'Lévy-Bruhl and modes of thought: a re-appraisal', *Mankind* 14/2 (1983), pp.112ff., and for modern 'resurrections' of the dichtomy, cf. C. R. Hallpike, *The foundations of primitive thought*, Oxford, 1979; M. Hollis and S. Lukes (eds), *Rationality and relativism*, Cambridge, 1982 (various).

63 M. J. Meggitt, 'The Mae Enga of the Western Highlands', in Lawrence and Meggitt (eds), *Gods*, pp.114–16.

64 OT: Munil of Bolbo, *Bolumdan* of the Danga tribe, 1973.

65 L. J. Luzbetak, 'Worship of the Dead in the Middle Wahgi', pp.85–88.

66 OT: Peter Kuiwan, *kunjeyi* 1975.

67 OT: Obed Posu, 1977.

68 OTs: Kunangel Yeki, Mani Opai, etc. 1976–77.

69 cf. Barth, *Ritual*, p.147.

70 OT: Amini La'a and others, 1973.

71 Augustine was a key figure in early Christianity questioning the appropriateness of applying traditional Graeco-Roman (even Hebrew) retributive logic to events on earth. Here I foreshadow my book *To Forgive and forget? the logic of retribution in early Christian historiography* (for The transformation of the classical heritage Ser.), Berkeley.

72 OT: Obed Posu, 1977.

73 Glasse, 'Huli', p.30.

74 cf. F. Jachmann, *Seelen- und Totenvorstellungen*, pp.166ff.

75 J. Nilles, 'Simbu ancestors and Christian worship', *Catalyst* 7/3 (1977), p.183.

76 H. Strauss, *Die Mi-Kultur der Hagenbergstämme im Östlichen Zentral Neuguinea*, (Baessler-Archiv, N.F., 16 [1962]), pp.145ff. See also ch. 9 below on the Halia, Buka Island.

77 Lawrence and Meggitt (eds), *Gods*, p.11.

78 See G. Fugmann, 'Salvation in Melanesian religions', in Mantovani (ed.), *An Introduction*, pp.279ff; cf. Trompf, 'Salvation'.

79 cf. esp. J. Strelan, *Searching for Salvation*, Adelaide, 1977, esp. chs 2–3; B. Schwarz, 'Cargo movements', in Mantovani (ed.), *Introduction*, pp.242–45.

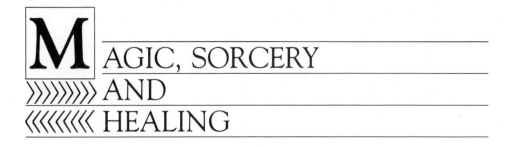

CHAPTER 4

MAGIC, SORCERY AND HEALING

If there are any 'appearances' (*phainomena*) in the known order of things which are guaranteed to leave the sensitive student of religion — especially of primal religions — wondering whether an adequate, complete account of 'cultural happenings' can ever be rendered, it is the alleged reality of so-called 'preternatural forces' or 'spiritual powers' affecting human affairs. The practitioners of traditional religions in Melanesia take these factors very seriously (though not enacting their rituals with a Calvinistic gravity!).[1] Yet it is precisely these elements which modern social enquirers usually find very difficult to face head-on, normally taming them as 'aspects of the belief-system' under consideration rather than immersing themselves in a strange, all-embracing '*Lebenswelt*'.[2] Such phenomena are considered typical of 'pre-scientific' (if not 'primitive') world-views, and thus primal peoples' claims about the appropriation of 'spirit-power' have not been readily taken at their face value. Most outside investigators will assume it preferable to interpret them 'naturalistically', by assessing their function as means of modifying behaviour, sanctioning power structures, providing psychological support, and so on.[3]

This chapter, deliberately designed to penetrate still further analytically, considers the relevance of the phenomenological method to the study of magic, sorcery and healing in traditional Melanesian religions. Some advocates for phenomenology suggest that one does not do justice to scientific endeavour itself if we do not first let even the weirdest experiences, including claims about them, communicate themselves to us in their own terms. Edmund Husserl, to cite phenomenology's leading exponent, called researchers to the prior act of 'bracketing' their prejudices and theoretical assumptions, and thus to attempts at contacting the world's happenings directly, with an 'eidetic vision'. For him a scholar should aim at representing 'the sense the world has *for us all*', the sense one 'obviously gets solely from our experience', before imposing abstract descriptive terms from the world of scientific constructs and philosophy.[4] Here, I at least go so far as to suggest that this method provides a juster, more open (and thereby more scientific) way of handling such phenomena we immediately connect with the terms (or concepts) 'magic', 'sorcery' and 'healing'. It follows, however, that the usages of these three terms reflect pre-judgements which phenomenologists should prefer to see temporarily cast aside. That makes the task so formidable. Words and experiences often seem inextricable: their nexus is the very nightmare of reality for any would-be objectivist.

Magic

Of the three terms under discussion, magic is recognizably broader in compass than the other two. I shall begin with it because debates over magic draw into sharper focus:
- some of the problems of language already introduced, more particularly those pertaining to definition and historical linguistics;
- certain difficulties for phenomenology (taking our cue from it that a natural, unadulterated grasp of things can only come by circumventing the modern scientific thought-world);
- the awkwardness of deciding whether certain techniques or actions, carried out on the assumption that extra-human power is being appropriated, do 'actually work' (as alleged by their practitioners) or can only be fairly explicated by referring to an other-than-ordinary matter of course.

'Magic' vs. 'Religion' in historical perspective

First, concerning the language question, one notes with dismay the endless efforts in cross-cultural studies to establish what is meant by 'magic', let alone what it is. Earlier this century Marcel Mauss produced a long theoretical treatise on the subject, only to leave various critics wondering whether it contributed more 'to the dissolution of "magic" as a category' than to its happy retention.[5] After dismissing Frazer and Lehmann for 'ignoring a considerable body of practices which are called magical (*magique*) by all those either performing or observing the rites' (as if the whole world spoke French!), the best he could do by way of definition is to claim as 'magical . . . any rite which does not play a part in organized cults'.[6] So much for the short idiosyncratic graces at the Protestant dinner table, and 'little arrow-like prayers' the Yoruba shoot up to Olodumare (who lacks a cult),[7] just to begin citing some tidbits from the utterly complex sphere of *un*organized religions! So much for those 'scenarios of magic' which clearly are organized by the group or 'churched' (to use Durkheim's quaint terminology), when each member of the Turcoman tribes, for instance, utters up a 'wish' on Hidirellez night, knowing it will come true if one just remains alert enough to glimpse the embrace of the star-Lords Hizir and Ilyas in the sky![8]

The more one analyses subsequent attempts to distinguish magic from religion, moreover, the more a sense of futility mounts. This is not only because anyone could justly argue for a certain interchangeability between them, or because many peoples possess no 'special words for religion and magic as mutually exclusive cultural entities',[9] but also because one can almost always find a term which will do just as well, if not better, and also appear friendlier, than 'magic'. This century's faltering attempts at precise definitions, indeed, along with its higher calibre of field research, all surely dictate great caution and a more sparing reference to magic as anthropology's vaguest object of enquiry.

Bronislaw Malinowski's psycho-mental approach to the matter exemplifies some of the conundra in the inter-war stage of the discussion. If it really is true that 'tension in his organism' drives the human 'to some substitute activity' (that is, magic), which issues from a distinctive 'mental attitude and a belief that hope cannot fail nor desire deceive',[10] then one might as well conclude that most of the world's documented rituals, public or private — or in other words virtually all 'religious ceremonies' — are performed in the hope and expectation that special efforts to link in with superhuman power will produce required 'definite ends'. In any case, in one of his later works Malinowski all but concedes magic is wish-fulfilment standardized by fixed rules: and one wonders why he does not honestly admit to his own half-hidden (in this case Freud-like!) reductionism — that both religion and magic are basically morale boosters against hardship, and that magic is little more than suggestibility hedged around by a cultivated mystery.[11]

The focus of the problem has shifted since those earlier days, when there was also a good deal of confusion about the relation between *mana* and magic.[12] On considering interpreters of so-called primitive cultures, most researchers have quietly shelved the harder issues, either just wanting to get on with the business of description, or maintaining that the heart of the methodological debate lies elsewhere.[13] Some favour the adjectival term 'magico-religious', one of those linguistic curiosities which, although hailing from two pioneer students of Melanesian cultures — Rivers and Seligman(n) — now rates more as a near-at-hand sedative for our mind-strain over apparently insoluble problems.[14] Others (and I suspect this is particularly true of a recent breed of specialists in Religious Studies) have tended to subsume magic almost completely under the rubric of 'primal religions',[15] noting magic as an aspect but with no unnecessary prominence. This is in part a response forced on them by the young national intellectuals of developing countries, who for too long have borne with conservative missionaries denigrating their traditions as merely 'magical' and 'superstitious'. Perhaps it is also a reaction against Western occult faddism, which has made it a new priority for sensitive observers to give back small-scale cultures the integrity of religion, rather than have them swallowed up in the new counter-cultural (partly consumerized) enthusiasm for 'witchery' and mysterious rites.[16] And certainly most of the learned literature over the past two decades appears friendlier and possibly less patronizing for talking more about rituals and rites — rites of increase, rites of passage (or critical rites), and so on — than 'magical practices'.[17]

In all the varying applications and intonations of the term 'magic' in social scientific study, I detect the constant yet elusive influences of our linguistic past. What has been at work is not only the process of transferring categories, from one or more European language-complexes to any one of a number of non-European ones, but also the extrapolation of terminology from the forums of traditional western theological evaluation into the arena of modern empirical ethnology. Unlike the terms *mana* and *tabu* (which were only recently expropriated from their pristine contexts in Oceania), yet like 'sorcery', 'witchcraft' and 'superstition', the term 'magic' had been subject to a long history of usage in theological polemic.[18] This usage of 'magic' was most noticeable in Reformation and seventeenth century diatribes and, so, was already contrasted with the Christian faith or 'the true principles of religion', well before Enlightenment thinkers ever stressed the plurality of religions and thus longer still before anthropologists drew their updated distinctions.[19] One of the central thrusts of post-Reformation theology in the West was to dissociate (true, official) Christianity from any intimation of magic (or its suspect 'associates'). This sword of purification, moreover, had two edges: one was designed to root out whatever paganisms and wrong-headed folklore still bedevilled the European countryside; the other, particularly when the sword fell into the hands of Protestants, cut away at the superstitious excrescences of Popery.[20] This general trajectory of thought, which has never strictly speaking disappeared from the modern history of Christian reflection, has had a crucial conditioning effect on subsequent discussion about the relationship between religion and magic — in at least two respects.

In the first place, because Christianity was more or less established by its modern advocates as a non-magical religion, there has been an automatic linguistic pressure to distinguish magic from religion in Western scholarship. The almost unanimously respected Christian norm stresses faith against manipulation: one is to accept with confidence 'the promises of God' but not pretend to cajole him by ritual technique. Here faith (or religion specially conceived) has preserved its own right of independent existence.[21] It has to be plainly admitted, however, that all those efforts to determine the will(s) of the spirit-being(s) — by appeasing, barter-like, apotropaic, 'technological' and (why not say it here?) magical means — all of which wary Christians have been likely to blacken as human in origin, are endemic to virtually all the other religions. Thousands of primal religions, in particular, reflect the needs of small-scale societies as concrete and fairly immediate — centring on material and bodily security — by displacing a vast host of procedures for influencing spirit-agencies in the interests of the group or individuals.[22] In this light, magic appears as an old-fashioned shorthand way of referring to the vast world of non-Christian belief and practice; thus, we might as well concede that it is probably fairer to describe this world as religious and be done with it.[23]

In the second place, however, because of the Protestant–Catholic conflict in modern Western history, there has been a tension within Christianity devolving around rites — a subject very much connected with the religion–magic dichotomy — which has contributed to the linguistic and argumentative structure of subsequent debates about magic in social scientific literature. According to the Protestant (and sectarian) challenge, Roman Catholic emphases on outward sacramental form have taken the church in strides toward magic. In other words, ritualism is seen to stand somewhere between (true) religion and magic; the extent of the use of rites thus becomes an index to the relative corruption (*Zauberzeichen* or indication of the level of magic) in religion, which should be purified of any suppositions about supernatural results '*ex opere operato*'.[24] Yet, because of this tension and because Christianity undoubtedly possesses rites, the whole Christian tradition has been justly ranged, since the emergence of the social sciences, with other religions. Many of these other religions, however, more particularly the so-called primitive types, have been unjustly treated as heavily magical — albeit at a decreasing rate over the last two centuries[25] — when it would be preferable to consider them as religions in which rites or 'sacred actions' are held to be more concretely, more immediately efficacious.[26] Magic can perhaps be salvaged as one of the various synonyms denoting this (alleged) efficacy, yet hopefully not with its former generic appeal, or with its old capacity to mislead, implicitly denigrate and potentially annoy.[27]

What can phenomenology concede to pre-scientific world-views?

These observations about language serve to preface the argument I intend to develop about the second problematic — phenomenology. It is intriguing how these investigations have taken us back behind the historic formulations of social scientific categories. It would be unfair, of course, to pass off the Reformation and seventeenth century distinction between (true) religion and magic as 'pre-scientific', since that is one of the several crucial steps towards the more complete naturalization of the cosmos, the subsequent 'secularization of consciousness' and thus towards the triumph of the 'scientific-outlook', that *sacra scientia* itself dared to traverse.[28] More to the point, however, is whether the whole world of awareness lying beyond the scientific bias towards objectification, classification and law-like generalization (that is, lying in temporal and geographical contexts which have not suffered the pillages of a scientific *Weltbild*), in some sense corresponds more closely to an eidetic vision of phenomena, an apprehension of the world in its own terms, or 'such as it is' (*als Solches*) without it being constantly related to scientific categories.[29]

There is no certain answer to this question. Edmund Husserl, who called researchers to what he termed a *natürlicher Weltbegriff*, or to a pre-scientific grasp of the events, was annoyingly uninterested in history, and it is up to those whose work is informed by his tradition to explore the possible historical implications of his position.[30] Some phenomenologists will prefer to argue that both the Western past and non-European societies are irrelevant to his position because nowhere can one find a pre-modern culture without its palpable prejudices, and without its categories of 'spirit-forces', which Husserl himself would have found very hard to accept.[31] Almost in spite of its founder and his overly philosophic protégés, however, the phenomenological method can be adapted to relieve us a little from this unsettling dream. At least we have learnt that, for Husserl, natural and direct apprehension can only arise by mitigating the subject-object dichotomy, dampening our tendencies to reify, to consider reality as *objectiv*, or to pursue the 'essence' of something or 'the Thing in Itself'. Phenomenology should take us back to 'facts', 'events', 'appearances' grasped pre-philosophically (*rückkehr zu den Sachen selbst*), as facets of experienced life and not categories of science.[32] Here one might as well note that it is the existence of an unblocked doorway between subject and object which allows for the distinctly religious sensibility of *not* reducing reality into a mere objectification. Room has been left for a natural knowing of the world as, at least in part, personal and spiritual — even possibly including the invisible agencies and efficacious power of the so-called 'primitive magician'. It would be a sheer extravagance to claim, however, that phenomenology is bound to uphold the claims for the religious outlook on life in general; it is sufficient that it leaves one worrying both about what has been deterred in consciousness, and what might have been left out of reality, by the epistemologies of modern science.[33] Thus, one comes to realize how consideration of this second problematic provides for some helpful manoeuvrability in our approach to the third.

The workability of so-called 'magic'?

A difficulty for the observer of cultural events, which is rather too often set aside as unmanageable, or even as unimportant in its own right, is the alleged *efficacy* of so-called 'magical' techniques (or of rites and special actions, including spells, charms, sorcery and healing procedures), as claimed by their practitioners. Admittedly, most well-trained university graduates will have good grounds for being sceptical about such claims. Not only may the rites be shrouded in such secrecy that the researchers will only learn about them through hearsay,[34] or from others who purport to have experienced their effects, but the varieties of cultures and repertories are such that some procedures are likely to look like charades beside others, some present themselves as quite untestable, and others fall susceptible to alternative, more respectable explanations. It is small wonder that anthropologists have preferred to establish magic's 'functional', 'structural' or cognitive place rather than its genuineness. Yet, that this avoidance is perfectly consistent with the reductionism endemic to modern scientific methods is a point hardly worth missing. In the important case of Claude Lévi-Strauss, in fact, this reductionism lexically backfires on magic itself, which is represented as a conceptual structuring, or mediation, of normally distinct spheres of activity, surprisingly generalized as a 'naturalization' of human actions![35] Here social science quite obfuscates the traditional, formal content of 'magic' — the supernaturalism usually attached to it in Western semantics — and while doing so, paradoxically exposes a certain inutility about magic as a category, thus advancing the cause for its negation as a real object of enquiry.[36] I return to my earlier point that it is better to concede how 'religious' most magic is, getting its general context straight before granting it an overly-independent status (as a 'pseudo-science', for example, which is both too pejorative and a phrase atheists could just as easily give to religion).[37] The struggle for better definitions, on the other hand, can hardly be debarred, let alone discouraged!

Recommendations? Without even pretending to confirm the ready availability of occult forces, I would suggest that science has probably domesticated so many of today's intellectuals that we are conditioned to be more closed than open to the existence of 'non-natural, non-empirical' dimensions. The clear implication one can tease out of phenomenology is openness — some mid-course between the extremes of crass occultism and secularist bigotry. Such openness, to go further, requires the backing of a new style of fieldwork, hitherto rather daunting. Without also pretending that we should all foster a band of mini-Carlos Castanedas, it is probably desirable, for the adequate representation of a primal culture, that some researchers actually seek training or co-participation at the hands of the adept — the self-avowed wielders of unseen powers — and not forever look pre-emptively for psychotic traits or self-conscious deception. Among anthropologists this agenda has barely begun to be followed.[38]

Magic in Melanesia

As the most complex anthropological theatre on earth, Melanesia has already hopefully taught learned researchers two simple home-truths, which pertain to the aforegoing discussion. First, there is the common inextractability of what some might have expected to be the separate phenomena of religion and magic.[39] Secondly, the typical Melanesian claim that the acquisition or control of 'individuating "power"'' any Westerners might describe as magical[40] was made possible only through the aid of spirit agencies (such as ancestors, deities, tutelary animal- and plant-spirits), not just through correct procedure or (as the first serious ethnographer in Melanesia superficially put it of Woodlark Island belief) 'the internal power of things'.[41] Thus, the general drift of latter-day ethnographic research — especially from the time when

Vicedom and Tischner found no differentiation between magic and religion in the world of the Melpa *Moka*[42] to the very recent omission of magic as a category of Fredrik Barth's study of the Baktaman[43] — confirms the need for careful attention to the linguistic and phenomenological questions so far raised. No one could deny, admittedly, that in most traditional Melanesian world-views, spirit-power can be harnessed and localized — in the Elema sorcerer's dangerous bundle of 'heat', for example, in the Fuyughe prophet's snaring of thunder between timber, pandanus leaves and bark cloth, or the Rovianas' increased access to *mana* through retaining the skulls of their chiefs.[44] Yet, that there are 'powers', 'principles' or 'occult forces' different from such agencies as 'spiritual beings' is a common preconception of virtually all the world's religions.[45] The question is whether such powers can be appropriated without calling on the intervention of spiritual beings, and whether, personal or impersonal, these powers are understood to be compelled to operate automatically, after the use of spells, charms, rites, and so on, as if spirits are incidental to human management.[46]

Limited though we are by a small compass, we can begin to isolate those key problem-points of ethnographic research in Melanesia which have been most implicated in our general discussion. First, there is the problem of *distinguishing spell from prayer* in Melanesia. Prayer has not been represented as a prominent feature of Melanesian religious life,[47] but this is consistent with the conditioned, expatriate propensity to expect 'the magical'. It may be that the observer can detect a phenomenological difference between prayer, spells, ritual formulae, chants, and perhaps certain songs invested with manipulative power; yet, lexically, they all may go under the same name in a given society.[48] Above all, because the object of articulating words (or sounds) in a set, apparently sacralized fashion, is generally so concrete (the desire for sickness to be removed, for success in a hunt, and so on), the Western observer is commonly tempted into talk of spell and magical potency.

To illustrate this aspect of the continuing nightmare brought on by phenomenology, let us consider three documented utterances, the first of which has already been alluded to. In 1889, when Bishop Navarre was fortunate enough to overhear those special words uttered by a Roro (Yule Island) fisherman on the beach before taking to sea, he described the whole effect in his journal as '*une prière*' (a prayer). What the villager had simply done, however, was to list the names of great ancestor fishermen and more recent dead relatives (including a woman), while knotting the net for a hoped-for number of fish. He thus created a 'rope of power' to bring success.[49] His likely use of this 'chain effect' in other situations, and the apparently muddled syntactical nature of the saying, might convince one that here we have a spell, the procedure in any case being reminiscent of a hundred-and-one Melanesian efforts at power-appropriation to bring increase or 'good luck'.[50] As for the second example, a Negrie man who disclosed a secret chant — for the bearing of heavy loads — as an untranslatable 'listing of pairs of men and animals that goes on and on', persuaded Patrick Gesch (1977) that this was a spell, because it was whispered over the leaf of a betel-nut tree; its chanter even suggested that it would be just as good 'to make a car get out of a bog'. Yet, on noting that the ancestors are invoked in the enunciation, 'as the very epitome of power and ability to get things done',[51] the interpreter's mind could easily turn from magic to thoughts of a characteristically Melanesian way of impressing oneself on the spirits. Roy Wagner provides two important *pobi* from among the Daribi (1960s), to take the third case. Here, *pobi* is translated as 'spell', there being no reference to prayer throughout Wagner's analysis. Yet both utterances contain significant references to the mythic cross-cousins, Iwai and Mawa, who are now said to carry the moon and sun across the sky, and their sway is evidently being articulated to stop or bring on rain.[52] The *pobi* are 'standardized', but one needs to have good reasons for distinguising such long, quite complex statements from the various set invocations we call prayers found in the great religious traditions.[53]

Wagner is likely to respond by an appeal to the *metaphoric* aspect to magic spells. One of his charts in *Habu* contains a thorough enumeration of how the content of a spell provides a so-called 'metaphoric link' between two ostensibly 'separate areas' of human experience, bringing them together into a 'desired effect'. Thus, before hunting, for instance, a spell is employed which alludes to thorny vines snagging leaves, and Wagner concludes that the separate areas of plants and animals are forged together, the 'metaphoric link' being the 'catching [of] forest products', and the 'desired effect' being to 'make dogs catch game'.[54] This is interesting hermeneutics and difficult to dismiss; on the other hand, it has the disadvantage of objectifying a structure which may not be a factor in Daribi consciousness. Of course it remains true that all language is reducibly metaphoric, and that no hermeneutics is possible without erecting frames of reference.[55] However, the point here is that the scientific interpreter has introduced the category of metaphor, which may actually obfuscate the perfectly 'natural', 'organic' way by which Daribi relate their words or explicatives to the needs of life, and thus to spirit agencies.

A similar problem presents itself with symbolic analysis.[56] Are symbols only what are recognized as such by those whose culture and grammar allow them to distinguish symbols from non-symbols? Or can symbols only be adequately identified by the trained observer who can fathom the 'operations' of the unconscious? Granted that science can uncover symbols in forms and actions where their creators have not perceived them (and Carl Jung, for one, would call this disclosure an exercise in phenomenology[57]), might not the result be some brilliant reflective objectification of what in actuality, or when observed 'as such', is 'natural' and not self-conscious? One may discover a European tenderly stroking leaves in a glass house, whispering words of care to a beautiful plant;[58] if such doings fail to impress themselves upon most Westerners as distinctly symbolic or magical, why should there by any greater tendency to invoke primal people in non- or super-verbal intrigue? When the Baktaman passes something which concerns him under his armpits, for instance, this may be for him the act of smelling or testing, and may thus be unjustifiably labelled as *symbolic* (though not so unjustly as sacralization).[59]

It is possible that each society's cultivated logic will suggest routes out of these difficulties; here I am only intent on setting forth the issues. And there are a few others worth citing before turning to sorcery — a subject no discussion of magic can do without, and a factor without which magic is much harder to redeem as a useful classifier. For one, care is required when power and magic seemed to be expressed univocally in a Melanesian tongue. Even if it is true, for example, that the Mekeo perceive *isapu* 'as a physical quality or force which is present in different degrees in various physical objects . . . considered to be hot'[60] (an outlook readily paralleled along the Papuan coast[61]), there ought to be good linguistic reasons and appropriate phenomena to persuade one that 'spiritual power' would not do just as well as any reference to magic. After all, *isapu* is applied broadly enough by the Mekeo to include the notion of inviolable authority,[62] there being analogues in other Melanesian belief-complexes calling for a similar caveat.[63]

Then there is the closely related issue of 'discernment', as Gesch terms it. Through initiation(s) and many experiences, young people come to learn how it is possible to achieve extraordinary things in the world, such as organizing a feast or harvesting a fine crop of yams — those accomplishments which appear as marvels to the young.[64] It could be that such a person has learnt and tried many techniques to appropriate super-added power, yet the step from being only a 'trier' to someone who has a sense of being in confident control only comes after having achieved much; it is only then that power, authority and formidableness have been integrated into that person's own secure being. If this is the case, why should we not retranslate notions and practices for which we were tempted to use the word magic into talk about 'mastery', a 'total efficacy' in handling the visible and invisible forces in the cosmos, or truly 'effective action'?[65]

Considering discernment in this fashion reveals the fallacy of bifurcating practical activity from magic, let alone religious from a magical consciousness. Reflect on Malinowski's rather circular argument in this connection. Where there is no danger, he asserts, as in 'lagoon fishing', a man being able to 'rely completely upon his knowledge and skill', magic 'does not exist', but with dangerous and uncertain 'open sea-fishing . . . extensive magical ritual to secure safety and good results' is employed.[66] Taking this assertion and the full range of Malinowski's own findings, we would like to know: where is religion all this time? In certain prayers uttered by lagoon-fishermen? Or lurking behind the prows built for virtually all Trobriand canoes, which had so much dedication and asceticism put into their carving? Besides, does it not usually follow that a larger output of human energy, religious and tech-nological (not just magical), will be manifested where the greatest need for power-appropriation applies? And if lagoon-fishing required no magic, why should the coral gardens require it? — with so many capable gardeners and nurturers around![67] Here we can begin to see the need for a more integrative approach, one which apprehends *homo religiosus* as a totality in which practical skill, ritual actions and belief result from the same consciousness, and are not incorrigibly dissected to fit scientific categories.

To elicit all these problems is not to dispense with magic as a category, but to demand a sound justification for retaining it. After all, there are certain styles of action — 'war magic', for instance, as it is often termed in anthropological literature, or 'love magic' and 'wealth magic' — which do not find their obvious parallels in some of the major religions. Consequently, these phrases have a greater capacity to stick, as also does 'war magician'. It seems to make sense, for example, to distinguish the Mekeo *fai'a* as a 'war magician' — a man who wields mystical powers against the group's enemies — rather than a sorcerer (*ungaunga*); and, likewise, the Wahgi *obokunjeyi* is a person using *kunje* (magic) for battle purposes (*ope*), not evil *kum* (sorcery) against his fellows.[68] In the Wahgi case, although the war magician and the sorcerer both wield harmful or death-dealing powers, the phrase appears suitable for the former since one can find a *kunjeyi* 'pure and simple' who divines sicknesses and prescribes cures, no highly distinctive term being used for such healers in particular. But the problems do not run away easily and, in any case, mention of sorcery and healing already suggests that our discussion should be deepened.

Constantly harping on terminological adequacy has not helped in that part of the phenomenological investigation concerned with whether or not so-called magic works. I suspect one probably needs the criteria of harming and healing, which will be utilized more in the following sections, to throw any bright light on this task. At least we can advise at this stage against the incautious assumption that most traditional Melanesian societies possess distinctly compartmentalized epistemologies of magic, the successes and failures of this magic being explicable within a closed system sufficient unto themselves. If there are no obvious results to a special ritual, in other words, the explanation for failure does not necessarily have to be found within magic's own frame of reference. Peter Lawrence has stressed the fact that, for coastal Madangs, magical techniques correctly performed must bring the desired effects; thus, any explanation for failure focusses on the likelihood of an improper performance.[69] As far as my experiences with a variety of other cultures are concerned, however, explanations can be more diverse, even if apparently standard, and need not always be derived from the 'conceptual province' surrounding 'magic' itself. A Roro such as the fisherman mentioned above may make all the necessary preparations for a hunt, linking himself to the ancestors; yet if, unbeknown to him and during the course of the hunting itself, someone arrives at his hamlet in search of him, he shall catch nothing.[70]

This reversal of hunting success is ascribed to a widely accepted, yet unmanageable and mysterious principle, which can cut across all human attempts to manipulate the spirit order in the hunter's favour. In various coastal and highland contexts, further, the failure of crops which have received appropriate 'rites of increase' can be attributed to the displeasure of the dead relatives — towards individual, family or larger 'security circle' — for failure to fulfil social obligations; or it can be commonly ascribed to sorcery.[71] Even if such overlapping and interrelationships may indeed be conceived, in a traditional world-view, to arise from interacting or conflict between different *loci* or 'departments' of power, some helpful, some harming, they are still far from neatly reflecting the two prongs of the 'magic–religion dichotomy' some would like to foist on the thought-forms from without.

But what of sorcery and curing in Melanesia? Are not most of their enactments examples of magic? Are they not cases of 'the pretended art of influencing the course of events', with sorcery being malevolent and thus hardly part of religion? Even just to touch on traditional epistemologies, it seems, leads us (like Steppenwolves!) into the remaining sequences of a little nightmare.

Sorcery

Sorcery is typically portrayed as the black side of magic (I have known Melanesians to be annoyed by the possible innuendo);[72] and if magic has been described as the bastard sister to either science or religion,[73] one half of her nature has generated a bad press and a good deal of fear. 'Witch crazes' and whole movements have centred on the urge to eliminate the 'black arts' and sorcery in Europe and Africa.[74] The Papua New Guinea Sorcery Act (1976) discriminates between black and white magic, declaring the former punishable by law for bearing harmful intent, while Fiji's 1969 Penal Code defined both sorcery and witchcraft as 'destructive magic'. Thus, two important general problems, one very hoary, immediately float before our eyes. First, does not the phenomenon of sorcery, if it has been called 'black magic' — and if fear and distaste toward it can be found even among pre-Christian practitioners of religions in Melanesia — justify the continued use of the term 'magic'? Second, if sorcery is claimed to be dangerous, how does the phenomenologist adequately describe its harmfulness?

In answer to the former question, it looks on the surface as if sorcery offers the best legitimacy for magic's retention. Sorcery, one could argue, defines magic like evil defines a dramatic plot: the spell, the exaggerated and often ugly-looking actions, the intensity of desire, which are all usually manifested in the most secret corners, all appear to provide the key model through which magic in general can be determined. This is actually a cogent point and one extremely difficult to brush off. Nevertheless, it is not one that should be used as a licence to read magic back into a culture with less circumspection, especially if thorough work is called for to establish what the sorcerers do and what (or whose) power they rely on for their deeds.

That old debate will go on, probably, and it is partly a side-show to speculations about the origins of religion, as to which rituals have created the paradigm for which — whether *group* 'rites of increase' have informed the styles of behaviour found in *individual* attempts at (omni)potence (so Durkheim) or vice versa (thus Frazer). But it is worth noting that 'rites of decrease', if acts of sorcery and black magic may be so renamed for a moment, are far less likely to be celebrated publicly. Once power-appropriation is 'individuated', in both senses of being harnessed by a single person and for a relatively specific end, it is therefore more liable to fall outside the control of 'normative religion'. This circumstance helps explain why, once the collective ceremonies of pre-Christian traditional religions collapsed, the 'shadow' of the religions, which we have come to call magic and sorcery (as well as witchcraft and superstition), and which could be more easily perpetuated as personal practices, remained behind.[75] This process only goes to show, however, that Westerners should elude their linguistic conditioning by first trying to place sorcery in relation to the wider socio-religious matrix of a society, without presupposing that sorcery is apart from the religion and the 'definitive statement' of the magical sphere. The sorcerer might be considered by a people to be quite 'outside the system', both malevolent and alien, as the two words *rangame* and *rangume* suggest, for example, among the Tangu.[76] Yet, he may well have a more or less institutionalized role, like the Mekeo *ungaunga*, who, although rarely found strolling down the main village walkway, is understood to be directed by the chiefs to maintain domestic order. If in both these cases (Mekeo and Tangu) one has little need to query the usage of the terms 'sorcery' and 'sorcerer', however, which seem fairly legitimate here (despite the whiff of theological error detectable in the English words), what is less clear is whether reference to the term 'magic' becomes more viable, especially when informants want to insist that, practised 'in or out of the system', sorcery is a prominent part of 'the religious scheme of things'.[77] A good rule of thumb for a better sleep over this issue is to test first the lexical situation in each culture. If there is one term (or more) shared in common between sorcery actions and other sacral activity, for example, 'magic' might be a defensible translation.[78]

A phenomenological assessment ought also come into the picture here. After all, in some societies one gains the impression that a person's very family members or that person's neighbours are all potential sorcerers; in such situations the 'mere hope or wish' for someone's 'ill' can be accepted as dangerously potent (as among the Orokaiva).[79] Or, to take another variable, the 'sorcerer' specialist can sometimes also be the very one to alleviate sickness (as with the Roro/Mekeo), by working counter-sorcery, and this kind of double role-play should make for a very cautious usage of specialist titles.[80]

As for the second question, about an adequate phenomenology of magic, we must begin by noting the tension between reductionist approaches to sorcery and those which take its effects to be genuine, or to be the wielding of real spiritual power. On the other hand, there lie scholars who emphasize sorcery as an instrument of 'social control',[81] quite apart from whether the members of a given people conceive it as alien or integral to their social life. The persons who fail to fulfil obligations, for instance, or make enemies easily, or combine their success with arrogance, or who attain to high authority (I think of the Halia chiefs for the last case — see chapter 3, n.22), lay themselves open to negative acts to check their irresponsibility or diminish their influence. Alongside this perfectly admissible social explanation of sorcery, one usually finds a stress on psychological factors. People fall ill because they learn sorcery is being directed against them, or get worse because their fellows have already explained the early symptoms as sorcery's inflictions. It may also be noted that, psychology aside, some sorcery is carried out by, as was pointed out before, literally offering the unsuspecting guest a poisoned potion, or by surreptitiously hiding a bagged snake (already familiarized with the smell of the victim) near a person's bed. On the other hand, most primal peoples themselves conceive sorcery to be the appropriation and effective direction of actual, harm-dealing powers (such as the ill-disposed dead or independent spirits or harnessed forces) against the unsuspecting (or against competing malevolences). The odd Western researcher is beginning to report, moreover, on uncomfortable experiences at the other end of sorcery rites, or in an interview situation with a sorcerer.[82] My own very first introduction to Melanesian religion came in 1962 through the late William Neil, who lost his missionary brother and his own left arm to Malaitan cannibals, and who vividly described the utter depletion of his physical strength when a Malu'u (Toabaita) sorcerer rushed at him in the bush with small, blunt carved objects.

The two bodies of opinion are in conflict to this extent: those who claim to have experienced some uncanny evil power, or are convinced by accounts of it, are not going to consider reductionist explanatory 'shortfalls' to be worth their salt. Phenomenologists can operate as mediators here. On the one hand, they should remind the scientifically and cerebrally oriented that they may either be culturally deprived from perceiving what is seen by others 'naturally', or be secularized to the point of excluding spiritual factors. On the other, they would do well to warn that some people are prone to fright, to project, and thus to give exaggerated accounts of so-called evil and its likely sources.[83] Openness is called for again. As the artist Pissarro once remarked, 'remember the natives, they are naive and knowing', and while it is reasonable for the scholar to be sceptical of claims made by isolated peoples unschooled in the halls of learning, it is hazardous to repress knowledge of non-empirical realities which most of the world can still 'touch', but which a small minority called intellectuals refuse to believe exist.[84]

Sorcery in Melanesia

To attempt an ethnographic survey of sorcery (and witchcraft) in Melanesia would be to duplicate the work already done (even if it is in need of some revision) by Mary Patterson and the contributors to important symposia on the subject.[85] Instead, I intend to concentrate on a small number of pressing methodological and phenomenological problems. In keeping with the immediately preceding section, these concern sorcery as viewed in the broader context of Melanesian religion; and a return to the subject of sorcery's workableness.

It should be clarified that, although modern legal regulations identify sorcery and witchcraft with the practice of black magic and declare it culpable, from traditional viewpoints most sorcery in Melanesia was considered helpful for dealing harm to outside enemies. Such recent legislation does not speak to the pre-modern situation; it is devised to clean up violence and deliberate acts of vindictiveness unacceptable in new nations.[86] Traditionally, however, every tribe or 'security circle' was its own micro-nation; and since the units were small, inter-tribal alliances being subject to shifts and re-alignments, there was a pressing need for internal cohesion and energetic cooperation. In pre-pacification circumstances the basic social units simply could not afford to have sources of instability in their very midst constantly undermining the sense of solidarity and military security. If the warriors had to be constantly alert, what agony to have to bear many additional worries about a neighbour who could scrabble some of your betel-nut shell, hair or fingernail leavings for malicious ends! Today, admittedly, there is considerable worry about the proximity of sorcerers (as we noted of the Papuan coast and the east Sepik region in the last chapter), but of course it is a strain now borne without the old fears about a surprise raid.[87]

We have already argued the case that most pre-pacification sorcery was outer-directed, and thus used as an aid in battle, or against enemies and disliked persons in other security-circles who were singled out for treatment during times of both war or peace. Once pacification was imposed, with the colonial (and mission) policy to integrate previously separated hamlets into villages, or to encourage economic cooperation between previously ill-disposed groups, being enforced,[88] the new menace was the social rupturing brought about by inner- (as against outer-) directed sorcery.[89] When most researchers entered the field, then, they entered societies in transition, and one particular phenomenological nightmare for them concerns the discrimination between tradition and 'neo-tradition'. The large Wahgi cultural complex nicely illustrates this. Where there is still military tension, as around Kup and the border between the (Wahgi) Kumai and the (Chimbu) Endugla, *kum* (sorcery) figures there as an action of inter-tribal conflict;[90] where warfare has ceased, one finds a much greater concern for detecting workers of *kum* within the group — identifying them as women whose bottoms glow in the night (witches), or more recently as men who put *botel* (glass, or sharp object) in food or cars (sorcerers).[91]

Even in societies, such as the Mekeo, where sorcerers are apparently institutionalized as tools of chiefly control, the earlier importance of outer-directed concerns show up. So, even among the Mekeo, significantly, sorcerers were primarily conceived of as protectors in pre-contact times. When the depleted Aipiana clans Fagu'opa, Faila and Inauefai — losing population in the 1870s owing to both warfare and sickness — each *lacked* an *ungaunga*, for instance, they requested the (by this time disaffected) large Veipa'a clan called Meauni to supply them with 'domestic sorcerers', so *unprotected* did they feel without them. Today, after mission opposition to all revenge syndromes and with rampant increase in sorcery, all these clans harbour no such image.[92]

Surveying extant ethnographies, therefore, it is always worthwhile establishing the degree of a society's interaction with expatriate influences before the anthropologist enters the field. One litmus test for anthropologies of sorcery is to gauge whether researchers have discriminated between the more strictly traditional and the adaptive, and have attempted to reconstruct the much tenser atmosphere of pre-contact days. Those were the old days when 'seized' Bena Bena payback runners would run over hill and down dale to isolate the hamlet of the sorcerer-killer without being arrested by police on the Highlands Highway, or when the Hube could daemonize themselves for vengeance against enemies by thrashing a corpse without the objections of missionaries. Thus, those were different days from the time when peace was to be ordained; in the later time there was much freer interaction between communities, as among the Toaripi in the inter-war years, and yet the old strife between groups was perpetuated at a spiritual level, through each village having its defender sorcerers.[93] And they differ again from the more recent phase on the coast when communities are divided among themselves because of sorcery threats (settling into a malaise of sheer boredom, or suffering from unfortunate quarrels between traditionalists and Christians).[94]

This paradigm hardly precludes the possible traditional role of sorcery effecting control within the sorcerer's own security circle, but the onus is on the researcher to show that this was a crucial factor before pacification (cf. n.79). The paradigm only serves to indicate where the emphases are likely to shift — to facilitate and not tyrannize over ethnographic analysis. Even so, it reminds interpreters that, should they wish to stress the element of social control of the maintenance of order, they have to make clear what is meant by the *society* (the whole linguistic matrix? one basic unit of it? or its leadership?), as well as answer the argument that, for many societies in post-contact times, sorcery became a destructive and criminal-like feature of life.[95]

If there are traps in treating sorcery ahistorically, it is also hazardous to consider sorcery in a vacuum, or within the apparently discrete boundaries of magic alone. In terms of traditional epistemologies, as suggested in chapter 3, sorcery falls into the much wider arena of retributive logic. There are fascinating logical and explanatory systems surrounding what Marshall Sahlins[96] has termed the 'negative' and 'positive' reciprocities of Melanesian societies, and the rationales for both (negative) payback and (positive) reciprocal activity are integrally tied in with consensus or standard explanations for significant events (such as disaster, sickness or death). Sometimes, in fact, sorcery appears to be *more* an explanation than a fact, since it can be difficult to establish whether some peoples actually do have sorcerer figures among them or not.[97] In other cases sorcerers are such an essential component of indigenous philosophy that no sickness unto death can be explained without reference to them, and so important in cosmography, as Daniel Shaw has recently shown of the Papuan Samo,[98] that they (the *booganli oosoo*) are the human mediums by which the evil (forest) spirits act out their part in a 'cosmic struggle'. The anthropologist ought to be wary, moreover, in view of the fact that the local epistemology will have been adapting as the status and function of sorcerers altered through post-contact time, while also simply taking these broader dimensions into account.

The second major problem concerns the alleged effectiveness of sorcery. Assuming the nub of this difficulty concerns cases which do not involve the direct planting of dangerous flora and fauna (in pathways or houses), or straightforward killing (through poison or other means), most scholarly researchers will probably feel the need for objective criteria before they would make a decision. Here the methodological nightmare continues without abatement, owing to lack of laboratory conditions on the one hand and a surfeit of secrecy on the other. Self-confessions will be of value — provided they are not forced out of the innocent! — and all the more if some indigenous divination technique (the diviner's log used by the Mengen and other island or coastal New Guineans, for instance, or the prophetess-diviner or *ga'in* among the Murik Lakes people)[99] has brought to light a sorcerer who acknowledges his or her guilt. An outsider, however, would have to be very lucky indeed to witness a spate of these. As for seeking apprenticeship with a sorcerer, the researcher would constantly find it awkward reconciling the exercise with the usual aims of scholarship! Overall, even while allowing that 'the logic of [a] belief system may well be self-contained', the temptation is to fall back on modern science (even a good missionary ploy at this point) and maintain that 'most beliefs in sorcery are empirically false',[100] when a lifetime of empathy, or even 'sharing the unconscious' of indigenous persons, might be the only means which one could really decide over verifiability.

Certainly, the whole subject demands more research: into various types of sorcery (as have been analyzed for the Mae Enga by Paul Brennan, for instance[101]), into the networks by which the members of one group will hire a sorcerer from another,[102] into the 'pattern of allegations' (as to whether one or two renowned sorcerers are being blamed for most deaths in a whole cultural complex), and so on. Another subject of enquiry concerns the role of those anti-sorcery techniques designed to cure the ailments purportedly brought on by sorcery. This brings us to the subject of healing, and especially to the thorny question of the 'psychosomatic connection', although it should be conceded that sorcery alone is a factor quite capable of bringing that connection into view. Fear and worry have a remarkable capacity for bringing on sickness, and thus sorcery can be a readily identifiable source of all three without recourse to 'mystical' interpretations. As Père Fastré once jotted in his fieldnotes, one of his Fuyughe acquaintances 'accidentally' brushed a cassowary with his leg and, apparently because he believed the bird was really a sorcerer, or 'cassowary man', a tropical ulcer later emerged on his limb and grew so huge that he subsequently died.[103] It would take a vision indeed, certainly something more than an unnerving dream, to prove that the man died by sorcery. But that is also to say we do not know enough.

Healing

Modern Western medicine has become very physically oriented; the practitioner concentrates on the bodily functions, the administration of drugs and the excision of unwanted parts. Folk medicine is still in some disrepute (even though it was the herb collectors and apothecaries of the seventeenth century which actually took medicine out of its over-theoretical doldrums!),[104] and most doctors sneer about the branch of their profession called psychiatry because it is the least scientific, or brings about the least effective results (despite its already top-heavy emphasis on medication).

Reactions to this 'pragmatic reductionism' are now gathering force, albeit slowly. Among others, the avant-garde in Californian medical circles have dared to rehabilitate the concept of 'healing', maintaining that the ideal aim of medicine is to heal and bring wholeness to the dis-eased person, not to function as a body technician.[105] According to this more recent strand of thought (or does it not have more than a touch of 'pre-scientific' outlooks?), human beings usually need their illnesses — their bodies telling them to stop and rest (by temporarily malfunctioning) just as a psychotic tendency will emerge to compensate for some over- or under-developed facet of psychic life. If, from Freud's history of psychoanalysis (1914) to the neuro-linguistic handbook called *Frogs into Princes* (1979),[106] the modern literature of psychiatry reflects numerous allusions to the world of 'magic and sorcery', it is becoming increasingly less difficult to find Western physicians interested in the possible links between different sicknesses and various outlooks on life.[107] The forums of modern and traditional primal medicine are to that extent moving closer.

Reckoning the human being as a 'somatic-psychic whole', or an 'integration of somatic, psychic and spiritual aspects', as Victor Frankl prefers to put it,[108] the newly oriented modern healer discovers common ground with the traditional practitioner of primal societies — in the concern to 're-make the whole person', and to treat emotional factors, including the breakdown of human relations, in the therapeutic act. Such a promising compatibility suggests that there may be much to learn from the *Lebenswelt* of 'archaic remedies' (which are not necessarily *un*scientific simply for having preceded modern science).[109] Ongoing dialogue may fly in the face of scorn, yet those engaged in it can at least rest assured that, for all the cupboards full of tablets and syringes, today's conventional Western medicine cannot provide all the answers to mortal frailty.

Healing in Melanesia

The range of diagnostic and healing techniques in Melanesia is rather too complex to admit easy generalization. Some cultures utilize highly impressive classifications of sickness, each matched by an appropriate explanation and treatment. Sibona Kopi is the first Melanesian to analyse indigenous medical knowledge — 'on a similar level of sophistication' to 'foreign scholars', as Nigel Oram rightly contends; he clearly demonstrates how, for the Motuan people, sorcery, disease and curative techniques are incorporated into 'a rational system of belief' and thus into their religion.[110] Along with recent detailed work by a few expatriate scholars,[111] his work opens up the hitherto inadequately explored field of religio-medical anthropology.

I am not so confident, mind you, that most other societies will be as profitable to study. It may be that a power-balance between sorcerer- and healer-figures is required in a society to produce a richer body of lore; as with the Motuan *babalau* pitted against *vada*, or the Wahgi *kunjeyi* (who follows a variety of divination procedures and should know all the sickness-causing spirits) against the *kumyi*.[112] Yet there are other Melanesian groups almost completely lacking in healers; one among the Toaripi who once presented himself to be interviewed was considered a rare specimen indeed, in a setting where every fatal sickness derives from sorcery, and the role of the sorcerer so prominent.[113] Nonetheless, herbal cures, prescriptions of plants for barren-ness and birth control, as well as instructions about foods to be avoided when pregnant or at a certain stage of life, and so forth, are an important part of the Toaripi corpus of knowledge.[114] How the material should be ordered, in any case, distinguishing between what is public and specialist ken, is a research art in itself, and there is a danger of reading in too much system where it does not apply.

Divination and healing techniques present many imponderables for phenomenology and, again, their range and complexity in Melanesia is extraordinarily diverse. Whether shamans are to be found in Melanesia depends on settling definitions; there are, certainly, motifs reminiscent of the Siberian shamanism (described by Eliade, Shirokogoroff and others) in various cultures.[115] Among other data, I think of the 'shaman's calling' documented by Herdt among the Sambia, the apprenticeship and schooling of the *opipi-ye* ('practitioner of [traditional] medicine') in the Kiripia region, and the hierophant 'Dabialok', of the Faiwol-Olsodoip area near Telefomin, who cured ailments after being 'shaken' by a place-spirit, and led others in a dance procession by carrying a rope, which they all held behind him (all these being Papua New Guinea highlands cases).[116] Here, we have the same old twin problem of deciding on the right terminology and wondering what to do with 'altered states of consciousness'. In this whole area of healing, too, I suggest much more research needs to be done — phenomena documented without preconceptions about typology; supposedly curative plants analyzed in laboratories; and even, perhaps, therapeutic processes undergone by an outsider imbued with the relevant language.[117]

We return, in conclusion, to the issue of workability, but still with no respite to offer from a weary round of problem-raising. Some comfort lies in the fact, admittedly, that traditional medicine often does appear to get results, since patients in modern Melanesian hospitals who have ailments undiagnosable by Western-style doctors are often relieved from dis-ease by a resident (even legally authorized) practitioner of the old ways.[118] When a very seriously ill child is driven to the hospital, however, the hospital staff usually lament the fact that the parents have put too much faith in traditional medicine, even if the number of effective cures at the village level simply go on undocumented. The phenomenologist sighs for lack of phenomena. And when a cure does seem to come and is witnessed, who is to deny that it was not on the way in any case? A Kerema woman (who had migrated to Port Moresby from the Papuan Gulf), for example, fell seriously ill with measles in 1973 and was taken from her home to the city hospital. No improvement showed for two days, and the doctors were worried. Yet throughout the proceedings she kept up her demands to receive a *puri puri* (sorcery/counter-sorcery) man. The doctors at last consented; the traditional healer came, counteracting the sorcery she felt was forced against her, and she was perfectly well the following day. Measles, however, do not last forever, and disappear quickly . . . who is to say? Many a Melanesian could retort, however, that since traditional sorcery, counter-sorcery or healing procedures are being carried out while a patient is in a modern hospital, the outcome can always be attributable to traditional causes and not to anything expatriates or strangers believe they can achieve. Thereby primal consciousness can completely bypass the astounding monuments, the precisioned instruments and the 'magic bullets' (called drugs)[119] produced through modern science. The phenomenologist remains open; not so foolish as to deny that penicillin does wonders for tuberculosis in both black and white bodies, nor so preemptive as to deny that the sick need familiar assurances, and a sense of 'total treatment'. Since the root cause of most sicknesses may well lie in fears and attitudes, modern medicines may only 'smash out the red light in the dashboard', as it were, before the trouble recurs on some later occasion, the exercise not being strictly healing at all as it misses the psycho-spiritual dimension. This is a dimension which, surrounded as they feel by a world of non-empirical agencies, primal peoples cannot afford to neglect.

In this light, phenomenology is more scientific for being open-ended in its methodical stance, and in its refusal to accept social scientific strait-jacketing, when both the limitations of words and the richness of phenomena make all attempts to reduce reality to the merely psychological, socio-economic, political, and so on (in order to manage it theoretically) look like abortive escape-routes from complexity with an (over-sharpened, eventually self-inflicting) Occam's razor. How many of our Western law-like generaliza-tions, let alone basic methodological assumptions can, strictly speaking, be verified? Do we have the proper tools to rule out the existence of spiritual and non-empirical factors which most peoples throughout a vast human history allege to be involved in facts as basic as harm, sickness, death, or deliverance from any of them? Only recently I was party to a fascinating conversation between a Western-educated Choiseul Islander and an initiated Aborigine from the Kimberleys (Western Australia), both healers (the former a very reluctant one), who discovered to their amazement a common awareness of a higher 'level of the mind' in the act of healing.[120] How can such a state be verified? Is it more 'scientific' to naturalize it (very impolitely), despite the self-avowals of two sensible men who seek to apply an unexplained gift rather than practise charlatanry? Enough questions asked.

NOTES

The material in chapter 4 is based on a paper given at a conference sponsored by the Research Centre for Southwest Pacific Studies, at La Trobe University (1982), 'Magic, Sorcery and Healing in Melanesia'.

1 Note the mistaken preconceptions (found, for example, in Karl Heider, *The Dugum Dani*, Chicago, 1970, p.167) that religion has to be acted out with due seriousness and a more than carefree manner if it is to avoid being dubbed 'almost impious'.

2 Where they have not rejected traditional religions outright as 'superstitious nonsense', missionaries (and missionary anthropologists) have an advantage in sensitivity here, since Biblical consciousness clearly assumes the existence of (at least some) good and evil spirits, as well as the spirit-based efficacy of sorcery, healing, etc. Yet cf. chap. 10. '*Lebenswelt*' is used here following Husserl — see n.29 below.

3 For historical background on the anthropological 'cast of mind', e.g., E. E. Evans-Pritchard, 'Religion and the Anthropologists', in his *Essays in social anthropology*, London, 1962, pp.30–45.

4 Husserl, *Cartesianischen Meditationen* (Husserliana 1) (ed. S. Strasser), The Hague, 1950, p.177 (sect. 62:15–19); cf. (as background), P. Ricoeur, *Husserl; an analysis of his phenomenology* (Northwestern University Studies in Phenomenology and Existential Philosophy), Evanston, 1967.

5 e.g. D. Pocock, 'Foreword' to Mauss *A General Theory of Magic* (trans. R. Brain), London, 1972, p.1.

6 Mauss, 'Esquisse d'une théorie générale de la magie', in *Sociologie et anthropologie* (Bibliothèque de sociologie contemporaine), Paris, 1968, pp.6, 16.

7 cf. N. Q. King, *Religions of Africa*, New York, 1970, p.16.

8 cf. Y. Kemal, *The Legend of a Thousand Bulls* (trans. T. Kemal), London, 1976, pp.15–16, 22, 39. For background on Mauss's colleague Emile Durkheim here, see Evans-Pritchard, *Theories of primitive religion*, Oxford, 1965, p.57.

9 Lawrence and Meggitt, 'Introduction', *Gods, Ghosts and Men*, p.7.

10 *Magic, science and religion and other essays* (ed. R. Redfield), Boston, 1948, p.60, cf. 51, 67.

11 cf. Malinowski, *Freedom and civilization*, London, 1947, pp.205–14. On Malinowski's opposition to Freud's theories elsewhere, cf. M. Spiro, *Oedipus in the Trobriands*, Chicago, 1982.

12 See esp. R. R. Marett, *The threshold of religion*, London, 1914 edn, pp.xii–xiii (preface to first edn, on the views of J. Hewitt, Mauss, etc.), pp.58–63.

13 W. La Barre, for instance, opts for a heavily psychological analysis of both religion and magic. cf. *The human animal*, Chicago, 1955, pp.286–87; *The ghost dance*, New York, 1970, ch. 9.

14 cf. Evans-Pritchard, *Theories*, p.33; cf. more recently M. Reay, 'The magico-religious foundations of New Guinea Highlands warfare', in M. Stephen (ed.), *Sorcerer and witch in Melanesia*, Melbourne, 1987, ch. 3.

15 Note the watershed article by H. Turner, 'The primal religions of the world and their study', in V. C. Hayes (ed.), *Australian essays in world religions*, Adelaide, 1977, esp. pp.27–29. cf. also H. Biezais, *Von der Wesenidentität der Religion und Magie*, Abo, 1978.

16 cf. N. Drury and G. Tillett, *Other Temples, Other Gods*, Sydney, 1980, pp.12–14 (on how Aboriginal religion can be treated as part of 'Australia's occult heritage').

17 cf., e.g., W. van Gennep, *Les rites de passage*, Paris, 1909; V. Turner, *The Ritual Process*, London, 1969.

18 Etymologically the term 'magic' can be traced to the Old Persian i.e. *magu* (from there into the Greek *magos*, and the Latin *magice/magicus*). For the early stages of the debate between Christianity and magic, e.g. J. M. Hull, *Hellenistic magic and the synoptic tradition* (Studies in Biblical theology NS 2:28), London, 1974, pp.142–45; E. R. Dodds, *Pagan and Christian in an age of anxiety*, Cambridge, 1965.

19 K. Thomas, *Religion and the decline of magic*, Harmondsworth, 1973, esp. ch. 9. For background, L. Thorndike, *History of magic and experimental science*, London, 1925, vol. 2; D. P. Walker, *Spiritual and demonic magic from Ficino to Campanella* (Studies of the Warburg Institute 2), London, 1958.

20 Esp. Thomas, *Religion*, ch. 3.

21 For a reinforcement in modern theology, note P. Tillich, *Systematic theology*, Welwyn, 1964, vol. 3, pp.104–147 (on faith vs the ambiguities of religion, which can include the demonic).

22 cf., e.g., W. J. Goode, *Religion among the primitives*, Glencoe, 1951, esp. chs 3, 5; and again Trompf, 'Salvation in primal religion', in Dockrill and Tanner (eds), *The idea of salvation*, pp.211–12.

23 J. G. Frazer's attempts to consider magic as clearly distinct and historically prior to religion, then, cannot stand (as was ably demonstrated nearly fifty years ago by R. H. Lowie, in *Primitive religion*, New York, 1924, ch. 6). cf. Frazer, *The golden bough*, London, 1911 edn, vol. 1, chs 3–4.

24 For background in late mediaeval and Reformation debates, cf. E. Seeberg, *Luthers Theologie in ihren Grundzügen*, Stuttgart, 1940, pp.145–46; H. A. Oberman, *The harvest of medieval theology*, Cambridge, Mass, 1963, pp.140, 148–51.

25 cf. E. J. Sharpe, *Comparative religion; a history*, London, 1975, chs 2–4.

26 Goode was moving in this direction (*Religion*, pp.54–55), when he wrote of magic and religion as representing a continuum, but he over-emphasized the notion that magical actions have *goals* when this is just as legitimately a feature of religions.

27 One way of confining the meaning of magic is to render it virtually synonymous with thaumaturgy (the working of miraculous events); cf., e.g., B. Wilson, *Magic and the millennium*, New York, 1973, chs 3–5 (though without sufficient explanation of his usages). The usage 'theurgy' as an alternative to magic also presents itself. For a show of annoyance toward Western (and prejudiced) emphases on magic in traditional African religions, O. p'Bitek, *African religions in Western scholarship*, Nairobi, 1970, esp. ch. 1.

28 Esp. J. Dillenberger, *Protestant thought and natural science*, London, 1961; cf. Trompf, 'Missiology, methodology and the study of new religious movements', in *Religious traditions*, 10 (1987), pp.96–97.

29 See Husserl, *Cart. Medit.*, sect. 62; cf. *Die Krisis der europäischen und die transzendentale Phänomenologie* (Husserliana 6) (ed. W. Biemel), The Hague, 1962, pp.99, 148–54, 179 (for the concepts of *Weltbild, Lebenswelt*).

30 For Martin Heidegger's rejection of Husserl's ahistorical tendencies, *Sein und Zeit*, Tübingen, 1967, pp.363–64, 372–97. For a good, earlier example of the historical phenomenology of religions, G. van der Leeuw, *Phänomenologie der Religion*, Tübingen, 1933.

31 cf. L. Kolakowski, *Religion*, London, 1982, p.86 on this issue.

32 Husserl, *Cart. Medit.*, sects. 24–29; cf. D. Carr, 'History, phenomenology and reflection', in D. Ihde and R. M. Zaner (eds), *Dialogues in phenomenology*, The Hague, 1975, pp.156–75; P. Janssen, *Geschichte und Lebenswelt; ein Beitrag zur Diskussion von Husserls Spätwerk*, The Hague, 1970, pt. 2.

33 cf. also P. Ricoeur, 'Hegel and Husserl on intersubjectivity', in H. Kohlenberger (ed.), *Reason, action, and experience* (Klibansky Festschrift), Hamburg, 1979, pp.13–29.

34 cf. P. Lawrence, 'Statements about Religion; the Problem of Reliability', in L. R. Hiatt and C. Jayawardena (eds), *Anthropology in Oceania* (Ian Hogbin Festschrift), Sydney, 1971, pp.139–46.

35 Lévi-Strauss, *La pensée sauvage*, Paris, 1962, ch. 8.

36 Note Wagner's just criticisms in *Habu*, p.58.

37 Thus, against the older view in E. Tylor, *Primitive culture*, London, 1903, vol. 1, pp.117–36, and Frazer, *Golden bough*, vol. 1, pp.220–22.

38 e.g., by Michele Stephen, 'Master of Souls', in Stephen (ed.), *Sorcerer*, pp.41ff. Other authors in the collection she has edited, however, generally evade these questions. As for earlier, 'unfair' psychologistic reductionism, cf., e.g., G. Roheim, *Magic and Schizophrenia* (ed. W. Münsterberger), New York, 1955; cf. La Barre, *Ghost*, etc.

39 Lexically, on the other hand, most researchers have found it easier to locate vernacular terms they could translate as 'magic' and few or none they would dare translate as 'religion'. Preconceptions about religion, however, and lack of training in comparative religion, have played a part here. Not even the Latin *religio* means what most Westerners conceive to be meant by 'religion'. For background to these problems, esp. W. Cantwell Smith, *The meaning and end of religion*, New York, 1963, esp. ch. 1.

40 cf. Wagner, *The Curse of Souw*, pp.47–57.

41 Curti, 'The Island of Muju', pp.38–39 (by kind permission of the translator Donald Affleck).

42 G. F. Vicedom and H. Tischner, *Die Mbowamb; die Kultur der Hagenberg-Stämme im östlichen Zentral-Neuguinea* (Monographien zur Völkerkunde 1), Hamburg, 1927, pp.339–42, 390–92.

43 Barth, *Ritual*, esp. p.288.

44 cf. F. E. Williams, *Drama of Orokolo*, pp.86–88, 103, 107, 111, 226–27; Trompf, '"Bilalaf"', p.62; E. Tuza, 'Silas Eto of New Georgia', in Trompf (ed.), *Prophets*, pp.116, 136–37. Perhaps one most commonly associates acts of 'magical power' in Melanesia with fire-walking (in Fiji, and among the Baining, New Britain).

45 For a *locus classicus* in primal religions, see H. A. Junod, *The life of a South African tribe (the Thonga)*, Neuchatel, 1912–13, vol. 2, pp.488–89, cf. 493–94. That *mana/minana* should have been turned into an abstract notion of independent power, however (see esp. R. H. Codrington, *The Melanesians*, Oxford, 1891, pp.51, 57, etc; F. R. Lehmann, 'Versuche, die Bedeutung des Wortes "Mana" . . . festzustellen', in K. Rudolph, R. Heller and E. Walter (eds), *Festschrift Walter Baetke*, Weimar, 1966, pp.151–58), is questionable. cf. R. Keesing's reappraisals, in 'Rethinking *Mana*', pp.137ff., with special reference to the Kwaio case. Note also *moira* and *dynamis* in Greek religious thought (and the latter in Christianity; cf. Luke 24:49b), and *karma* in the Vedic–Jain–Buddhist trajectory. On so-called magic in the Vedic tradition, cf. *Atharva Veda*; and in Theravada Buddhism, see esp. L. A. de Silva, *Buddhism; beliefs and practices in Sri Lanka*, Colombo, 1974, ch. 13.

46 For discussion, Lowie, *Primitive religion*, p.136.

47 Malinowski, 'Introduction', to Fortune, *Sorcerers of Dobu (1932)*, New York, 1963 edn, p.xxix, cf. Fortune, p.101.

48 On a case of lexical uniformity, see e.g., Barth, *Ritual*, p.17 (on the Baktaman); cf. also on Melpa, A. and M. Strathern, 'Marsupials and Magic, a study of Spell Symbolism among the Mbowamb', in E. R. Leach (ed.), *Dialectic in practical religion* (Cambridge papers in social anthropology 5), Cambridge, 1968, p.181; and on Lamassa OT: Jason Isiop, Oct., 1985. I foreshadow here the publication of collections of traditional Melanesian prayers made by Father Theo Aerts M.S.C.

49 Mgr Navarre, Notes et journal, pp.90–91. Joshua Daimoi has pointed out to me a Sentani parallel (from west New Guinea/Irian Jaya) (OT: Sept., 1976).

50 Each one of these efforts, however, should be subjected to phenomenological reflection or testing. I must admit, for example, that when I first saw so-called 'magicians' murmuring inaudibly over specially selected bananas in a peacemaking ceremony among the Kumai (Wahgi, 1976), the word *magic* did not occur to me. In the act of *taukunje* (banana-'magic'), the specialists blew on the bananas, spat ginger into them, while separating parts of them with an arrow and *tanget* leaves, before this special food was mixed in with the whole cooking-pit full of food to be consumed. The words and actions suggested simply sacralization or consecration of a meal they hoped would bring about peace, but they admitted they had no guarantee that their enemies were (as they should have been) doing precisely the same thing. On the other hand, on witnessing an informal, non-specialist attempt at 'rain-stopping', with hands raised to the sky, I immediately thought of magic. I cite these examples to illustrate, not only the importance of first impressions, and the need for further probing, but to ask whether something like an official/non-official, religion–magic difference might not apply in certain primal societies as it seems to in major traditions. See also below on the Wahgi.

51 Gesch, 'Magic as a process of Social Discernment', in Habel (ed.), *Powers*, pp.140–41.

52 Wagner, *Habu*, pp.62–63, 109.

53 See van der Leeuw, *Phänomenologie*, sects 34:6, 62, for examples.

54 Wagner, *Habu*, pp.63–64 (table 2). cf. also p.57 (on Malinowski).

55 For background, R. Ricoeur, *La métaphore vive*, Paris, 1975; E. R. MacCormac, *Metaphor and myth in science and religion*, Durham, 1976; J. Derrida, 'The copula supplement', in Ihde and Zaner, *Dialogues*, pp.8–13.

56 For background to the issues here, cf. R. Firth, *Symbols; public and private*, New York, 1973; J. Skorupski, *Symbol and theory: a philosophical study of theories of religion in social anthropology*, Cambridge, 1976; D. Sperber, *Rethinking symbolism* (trans. A. L. Morton), Cambridge, 1975.

57 See esp. Jung, 'Aion: the phenomenology of Self' in J. Campbell (ed.), *The Portable Jung* (trans. R. F. C. Hull), New York, 1976, pp.139ff.

58 cf. P. Tompkins and C. Bird, *The secret life of plants*, Harmondsworth, 1974, pp.37–51, etc.

59 cf. Barth, *Ritual*, p.67. I have only 'scratched the surface' of a vast problem here, of course, and there is much more besides to say about the relationships, similarities and fusions between sociolects, idioms, parabolic style, and both metaphor and symbol (see above n.55). My approach here is not unrelated to writing on Erave metaphor and religion by M. MacDonald which is not yet published; yet cf. her 'Symbolism and myth', and 'Magic, medicine and sorcery', in Mantovani (ed.), *An Introduction*, pp.123ff., 195ff; and on a phenomenological approach to mythopoesis in another highland culture, J. Mimica, Omalce (doctoral diss., ANU, Canberra 1980). I thank Deane Fergie for referring me to this work.

60 M. Stephen, Sorcery, magic and the Mekeo world view', in Habel (ed.), *Powers*, p.155.

61 See n.44 above. Note the connotations of the well known Motu word *siáhu* in this regard.

62 Thus E. Hau'Ofa, Mekeo (doctoral thesis, ANU, Canberra 1975), p.243; D. Fergie, 'Prophecy and leadership: Philo and the Inawai'a movement', in Trompf (ed.), *Prophets*, p.152.

63 For background, esp. Codrington, *Melanesians*, p.191, cf. 51 (on Solomon cases).

64 Gesch, 'Magic', pp.145–48, cf. his *Initiative and initiation*, esp. ch. 14, pt. 1.

65 Gesch, 'Magic', p.145.

66 Malinowski, *Magic*, ch. 2 (I follow Wagner's criticisms here, see n.54 above).

67 Malinowski, *Coral gardens and their magic 2: the language of magic and gardening*, Bloomington, 1965 edn, pp.70, 238–39: My points also relate to the differences of opinion between Malinowski and A. R. Radcliffe-Brown about religion, magic and crisis, cf. W. A. Lessa and E. Z. Vogt (eds), *Reader in comparative religion; an anthropological approach*, New York, 1979, pp.36–56.

68 One could decline use of the term 'magic', however, in favour of something like 'protective power', if rites performed are basically concerned with repelling evil spirits. So, against L. Pospisil, *Kapauku Papuans and their Law*, p.28.

69 e.g. Lawrence, *Road*, pp.17–18, 23–25, etc; cf. also his *'De Rerum Natura*: the Garia View of Sorcery', in Stephen (ed.), *Sorcerer*, ch. 1, and Lawrence and Meggitt (eds), *Gods*, pp.18–22.

70 OT: Makuri Wani and others, Delena, 1974.

71 See, for few among very many examples, Meggitt, 'The Mae Enga of the Western Highlands', in Lawrence and Meggitt (eds), *Gods*, p.114; Stephen, 'Sorcery, magic', p.153.

72 The association between magic and black may go back to the use of black African (Nilotic) officiants in pagan (especially Egyptian) cults in the early Christian centuries. cf., e.g., M. J. Vermaseren, 'Paganism's death struggle', in A. J. Toynbee (ed. A. J. Toynbee), *The crucible of Christianity*, London, 1969, pp.240–41; and for a very influential early use of the distinction, Augustine, *De civitate Dei*, X, 9.

73 Frazer, *Golden bough*, vol. 1, p.222; E. B. Idowu, *African traditional religion*, London, 1973, p.191.

74 For background, Thomas, *Religion*, esp. ch. 14; M. Wilson, *Religion and the transformation of society; a study in social change in Africa*, Cambridge, 1971.

75 cf. Thomas, *Religion*, ch. 18.

76 Burridge, *Mambu*, pp.59–60; cf. 'Tangu, Northern Madang District', in Lawrence and Meggitt (eds), *Gods*, pp.230–36.

77 Hau'Ofa, Mekeo, p.260; Stephen, 'Sorcery, magic', p.150; Fergie, 'Prophecy', p.151.

78 As in most coastal Gulf and coastal-hinterland Sepik societies; cf., e.g., H. Brown, 'The Eastern Elema', chs 3–4, 8; Gesch, *Initiative*, ch. 12 (for two of the more detailed analyses).

79 F. E. Williams uses the phrase 'magically potent'; cf. *Orokaiva Magic*, London, 1928, p.180. W. Jojoga Opeba informed me of an Orokaiva proverb expressing fear of sorcery by one's very own brother, yet admits that this was more an encouragement to be extremely wary in general, rather than constantly fearful of one's own kin; though in personal communication Ross Border argued that fear of sorcery [= poisoning] within the very bosom of Kwoma families, in the Sepik, was expressed with specific seriousness even in pre-contact times — cf. his 'Sorcery, Illness and Social Control in Kwoma Society' in Stephen (ed.), *Sorcerer*, ch. 6.

80 Trompf, Fieldnotes, 1972–74 (along with a recent joint analysis of Mekeo beliefs with Andrew Kavana, University of Sydney, 1982).

81 For background, esp. M. G. Marwick, *Sorcery in its social setting; a study of the Northern Rhodesian Cewa*, Manchester, 1965, ch. 8 (and literature cited there). And already see notes 77 and 79 above.

82 OT: L. Aitsi and D. Fergie (for the Mekeo); cf. Fergie, 'Prophecy', p.169.

83 For background, esp. S. Freud, *New introductory essays on psychoanalysis*, in *The standard edition of the complete psychological works of Sigmund Freud*, London, 1964, vol. 22, Nos 32, 35; R. Ricoeur, *La symbolique du mal*, Paris, 1960.

84 How to develop a *scientific* methodology accounting for these realities is a crucial question. Carl Jung is a watershed figure in this respect (within the twentieth century), and has given the cue to examine the power of the Unconscious or 'the universal structures of the imagination', recently taken up by Stephen (see n.38).

85 For Patterson's work, see her 'Sorcery and Witchcraft in Melanesia', *Oceania*, 45 (2–3), 1974–75, pp.132–60, 212–34. See also notes 38 and 89 for symposia.

86 e.g. *Independent State of Papua New Guinea (Statutes)*, Chapter No. 274; Sorcery Act, esp.

pp.7–8; cf. Fijian *Penal Code* (Amendment) Act, 1969, sect. 262A.

87 For literature and general analysis, J. Parratt, *Papuan belief and ritual*, pp.27–37; and see notes 44, 81 above.

88 cf. esp. C. D. Rowley, *The New Guinea villager*, Melbourne, 1972 edn, ch. 4.

89 Note esp. contributions in M. Zelenietz and S. Lindenbaum (eds), *Sorcery and social change in Melanesia* (*Social analysis*, Spec. Issue, 8, 1981).

90 Trompf, Fieldnotes, 1976–78. cf. M. Reay, *The Kuma*, Melbourne, 1959, pp.145–47.

91 Trompf, Fieldnotes, 1977; cf. (for the Mendi), R. Lederman, 'Sorcery and Social Change in Mendi', in Zelenietz and Lindenbaum (eds), *Sorcery*, pp.21–23.

92 Here I rely on the tradition deriving from Aniau Kavo of Aipiana (probably the most feared sorcerer among the Mekeo in the 1930s), and preserved by his grandson Andrew Kavana (cf. n.80 above). In this and other cases, however, I do not mean to deny that sorcery did not contribute to the history of 'schisms' and rifts between communities that produced more and more separate clans and tribes in the past, as evinced by Roro and Mekeo oral histories themselves. See, e.g. P. S. Swadling, L. Aitsi, Trompf, et al., 'Beyond the oral traditions of the Austronesian-speaking people of the Gulf and Western Central Province', *Oral history* 5/1 (1977), pp.50ff.

93 V. Koroti, 'Explanation for Trouble, Sickness and Death among the Toaripi'; C. Siaoa, Gods, Spirits and Religion among the Eastern Toaripi (handwritten MS, UPNG, Port Moresby, 1976). Yet cf. Brown, 'Elema', pp.92, 231ff. Correctly using Chalmers's assessments at the end of the last century, Marcel Mauss got these matters right ('Esquisse', *Sociologie et anthropologie*, p.23).

94 Trompf, Fieldnotes, 1972–74, 1977–78.

95 On the need to study individuals, cf. Stephen, 'Master of Souls', and '"Bilalaf"', esp. pp.49, 96.

96 Sahlins, 'On the Sociology of Primitive Exchange', in *A. S. A. Monographs*, pp.139–236.

97 cf., e.g., A. Forge, 'Prestige, influence, and sorcery; a New Guinea example', in M. Douglas (ed.), *Witchcraft confessions and accusations*, London, 1970, pp.259–60 (on Abelam, Sepik).

98 D. Shaw, 'The good, the bad, and the human; Samo spirit cosmology' (forthcoming) (with kind permission).

99 On pole divination, OT: L. Longi and others, November, 1981 (Mengen); cf. K. Namaleu, Wok bilong Yali (taperecorded lecture), New Guinea Collection, UPNG, Port Moresby, 1974 (on the evident spread of this technique to the Madang area); P. Maralis, A Descriptive Study of the Persisting Nalik Traditional Religion and its Future (BD thesis, Rarongo Theological Seminary, Rarongo 1981), pp.26–30 (by kind permission) (New Ireland) (for rites preparatory to this technique). On divination by a prophetess, M. Tamoane, 'Kamoai of Darapap and the Legend of Jari', in Trompf (ed.), *Prophets*, pp.206–07.

100 So, Young, *Fighting with Food*, p.128 (Massim).

101 Brennan, *Let sleeping snakes lie* (Special studies in religions 1), Adelaide, 1977, esp. pp.46–47.

102 cf., e.g., Forge, 'Prestige', esp. pp.263–64 (Abelam).

103 Fastré, Moeurs, pp.187–88.

104 Thomas, *Religion*, pp.12–15.

105 For a watershed conference, K. R. Pelletier and D. E. Bresler (co-chairs), *Healing* (Symposium, University Extension, University of California, Santa Cruz and Los Angeles, with Gladman Memorial Hospital, Oakland) (Prog. X430.1 and 2), Santa Cruz, March–April, 1975. cf. D. J. Jaffe (ed.), *In search of a therapy*, New York, 1975.

106 Freud, *Collected Papers* (trans. J. Riviere) (The international psycho-analytical library 7), New York, 1924, pp.321–22, etc; R. Bandler and J. Grindler, *Frogs into princes; neuro-linguistic programming*, Moab, 1979; etc.

107 cf. such a journal as *Culture, medicine and psychiatry* (ed. A. Kleinman); as well as anthropology with new perspectives, e.g. A. Kiev (ed.), *Magic, faith and healing*, Glencoe, 1964. C. F. Sargent, *The cultural context of therapeutic choice* (Culture, illness and healing 3), Dordrecht, 1982.

108 V. E. Frankl, *The unconscious God*, New York, 1975 edn, pp.28–29.

109 cf. M. Opler (ed.), *Culture and mental health; cross cultural studies*, New York, 1959. For various points in the above section I am indebted to Dr R. R. Trompf. cf. also D. C. Jarvis's well known *Folk medicine*, London, 1958.

110 Kopi, '*Babalau* and *Vada*: religion, disease and social control among the Motu', *Oral history*, 7(3), 1979, pp.8–64 (cf. Oram's introduction, p.2).

111 e.g. G. Lewis, *Knowledge of illness in a Sepik society* (London School of Economics monographs on social anthropology 52), London, 1975 (Gnau); S. Frankel, *The Huli Response to Illness*, Cambridge, 1986. Note also B. G. Burton-Bradley, *Stone age crisis; a psychiatric appraisal*, Nashville, 1975 (with caution).

112 Kopi, 'Explanation'; Trompf, Fieldnotes, 1976–81.

113 i.e., Josef Oro, Lese Oalai, 1974; see ch. 5 below.

114 Br. A. Miva, What the Lese Oalai people of the Eastern Toaripi (Gulf Province) believe about magic, sorcery and life after death (unpublished typescript, Holy Spirit Seminary, Bomana, 1977), esp. pp.7–8.

115 M. Eliade, *Shamanism*; S. M. Shirokogoroff, *Psychomental complex of the tungus*, London, 1935; cf. I. M. Lewis, *Ecstatic religion*, Harmondsworth, 1971.

116 We await publications by Barbara Jones on this last case. For the others, G. H. Herdt, 'The shaman's calling among the Sambia of New Guinea', *Journal de la Société des Océanistes*, 33, 1977, pp.153–67; M. Kolandi, 'The traditional treatment of illness in the Kiripia area', in Habel (ed.), *Powers*, pp.91–96; B. Jones, cited in Trompf (ed.), *Prophets*, p.63, n.170.

117 cf. Kopi, '*Babalau* and *Vada*', pp.57–60.

118 e.g. *Hansard*, National Parliament of Papua New Guinea, 18 March, 1976, 261ff. The Nonga Base Hospital is famous for its hospitality to 'proved' traditional practitioners. See also D. K. Holdsworth, *Medicinal Plants of Papua New Guinea* (South Pacific Technical Paper 175), Nouméa, 1977; D. F. Parsons-Claire (ed.), *Healing Practices in the South Pacific*, Honolulu, 1985.

119 cf. M. Diesendorf (ed.), *The magic bullet; social implications and limitations of modern medicine; an environmental approach*, Canberra, 1976.

120 M. Fazeldean, 'Aboriginal and Christian Healing', in Trompf (ed.), *Gospel not Western*, pp.102–05. For further theoretical reading in connection with this chapter, esp. F. R. Struckmeyer, 'Phenomenology and Religion; Some Comments', *Religious Studies*, 16, 1980, pp.253–62; J. Patocka, 'Was ist Phänomenologie?', in Kohlenberger (ed.), *Reason*, pp.31–49.

DREAM, VISION AND TRANCE IN TRADITIONAL AND CHANGING MELANESIA

This last chapter on matters traditional considers the thorny subject of altered states in so-called 'primitive' contexts. Once again an interest in varied ethnographic data will be combined with methodological concerns, especially with appeals for linguistic discretion and an avoidance of reductionist or monochrome frames of interpretation. In a diehard neo-positivistic ethos, for a start, it is rather too readily presumed that dreams are mere illusions or personal fantasies and so-called visions are hallucinations; that claimed possessions are cases of individual or collective hysteria, and glossolaly is induced gibberish; that other altered states, such as shamanic 'voyaging', are symptoms of catalepsy, psychosis, and so forth. The very mention of psychosis, moreover, calls to mind that at least one well-known anthropologist, Weston La Barre, maintains that 'qualitatively there is no discernible difference in content between a culture and a psychosis'[1] — a jump which should make us wary that some observers are now not ready to distinguish 'altered' from 'psychopathic' states of consciousness, nor to give the alleged ecstasies, clairvoyances, trances, ordeals, and so on, of ten thousand different cultures an *other than* (socio-) psychological account.[2]

On the other hand, no hardy scholar can afford gullibility, as if the parochial or indigenous understanding of unusual phenomena should always be accepted at its face value. Not a few times will Occam's razor be useful in cutting away unnecessarily supernaturalistic explanations; and who should not heed David Hume's old warning that rumours of miracles tend to run wild, or even the neo-positivists' latter-day plea for (at least an attempt at) verifiability. Has any society not known its tricksters? Or those whose ploy is to claim for themselves experiences and powers which will enhance their prestige? Thus, researchers will be left without essential tools of trade if leaving behind their serpent cunning and a sense of discrimination. Yet if, conversely, they have cramped a certain naïveté, even some unrestrained moment of empathy, out of their systems, they may colour their assessments with prejudgemental scepticism. If their descriptive work may still look accurate, indeed, their powers of evocation will have been impoverished and their theory full of 'blind-spots'.

The general subject of 'altered states' in traditional Melanesian religion is vast, encompassing such topics as dreams, visions, trance and possession, xenophonic behaviour, divination, shamanism, prophetic oracular activity, clairvoyance and bilocation, clinical death experience, drug ingestion, special states of meditation, rituals of extreme physical ordeal, and certain key types of apparent psychopathology. To choose the order in which to deal with such matters can only be arbitrary and, because in any one cultural complex there can be highly intriguing mixtures of otherwise distinct phenomena, even the separating out of these topics could be methodologically faulty. In this chapter, for manageability's sake, discussion will be largely limited to dream, vision and trance. Even such a brief excursion, with its imposed limitation, should allow the glimmerings of a putatively balanced hermeneutics to shine through. This will, thus, reveal how we consider further open-ended research ought to be conducted. Once again post-traditional developments will not be neglected, more particularly because shortly, in the second part of this book, we shall pass into the study of rapidly changing modern Melanesia.

Dreams

No one will question that Melanesians dream dreams. The phenomena of others' dreams, however, are forever inaccessible — as the unique experiences of private minds — to outside observation. One is left only with reports from the dreamers; thus, investigatory questions tend to turn around how dreams are interpreted or used by individuals or social units. First, we can consider *the general understanding of dreaming vis-à-vis the wakeful state*, before particular explications of particular dreams. In collecting responses by informants from a wide range of Melanesian societies (over one hundred),[3] I have not come across a cultural group which fails to draw a distinction between dreaming and being awake. On the other hand, neither have I found any analogous concept to the 'unconscious' or 'sub-conscious' as found in Western philosophical and psychoanalytical literature over the last two centuries.[4] Cautiously stating it (because the English word 'consciousness' and its European cognates may already be 'loaded'), pre-contact and village-raised Melanesians have tended to accept dreams as another form of consciousness, the vital or undecaying attribute of the human, even sometimes the 'total human' (or 'man/woman under consideration') being understood to go frequently and 'actually' to 'places' other than those known in wakeful life. Note that I talk about vitality (or such terms as 'soul', 'spirit') or the whole human being, rather than about the 'mind', because only in rare cases do traditional Melanesian psychologies place the seat or controller of sensory and experiential capacities in the head, as against the stomach, heart, or other parts within the torso.[5] Although one may find the conception, as among the Daribi (lower Chimbu), that the soul (*noma/bidinoma*) leaves the body through the coronal suture (or nose) for dreaming to occur, nonetheless the soul in Melanesian traditions is normally located away from the head (for the Daribi in the heart, liver and lungs).[6] Upon returning from the dream world, moreover, members of varied traditions often related experiences which are apparently just as real (even if sometimes more profound and indelible) as those known in an awakened condition. The subject of dreams worth reporting is typically conceived as a complete 'I', not just as a bodiless observer moving around ethereally, with the events actually taking place rather than being illusions. This alone should make us appreciate that alleged 'soul-flying' (as found among Mailu or Suau witches), as well as divination, and bilocation, are very much akin to (and on close investigation may often be found to be the same as) dream experiences.[7]

Social significance of dreams

Before moving on to consider the social role of dreams, then, or how they are interpreted, these prior comments raise the question as to whether the *ethos* of a primal or archaic society bears a higher likelihood of vivid dreaming, or individual adeptness at 'riding dreams through to an end' with an awareness that can be taken back into ordinary wakefulness.[8] Roger Bastide's researches in Brazil may be invoked here, his *La transe, le rêve et la folie* being the only general sociology of dreams currently available. Interestingly, his sample of middle-class Sao Paolo suburbanites, mostly of Portuguese heritage, usually took their dreams to be in jumbles of no personal significance; the dreams of the descendants of black slaves and indigenous Indians, by contrast, were typically vivid, pregnant with meaning and taken to give direction in life.[9] It requires asking, therefore, whether the social significance of dreams in Melanesia derives from experiences which many outside, especially Western observers, have not been in the best positions to evaluate soundly, with properly suited and open minds.

Concerning the social dimension, we note that there is a common tendency in traditional Melanesian societies to share dreams among close kin, especially in the mornings. In this way there have grown up special patterns of behaviour to cultivate dream life, along with methods of discriminating between types of dream experiences, and distinct styles of dream interpretation, in each society or social unit. Concerning the *sharing of dreams* one should not exaggerate. We have not come across a Melanesian culture in which dreams are carefully and systematically analyzed by a group on a day-to-day basis, as is apparently the case among the Malayan Senoi, whose families organize themselves into something like a 'breakfast dream clinic', 'with the father and older brother listening to and analyzing the dreams of all

the children', the complete findings then being reported to 'the male population' gathered 'in the council'.[10] Melanesian situations are much less formal,
and those who feel they have something important to declare, or who are
better known for their dreaming (note the pidgin, *driman*), tend to dominate
discussions unequally. Traditionally, in societies known for their male long-
(or club-) houses, in which initiated warriors were separated from most
women and children, this informal dream-sharing did not usually involve the
adult men and the others together, and time devoted to it was in any case
conditioned by the relative tenseness of inter-tribal hostilities (a tenseness
conspicuously absent in Senoi territory).[11] Special discretion about relating
dreams could also be called for. Among the Erave (north-west Gulf), for
instance, the person who dreams about the death of a kinsman or who sees a
kinsman walking in the presence of recognizable people already departed this
life, will try to keep what he or she noticed a secret, confiding it quietly only to
other trustworthy members of the family or lineage rather than the relevant
person himself.[12]

The *cultivation of dream life* follows from the seriousness with which
dreams are taken. Among the Jaua (an Orokaiva grouping of Papua), for
example, it is presumed that one's ancestors are the givers of sleep experiences; for this reason, food is left out for them within the house overnight
— in the hope of some clear, revealing dream.[13] Such actions already
imply the distinction they draw between those parts of dreaming or kinds of
dreams which are not as coherent, memorable or easily interpreted, and those
dreams or parts thereof which are recognizably significant. Methods of
discriminating between types of dream experience, thus, need to be taken into
account. At dawn in the men's long-house during a period of tribal fighting, at
Kup (New Guinea highlands) for example, I found Wahgi warriors insisting
that only those dreams they had *just before* waking were significant and worth
sharing among themselves for the coming day; the rest might as well be
forgotten (a view the Jaua and other Orokaivan groups, for a start, would not
be prepared to accept). The Fuyughe (Papuan highlands), along with their
neighbours the Tauade, distinguish ordinary dreams from the nightmare. The
latter kind of episode is often consequent upon sickness; the person who is
unwell, perhaps feverish, finds himself struggling with threatening and armed
enemies, or with evil-looking or monstrous spirits (and among the Tauade it
seems peculiarly fearful to encounter someone with long, European-like
hair).[14]

With most peoples individual dreams are distinguished as highly significant when dead relatives appear in them, perhaps returning via sleep after
a death to make known their killers (as among the Kamano, eastern highlands), or perhaps showing the dreamer some unusual, supernaturally charged
object to ensure success in his activity (as with the Wola, southern highlands).[15] With other cultures again, as among the Dobu and various other
south-east Papuan groups, a special status tends to be given to the dream of a
journey to the land of the dead. The genuine facility for spirit-travel to this

place is held to be the special preserve of sorcerers and witches, who in turn can send forth spirits from *Bwebweso*, the Dobuan hill of the dead, to make some sleeper fall in love with someone or to bewitch her with a nightmare.[16] For the Dobuan, if follows, sleep-walking is the enticement away of a living person's spirit by an errant ancestor, while the Tauade, by comparison, describe both madness and sleep-walking with the very same phrase — *etalal la* (to dream walk).[17]

Dream interpretation

This discussion already suggests that each culture possesses its distinct styles of dream interpretation. In some cases, as among the Jaua mentioned above, the dream is reflected upon in terms of current difficulties or unanswered questions demanding solutions; these problems tend to fall into two, however, and concern either the past or the future. Some events *have* happened, such as a sickness, death or calamity, and a dream can reveal why; on other occasions there are anxieties about the future (to do with obtaining enough food or exchange valuables, the outcome of warfare, for instance), and the dream will contain proleptic insights.[18] Some traditions, interestingly, place more emphasis on this premonitory element than others. Dreams are shared among the Begesin (hinterland Madang) at dawn, for example, primarily to prepare the security circle for what is ahead. It is possible, though, that a dream reported may lead others to the conclusion that the sleeper did not act on his dream quickly enough. 'I dreamt I killed a pig last night.' 'You should have gone hunting' (in other words, Why didn't you get up earlier and respond to what you saw?).[19]

In this last case we find that the experience of a pig being killed is taken *literally*. In the Erave example given earlier, too, someone's recognition of a known villager among the ancestors in a dream was taken as a plain signal that that person would die. Yet not all Erave dreams are interpreted this way, and a little way further to the east, among the Daribi, dreams to the effect that one has done some violence or engaged in sexual intercourse can be explained '*metaphorically*' or '*symbolically*' to refer to the prospect of a good hunt. In trying to understand why the Daribi connect a given dream subject with some action in ordinary life, Roy Wagner insists that the uniformly successful method of de-coding is to uncover the working metaphors, most of which are somewhat unlikely by Western, even cross-cultural standards.[20] His account is persuasive, though perhaps rather too forced. Two young researchers working on dream symbolism among their own people (on the border between the Melpa and Tumbuka, central New Guinean highlands), by contrast, have shown that whereas some metaphoric relations in local dream interpretation are idiosyncratic, others make obvious sense in the complex world of comparative symbology. A little space should be afforded to some of their interesting results.

Examining dream interpretation methods employed by the elders in

Manjika and Ramdi tribes of this Melpa-Tumbuka complex, they note that dreams fall into five basic kinds:

1 Good Dreams   – *(kump kai)*
2 Bad Dreams   – *(kump kit)*
3 Adult Nightmares   – *(urukump kit)*
4 Children's Nightmares – *(kangambulga etepa hau enfetam urkump)*
5 'Just a Dream'   – *(mi kump)*

The results of their analysis of the symbology used for making sense of the first two categories (Good and Bad Dreams) may be sketched out diagrammatically as shown in table 5.1 below. As with the Begesin, all dreams are proleptic, except in the sense that dreams of future warning can be taken as neglect of obligations in the past. Only selected examples are given.

TABLE 5.1   MELPA-TUMBUKA DREAM INTERPRETATIONS

Type of Dream	Content	Meaning	Symbolic Suggestion
kump kai	bird	good time, leisure	birds are free to fly
	taro, sweet potato	good health, strengthening	idiosyncratic traditional association (did occasional meat ingestion loosen the excreta?)
	someone whose name suggests *kai*, or things associated with it	good things, luck, good luck	straightforward semantic suggestion (*kai* means 'good')
kump kit	running	death	life has been drained
	something slippery (e.g. fish, eel, or *kelip* tree, which is slippery under the bark)	misfortune, not getting what you want	something slips away from you
	frog	losing	'you will urinate like a frog', be upset and sitting while achieving nothing
	member of an enemy tribe; cassowary	trouble	the enemy spells trouble; freed cassowaries can kill people
	roasted or cut-up pork	bad luck	idiosyncratic traditional association

Good and bad dreams (types 1 and 2) are shared, usually by someone who recognizes the dream is significant enough to pass on. Warriors in long-houses during battle periods were particularly eager to share such dreams as signs of propitiousness or otherwise.[21] Adult nightmares (type 3) are deemed useless and too difficult to work out, but nightmares in children (type 4) are considered good for them: the children are calmed with the assurance that such experiences will make them grow — nightmares will enlarge a child's lungs or liver, for instance. The fourth type only arises contextually. If two or more dreams 'compete', for instance, the less significant or minority experiences will be passed off as 'just dreams', while a bigman could pitch his leadership claims and rhetoric against a less influential man appealing to the 'authority' of a dream.[22] The two researchers claim that this is just a small part of the story, and that the rules of symbology can get much more complex and subtle.

In Melanesian societies one sometimes finds distinction drawn between *individual* and *collective* dreaming. It may take more than one dream suggesting a successful catch, for instance, to bring out a whole hunting party. Dreaming about such matters, in any case, is often treated as of less consequence for the whole group (family/lineage/security circle/sub-clan) — and thus more to do with personal achievement — than dreaming experienced or deliberately sought to solve serious problems. This is certainly true among the Mendi (southern highlands), who organize impressive collective dream-sessions in times of crisis, and thus distinguish the results of these sessions from dreaming in relative isolation. After a death by supposed sorcery, to illustrate, the bereaved kinsfolk lie in a line under a 'dream shelter' on a mountain-top. They are tied together by the arms and across the chest with cordyline and sleep under the supervision of a 'dream master', who tugs at the rope during the night — to wake everyone — when one of the sleepers show signs of having experienced something disturbing. Traditionally, the corpses of the recent dead were deposited in nearby graves on the heights; a bamboo tube was inserted through the earth to a buried person's skull, and the living would whisper down questions about his or her death before the dream sessions began.[23] Perhaps here we have the nearest thing to the Senoi 'clinic', the onus being on all those involved to contribute to a consensus interpretation. And it is the Mendi, you will recall, who hang *'mandala*-looking' clay discs (of the sun) at the entrance to their spirit houses.

Much has already been written about *the role of dreams in socio-religious change or innovation*. This role became evident in the investigation of various 'cargo cults', cult leaders deriving their legitimacy from some privileged insights into the spirit order through dreams or visions.[24] Such an assessment relied on the data of religious life as affected, in varying degrees, by missionary activity and European intrusion, and it was not until Willington Jojoga Opeba's reappraisal of the Orokaiva taro and Baigona cults (of the 1910s) that good examples were found to confirm how dreams or visions experienced by potential leaders in the past could spawn substantial readjustments to the ritual repertoires of pre-contact situations.[25] This is not to deny that there is as much change in content as there is essential continuity in the dream patterns of an adjusting, 'modernizing' Melanesia. While researching a so-called 'revival movement' among the Begesin, for example, Alois Yagas has noted shifts in 'dream emphases' among villagers in his own lifetime. During the 1940s, dawn and breakfast dream-sharing was an important ingredient in community life, especially for the elders. According to Yagas's assessment, dreams about the coming of Cargo or European-style goods (pidgin: *Kago*) were frequent in those days because the real chances of getting to European goods were limited; by the 1970s, however, consistent dream-sharing had given way to the odd discussion in small groups (or the occasional gathering under stress), and the Cargo motif had dissipated now that there was road access to Madang and an increased availability of European-style goods.[26]

What of dreams among those who come in to the cities from the villages? Is there anything to confirm a similar pattern to the one established by Bastide for black migrants to Sao Paolo? Certainly. In my own research, many city-dwellers have reported to me that they or one of their relatives have known through a dream that their close ones had died or fallen into trouble, or did so soon after the dream itself. Virtually all these people grew up in villages, and most pay regular or annual visits back to their home places. In the study which follows, moreover, Remi Dembari shows just how resilient the dream life and interpretation of the village can be among those who have left it. His survey enriches what has already been said about dreams in traditional settings, but shows how dream signification established in a rural area persists in its import among those in situations of change who have need of a stable world of meaning.

'Dream survey' among the Tainyandawari

The main aim of this short survey is to uncover the common perceptions and understanding of dreams among the Tainyandawari people, who make up one of the cultural blocks or complexes in the Northern or Oro Province of Papua New Guinea, placed under the nomenclature 'Orokaiva'. To a lesser extent the traditional neighbours to the Tainyandawari, another Orokaivan group called the Binandere, will be considered. A secondary, but no less interesting, object of this survey is to test the resilience of shared traditional views about dreams by educing reponses from a representative number of Tainyandawari (and Binandere) living in the capital, Port Moresby (and thus in a situation of rapid social change), where the survey was, in fact, conducted.

The sample

The sample population was of forty persons, who were all given simple questionnaires.[27] The haphazard method was used. The people interviewed were those known to the researcher to have come from the above two areas to Port Moresby. The random selection procedure was not used because most of the potential respondents were in the workforce and it was not clear whether all those randomly selected would be available. Thus, the selection came to be based on availability. Of the sample population 77.5 per cent were from the Tainyandawari area; the rest, 22.5 percent, from Binandere. Both areas, however, share the same 'general culture', as the results will bear out. As for social roles, the population included urban workers, housewives and migrants recently from the villages.

Village distribution of the sample population — according to the home villages, this was as follows: 31 from the Tainyandawari area, and 9 from Binandere. Of the former number as many as 6 persons originated from Bindari village, and 4 each from Iwaie and Katuna. The number of Tainyandawari villages involved in the study represents more than half of the total villages in the area.

Age groups — as the majority of the respondents simply did not know their age, the interviewer had to do the estimating. With some subjectivity allowed for, the age distribution of the forty respondents was: three below 20 years; three, between 20 and 25 years; thirteen, between 26 and 30 years; ten, between 31 and 35 years; five, between 36 and 40 years; and six, over 40 years. Thus, most respondents were from the middle age range. Because most people in the category of 'below 20 years' were still at school and, thus, not available, very few of this group were included in the survey.

Educational levels — generally there is a large variation in educational attainment among Papua New Guineans, and this is particularly true in the Tainyandawari area.

As table 5.2 indicates, the level of educational attainment is strongly correlated with age: the older the respondent, the lower the educational level; the younger the respondent, the higher the level of educational attainment. All the respondents below the age of 30 years had been to school. About 28 per cent of those above the age of 30 years had never been to school. All the respondents below 20 years of age had been to Grade 10 or above.

Occupational and sex distribution — in simple terms, this broke down as twenty-seven workers (all males), ten housewives, and three (male) villagers on extended visits to Port Moresby. It should also be noted that most of the respondents who have been away from their villages for periods exceeding six to ten years were over 30 years old.

TABLE 5.2   Educational Attainments of Dream Survey Respondents

Age Range (in years)	Educational Level					Total
	No School	Below Grade 6	Grades 6–9	Grade 10	Above Grade 10	
Below 20	–	–	–	2	1	3
20–25	–	–	2	–	1	3
26–30	–	2	9	2	–	13
31–35	1	4	5	–	–	10
36–40	1	3	1	–	–	5
Above 40	4	2	–	–	–	6
Total	6	11	17	4	2	40

NOTE: Grade 6 is the highest level in the Primary/Elementary school system.

The alleged causes of dreams

In the questionnaire used, the respondents were asked to consider what or who instigates dreams. In answering the few questions relevant to this, there were 40 mentions of dreams resulting from the soul of the dreamer having contact with ancestral and dead spirits, 34 mentions relating dreams to digestion problems, 40 to growing up, 40 to wish-fulfilment and none to other possibilities, making a total of 154 attempted responses. There seem to be only four specific causes of dreams known among the people of the area under study.

Recognizably common dreams

Common dreams are the dreams that are common within a society. In the Tainyandawari area the people have well-known dreams which are experienced by everyone. These dreams are said to be very significant.

Common dreams reported by the respondents concerned:
1 death;
2 gardens being destroyed by pigs;
3 charms, new knowledge, techniques or advice being received;
4 problems being solved;
5 sex;
6 wish-fulfilment;
7 growing up (flying, falling).

For all of the seven cases there were forty mentions in the questionnaire answers, all the respondents agreeing about the commonality of the above dream-types in the Tainyandawari area. From the responses, moreover, we can list the most commonly identified dream motifs and the consensus meanings virtually always accompanying them. Most of the common dreams and their interpretations are shown in table 5.3.

TABLE 5.3   Tainyandawari-Binandere Dream Interpretations

Dreams	Meanings
1 Coitus in vagina	Hunting trip will be a successful one.
2 Canoe splitting in the middle	Somebody will die.
3 *Sing sing* (dancing and singing)	Mourning over dead. Somebody will die.
4 Holding a feast or some sort of festival	Burial ceremony. Somebody will die.
5 Man or woman dressed in finery	Dressing the dead before burial. Somebody will die.
6 Death of a female	A male will die.
7 Death of a male	A female will die.
8 Death of a family member	A person from the family will die.
9 Painting body	Someone will die.
10 A new canoe being launched for trial	Someone will die.
11 Canoe sinking	Someone will die.
12 Pot breaking	Someone will die.
13 Sago breaking	Someone will die.
14 Being naked	Seeing a pig. The hunting expedition will be successful.
15 Spearing a person	Related to sorcery. This means a member of the spearman's family will die of sorcery.
16 Seeing a girl regularly	The girl is after the dreamer.
17 Pigs eating taro	Pigs destroying the garden of the dreamer or his family.
18 Flying	Resembles going up higher. Growing up taller.
19 Falling	Growing up.
20 Vagina	The dreamer will have a very big or significant success.

Apart from the common dreams, listed in table 5.3, there are also unusual dreams, which are known to be experienced by individuals and are personal. As these dreams are not taken to be so significant, the dreamers don't feel the same need to reveal them to others that they do with the common dreams. Most dreams in the unusual category contain a mixture of contents and are easily forgotten.

The common dreams are known as 'true dreams' (dream = *aturo*; thus, *aturo be*) and the unusual dreams, as 'false dreams' (*aturo pitawa*), although there are cases when uncommon dreams can be deemed true — if they are systematic, clear, and the contents are easily remembered by the dreamer. Whatever the content is, it will turn out to be real in the waking life; thus, dreams reveal the future or the need for future action because an event, such as a death, has occurred in the recent past.

Individual dreams

Below are documented a selection of the dreams told by the respondents.

Dream 1 — about death

Edwin Dagina from Iwaie village had this dream about death.

> My father was the master of a feast. He ordered everyone in our family to make big gardens and prepare for the proposed feast when we will give the food to another family in the village. When the garden was ready for harvest, somehow all the people in the village were going to take part in making the feast. This time, the Iwaie people were going to give the feast to Deboin people.
>
> When the Deboin people finally came to the feast at Iwaie, they were all dressed in their finery. The men wore colourful feathers on the head but somehow some women were covered in mud. All their canoes were newly made and beautifully painted. The canoes just before making it ashore, they were walloped by big waves appearing from nowhere. A great majority of the canoes split in halves. The people were swimming in the sea everywhere. There was a lot of *sing sing* in the village.

This was a symbolic dream as it contained a lot of symbolic things (people dressed in finery, new canoes, canoes splitting into halves, canoes sinking, ladies painted in mud, feasting and dancing). It was one of the common significant dreams. Edwin had the urge to share the dream with others the next morning.

Interpretation: Edwin and the people who listened to his dream interpreted it as meaning that someone in Iwaie will die soon. A few days later, an elderly man — from the family for which Edwin's family was to prepare a feast — passed away.

Dream 2 — growing up

William Kaipa of Katuna village had this dream when he was about 10 years old.

> I was flying to some unknown destination. On the way, I passed some very tall mountains and trees. As I was beginning to feel tired, I decided to take a break of a few minutes on the branch of the nearest tallest tree. When I landed on the branch, it broke and I had this terrible falling feeling as I woke up.

Interpretation: 'I was growing bigger'. This flying dream is mainly dreamt by kids of early teens and below. William and the others interviewed all reported having multiple flying and falling dreams when they were very young. They also noted that they hardly ever have those dreams now that they were older.

Dreams 3 and 4 — receiving charms, new knowledge, and problem solving

Cyril Gegora from Iwaie (now a villager) relates two dreams and an experience he had when he was in Samarai in 1962: at the time he was out of a job.

In the first dream one of his bicycle tyres was out of order and he was not able to purchase a new one. Of all the brands of tyres available at Burns Philp store he preferred a particular one, which cost 12 shillings and 6 pence. Every day Cyril used to go to BP's store, stand near the counter and contemplate that tyre.

Cyril then had an experience, which was followed by another dream. One day he went into BP's store and leaned against the counter near the tyre that he wanted. For a long while he stood there without anybody near him, wishing he had the money to purchase the tyre.

> As I was leaving, I saw a wallet on the counter just in front of me. I looked around to see if there was any customer around but there was no-one. I put the wallet in my pocket and went out. I went to the beach near the wharf to check the contents of the wallet. To much amazement, in the main pocket I found exactly 12 shillings and 6 pence. In the small pocket I found a piece of dried ginger (*roriwa*) and dried bark of a vine (*dongo ainto*).[28] I got the money and I threw the rest of the contents of the wallet into the sea under the wharf. Because of the reputation of Milne Bay people practising sorcery and magic I was frightened that the things belonged to a Milne Bay person. They might find out about my act through dream and kill me; so, I had to get rid of the *roriwa* and *dongo ainto*.

That night he had his second dream.

> My father[29] told me that he saw my worry and he helped me to solve it. About the *roriwa* and *dongo ainto* I threw into the sea, he said: 'Those are my luck charms for gambling and attracting girls that you rejected. I gave them to you to use if you need money or if you want a girl.' As my father was leaving, I was filled with a feeling of disgust and sadness, then I woke up.

Years later Cyril returned to the village. A man gave him a piece of dried *roriwa* and a piece of dried *dongo ainto*, telling him that those charms belonged to Cyril's own father. When Cyril's father was dying, he gave the charms to that man and asked him to pass them on to Cyril and his elder brother when they grew up. According to Cyril the *roriwa* and *dongo ainto* were 'exactly the ones' that he tossed into the sea at Samarai.

He commented that if you are running into problems and you have no way of escaping it, the ancestral and dead relatives' spirits will solve it for you. He went on to say that you have to be a good person before the spirits decide to help.

Dream 5 — sexuality and achieving prosperity

This was dreamed by Aidan Oure from Iaudari village (Binandere Complex).

In the 1960s Aidan, who was then a young man working in Lae, used to give his money to an elderly man from Buna (in the Northern Province) to look after. (There was no concept of banking among Papua New Guineans in those days.) He had never ever gambled until one particular Friday night when he went to watch a very big gambling tournament in which his *wantoks* (those from the same area or speaking his language) were taking part. He watched them lose all their money to a man from Central Province. Aidan thought to himself that the lost money somehow must be retrieved. He had £10 and he decided to try gambling. That man from Central Province won Aidan's £10.

Disgusted with himself for having to take part in gambling and losing the £10, he was really worried and left to sleep.

In the dream he saw his father (already dead) giving him directions to a location where he could find a vine (*dongo*), which was a lucky charm. He was instructed how to use it.

> My father told me to leave at five o'clock in the morning to go and find the *dongo*. He told me that a very long *dongo* would be sticking out of the tree canopy on my right. My father instructed me how to use it,[30] and how not to go near ladies when I am using it. My father said that when I used that *dongo* I would win back all the money from that Central Province man. However, he warned me that during the process I would face a strange incident.

> I left early in the morning following the track that I saw in the dream. Suddenly I heard a cracking sound on my right side. When I looked up, I saw exactly the same *dongo* described in the dream sticking out of the canopy. I went through the ritualistic procedure I learnt in the dream, got the *dongo* and went back. On the way to the gambling location [gambling was still continuing on during Saturday morning] I felt very hungry, so I went to the house to find food. But in the house there were three women, all asleep while their husbands were out gambling. The newly married woman heard me making a noise and came to the kitchen to see what was happening. When she saw me, she just stood there speechless, staring at me. I told her that I was hungry so I was eating bread. When she returned to bed, another women came out and did the same thing. When she saw me, but before she left, she commented that I looked different. The last women came out to see me. She was really surprised with the way I looked. She told me that I had changed drastically overnight and looked very big. Now, I realized that I had not followed my father's advice.

> That woman retired to the room, had a talk to the other two and they all came to the kitchen together. The first of the three who saw me said, 'Aidan, we want you to have coitus with all of us'. I broke my father's advice. Anyway, I took them to the room. They all stripped and lay down and I told them what had happened to me. I confessed that it was my fault, and then I 'went over them' (*darutegari*)[31] to wipe out their burning desire of me. I then left to gamble.

As soon as I started, I hit the winning score, not giving a chance to anybody before they finished paying the last penny. The total amount I won was well over £4000.

The Central man offered me his daughter, who happened to be right at the scene, to marry me, and she was already sitting by my side when the father made the announcement. But an older *wantok* said that I was too young to marry and we left.

Aidan had been warned he would run into a strange incident, and it was this offer of marriage.

Aidan seriously told me that if you are really worried and face a problem, the spirits of your dead will come to the rescue. However, first of all, we must be 'nice guys'. That is, we should respect our dead people at all times. He was really worried for others and genuinely expected his dead spirits to retrieve his £10, and so he was helped.

Dream 6 — about a pig destroying a garden

Cyprian Duimba, from Bindari, reported this dream.

> I went with my wife to one of our gardens. During the day we fenced that garden to keep pigs away. When we came back to the village, somehow, I hit my wife and broke her arm. My father-in-law was really angry. He said something bad towards me and told me that my garden will never produce enough food. Then I saw a group of village pigs jumping over a fence in the village.

He said that, when he woke up, he knew that one of his gardens was destroyed by the pigs. He went early in the morning to check all his gardens (the gardens all being within the compass of about half a mile or 1 km.) One of the two gardens without a fence was destroyed.

Dream 7 — an uncommon dream but significant

Edwin had been married for about six months and his wife was about less than two months pregnant at the time of the dream. He had this dream when he was sleeping in a separate room.

> I went with Martha [his wife] to her village. When Martha's mother saw that she was pregnant, she was very angry and scolded Martha. Martha started crying, then I woke up.

When Edwin woke up, he heard somebody crying. He lay down, still thinking that it was part of the dream, and that he was still dreaming. Realizing that the crying was not far from his room, he got up and went into his wife's bedroom. To his surprise, he found his wife crying. He woke his wife up, and asked what was wrong with her. She told him that she had had a terrible experience in the dream. To their astonishment, they found that they had had exactly the same dream at about the same time.

Interpretation: Martha's uncle who works in Port Moresby, had been to the village recently. Martha's mother sent her a message with her uncle. Her uncle had not yet conveyed the message. The spirits of the dead indirectly forced her to go and visit her uncle and get her message.

They both later insisted to me that this interpretation was true.

Dream 8 — wish-fulfilment

Taylor Deburu dreamt about the Oro provincial government candidate for the North Coast (Tainyandawari being part of this electorate). The particular candidate was endorsed by Taylor and his group.

> I was going with Sylvanus [the candidate] to Ambari [the head station of Tainyandawari area] and we ran into bad weather at Kumusi river. We had to cross the river by a speed boat. Other people were at a loss trying to cross.

> Somehow the river was so rough that it had big waves like the sea. I urged my friends that we must attempt it or else we would get nowhere. When we were in the middle of the river, dark clouds hovered above us and covered us. We could not see a thing beyond the sides of our dinghy. We managed to reach the other bank somehow. The clouds immediately cleared and we saw that we were the only ones who were successful.

Interpretation: Taylor readily interpreted that having to struggle to the other side was simply Sylvanus fighting against other candidates to win the seat. Reaching the other side successfully while the rest of the group failed meant that Sylvanus would in the end win the struggle for the seat of North Coast. At the time of the interview, some time before polling was to take place, Taylor expressed confidently that his candidate (Sylvanus) would win the election.

Some experiences are perceived in the same way as dreams. The Tainyandawari people relate strange experiences to dreams. This is so in the sense that one sees the spirits as the major source of such experiences.

Below is an example of an experience which is very much related to dream.

Special experience related to sleep

This was also reported by Cyril Gegora and was experienced in Samarai in 1963.

Two young men from Bindari village took their village-people's copra to Samarai for sale. The total amount earned was £75. The young men did not want to go back home quickly; so, they gave the money to Cyril to look after (remember that then there was no concept of banking among Papua New Guineans). Cyril used to keep the money in his pocket during the day and put it under his pillow when he was going to sleep.

One man from Cyril's village, however, somehow knew that Cyril was in possession of a large amount of money. That man was an addicted gambler and he decided to steal the money.

One night when I was asleep, that man crept to my bed and as he was just about to reach the bed I opened my eyes as if I had been awake. I asked him what he was doing there and he left. A couple of nights later, the culprit returned. Once again as he was reaching the bed, I suddenly opened my eyes and saw him face to face. The culprit retired. Some more nights had gone by and he returned. This time he was very close to getting the money. When he was just about to slip his hand under my pillow I suddenly sat up as if I had been awake. I caught him in the act, so that he gave up completely.

Interpretation: 'Our ancestral and dead spirits and our souls look after us when we are sleeping. When someone is going to kill us, rob us, or something of that sort, our soul and spirits report to us. In the case discussed my spirits brought me back to the state of being awake as the culprit crept closer and closer to my bed.'

He reported that whatever we do we are not alone. The ancestral and dead spirits always guard us, and this is good reason why we must show respect to them all the time.

Results of the survey

It can be fairly assumed that the sample population forms a representative group of the Tainyandawari, being distributed across virtually all the villages of the area. On the other hand, because the respondents have different educational backgrounds, ages, occupations, and lengths of absence from the village, one may expect them to have differing views on dream. The fact that they were all now resident in Port Moresby, moreover, already led one to suspect that new ways of life there might have undermined the outlook on dreams they inherited from the village.

As it turned out, however, differences in personal background and the reality of the new urban location have not significantly affected Tainyandawari and Binandere views on these matters. Apart from the recognition of 'digestion problems' (which 85 per cent of responses had as one of the causes of dreams, and which might indicate the influence of more secular 'town talk' about dreams and the effects of non-traditional foods), all the rest of the recognizably traditional causes seemed to be known and accepted by each one of the respondents. This shows not only that the Tainyandawari people all hold the same traditional views of dream life but that these views have stood the test of social change.

Even if a number of causes for dreams was mentioned, the most distinct and lasting impression gained from the respondents was that dreamers are able to receive and comprehend the message because of communication between the soul and the spirits. A recurrent theme was: 'when we go to sleep our souls guard us'. 'If there is any danger or anything significant happening, the spirits inform the soul and the soul in turn comes into us again and communicates the message to it.' The belief among the Tainyandawari people that the dreamer's soul leaves the body and communicates with the spirits is consistent with 'the classic position' about dreams in most other Papua New Guinean societies.

The dream motifs of interest to these people appear to be consistent with concerns known throughout Papua New Guinea and even wider Melanesia. I refer here to dreams about the receipt of charms, new skills and special knowledge, as well as about hunting, the destruction of gardens, and death. Very common in Melanesia, furthermore, is the understanding of dream as revealer of the cause of anyone's death, or as indicator that someone will die.

Having considered the writings of Sigmund Freud and Carl Jung on dream interpretation, I agree more with Jung's emphasis on various archetypal elements. Certainly, to reduce the motifs to suggestions of sexuality, in Freud's sense, is not confirmed by the evidence gathered in this research. On the other hand, what the Orokaivan peoples recognize is symbolic in dreams is naturally not thought of as expressions of the collective unconscious (as Jung describes it), but as insights or principles passed on from generation to generation. Significant for the Tainyandawari is the distinction between true-common and false-unusual dreams, with dreamers recognizing that the contents of the former are highly informative and can be effectively interpreted. There is no need to use special dream interpreters, however; for, all those people who reported dreams had, themselves, answers to them readily available. The significant dreams being so common and occurring frequently, everyone knows their meanings.

One interesting thing worth stressing concerns how the Tainyandawari reported on dreams being effective in the waking world. They seem to have proof in believing certain types of dreams 'come true'. As indicated by the dreams and experiences of Aidan and Cyril, people partly depend upon their ancestral and dead relatives' spirits. It seems that a good portion of the Tainyandawari's day-to-day activities are directed by dreams, and priority is given to their disclosure and interpretation to deal with practical realities. This obviously helps explain the resilience of dream interpretation (and also of traditional religion, or that aspect of it to do with the relations between the living and the dead). In dreams the worker and migrant in Port Moresby, though far from his ancestral home, can still experience the closeness of those who made his or her people what they are.

This survey by Remi Dembari, however, does not require us to deny or lessen our concern for the emergence of 'modern' content in dreams, whether in the village or town. What also has to be monitored is whether the new content takes on a new significance of its own or is interpreted through a traditionalist lense. Two closing examples illustrate the need for this new attentiveness. Yagas, for example, when employed as a public servant by the Papua New Guinea National Broadcasting Commission in Port Moresby, had two vivid dreams about being killed in car crashes. Shortly after, on both occasions, one of his relatives died by road accident. According to Begesin tradition, dreams are usually proleptic; yet, the subject of the dream is not necessarily oneself at all, and could just as easily be someone who is close kin and 'of the same blood'. The local interpretation, then, did not so much scare him or lessen his own sense of security as prepare him for traumatic events affecting relatives. Again — this time to treat the more distinctly religious sphere — there is the interesting case of a Yabim man (Finschhafen, Morobe) who dreamt he was protected from the sword of the Devil by a tiny Bible, which he wielded as a weapon and then held close to his heart upon falling before his assailant. The Devil eventually gave up in disgust. The dream left such an indelible impression that this man has made the story of his escape the convincing, experiential basis on which to spread the Christian message, and to orient his own life. Here, the dream of a struggle with the Devil may bear archetypal (or symbolic) correspondence to the battle with threatening 'bad spirits' (following Carl Jung's style of approach); yet, the dreamer has conceived his dream experience in terms of opening up a radically new (in his case somewhat anti-traditionalist) outlook on life.

Clearly, to conclude this section on dreams, the material we have been examining is susceptible to psychoanalytical investigation. Despite allusions to Freud and Jung, however, it has not been an intention here to test the hermeneutic's of any psychoanalytical school against the above data. Suffice it to re-iterate that a Freudian approach, does not fare so well as the more cross-culturally attuned interpretations, such as those of Carl Jung and his sympathizers.[32] That the above data reflect either the 'omnipotence of thought' among 'primitives' (thus, Freud), or a primitive state of pre- (or half-awakened) consciousness (so, Jung), is another matter.[33] We can admit the importance of the Unconscious, but there is nothing in the evidence to suggest that a primitive/modern distinction should be laboured, only that primal peoples are relatively more open to the inroads to 'psychic influences' beyond 'ordinary consciousness'.[34]

Visions

The subject of visions is much more difficult to analyze. Not only is there a paucity of solid data but both indigenous frames of reference and modern scholars differ widely over the use of the category. Significantly, the index to the edited collection *Gods, Ghosts and Men in Melanesia* contains no reference to visions at all.[35] This is not such a travesty if one considers that many informants, when they insist they have seen somebody from (or even some event in) 'the spirit order', talk about it as a concrete occurrence, to that extent comparable to an ordinary life experience, and not as a flimsy apparition. Mythology, lore and vocabulary have a lot to do with this. Mae Enga myths make it possible for mortals to encounter 'the sky people' (*yalyakali*); Lakalai men have their nettles to distinguish real women from female ghosts, who feel no pain; in a good many (if not most) Melanesian languages, further, the same verb refers to seeing the spirits as it does to seeing anything else, just as the English term vision leaves one to decide whether it is being used in a common-or-garden or technical sense.[36] Thus, the intrusion of being[8] from 'the (normally) non-empirical side' can be taken at face value by many Melanesians in such a way that it is only the unusual content of the reported sighting and not the context, aura or general atmosphere which would make researchers think in terms of visions. When they do, in any case, most Western social scientists would suspect self-deception or trickery.

In order to deal with this problem, one should at least start by shedding culturally-conditioned prejudices. As Jung usefully instructs, it makes sense to at least distinguish '"vision" (*Vision*) from "hallucination" (*Sinnestäuschung*) because the former is by no means peculiar to pathological states' (or to times of ingesting hallucinogens).

> Even people who are entirely *compos mentis* and in full possession of their senses see things that 'do not exist'. I do not know what the explanation is of such happenings. It is very possible that they are less rare than I am inclined to suppose. For as a rule we do not verify things we have 'seen with our own eyes', and so we never get to know that actually they did not exist.[37]

We might venture a little further, without being the slightest bit less scientific, by asserting that 'things' or 'persons' sighted which 'do not exist' are nonetheless realities for those who saw them, some people being more prone (why not even say, adept or 'open'?) to seeing them than others: these realities, for all we know — to give a newer twist to some diehard Cartesian logic — could actually exist on another plane. To abandon an empirically-controlled criticism in the course of one's investigation, or even to arrive at a reductionist universal-scientific vocabulary to cover each and every case, amounts to foolhardiness. When La Barre bundles 'revelation, vision [and] divination' altogether as 'mere "supernatural" functions of the *sub*conscious, when the critical conscious mind is lowered in dissociative states',[38] we should rightly suspect verbal (rather than any adept's) trickery has been in play.

The more the oral historical evidence is unveiled, in any case, the more crucial visionary experiences are said to be in determining religio-cultural directions. Of great interest, but presenting difficult materials for the historian, are those traditions of 'visionary disclosures' graced to culture-heroes — such as Manamarkeri of the Biak-Numfor region, who is conceived not only to have founded many settlements but also to have been taken under the earth to see *Koreri* (the true source of the islanders' wealth); and Papua's Edai Siabo, whose spirit-led descent to a rock in the ocean depths results in the finding of the *lagatoi*, the great vessel to take the Motuan trading expeditions to the Gulf and thus ensure their people's survival.[39] We are now fortunate to have highly publicized cases of visions experienced by leaders in traditional movements of socio-religious adjustment. This refers to the alleged appearance of ancestors to Buninia (a Taro cult 'founder' among the Orokaiva), when he was supposed to have been 'struck down spiritually' by his departed father, and to the claim of Kosivo, Buninia's sister-in-law, that spirits of some recently killed enemies had copulated with her.[40] These examples, Jojoga Opeba for one would argue,[41] belong to a pre-contact ethos. These and other experiences in this context were all presented as 'actual happenings'. In the light of what has already been said about dream adventures often being represented as actual adventures that does not make it easier to distinguish 'special sights of the other side' from dreams; but their distinguished importance makes them a tantalizing subject for cautious study.

To isolate specific difficulties here, one could take the well documented case of the *peroveta* (prophet) Genakuiya of Buna (an Orokaiva of the Jaua grouping). Genakuiya (recently deceased) was believed to be able to visit invisible realms, more specifically the land of the dead (as well as the heaven and the gates of hell talked about by Christians). The genuineness of her experiences aside, we should note that Genakuiya retired, lay down and shut her eyes when she visited these other places, entering through what she described as a 'deep sleep' (yet not *eturo*, 'dream', or *evari*, 'ordinary sleep').[42] It was important for her clientele that she was not having ordinary dreams but being permitted a special witnessing (what we would normally call a 'vision'). Her retirements, furthermore, came not from tiredness at the end of a long hard day, but from her avowed ability to fall into a state of strange awareness quite other than consciousness.[43] Here one can get stuck, wondering whether trance, not only dream, might be as equally appropriate a category for her experiences as visions, but I have already foreshadowed the problem of mixtures and category 'breakdowns'. This kind of problem has been occasionally noted elsewhere. As Reo Fortune once commented about the phenomenon of 'seeing' on Manus Island:

> Some of these seers merely stare into vacancy and, without compulsive evidence of possession, act as oracles that are believed to be possessed. Others of the Usiai seers practise through alleged dreams that are taken as oracular.[44]

Some of these issues discussed here are highly relevant to the study of cargo cults and new religious movements (which will be taken up in chapters 8–9 especially), and it is only in this connection that we have been forced to sort out some of the phenomenological difficulties which can arise. Many of the vision encounters the author personally discussed with leaders of such movements are of a highly traditional nature, albeit with some twist that reflects adaptation to new changes in the cosmos. A former cultist, Luliapo Brugua (of Liorofa, among the eastern highlands Bena Bena), for example, told me of his direct encounter with a spirit-ghost (*f^{e}re*) at night in 1969. Others in his hamlet admitted such a sighting was not new in his culture, but what got Luliapo moving, and led him to initiate and direct a cult, was the spirit's presentation of a £10 note. That bespoke great changes ahead, for which he fostered group expectations.[45] For another case, read the autobiography of the

Toaripi Kae Fo'o (coastal Papua) about his activities 'before inaugurating a cargo cult'.[46] Admittedly, this could be a case of a person turning his own life into a legend, and it is the story of someone caught between the two worlds of traditional 'magic' and the mystery of the 'whiteman'; but on close inspection it nicely reflects the kind of consciousness which European littérateurs would dub 'dream-like'. Kae moves in a world in which twelve corn cobs grow out of a single comb, a strange red plant on a mountain-top turns into a cabbage, and a white falcon falls miraculously to the ground before the hunter. The man is in no obvious pathological condition — he could sit concentrating long enough to tell his story in the one day-long session. Yet, no one at Kavora village attracted by his talk would pretend to have perceived for himself the kinds of things Kae had seen — all of his images being from some liminal zone between the worlds of blacks and whites. We are left either with a trickster, and a clever cunningly rationalizing, manipulative one at that, or a person with an unusual window on reality.

That the content of visions has changed in various areas following the impact of Christianity can hardly be denied, and openness to different, newer types of appearances could well have something to do with the ethos of different churches. Kae Fo'o, for instance, possibly because he grew up influenced by the Protestant London Missionary Society, makes no mention of angels or Maria, but it is probably of some significance that Josef Oro, a fellow eastern Toaripi from a neighbouring village, claimed to me that he had been summoned to be God's healer in an invidious world of sorcery (c. 1955) by an angel. The angel was surrounded by 'dazzling light', and holding a 'croton bush in his hands'; Josef conceiving Catholicism and tradition as wedded in this experience, since the croton is associated both with magic and the decoration of church altars.[47]

Such varied sightings, together with hints of religio-cultural conditionings affecting them, tend to leave us without steady controls. Yet the experiencers' insistencies remain. Occasionally we are severely shocked out of a tempting skepticism. On an airplane flying from Wewak to Port Moresby in 1981, one of my university students, a Manus, admitted to me that he had once seen a vision. He was quick to add that he had hardly ever been to church in his life, and was trying to be very respectful of the traditions of his people. But 'one day', he said: 'I saw the heavens open and a group of angels in white clothings [sic] high in the sky. I saw it with my very own eyes. Although I have not done anything about it, the experience has never left me and I have tried to think about things of religion ever since.'

Trance and possession

The term 'trance' can be used of a dream state or of being transfixed by visual or auditory experience beyond one's reckoning; but I have coupled it to 'possession' here with the intention of focussing on relatively active behaviour which does not appear to be under the conscious control of persons enacting it, that is, the controls evident to others in normal circumstances. The phenomena of trance and possession in Melanesia are more varied than one might expect. To begin with, one should take note of the different contexts in which they are manifested, the differing precipitating factors, the signs of the relevant 'altered state', and whether the phenomena are experienced by individuals or collectively. Other issues which necessarily follow concern the researcher's 'steering equipment' and 'agreed criteria' for interpreting what is going on, and also the role of social change in altering the 'face' of the phenomena one way or the other.[48]

As for the *contexts*, no general rule can be applied, unless one talks in vague terms about a link between possession states and 'crisis situations'. On San Cristobal (Solomon Islands), to illustrate, some clans will not go to war unless one of their number shows evidence of being possessed by the war god. Among the Bena Bena, as we have already seen, the spirit ($f^e re$) of a person who had died by sorcery is taken to enter someone's near-of-kin like a wind (*bunemeha'a*), so that they shake (involuntarily) and then race off under this intervening spirit's guidance to the hamlet of the culprit sorcerer. Among the Central Wiru language group (south of Pangia, southern highlands) by comparison, the occasion to 'shake', under the irrupting influence of the ancestors, and to do so as a group of men and women, is at a time of general adversity, when harvests are bad, pig herds low and human sickness too prevalent.[49]

Concerning *precipitating factors*, one finds that, apart from general circumstances which may suggest the need of contact with the spirit order, apparent trance and possession states can be brought into operation through a variety of means. It might be through drumming (as with Etoro shamans before battle, Western Province of Papua), continuous dancing (as among the Wiru), blowing out scented breath or smoke (as did a Jaua master-of-ceremonies in a local taro cult, using the wild strawberry leaves he chewed as a vehicle for transmitting *jipari* 'dance trances'); or it could perhaps be through ingesting stimulants, or participating in numinous moments, such as sacrifices, initiations, séances or 'shamanic-looking' consultations.[50]

Even though such numinous moments are charged with spiritual power, as they allegedly are, it is not the case that the same impressions or expectations as to the *signs of possession* are found among different peoples. In an important ritual called *Fan Nanggi* ('feeding the sky') on Biak Island (Irian Jaya), for instance — carried out 'in times of scarcity and uncertainty' — participants knew the *mon* or 'shaman' performing the rite had had his sacrifice welcomed when they saw the 'vibration of his arms'; this was, thus, the sign that he was in 'a state of trance, possessed by *Nanggi* the sky deity'.[51] At Mumeng initiation ceremonies (highland Morobe), by comparison, the role of the sorcerer–initiator (*sindang*) is to paint a specially prepared, be-spelled solution of *wawe* (or red pandanus paste) on the chest and upper arms of the young initiates. So, daubing *wawe* in this context is a sign that each potential warrior is being possessed and thus protected by the war god. It is believed that the solution will cause death if it touches the mouth, hands or lower parts of the body. Just to feel it running on the body, then, has 'made' people fall unconscious, the occasional youth even dying, and such events are interpreted as the tokens of the god's control and wishes. As the painted warriors burst out of their seclusion, painted with *wawe*, women hold their babies as tightly as possible, consulting a *sindang* if a child coughs or vomits, for fear the god may seek to take the infant's spirit away.[52] Among the Roviana (New Georgia, Solomons), as one example of a consultation, a specialist practitioner under *sabusabukae* ('spirit possession') would wave armlets and shell-money about, 'requesting his ancestral spirits to give answers' to his questions (about disease, and so on). The reply soon came 'when he began to feel a great weight from his arm moving towards his whole body'.[53] In other cultures, persons are understood to take on spirit power simply because of the ceremonial role they play: a Fuyughe *utame* chief for example, dressed up to participate in a feast, does not have to manifest unusual behaviour to convince others that he is a special locus of spiritual power; this is because it is believed the human cosmos would collapse without him.[54]

Most of the examples just touched on rightly suggest that there is much more evidence of *individual* rather than *collective* possession phenomena in traditional Melanesian societies; even then, Hans Nevermann may be correct in surmising that 'possession states' of any kind are not really characteristic of Melanesian cultures across the board.[55] From only one set of interviews, which was from Wiru informants, have I learnt of collective shaking (pidgin: *guria*) clearly being a vital part of pre-contact tradition (see n.49). There is, on the other hand, Ronald Berndt's account of the *Zona* or 'cold wind' which was reported to have affected many people from Kamano to Fore, before Europeans were actually known to the areas.[56] The *Zona* caused them to 'shiver and shake' in groups — somewhat like those who had 'sorcery sickness'. And we have Jojoga's arguments that *jipari* was an instance of pre-contact innovation. Most of the information about collective agitations, nevertheless, or the phenomena of shaking, quivering, head-jerking, and so on — too often in the past depreciated as convulsive, paroxysmal, mass-hysterical, over-emotional, and the like — hails from studies of cargo cults and other new religious movements.[57] These cults or movements may provide some indications as to what may have happened at moments of very severe crisis in times gone by, but there is little oral historical proof to go on, and they are probably best taken as 'transitional' rather than 'traditional' expressions of Melanesian religions.

At least some of the phenomena of these new movements help us to sharpen our critical insights with regard to claimed 'possessions'. There can be no doubt that some groups have deliberately worked themselves up collectively (especially in prolonged dancing, to an extreme not known in their traditions) to make things change, to transform their world and bring in the

Cargo — or the new goods of the whites. It is fair to argue this of certain 'Adventnachten' ('advent nights') of the Koreri movements — particularly of one in 1938, when many Shouten Islanders were 'so sensitive' to the drumming, and singing, many of the songs being composed by the remarkable prophetess Angganita, that they were 'overcome of their own accord' and began 'to tremble and sometimes . . . speak with strange guttural sounds'.[58] It is also reasonable to maintain that one high-point of the so-called 'Mur Madness' among the Wahgi (in 1949) was an exaggerated *Kongar* (or pig-kill) dance and 'mock battle', with warriors eventually rushing around frantically in a pallisaded *sing sing* ground trying to transform stones, wood and banana leaves into European goods.[59] A comparable state of affairs can be found from Mengen history (east New Britain), when in 1961 two nude men, among a host of excited, boundlessly energetic dancers at Maihuna, bellowed to a worried local *luluai* (an indigenous government official) that their 'skins felt hungry for cargo'.[60] In these cases it is fair to speak of over-excitability; if anything like trance conditions are evident, they can be at least partly explained as the results of people wanting to pass into an 'altered' condition of being.

On the other hand, there are some occurrences of involuntary behaviour which take place *against* the wishes of either individuals or groups, and these ought to be considered carefully to decide whether we might have good reasons for taking indigenous conceptions of possession more seriously than most social assumptions would allow. What we need is a sprinkling of situations in which recourse to typical naturalistic explanations is not easy. The Anglican missionary William Neil, for instance, has reported how a group of Toabaita neophytes begged him to come quickly to cast out an evil spirit (north Malaita, Solomons). On arrival at the relevant village he found an elderly woman who had long lost her legs, and only possessed mere stumps in their stead, jumping some 3–4 feet (or approximately 1 m) above the ground. Completely bewildered, he shouted for the force to depart (invoking Jesus, as he thought he should!), and the prodigy subsided.[61]

Another small object lesson for dogmatic anti-supernaturalists comes from an unaffected eye-witness, Koroti Kosi, at the tale-end of the so-called 'Vailala Madness' (pan-Elema, Gulf of Papua). Kosi, who became paramount chief in Lese Oalai (eastern Toaripi) reckoned himself to be 10–12 years of age in about 1920, when the incident occurred. Along with men, women and children from Kavora and others from his own village, he was standing on the sand-bar which stretches westward from Kavora towards Elema country. They were discussing their fishing catch. Then, in the distance, along the beach to the west two men could be seen running towards them. There was no way the two could reach the party by foot. The sand-bar ran into deep water, and part of the Miauru River mouth thus severed the fishing party from the strangers by a good hundred yards (or about 90 m). Running toward the water's edge, the two newcomers burst out: 'It's coming! It's coming!

Something terrible has happened to the west!' And in an instant, so Koroti vividly remembers, all the adults — but, curiously, none of the children (around 12 years or under) — were caught up in a series of uncanny bodily movements.

People's arms were impelled behind their backs, their wrists being uncontrollably fastened as if a jailor had tied them together, and their ankles were likewise linked in a way that made them stumble and sometimes fall. Whether sitting or standing, this 'wrist-and-ankle locking', accompanied by bodily shuddering, was at its height for some hours. At times it was unpredictably broken by individual men rushing off into the bushland between the beach and Kavora to listen for cicadas (these insects being traditionally held to mark the presence of ancestors). But most of the people remained caught in the locked state, speaking apparently unintelligible words, 'seeing' white-skinned ancestors, cargo ships and submarines, jerking while sitting or standing, while the frightened children watched in amazement, though some went for help. Although the affected people were conducted away from the exposed area, they went totally without food for three to four days and hardly slept. The elderly began to look emaciated, and the more agile sometimes burst into hyper-activity, including jumping from house roofs. The tension involved seemed to ease off at the end of each day, and eventually the whole experience 'wore off' for the initial group. However, Koroti's father organized the preparation of food on the expectation that the 'wind' would affect others — and he was right. After several weeks of sporadic eruptions like these (which also had some impact on social organization), the whole business passed.

The consensus among the experiencers was that it had been spirit-possession; but it is fascinating that, whether or not they had earlier heard rumours about the Vailala phenomenon to the west (and Koroti, for one, did not think they had), they did not put the occurrence down to the visitation of the ancestors (as many seem to have already done in the Vailala area itself). No. This was instead a most unwelcome episode, brought by evil spirits (*arahoha maealoro*). After recording the whole account I passed it on to a psychologist, who described it as a clear case of 'mass hysteria'. This summation of the matter, however, appears all too glib, and more a labelling than an explanation, especially because the 'wind' passed through haphazardly, unpredictably, usually avoiding children and by-passing odd villages in its path along the coast to a point as far east as Oiapu.[62] That being the case, the whole episode could be just as important for reconstructing possible variations in the responses to such phenomena in the traditional past as it is for understanding psychic adjustments in recent times.[63]

More could be said about collective possession phenomena in connection with new indigenous churches and pentecostalist movements erupting throughout Melanesia at the present time, but then such incidences are intimately bound up with verbal curiosities, or so-called glossolalia.

Xenophonic behaviour and glossolalia

Most of us would be prepared to define a language as a series of articulated sounds which make sense to another party and which can be reciprocated by following the same rules. We are tempted to dub an unpredictable volley of mouthed noises as 'incoherent babble', 'gibberish' or 'nonsense syllables' if the vocalizations make no semantic sense in their setting, even to those sharing the same experience, and if what is spoken accompanies symptoms of stress (such as groans) or of (psycho-) pathology (such as rolling of eyes).[64] This general distinction, I maintain, though not unhelpful, is somewhat unsubtle for the purposes of studying 'altered states of consciousness'. If I may appeal to old, rather sadly neglected patristic categories, one can seriously and less preemptively discriminate between *xenophonia* ('strange utterance') and *glossolalia* (a nineteenth century neologism for 'speaking in tongues') in the phenomenology of religion.[65] Xenophonic behaviour is distinguished for its striking anomalies — it can be high-pitched, guttural, and full of staccato — and it is more than often accompanied by unusual bodily actions. Glossolaly, in contrast, if its forms are not actual languages, has been found upon careful analysis to reflect the structure of actual languages.[66] Even though its use may be found among emotionally oriented congregations and sects (of the Christian world in particular), there is no doubt that it can be appropriated by well integrated persons, employed with noticeable serenity and liturgical sobriety, and sometimes de-coded in a church setting by someone having 'the gift of interpreting tongues' (cf. I Cor. 14 : 26–27). Occasionally, though now undeniably, there are times when people find themselves speaking sentences which, to them, are completely foreign in meaning but are nonetheless intelligible to hearers, sometimes to specialists in archaic or non-extant languages.[67]

Evidence of cases of xenophonia or glossolalia in pre-contact, traditional Melanesia is rather skimpy, and I have only come across individual, not collective, behaviour of this sort. Traditionalist prophetesses among the Torau (Bougainville), to take a most interesting example, are understood to be seized by the ancestors when they fall flat and frontwards to the ground. While lying, they moan or screech out expletives which are unintelligible to virtually all surrounding onlookers. Sometimes women associates interpret the noise (in a proceeding not so dissimilar to the Delphic Oracle), and at other times the prophetesses themselves disclose the future, after these gripping 'visitations' from the spirits.[68] Here we seem to have xenophonic behaviour preceding proleptic statements, a two-phased process operating in the one person, which recalls some interesting parallels in the history of religions — the Phrygian (female) prophets of Montanism, for a start.

As for collective phenomena of this kind, on all accounts it is surprisingly recent and tied in to the trance phenomena of new religious movements already mentioned. What transpired in earlier movements, however, is now hard to gauge. F. E. Williams could not take a tape-recorder to the scene of the so-called 'Vailala Madness', and so no linguistic analysis of the various curious utterances involved were carried out. Perhaps our only hope is a Vailala man living at Bereina who at odd times, all-too unpredictably, has headaches which make him revert to the palaver they used at the very start of the Vailala movement in 1919.[69] Usually we have to make do with competing modes of description — especially regarding cargo movements: some resting on more pejorative terms (like Williams on 'jibberish . . . stuttering and mumbling'), and others (like F. C. Kamma) oscillating between references to 'gibberish' and the more charitable 'glossolalia' in the Koreri movement outbursts.[70] It is now high time for investigations of such matters to become both more intense and sensitive.

John Barr is probably on the right track when he argues that, along with shared dreams and visions, and the bodily agitations of many new religious movements in Melanesia, glossolalic-looking expressions function as rites of passage in the world of apparently discredited tradition and of pressures on people to change their general orientations *qua* social groups.[71] In that case they certainly belong to a very important story of changing Melanesia over the last century or more, yet perhaps also provide a glimmer of what may have happened in times of crisis even earlier. It is hard to pontificate. We can talk of 'psychically stabilizing ecstatic' activity as viably as 'temporary psychosis' (with a people having to work through madness for the sake of eventual social health). There is still room, too, for the view that such phenomena in earlier times acted as a preparation for the so-called 'Holy Spirit' movements prevalent in Melanesia today, which reflect the impact of Christianity and the yearning to indigenize it — both of which will be taken up in the second part of this book.

There are many other, and varied phenomena that could also be cited. Since we have considered visionary experiences, why not also aural ones (or the so-called 'auditory hallucinations'), for instance? Might it not be that primal peoples can 'see' and 'hear' the 'other side' (= the 'spirit order'? the 'Unconscious'?) more readily than Western urbanized peoples?[72] A list of such additional phenomena would certainly have to include traditional Melanesian 'prophetism': it might also include shamanic *ekstasis* and 'soul-journeying', and alleged cases of clairvoyance and bilocation. And, from these, there are others that automatically suggest themselves: divination, meditation and special states of concentration, curious ordeals (such as Baining fire-walking, east New Britain), hypnotic fascination, clinical death experiences, running *amok*, 'wildman' behaviour, and so forth.[73]

However, it is not the role of this book to exhaustively detail the full range of Melanesian ethnographic data. And now, having drawn to the close of the first part of our survey, it is high time to consider what we have been frequently foreshadowing all along — a changing Melanesia under the influence of Christianity and 'modernization'.

WAHGI SPIRIT STONES. These stones, although worked by some group long predating the Wahgi, were assumed by the Wahgi to have spiritual significance.

Photographed by the author, at Fatima Museum, central highlands, New Guinea

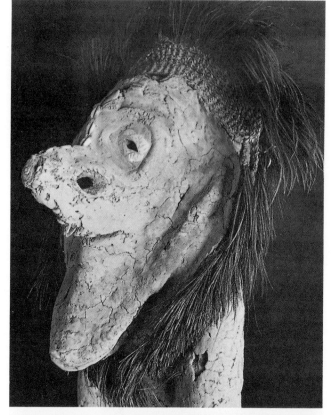

VLISSO, GOD OF WAR AND HUNTING.
This snub-nosed deity comes from
the Yuat River, Sepik River region,
New Guinea.
Plate from *Oceanic Art: masks and sculptures
from New Guinea* © Unesco 1968.
Reproduced with the permission of Unesco

ROVIANA WAR GOD. This ear-ringed
figure, from New Georgia, western
Solomons, was photographed in the
1930s standing in its original
position, with its offertory shrine
(*foreground, left*).
Photo courtesy of Bishop David Pratt

ABELAM HAUS TAMBARAN ('SPIRIT HOUSE'). This *haus tambaran*, in the east Sepik River region, New Guinea, was still in use when photographed by Antony Forge in 1959. The women (*in the foreground*) are removing yams that were displayed on ceremonial ground, at the end of a debate and feast.

Photo courtesy of Antony Forge

VIEW OF A MELANESIAN 'TEMPLE'. This nineteenth century lithograph represents a Dutch artist's impression of a 'temple' in the Biak-Numfor region, west New Guinea (now Irian Jaya). Today, few traces remain of such structures there.

INTERIOR OF AN ELEMA ERAVO. This cathedral-like edifice was photographed in the Papuan Gulf area in the 1930s. The *gope* boards (the elliptical discs, *upper left and right*) can be clearly seen.

Photo by Frank Hurley, from the Australian Museum Collection (V.4784)

ASMAT SHIELD. An example of the striking designs employed for these shields, from the south coast of west New Guinea (now Irian Jaya).

Photo by Robert Mitton, courtesy of George and Lil Mitton

FUYUGHE WAR CLUBS. The pineapple-shaped heads of these clubs, from the Papuan highlands, are carefully carved in stone before being fixed to the wooden handle.
Photo by the author

SILAS ETO. The prophet of the Christian Fellowship Church is shown (*seated right*) wearing his ceremonial robes, at Madou, New Georgia, western Solomons. With him are his wife (*seated*) and his secretary (*standing*).
Photo by the author

JOHN TEOSIN. The Hehela leader is standing in the open area in which Hehela ceremonies are often conducted. In the background is his unfinished, two-storey house, on Buka Island, off Bougainville, New Guinea.
Photo by the author

NOTES

Chapter 5 has been written in association with Remi Dembari and is also partly based on a paper given at a conference sponsored by the Research Centre for Southwest Pacific Studies, at La Trobe University (1983), 'Dreams and Altered States in Melanesia'.

1 *The Human Animal*, p.246.
2 cf. also La Barre's *Ghost*, esp. chs 7–8, 10, 12–13; cf. *Culture in context*, Durham (USA), 1980.
3 G. W. and R. R. Trompf, Dream survey (unpublished collection of field and clinical notes, largely from Papua New Guinea, 1973–85). Dr R. Trompf's work involved dream analysis as acting superintendent of the National Psychiatric Hospital, Laloki, 1985.
4 On the unconscious in the works of Sigmund Freud and Carl Jung, and before Psychoanalysis, see Trompf, *In search of origins*, pt. 1, chs 4–5.
5 The Hula-Aroma-Velerupu tradition of coastal Papua, then, which locates the source of human vitality in the head is rather exceptional. Trompf, Fieldnotes, 1974. For an overemphasis of the affects of a non-cerebral 'traditional anthropology', however, see A. R. Hallpike, *Bloodshed and vengeance in the Papuan mountains*, Oxford, 1977, pp.77–83.
6 Wagner, *Habu*, pp.68, 130–31; cf. also Glasse, 'The Huli of the Southern Highlands', in Lawrence and Meggitt (eds), *Gods*, p.30.
7 On the Papuan witches, W. J. V. Saville, *In unknown New Guinea*, London, 1926, p.215 (Mailu); Seligmann, *The Melanesians of British New Guinea*, pp.640ff. (Suau, Massim); on divination, e.g., Roro, see above ch. 2 and n.17; on bilocation, K. Carley, 'Prophets old and new', in Trompf (ed.), *Prophets of Melanesia*, pp.152ff.
8 A capacity analyzed and considered experimentally in the Spring Quarter Workshop on Dreams (unpublished materials, University of California, Santa Cruz, 1975).
9 Paris, 1972, pt. 1; cf. also his 'Sociologie de rêve', in R. Callois and G. E. von Grunebaum (eds), *Le rêve et les sociétés humaines* (Bibliothèque des Science humaines), Paris, 1967, pp.177ff.
10 K. Stewart, 'Dream Theory in Malaya' in C. T. Tart (ed.), *Altered states of consciousness; a book of readings*, New York, 1969, p.160; cf. R. Noone, *Rape of the dream people*, London, 1972. However, we await John Wren Lewis's challenge that Stewart's work amounts to a hoax.
11 e.g. the Wahgi, Trompf, Fieldnotes, Kup, 1976; cf. Stewart, 'Dream Theory', p.161.
12 OT: Obed Posu, Sept.–Oct., 1977.
13 OT: Jojoga Opeba, July 1983.
14 Hallpike, *Bloodshed*, pp.261–62. Near the Tauade, certain Fuyughe place gods are known to have been decorated with long hair (taken from the whites?).
15 R. M. Berndt, 'The Kamano, Usurufa, Fate and Fore of the Eastern Highlands', in Lawrence and Meggitt (eds), *Gods*, p.86 (Kamano); P. Sillitoe, *Give and Take; Exchange in Wola Society*, Brisbane, 1979, p.165.
16 R. Fortune, *Sorcerers of Dobu*, p.181.
17 OT: Carolyn Brunton, Sept., 1985 (Dobu); Hallpike, *Bloodshed*, p.261 (Tauade).
18 OT: Jojoga Opeba, July 1983; for comparative emphases in other Orokaivan groups, see Dembari below.
19 OT: Alois Yagas, August 1983.
20 Wagner, *Habu*, pp.68–71. On metaphors more generally, ch. 4 above.
21 Dreams are gifts from the dead (as among the Orokaiva, see Rembari below).
22 The two researchers are Robert Nonggor-r and Clitus Topa. On bigmen passing off dreams as 'just dreams' in political situations elsewhere, see D. L. Oliver, *A Solomon Islands Society*, Boston, 1955, p.225 (Siwai)
23 D. Eastburn in L. Lornley, The Mendi (unpublished book in typescript), Mendi, 1976.
24 An important theme in such basic works as Lawrence, *Road*, pp.162, 167, 190, 194, 243–51, etc; P. Worsley, *Trumpet shall sound*, pp.64ff., 85ff., 111ff., etc.
25 Jojoga Opeba, Taro or Cargo (in 1976), before studying under Michele Stephen; cf. her 'The innovative role of altered states of consciousness in traditional Melanesian religion', pp.3ff. Slightly ahead chronologically in the whole field: V. Lanternari, 'Dreams as Charismatic Significants: their bearing on the Rise of New Religious Movements', in A.

Bharati (ed.), *The realm of the extra-human; ideas and action* (World anthropology), The Hague, 1976, pp.321ff. (apparently unknown to Stephen, who refers more to my edited collection *Prophets*, (1977) on pp.18–19 and especially Opeba's chapter in it).

26 OT: Yagas, August 1983.

27 The questionnaire was designed in English but the actual interview was conducted in Tainyandawari vernacular. When the respondents did not appear to understand a question, the question was rephrased. Apart from preliminary queries, to do with name, village of origin, occupation, etc, the questions concerning dreams were as follows: What do you think causes dreams?/What type of dream is common among your people?/What types of dreams do you dream?/How do you interpret your dreams?/Are all the dreams significant?/ What do you do after the interpretation of your dream?/Do you believe in your dreams?

28 *Roriwa* and *dongo* are used for many purposes. They are used as lucky charms, magic, sorcery, poisoning (*kae*), treatment, and advancing in sports, employment etc. However there are different types of them serving different purposes.

29 When the Tainyandawari people are talking about the dead people, they do not say 'my dead father' or 'my dead mother'. Anybody who says 'my dead father' will be seen as not respecting his father. Culturally, it is unacceptable. (Cyril's father, however, was dead at the time of his experience.) The dreams are told as if something true had happened and not as mere dreams.

30 When people are talking about lucky charms, magic, or sorcery, they do not reveal everything about it. When Aidan was telling me the dream, he avoided telling me the procedure used to make the charm effective.

31 *Darutegeri* — literally it means walking over other people. However, in this context it was used as a ritualistic method of treatment.

32 cf. S. Freud, *The interpretation of dreams* (trans. and ed. J. Strachey), (The Pelican Freud library 4), London, 1976 edn; Jung, *Dreams* (Bollingen Ser. 20) (trans. R. F. C. Hull), Princeton, 1974.

33 Freud, *Totem and taboo* (trans. A. A. Brill), London, 1938, ch. 3; Jung et al., *Man and his symbols*, London, 1964, pp.30ff; cf. critique in Trompf, *In search of origins*, chs 4–5.

34 Here is foreshadowed G. W. and R. R. Trompf, *Carl Jung and the study of religion* (Religion and Reason ser.), Berlin (forthcoming).

35 Yet cf. Lawrence, *Road*, p.292, s.v. 'Visions'.

36 See R. Lacey, 'A Glimpse of the Enga world-view', in Trompf, *Mel. and Judeao-Christ. relig. trads*, pt. A, pp.52–53 (Mae Enga); Chowning, see chap. 2 above and n.15 (Lakalai); and for my generalizations about seeing the spirits I rely on a diversity of materials and oral testimonies available to me at the Summer Institute of Linguistics, Ukarumpa, October, 1977, where I delivered lectures on Melanesian religion.

37 *Civilization in transition* (trans. Hull) (in Collected works, Bollingen ser. 20), Princeton, 1970 edn, p.314, n.1 (first quotation), p.315 (second and longer); cf. also *Man and his symbols*, pp.30–31.

38 'Anthropological perspectives on hallucinations and hallucinogens', in R. K. Siegel and L. J. West (eds), *Hallucinations: behaviour, experience and theory*, New York and London, 1975, p.41.

39 See esp. Lacey, 'Journeys of Transformation', in Trompf (ed.), *Cargo cults and millenarian movements*, ch. 4.

40 Worsley, *Trumpet shall sound*, p.40.

41 OT: Jojoga Opeba, April, 1983, cf. his 'Melanesian cult movements as traditional and religious responses to change', in Trompf (ed.), *Gospel not Western*, pp.50, 54–55.

42 OT: Jojoga Opeba, April, 1983; cf. his 'The *Peroveta* of Buna', in Trompf (ed.), *Prophets*, p.134.

43 cf. ibid., p.135.

44 *Manus religion*, p.165. The Usiai constitute the inland Manus cultural complex.

45 OT: Luliapo Brugue, esp. Nov. 1973, August 1977; cf. also G. B. Blumenthal, 'Cargo Cult Movements', in T. Ahrens (ed.), *A study of the Lutheran Church in the Bena area*, Goroka, 1974, esp. p.15.

46 Trompf and V. Koroti (as translator), 'Kae Fo'o and his account of his life before inaugurating a cargo cult', in Trompf (ed.), *Mel. Judaeo-Christ. relig. trads*, pt. 3, c1, pp.89–93.

47 OT: Josef Oro, June 1974, interview translated by V. Koroti (unpublished handwritten MS, UPNG, Port Moresby, 1974) p.5. Oro also claimed to have seen the Morning Star as Spirit (p.3), a phenomenon of traditional importance but with some Biblical connections (cf. Rev. 22:16). Here, in Oro's story, incidentally, I caught no suggestion of psychosis at all; not only because his experiences were culturally acceptable but because of his whole personal bearing. There was also no history of bodily deprivation (cf. La Barre, 'Anthropological perspectives', p.16).

48 For some background, F. Goodman, J. Henny and E. Pressel, *Trance, healing and hallucination: three field studies in hallucination*, New York, 1974.

49 H. Nevermann et al., *Les religions du Pacifique et d'Australie* (trans. L. Jospin), Paris, 1972, p.133 (San Cristobal), ch. 3 (Bena Bena); OT: J. Wer, Oct., 1977 (Wiru). For pertinent data north of the Wiru, and in connection with adjustments to socio-cosmic change and the whites, see Meggitt, *Studies in Enga history* (Oceania monographs 20), Sydney, 1974, esp. ch. 1.

50 e.g. J. Hides, *Papuan wonderland*, London and Glasgow, 1936, pp.49–51 (Etoro), n.49 above (Wiru); Jojoga Opeba, Taro or Cargo?, ch. 3 (Jaua); F. Steinbauer, *Melanesian cargo cults* (trans. M. Wohlwill), Brisbane, 1979, pp.95, 131–32; and we await the work of T. A. Wyatt on betel nut chewing and altered states (UPNG) (coastal Papuan cases). Of particular relevance regarding stimulants here, M. Reay, 'Mushroom madness in the New Guinea highlands', *Oceania*, 31 (1960), pp.137–39.

51 F. C. Kamma, *Koreri: messianic movements in the Biak-Numfor area*, The Hague, 1972, p.14.

52 OTs: Tapei Martin and others, July, 1983.

53 E. Tuza, 'The demolition of church buildings by the ancestors', in Trompf (ed.), *Gospel not Western*, p.76.

54 P. Fastré, Moeurs, ch. 1; and OT: D. de Guise, May 1983 (following fieldwork on feasts in the Chirima valley).

55 Nevermann, *Les religions*, pp.132–33.

56 'A cargo movement in the Eastern Central highlands of New Guinea', *Oceania*, 23 (1952), p.57.

57 In this connection M. Stephen, *Cargo cult hysteria: symptom of despair or technique of ecstasy?* (La Trobe University Research Centre for Southwest Pacific Studies, Paper 1), Melbourne, 1977 and the literature cited there.

58 Kamma, *Koreri*, p.164.

59 Trompf, 'Doesn't colonialism make you mad?' in S. Latukefu (ed.), *Papua New Guinea: a century of colonial impact, 1884 to 1984*, Port Moresby, 1990, pp. 247ff.

60 Trompf, 'Keeping the *Lo* under a Melanesian Messiah', in J. Barker, *Christianity in Oceania; ethnographic perspectives* (ASAO Monographs 12), Danham, 1989, ch. 5.

61 OT: W. Neil, 1962.

62 OT: Koroti Kosi, May 1974. For background F. E. Williams, *'The Vailala Madness' and other essays* (ed. E. Schwimmer), Brisbane, 1976, chs 5–6.

63 Taking the cue from La Barre, *Ghost*, ch. 8, but not his glib conclusions.

64 cf., e.g., W. Sargent, *The battle for the mind*, London, 1957, esp. chs 2, 5–6.

65 Following Eusebius, esp. on Montanism, in *Ecclesiastica historia*, V. 13.16–18.14, cf. R. Knox, *Enthusiasm*, Oxford, 1959, ch. 3, F. L. Cross (ed.), *Oxford Dictionary of the Christian Church*, Oxford, 1958 edn, p.564.

66 See N. G. Holm, 'Ritualistic pattern and sound structure of glossolalia in material collected in Swedish-speaking parts of Finland', *Temenos*, 11 (1975), pp.43ff.; cf. his 'Tungotal och Andedop' (doctoral dissert., University of Uppsala, Uppsala, 1976).

67 The literature on glossolaly in modern church contexts is vast. For the most helpful introduction, F. D. Goodman, *Speaking in tongues: a cross-cultural study of glossolalia*, Chicago, 1972.

68 OT: Mary-Luke Garuai, unpublished seminar presentation, UPNG, 1975.

69 My efforts and those of Louise Aitsi to taperecord these regressions have so far failed.

70 Williams, *'Vailala Madness'*, p.335 (cf. p.336 on the 'head-whirling' affects of the whole Vailala phenomenon); Kamma, *Koreri*, pp.135, 163–64, 180, 191.

71 Barr, 'Spiritistic Tendencies in Melanesia', in W. Flannery (ed.), *Religious Movements in Melanesia 2* (Point Ser. 3), Goroka, 1983, pp.1–34. For a more Melanesian view of

glossolaly in distinctly Christian or conversion contexts, S. Namunu, 'Spirits in Melanesian tradition and Spirit in Christianity', in Trompf (ed.), *Gospel not Western*, pp.112–15, and M. Maeliau, 'Searching for a Melanesian way of worship', in ibid., pp.125–26.

72 Note the issues raised by J. Jaynes, in his *The origins of consciousness in the breakdown of the bicameral mind*, Boston, 1976, esp. pp.339ff., 357ff., although he is weak on modern ethnographic materials.

73 On prophetism, Trompf (ed.), *Prophets*; on shamanism, we foreshadow Trompf, 'Shamanism in Melanesia?' prepared for *Temenos*; on bilocation and divination, see n.7 above and chaps 2–4, for other pertinent examples; on meditation, we await further work by Sibona Kopi on the western Motu (for his doctoral dissert., UPNG); on fire-walking, K. Hesse and T. Aerts, *Baining life and lore* (ed. T. Aerts), Port Moresby, 1982, pp.66ff.; on hypnotic fascination, e.g. E. Bozzano, *Übersinnliche Erscheinungen bei Naturvölken*, Bern, 1948, ch. 6; on clinical death experience, we await a publication of materials by W. Flannery; on running *amok*, B. G. Burton-Bradley, *Stone age crisis*, ch. 4; on 'wildman behaviour', W. C. Clarke, 'Temporary madness as theatre: wild man behaviour in New Guinea', *Oceania*, 43 (1972–73), pp.198ff., etc. Note: during the same conference at which this chapter was presented in its original form, S. Kopi gave a personal account of his 'seeing' of a dead relative in a Motuan cemetery (while he was meditating), describing in detail that 'chilling sensation', alteration of visual field, etc. to a staggered audience of anthropologists. His lecture was pregnant, it follows, with great methodological significance.

PART

2

THE
NEW TIME

MAP 3

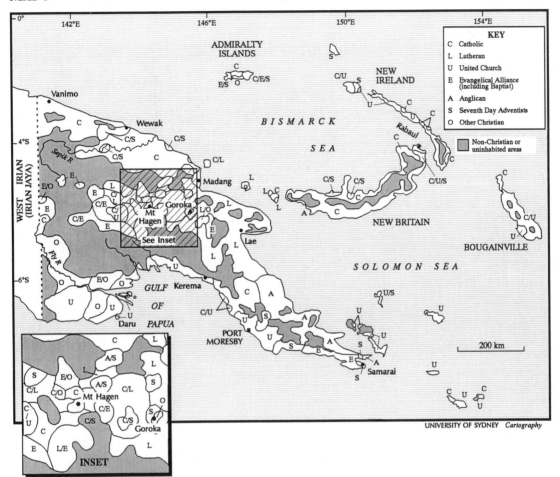

MISSIONARY IMPACT ON PAPUA NEW GUINEA BY 1971

THE COMING AND THE CONSEQUENCES OF THE MISSIONARIES

Europeans did not learn of the great Pacific ocean until the beginning of the sixteenth century. As for Melanesian waters, they were at first only traversed by voyagers bent on forging trade routes between Europe and the famed Spice Islands (the western outliers of Halmahera).[1] After some Portuguese sightings, Spanish ships ran closer to the islands inhabited by dark-skinned peoples, and from 1528 (when Saavedra anchored in the Manus or Admiralty Group) to 1595 (when Alvaro de Merdaña led a second expedition in search of the 'real' Isles of Solomon), there were opportunities for European colonial enterprise. Little of great moment befell the islanders, however, while the Pacific was a 'Spanish Lake'. Even after the Jesuit Francis Xavier arrived in the Moluccas in 1546, Christian missionary activity further along the chain of islands had to wait for another three hundred years.[2] The Sultanate of Tidore still kept nominal control of regional trade with the westernmost tip of New Guinea (and thus reflected Islam's easternmost point of expansion), and all Spanish attempts to make a 'Christian' impression upon Melanesia's Pacific side were desultory. The first Catholic Mass celebrated on Melanesian soil was at Sedeia Island (south-east Papua) during an expedition under Luis de Torres in 1605, and a few captives he took from among the Mailu in the following year may be rated 'the first Christians of the region' well ahead of time.[3] The really significant impact by outsiders was to wait until the nineteenth century, especially during its second half, when European colonial pretensions mounted to their highest, and missionary work experienced a heyday.[4] And, of course, the mission phenomenon has to be considered within this context of imperial expansionism and colonialism.

Research into missions cannot be limited to the study of interrelations between incoming proclaimers and indigenous hearers. There are also other expatriate actors upon the colonial scene — such as traders, explorers, miners, government officials and settlers — whose motives for entering the region were usually quite different from those of the missionaries, and who, together, represent the more 'secular front' of the Great Intrusion.[5] Nor can missionary activities be understood without assessing existing power relationships between expatriate groups (both locally and at large). The Melanesians, for their part, were quite capable of distinguishing between the types of new arrivals in their midst (and the missionaries earned their respect more than most), but they also had to make sense of the New Time (including the White Phenomenon and remarkable European technology) as a whole, so that their appraisal of preached Christianity was affected by its association with new wealth.[6]

It is not, however, the role of this book to provide a detailed assessment of all these factors. The next two chapters concern the planting and development of the Christian missions throughout Melanesia: this chapter concentrates on developments in Papua New Guinea (one of the most intensively missionized countries in the world) and the next chapter, on the work of the Catholic missions in particular (as the largest set of missionary operations in the region). The rest of the book considers the immense influence of the missionary message in the recent history of indigenous thought and practice. So, by way of introduction, we shall look at how and when missions were started in wider Melanesia.

Missionaries in Melanesia: the foundation years

However much more isolated the islands of eastern Melanesia now appear to be, it was almost inevitable that eastern Melanesia should receive missionaries before the great island of New Guinea. This is because both Catholic and Protestant missions were established in Polynesia (and Micronesia) during the first half of the nineteenth century. It was originally Tahitian teachers trained by the inter-denominational Protestant London Missionary Society, and then a succession of Tongans (prepared by the Wesleyans or Methodists), who first brought the Christian teaching to Fiji, in 1830 and 1835 respectively. As the century progressed, more and more Polynesians were to be trained and encouraged to take the Gospel that had been so successfully planted in their own fields to the untouched dangerous-looking 'black islands' further south-west.[7]

Before Papua New Guinea (or the eastern half of the main island of New Guinea and its outliers) was penetrated, however, mission footholds had been secured in Vanuatu or the New Hebrides (first by John Williams, of the London Missionary Society, who left Samoan teachers on Erromanga and Tanna, 1839–40), and then in New Caledonia, with Samoans representing the London Missionary Society being dropped off on the Isle of Pines in 1840 and French Marists arriving at the top end of the main island by 1848.[8] Far to the west two German Lutherans, sent on behalf of Utrecht Missionary Society of Holland, landed in 1885 at Doreh Bay in the Biak area of West New Guinea (or Papua). They were to prepare the way for a long line of Dutch Reformed missionaries, just as the training of Ambonese teachers by the London

Missionary Society in the Moluccas was eventually to have its effect on the south coast of Vogelkop and still further east.[9] By 1861, in New Zealand, the Anglican bishop, George Selwyn, had consecrated Coleridge Patterson as bishop of Melanesia and, following the failure of Catholic orders in the Solomons over the two previous decades, the two men sowed the seeds of Solomonese 'high church' Anglicanism.[10] Only New Guinea, and especially its eastern half, remained as the last frontier, and it was in the 1870s that great opportunities there began to present themselves. By that time the thriving colonial governments of Australia were showing increasing interest in the 'unpossessed' tropical land mass to their north.

Missions in Papua New Guinea during the nineteenth century

Missionaries bringing the teachings of Christianity were on Papua New Guinean islands as early as 1847. A Roman Catholic mission was established at Woodlark or Muju Island by the Marist order in that year, but it only lasted for eight years because of sickness, lack of food gardens, sheer isolation, and because two priests were killed. Besides, the local people were not really interested in what the missionaries had to offer and remain among the few Melanesian peoples still showing disinterest to this day.[11]

Over ten years after the Woodlark mission withdrew, a small wave of missionaries arrived on Papua New Guinea's coasts during the 1870s and 1880s to lay the foundations of those major missions and churches which are still such an important influence in the country. The most famous pioneer missionaries and the places at which they began work are well enough known — W. G. Lawes of the London Missionary Society worked in and around Port Moresby with helpers from Polynesia (1874 on); George Brown, the Methodist, came with Fijians and Samoans to New Britain and New Ireland (1875); Father Navarre, after work at Rabaul (1882) joined Father Verjus and his Filipino companions to set up the well known Catholic mission on Yule Island (1885); Dr Flierl, the most renowned of Lutheran missionaries in the region landed at Finschhafen in 1886 and the Anglican, Copland King, started his difficult work at Wedau in 1891. Their coming has often been characterized by the local peoples as a transference from darkness to light, and the time of the pioneer missionaries in particular has often been hallowed as the best time in the known past.[12]

We are forced to ask some important preliminary questions at this point. For, after all, why did these newcomers actually want to come and work in Melanesia? What were the first meetings between the 'indigenes' and these 'outsiders' like? What did the early missionaries try to do, and did they create any problems for the people among whom they worked?

Why missionaries came to Papua New Guinea

'Mission', as the work of 'being sent' (by God) to proclaim the 'good news' (or Gospel), is as old as Christianity itself. We only have to think of the renowned journeys of St Paul between Jerusalem and Rome for confirmation. By the eighth century AD, Christian missionaries had carried their message to the cold, northern reaches of Europe and, although having less impact in the East, they had established churches as far away as China. Centuries before the European penetration of New Guinea, what was learnt about India and south Asia, America and other parts of the Pacific (in the fifteenth century) left certain Christians worrying that the teachings of Jesus and the Bible were not being taken to all nations. Some felt called to help peoples who were being mistreated by the Europeans; the Jesuit, Father Peter Claver, for example, devoted his life to helping the suffering slaves in South America during the seventeenth century. Some simply wanted to convert people who had not heard of Christ; for this reason John Wesley went to teach the American Indians in the 1730s.[13] Others believed that God's (millennial) rule over the world would not come 'until the Gospel had first been preached to all nations' (Mark 13:10). All these motives and beliefs can be found among the missionaries in the Pacific: they wanted to help people; they wanted to turn people from 'ways of darkness and savagery to the way of light' (which, as a result of their cultural assumptions, included 'civilizing' them), and to do so before the End of the World.

Different records show how missionaries felt the call of God to work in the Pacific, or Papua and New Guinea in particular. James Chalmers, or *Tamate* ('King') as he came to be known by the coastal Papuans, recalls how far away in a community of poor Scottish crofters, a preacher in his church asked a very awkward question: 'I wonder if there is a boy here this afternoon who will yet become a missionary, and by-and-by bring the Gospel to cannibals?'. Chalmers then and there said to himself 'Yes, God helping me, I will', although only after a special conversion experience was he driven into action, becoming a worker for the London Missionary Society.[14] It was common that such men were 'called', or else they joined and put themselves at the disposal of a religious order or mission society, to go willingly where they were sent. And it was not just Europeans who made such momentous decisions; the newly fledged Christians from the Pacific itself always have to be kept in mind. In fact, if we were writing of the London Missionary Society and Methodists alone, we would find that there were many more South Pacific islanders who did hard, pioneering work than Europeans.

Encounters between missionaries and the people

Men and women of strong will, then, who wanted to preach their message and who wanted to change people's lives, tried to settle down among the communities of Papua New Guinea. What were the local reactions to this? Naturally enough, an early (and traditional) response was suspicion — but mixed with plain curiosity towards people with strange skin and hair, funny dress and impressive boats.

Let us contemplate some early encounters. Take the pioneer Lutheran missionaries, for instance. The first of them, who landed on the north coast of New Guinea's main island, were soon killed by warriors. Afterwards, when John Flierl took his companion and set up a little tent at Simbang, near Finschhafen, the local people were most unhappy (1886). The visitors looked as if they wanted to settle in; so, the villagers planned to drive them off. These reactions owed much to the fact that some of their people had been badly treated earlier by the whites who had absconded from the German New Guinea Company.[15] During the night, then, they heaped faeces and rubbish around the missionaries' tent as a sign of their displeasure. But this failed to drive Flierl away. The next day one local, named Ngakau, stole an iron axe and nearly hit Flierl with his own stone axe when the missionary came to recover his property.[16] But it was decided not to kill the newcomer and he was allowed to build a permanent house on Simbang land, even though 'any sort of land sale' to foreigners was 'unlawful' as far as the villagers were concerned.[17]

We can compare this encounter with another one. The Balawaia group of Papua (some 43 miles, or 70 km east from Port Moresby), while they had been fighting with their neighbours in the 1870s, had become increasingly curious about large sailing boats which passed their bay beyond the reefs but never came to shore. The Balawaia had heard rumours about a 'Misi Lao' (Mr Lawes) for some time. Then, one day in 1876 Lawes actually brought in the London Missionary Society vessel and landed with Chalmers and a Polynesian helper named Rau. The people shouted 'Maino! Maino!' catching hold of their noses and pointing to their stomachs, perhaps offering a special greeting or perhaps declaiming their own food shortage.[18] They were given gifts of rice and tobacco, which they took to be white ants' eggs and dog's dung; they were also very interested to see Chalmers strike some matches and show off his white arms and chest! Here the element of curiosity was a very strong reason to relate to the newcomers, just as it was, for another case, with the Anglican, Copland King. King was remembered for many years by the people of Sinapa, Collingwood Bay (in the Milne Bay area), for his bicycle riding and his hat, and also, interestingly enough, for the long black coat he wore as 'a mark of respect' when an old chief had just died.[19]

But curiosity did not necessarily last long. When the Polynesian, Rau, returned to the Balawaia, for example, he was forced to use his rifle (which missionaries were advised to take in case of a surprise attack).[20] However, he simply shot it into the air, and soon after was able to make peace with the clan leader by giving him a special cane.[21] Making peace was of critical importance at the time when missionaries began work in a new area. Once the Catholic Mission had established itself on Yule Island, and the missionaries were accepted among the coastal people, three Fathers, including Alain de Bois-menu (later head of the whole Catholic Mission in Papua New Guinea), dared to enter into the mountainous inland country of the Fuyughe people. They soon turned back, however, because a warrior band stole everything from their bags! Some months later, miners took the same path looking for gold and were killed. The administration, naturally not liking this at all, sent officials on a punitive expedition. The missionaries protested because they suspected such an act would affect future relations, especially since the policemen, as was typical, shot the wrong people in reprisal. It was not until 1904 that de Boismenu ventured back to Fuyughe country, and for some mysterious reason which the missionary believed was God's work, the people had no desire for payback, but willingly made peace with the visitors.[22]

What the early missionaries were trying to do

The early missionaries wanted above all to teach the Gospel, and persuade their listeners to live as Christians. Their strongest insistence at the start was that people should live in peace; yet, keeping the peace was far from easy. Groups who were traditional enemies and whose cultures actually depended on head-hunting and ambush as an impetus to group esteem, planting, building, even their art, had every reason to keep on fighting. Sicknesses along the coast, moreover, many of them epidemic and brought by the foreigners, were characteristically ascribed by warring groups to 'someone' not 'something', so that conflict between 'blamers' and 'blamed' continued at an apparently heightened level.[23] Missionaries, often without the help of the administration, tried to stop such skirmishing — as Father Verjus did, for example, when he mediated between two Mekeo groups and planted the cross of peace at 'Jesubaiba' (now the site of a new village), and Father de Boismenu, when he persuaded hostile Fuyughe chiefs to burn their spears in the fire.[24] And sometimes trouble between locals and white men had to be averted. I can think of Ruatoka, a physically weak but very willing little Rarotongan who, with his wife, and Chalmers and other south sea islanders, arrived in 1877. A year after he arrived, he went out with a small band of faithful Motuans to stop a 'great gathering of armed men' from killing some miners. At first the warriors threatened him, but he answered them back very strongly: 'Why do you want to kill me? What have I done?'. According to Chalmers, 'he then reasoned with them, preached to them, prayed for them [presumably he had learnt Motuan well!] and in the end they all dispersed to their homes'.[25]

From this we can see how missionaries seized onto some of the tensest situations to teach new ways. It was all very puzzling, sometimes traumatic for Melanesians. Ruatoka, for instance, actually carried people who were nearly dead to get them help — an act usually avoided by Papuans, for fear that the spirit might afterwards haunt the carrier, if the sick person died. Preaching against unnecessary fears, various bearers of the Gospel dared to enter the 'hideouts' of dangerous place-spirits and emerge unharmed, and even began churches on sacred ground for which the custodial spirits might be expected to fight.[26]

Other missionary activities were more impressive, however, even if sometimes unacceptable — the giving of gifts for instance, including clothes, the building of a church or mission house, and the attempts to gather the people together as a 'new flock.' Admittedly, the missionary message often made no sense or was very worrying: 'Who is this Jesus from a far away land or up in the heavens above?' 'Why should we feel so ashamed of ourselves?' 'How is it that we have done so much evil that we need to be saved through the death of a man who died a nasty death on a cross?'[27] Thus, were not the missionaries also harbourers of unnecessary fears? Some peoples, however, found the new ideas very congenial and intelligible. Roro informants will tell you that their forebears responded to the new teachers by declaring that they already had God (*Riripi*), and also knew Jesus (*Oarove*), who was miraculously born long, long ago in the bundle of wood carried by a deeply respected woman.[28] Around Madang, to take another case, there had also been a belief in a creator god, but there it was especially the teaching that Jesus would come again which was attractive, tying in with an expectation that one of the culture heroes (either Manup or Kilibob) would someday return.[29] In general, as the literature almost boundlessly attests, the tone of the early missionaries was one of love (albeit usually coated with paternalism) and hope, rather than sombre threat.

Some problems brought by the early missionaries

Because the missionaries expected great changes, they posed many problems for peoples who followed the traditional way of life. It would be useful to list some of these problems.

When a village received a missionary or even became Christian, it could incur the jealousy and anger of more powerful neighbours. Surprise attacks could result, then, and missionaries generally tried to persuade the victimized village against taking payback measures. The converted coastal and fishing-oriented village of Hula suffered in this respect in 1881, when twelve persons, including mission teachers, were killed in a raid from the larger, agriculturalist village of Kalo. On this occasion the British navy took retributive measures, and only after two generations had passed did Kalo's proud traditionalism succumb to pressure from Hula and other Christianized settlements.[30]

Problems also arose in numerous places where it was only individuals or families who became Christians and these people were in danger of becoming outcasts in their own society. Flierl's work around Simbang suffered in this respect, as did the whole Lutheran enterprise in fact, including the Neuendettelsau Mission (which sponsored Flierl) and the German government-backed Rhenish Mission. It was not until the coming of Christian Keysser, who concentrated on gaining access to a given society as a whole, through the chiefs, that significant numbers turned to the new faith.[31]

There were problems associated with the missionaries' style of life, too. Their houses, commonly very large, were often built away from the village; they sometimes lived in a manner quite luxurious in comparison to the villagers. Some of the missionaries, moreover, refused to eat with the people and usually had access to European-type food. Their wives, brought up with Victorian scruples about cleanliness, found it hard adapting to the dirt and grease, occasions naturally arising when they would rush off and wash after shaking many of the villagers' hands — these pioneer wives came to constitute a very impressive group, nonetheless.[32]

Problems occurred too, when missionaries frequently insisted on rather drastic changes in the people's customs. Not only did they prefer people to be clean and clothed, for example, but they were usually very strict on certain points of personal morality, such as monogamy, homosexuality and pre-marital intercourse. The old festivities and dances, moreover, connected as they typically were with the veneration of ancestors and the hopes of future fertility, were worrying to the missionaries, although attitudes varied. With the London Missionary Society along the Papuan coast, the south sea islanders succeeded in introducing Polynesian dances and prophet songs as expressions of Christianity; with the Catholics and (to a lesser extent) the Anglicans by comparision, there was more concern to preserve as much of the original dancing as possible, whilst re-orienting the people's values and outlook at the same time.

In the early interaction between missionaries and people, then, the Papua New Guinean response was naturally a mixed one. It took time for people to sort out what the issues were, to separate Christian beliefs from the strangers who brought them, even to love these strangers who were prepared to lose their lives just to bring 'good news'. It took time, as we shall see, for the new-born churches to grow, and for the message to be taken through the impenetrable jungles and across the extraordinary ruggedness of the New Guinea mainland.

Spheres of influence

By the year 1890 the missions of the larger Christian denominations of Western Europe had gained a promising foothold on the coasts of Papua New Guinea. In the earliest phase, significantly, each denomination started work in separate areas so that their efforts did not double up or openly compete. Such matters were geographically relative, however, and there was a competitive aspect to mission activity nevertheless. Other areas missionized from the sixteenth and nineteenth centuries — the Americas, southern Africa, parts of China, for instance — often witnessed an unhealthy conflict between Christian groups, either because of serious differences of opinion over the nature and faith of the church or because missionaries in a given area were from different nations, which had competing imperial pretensions. If many have come to think of present-day Papua New Guinea as a country blessed by effective cooperation between most church groups, such a clash of opinions and interests has still affected the whole Melanesian scene historically. Before the Second World War there was certainly a mutual animosity between Catholic missionaries (with their acceptance of the Pope's authority, and their pre-dominantly central European background) and the Protestants (with their insistence that the Bible was the sole repository of faith, and their decidedly Anglo-Saxon heritage)[33] — a typical carry-over from a longstanding dispute going back to the time of the Reformation. When, in 1890, different denomi-nations were settling into their chosen areas, the possibility of conflict and unbecoming rivalry had to be handled politically. The British administrator, Sir William McGregor, believed this problem could be avoided (at least in Papua, for New Guinea was under German control until 1914). He encour-aged key representatives from the Papuan missions to come to a 'gentlemen's agreement' as to their 'spheres of influence'. Even though the Roman Catholics sent no one to his 1890 conference, it was soon to be widely accepted that the Methodists were to take the Louisiade and D'Entrecasteaux Islands and a small portion of the mainland; the Anglicans, the north coast; and the London Missionary Society, the south coast excluding those parts already taken by the Catholics.[34] This arrangement, together with area divisions worked out in the course of events by Lutherans, Catholics and Methodists in German New Guinea and the New Guinea islands, has greatly determined the general territorial influence of the greater missions as it reveals itself on a modern map of religious affiliation in Papua New Guinea (see map 3).

Between 1890 and 1940 (the Second World War), of course, other entrants into the new mission fields of Papua New Guinea appeared. The Seventh Day Adventists, after pressing for a suitable area from 1908 on, eventually circumvented the 'spheres of influence' policy to begin work amongst the Koiari, inland from the London Missionary Society-dominated Moresby area, and had established as many as 101 stations in the country by 1940.[35] The Unevangelized Fields Mission[36] braved the jungles of the West-ern District (from 1932 on). When the central highlands were opened up in the 1930s, the regions which seemed to call out for the Gospel were so many and vast that still more Christian groups were to be enticed, though only Catholics and Lutherans made any inroads (on the north-eastern and far eastern fringes) before the Second World War.

The missions at work between the wars

A case study: Father Jules Dubuy

Rather than attempting to cover all the many developments in the history of missions, from the time of McGregor to the Japanese invasion, it is probably more useful to take, as an example, an interesting missionary from this period, examine his labours in some detail and discuss the interaction between this man and the people he was trying to evangelize. Our figure is Father Jules Dubuy, missionary of the Sacred Heart (Catholic) Order, who was sent to live in Fuyughe country in the Papuan mountains. Father Dubuy is a suitable choice, both because too little has been written about him (although there is a French film about his activities) and because his experiences and activities, successes and failures, are of great fascination.[37]

A Frenchman from Provence, Dubuy came to the hill village of Ononghe (about 15 miles, or 24 km, from present-day Woitape) and founded a station nearby in August 1913. He died at the same place almost forty years later, in 1952. To visit Ononghe today is a breathtaking experience. The station overlooks a network of great, deep, even awesome valleys, which seem to cut their way through majestic, steep-sided mountains. In and around this place Dubuy spent most of his working life, both building up the mission and encouraging people to associate with it. The task proved very difficult, but he was a man of remarkable energy. First, he had to master the local language and begin communicating as best he could with the people. Along the deep valleys each Fuyughe tribal group was separated into their strategically located mini-regions and, although neighbouring groups traded, their members were reluctant to travel outside their own valley or outside the confined sphere of protector spirits. These groups were constantly in conflict with each other over thefts of women and pigs, and payback killings followed; Dubuy noted, too, that cannibalism was practised not far from Ononghe, apparently on the bodies of enemies. The missionary had to devise means of relating to these tough folk who enjoyed a good battle, and who dwelt and gardened in such perilously steep places; the tribespeople themselves, who had apparently received news of a 'special kind of white man [or being]', were waiting — partly in hope, yet probably mostly in suspicion, to see what moves he would make.

In general terms, the Fuyughe saw Dubuy as a man who was not afraid to wander through places associated with enemy groups or spirits or tabu objects, which they themselves had worried about. As a matter of policy, Dubuy (and then those who were sent to help him) walked through the valleys surrounding Ononghe once or twice a year, and in 1926 he dared to venture into 'unexplored' territory to make contact with tribes little known to the administration. Again, Dubuy showed himself to be quite different from other white men who entered the area. As early as 1916, for instance, government patrol officers burned down two big Fuyughe villages in an effort to stop fighting; Dubuy, by contrast, was not a man of violent reaction. Actually his own house and the station were accidentally burnt to the ground by a bushfire a year later and, like the locals themselves, he was forced to start building all over again. He emerged as a man of peace and resilience. And Dubuy was very practical. Unlike government officials (the *kiaps*), whose tasks mainly consisted of giving orders to clean up dirty villages or of arresting those who broke the administration's laws, the Father built things which he suggested would better local conditions, often rubbing shoulders with tribes-men to reveal a new world of techniques and activities. He built a sawmill run by water because electricity was lacking; wood was sawn into building planks and then taken off to the station in small Merovingian-looking carts with strong wooden wheels made at the mill. In addition to an imposing church and other mission houses, a wood-working centre was erected, and a school. In the wood-working centre young men were invited to come to learn how to cut and build with planks, with a view to making more permanent houses and furniture. In the school Dubuy and his helpers taught children sent by those parents who were interested in what the mission had to offer. The education, of course, was mostly about the Catholic faith, and the Father had hopes that, from among a few of the older ones who desired to become Christians and among his young educated group, he would draw out his first cluster of catechists. By 1929 there were twenty-nine auxiliary catechists, who took a few prayers in the mornings and evenings in the villages. One distinct disadvantage for him was that the sons of chiefs were not sent to the school. This was owing to the belief that, as the *utam* (or what we might describe as a kind of 'Platonic form') of their society, a member of the primogenitive chiefly lineage would incur a cosmic catastrophe if he walked outside his own tribal territory.[38] Yet the eastern Fuyughe came more and more under the mission-ary's new influence; those of their own blood and background relayed to the villages the likes and dislikes of the Christian teacher, encouraged their number to respond to the distant cowhorn that called them from the hilltop to Sacrament on Sundays, and made them aware, as their knowledge of the outside would widen, of objects, changes, improvements, and benefits beyond their wildest imaginings.

1930 was the one year Dubuy spent away from Ononghe, when he sailed home to France. On his return he brought with him 16 tons of cargo for the mission and, because no one was prepared to land it on the Papuan mainland, he sent for help from Fuyughe country; hundreds of strong men and youths then trekked over 40 miles (64 km) to the coast and carried the goods in procession back home. Among the more notable items he brought were slide pictures of the Bible stories, to be shown through a lens which caught the rays of the sun, and also probably the first movie projector ever brought to Papua New Guinea — a hand-operated one. Dubuy believed that his message would only be grasped in a non-literate community through visual aids; certainly, many people came to sit in the darkness of his special picture showroom, set up inside the roof of his house. He had also brought a very large mechanical clock to chime each hour from the church bell-tower; but, more significantly, he brought picks and shovels and other road-making equipment, too. Amongst the Fuyughe, 'Dubuy' is a byword as far as road-engineering is concerned: the long and winding 'Dubuy trail' is still the only effective road link between the Papuan highlands and the outside world. By hard work and much persuasion over many years, Dubuy and his best known companion,

Father Alphons Bohn (who came in 1933), convinced the people that gentle sloping roads around the edges of the valleys would be even more useful than their mountain tracks, which required a sure foot and strong constitution! Now, miles and miles of horse trails run through the area, allowing for trade and reasonable contact by the administration, as well as access to Moresby.

Father Dubuy, then, combined worship and teaching with many practical exercises, and a person of such energy was bound to have a considerable impact. An honest assessment still has to be made, however, and Dubuy himself would be the first to admit both that the formation of a new Christian community was hard going and that he made many mistakes. Contact between missionaries and the many villages could not be everyday and constant and the mission, although very important to the people, still seemed to them to be a separate, outside influence, generally without as powerful a pull on their lives as their traditional beliefs and practices. The Fuyughe had their special feast times, when some of the most dramatic dancing and singing in Papua New Guinea were performed. Before each important ceremony, which was centred around some point in the human life cycle, concentrated work was necessary to harvest the gardens and prepare the *sing sing* ground; if such work had to be done on a Sunday, church was temporarily forgotten.[39]

Dubuy, moreover, had a fascinating competitor — a man who emerged to prominence in a valley on the outskirts of mission influence. This was Ona Asi, an interesting figure for the development of his ideas (which we looked at earlier) and whose biography I have recounted elsewhere.[40] Ona Asi was remarkable, too, for his oracular presages of future change when possessed by the snake spirit 'Bilalaf', and doughty in his effort to reinforce the threatened traditions of the Fuyughe. He introduced ritual techniques to enhance the fertility of the pigs and gardens, and developed a cause to keep his fellows from contact with the whites (on the pretext that a cosmic upheaval would result). He was held to be a 'super-man' of great, mysterious powers both at feast times and in cultic situations he organized within various outlying villages. He was also not afraid to learn a thing or two from the missionaries in an occasional conference, if only to confirm to his peers that he had access to powers which could match those of the outsiders.

The very existence of the Catholic Mission among the Fuyughe also brought increasing local interest in the acquisition of European items, which were symbolic of a new time and realm of power. Like most pre-war white men, however, Dubuy lived in a house apart from the hamlets, ate from a table rarely graced with the presence of local people, and his food came from the virtually self-sufficient mission farm he supervised — home-made bread baked by the sisters, vegetables from a well-cultivated patch, milk and meat from a herd of imported cattle. The white man's life was a very distinct one; to the people he seemed to have not only the 'secret' of a new way of looking at the world[41] but also an unfathomable access to foods and cargoes quite beyond the ken of the local people. It was natural, then, that many of the local people, who still felt strongly about the continuance of their group's material welfare and about the spiritual forces believed to sustain it, looked to the mission simply as another way of securing their survival or of obtaining extra material benefits which could bring prestige. It was one thing if the administration could recruit people to be policemen or carriers for these motives, but when people joined the church for 'materialistic' or not 'genuinely spiritual' reasons, the missionary began to wonder whether he had succeeded in creating a new Christian community after all.

Pre-war mission work more generally

Father Dubuy's situation, with all the complex interaction between two types of people and cultures it involved, each with two differing sets of expectations about life, provides a good picture of what the pre-war mission scene was like as a whole. From this, then, some important aspects of pre-war mission activities can be picked out.

Firstly, it is important to appreciate the difficulties of communication and travel during this period. The network of air-links for which Papua New Guinea is now quite famous existed only minimally before the war.[42] Travel to and from the country was almost exclusively by ship; within the land itself, by foot or horse. Missions had to have their own sea-going vessels, of course, to bring goods and messages from the outside world to outposts, and to reach untouched fields. The Anglicans were in very special need of good boats, because their main centre, Dogura (Milne Bay) was so far removed from any up-and-coming township.[43] And rare indeed was it to find missionaries in cars! In the late 1930s, as an example, we find the Roman Catholic bishop, de Boismenu, using what was the nearest thing to a four-wheel drive vehicle — perhaps the first in this country — a car with its back wheels like a tractor's.[44] On the whole, then, communication between areas was very poor, travelling time was long and frequently dangerous, and radio links were more than often inadequate.

Then, there was the question of language. When missionaries began their work they were expected to learn the tongue of the people to whom they ministered. In hours they could spare, many of them translated the Bible into local languages, reading from these translations in church and in discussion. Matters began to get very complicated, though, when newcomers found that numerous different languages were spoken in relatively confined areas. When planning to expand their work, they knew that they could not master all the languages around them, and they also realized that local peoples who formerly had no real contact needed to be able to talk readily to each other. Existing trade languages, then, or else the languages which the missionaries first learned, were encouraged as a means of inter-regional communication. Both the London Missionary Society and the Papuan administration made much use of elementary Motu (which was distinct from but had its precedent in a trade language from the *Hiri* trade cycle); the Anglicans chose the simple and rather beautiful Wedau tongue as a 'common denominator' around their central station; similarly, the Lutherans in New Guinea employed the Kote and Yabim languages as they expanded on and around the Huon Peninsula, up the Markham Valley and on into the highlands.[45] Such developments, as well as the growth of pidgin English,[46] were of preparatory importance for a united nationhood.

It should not be forgotten, either, how missionaries in Papua New Guinea often turned out to be explorers, that is, they ventured into un-mapped territory. But no matter which names we think of — whether or not they are as well known as the London Missionary Society pastor, Bert Brown, who challenged the bush trails inland from Toaripi country (1941),[47] or the Divine Word missionary, Father Schaefer, who trekked down the gorge of the Chimbu River (1933) — it must be stressed that such men were taken or accompanied into new areas by helpful and courageous Papua New Guineans. 'Some of our wives are of a people who live over these mountains', Bundi warriors (Madang highlands) told Schaefer as they pointed to the south. 'There is a grassland valley there and many, many people. We go over and visit and trade with them. The tracks are not bad. We can take you and with us you can travel safely.'[48] Such words are a tell-tale sign of how important the Melanesians themselves were in the spread of Christianity.

Keeping the church going often was difficult. Like Dubuy, missionaries in general strove to train catechists — that is, converted people who could take the Gospel to the villagers. They relied heavily on faithful men and women who could establish and maintain friendly relations with surrounding villages, who were patient enough to learn the missionary's language and to teach the local one, and who were brave enough to turn Christian. Then again, the newcomers were likely to fall sick in the fever-ridden jungles and swamps. Percy Chatterton, writing on the history of the Roro village of Delena, noted 'the continued high rate of death and sickness among the Polynesian pastors'. In this kind of difficult situation, a handful of people kept the church alive, but it was hard doing so because traditional belief so often had it that men died on account of some evil they had done, or because they were overcome by a sorcery more powerful than their own.[49]

Education was also an important aspect of missionary activity. As with Dubuy, missionaries almost always concerned themselves with elementary education and sometimes with the teaching of certain practical skills. Schools were usually conducted in English or the European language of the missionary and had a strongly religious bias. There was an unfortunate tendency to believe that the schooling appropriate to Western civilization could be trans-planted with ease, as if Papua New Guinean children already knew of pens and inkpots, and ought to learn about how to buy sausages at the shops.[50] But much was learned by *both* 'stranger' and 'native' in their interaction, even though the white teachers usually convinced themselves that they were by far the superior beings in the exchange. It was undoubtedly through the education of the young that missionaries and their supporters were most distinctly the agents of cultural and social change;[51] by 1939, it should be noted, 95 per cent of Papua New Guinea education was in their hands.

Concerning the teaching of practical skills, we may note that Dubuy was not alone in this: a mission much more famous in this connection was Kwato in the Milne Bay district of Papua, under the London Missionary Society missionary, Charles Abel. Abel believed in the fostering of industrial as well as spiritual life in Papua New Guinea; from 1900 on, he put a case to the London Missionary Society to accept his ideas on the creation of an industrial mission at Kwato, which concentrated on the teaching of carpentry, house construction, boat-building and furniture-making. Although winning over almost all of his missionary colleagues working in Papua, financial support from the Society in London was withdrawn in 1911, and Abel was forced to carry on as head of an independent mission.[52]

Relations between missions and the administration were often complex. By and large, the Australian government (1914–40) relied very heavily on the missionaries for information about the peoples under its control and for support in securing obedience to the colonial administration and its laws. Just as schooling was one medium for inculcating a new conformity, another lay with health measures — 85 per cent of medical facilities also being mission-run by 1939. As we have already indicated, secular authorities and churches did not always appreciate each other. Government personnel often resented the independent influence of missions, and tension could easily brew between proponents of 'love and mercy' and those (including settlers) who considered the natives needed to be taught lessons by brute force.

Finally, it can be seen that, by 1940, the missions had had a powerful impact on the lives of Papua New Guineans. The old religious beliefs and practices had either been driven 'underground' or seriously modified in missionized areas. More and more, men and women looked to the Christian missions as a new source of spiritual and personal inspiration, either as a means of widening their narrow horizons or of improving their lot, socially and economically. Many became very dependent on the missions for their future — perhaps too dependent, as in the case of Kwato (for prospective young businessmen had to rely too heavily from the start on mission backing[53]). The programmes of the missions, nevertheless, created the possibility of a new kind of leadership in the country as a whole — as pastor or evangelist, as medical officer or government official.[54]

Reflecting on all these developments, though, one has to be realistic about the nature of Christian influences. Many people turned along a new path, for example, because there seemed to be no other meaningful alternative. How could one turn one's back on 'the white man', who not only brought 'the true God' but also possessed such extraordinary things — from iron axes to aeroplanes? The situation in Papua New Guinea, too, could lead to many misunderstandings, and to the joining of a church for 'wrong reasons'. Men could associate Christianity so strongly with Western technology (as they 'arrived' simultaneously) and imagine the former to be the ritualistic means of procuring cargo. They could listen freely to the Christian message and yet take it back to their village as one set of beliefs to be curiously mixed up with their own traditional ones. And, in addition to such 'cargo cultists' and 'syncretists',[55] who usually had their vital leaders, there were other movements — led by men like Ona Asi — to preserve and revitalize their old ways. Most others, however, over time and through experience — by living ten thousand years in a lifetime, as Albert Maori Kiki expressed it — came to grasp the special uniqueness and universality of the Christian message for what it was, even if inevitably interpreting it through their cultural lenses.

Opening up the central highlands

As already indicated, missionaries entered the central highlands in the 1930s. After Schaefer's journey down the Chimbu River in 1933, the renowned Canadian, Father William Ross, established the Catholic mission at Mount Hagen during the following year.[56] At this time, too, the first Lutheran expeditions were being made into the same western highlands region. A whole new missionary frontier had emerged again; a whole new cycle of peacemakings, of struggles to learn different languages, of complex interactions and misunderstandings, of exhilarations and tragedies, had once more been set in motion. And then, very unexpectedly, and for such an 'untouched' country, most incongruously, came the terrors of the Second World War.

Missions and churches in Papua New Guinea: from wartime to the present

The Japanese invasion along the northern coasts and outlying islands of New Guinea brought death and property destruction in its wake. Many mission personnel were evacuated in good time; yet, many, both with and without Australian citizenship, chose to remain in the field. The years of Japanese control (1942–45) thus inevitably brought martyrdom and other unfortunate deaths.[57] The ordeal was felt sorely by the rank and file of the churches, who had to manage without the expatriate guidance upon which they had been dependent. That straitening, however, was in itself healthy, and out of the fire shone Melanesian martyrs and inspiring heroes who were to lay the basis for great indigenous involvement in church life in the years ahead.[58] Not that the war brought less confusion. Some villages were happy to go over to the Japanese in reaction to Australian overlordship, only to find themselves under suspicion at the end of the war. Whether loyal to the Japanese or not, some villages were also bombed flat (because of the Allied 'scorched earth' policy) if the enemy was thought to be using them. And both the horrendous effects of armaments and the huge quantities of armed servicemen and their instruments of power were astounding sights, from which local prophetic visions of 'coming Cargo' would gain more credence.

Since the war Christian influences have widened and strengthened. In 1947, for example, the great Wahgi Valley of the central highlands was again made accessible to the missions, thus ending the enforced period of pacification often referred to by the local people as *Jim Tela* (Patrol Officer Jim Taylor's 'Rule', c.1935–46).[59] The most populous region in Melanesia, the highlands, became attractive to settlers and missionaries alike. At first it had been a highly dangerous zone, in which only a few white 'soul-savers' were willing to risk their necks, and various indigenous and coastal evangelists — such as Yabim Lutherans in the eastern highlands, and Gogodala representatives of the Unevangelized Fields Mission in the southern highlands — prepared to eke out a precarious existence among hostile tribes.[60] But, as plantations came to be established, small towns grew up around government outposts, and roads were built, a hundred-and-one minor missionary organizations rivalled the usual 'mainline' churches in bringing 'salvation to the lost'. In 1962, when an Australian official shot a starter gun to open up newly gazetted land at Porgera in Enga country (then the western highlands), missionaries actually ran off as competitors for the best station sites.[61] By the early 1970s, furthermore, the eastern highlands had all the appearances of being the most missionized province on earth — over eighty Christian denominations and sects of one sort or another being represented there. And, in the more recently contacted southern highlands, the presence of too many missions brought allegations not only of confusion (even serious psychological problems) but also of a clever playing-off of one mission against another by power-broker bigmen.[62]

Papua New Guinea has been specially vulnerable to 'mission pluralism', making it very difficult to write the recent religious history of certain areas (including the Sepik, along with the highlands). Not only that, beyond Papua New Guinea itself there have been other less well known missions which have been active further afield, including: the Presbyterian Mission on Vanuatu; the South Sea Evangelical Mission on the Solomons (especially Malaita), which traces its history back to the Queensland Kanaka Mission of the 1880s; the Church of Christ in Espiritu Santo; various Baptist and evangelical groups in central Irian Jaya. The South Sea Evangelicals, various Baptist missions, as well as Brethren and Pentecostalist ventures, are also part of the current Papua New Guinea scene.[63]

The scene is also complicated by the special unities and divisions that have emerged in the major churches since the 1960s, and by the development of new bodies that co-ordinate the work of both large and smaller missions in effective ways, as the following examples will show. In 1963 the London Missionary Society and Methodist work in Papua was combined in the *Papua*

Ekalesia, and then again in 1968 into the United Church of Papua New Guinea and the Solomon Islands, thus incorporating the Methodists from New Britain to New Georgia.[64] Still earlier, in 1956, the Evangelical Lutheran Church of New Guinea was born; yet, the New Guinea Lutheran *Mission* was still in operation even if at a greatly reduced scale and in 'frontier-type' areas. Back in 1948, moreover, what was then called the New Guinea Lutheran *Mission* established itself in the Enga region and produced what is now called the Wabag Lutheran Church[65] — a venture derived from the Missouri Lutheran Synod in the United States of America. Although the Wabag Church has generally cooperated strongly with the Evangelical Lutheran Church of New Guinea, it is a separate entity. Their relations were, however, somewhat complicated as a result of a heated debate at Concordia Theological Seminary, Missouri Synod (in the United States), when there was a split between more conservative and more liberal approaches to the Christian faith, but the turmoil in this world-famous seminary has not destroyed Lutheran unity elsewhere. Conservatism in this context, incidentally, mainly means a literalist or fundamentalist approach to the Bible, that is, the belief that the Scriptures, as the holy word of God, are inerrant, and to be confirmed as faultless by Bible scholars or students.

A comparable theological conservatism, to proceed with the complex religious history of modern Papua New Guinea, is shared by many of the sectarian Protestant groups missionizing in the country. This is why a number of such groups have become affiliated with what is called the Evangelical Alliance, with its headquarters and training centre at Banz (in the Western Highlands Province).[66] The biggest component of this Alliance is a variety of Baptist missions, who have for long insisted on the baptism of adults by full immersion, and who claim that the baptism of infants is nowhere mentioned in the New Testament. The major churches (or missions) — that is, all those with the longest history in Melanesia (except the Seventh Day Adventists and the Unevangelized Fields Mission [now Evangelical Church of Papua]) — have become affiliated with the Melanesian Council of Churches and related organizations. These churches, which have very big seminary institutions in the country, have come to adopt a stance of liberal tolerance toward each other, and one of open dialogue and living relations, even though they have tended to rate the Melanesian Council of Churches as rather secondary on their agenda. The Salvation Army, a relative latecomer, is also a prominent member of the Melanesian Council of Churches. Still another, if smaller, exercise in organizational cooperation is the Pentecostal Alliance, making its presence felt in the 1980s to further the shared spiritual interests of those groups (such as the Assemblies of God, Four Square Gospel Mission, to name two better known ones) which emphasize the gifts of the Holy Spirit (speaking tongues, healing, prophecy, and so on).

Another aspect of the complexity, of course, is the very scale of church life and its influence in Melanesia since the war, especially in the socio-

economic development of the Melanesian region. The churches have made
their impact in so many areas: education, health services, transport services
(shipping and air), the translation of languages (note the Summer School of
Linguistics), printing, plantations, stores (for example, NAMASU), and
many urban organizations serving special needs, including needs at the
University of Papua New Guinea.[67] The background influence of the churches
in national politics is undeniable. Most of Papua New Guinea's national
leaders owe their education to the churches, and some members of parliament
have sought to represent religious interests in the House because of its
importance at the village level and in their constituencies.

NOTES

Chapter 6 is based on material originally contributed to University of Papua New Guinea
Extension Studies booklets.

1 F. Hezel, *The first taint of civilization* (Pacific Islands monograph Ser. 1), Honolulu, 1983,
ch. 1.
2 C. Jack Hinton, *The search for the Islands of Solomon, 1567–1838*, Oxford, 1969; O. H. K.
Spate, *The Spanish lake*, Canberra, 1979, cf. H. Jacobs (ed.), *Documenta Malucensia I*
(Monumenta historica Societatis Iesu 109: monumenta Missionum Societatis Iesu 32), Rome,
1974.
3 J. L. Whittaker, N. G. Gash, J. F. Hookey and R. J. Lacey (eds), *Documents and readings in*
New Guinea history: prehistory to 1889, Brisbane, 1975, pp.207–208, cf. 188–90; Lacey,
'Journeys of transformation' in Trompf (ed.), *Cargo Cults and Millenarian Movements*, ch. 4.
4 For background, e.g. W. P. Morrell, *The great powers in the Pacific* (Historical Association
gen. ser. 54), London, 1963; S. Neill, *Christian missions* (Pelican history of the Church 6),
Harmondsworth, 1964, s.v. 'Pacific Ocean' et passim.
5 cf. Trompf, 'The coming of expatriates to Melanesia', in Trompf (ed.), *Mel. and Judaeo-*
Christ. Relig. Trads, bk 1, pp.105–10 for a simple introduction; cf. J. Griffin, H. Nelson
and S. Firth, *Papua New Guinea: a political history*, Melbourne, 1979, ch. 1. For a detailed
study of the social background and predispositions of missionaries (to Papua), D. Langmore, *Missionary Lives; Papua 1874–1914*, (Pacific Islands Monograph Ser. 6), Honolulu,
1989.
6 The Old/New time distinction used in this book has been suggested by a reading of F.
Tomasetti, *Traditionen und Christentum im Chimbu-Gebiet Neuguineas* (Arbeiten aus dem
Seminar für Volkerkunde der J. W. Goethe-Universität 6), Weisbaden, 1976.
7 On Fiji, J. Garrett, *To Live among the stars: Christian origins in Oceania*, Geneva and Suva,
1982, pp.102–105. The London Missionary Society (LMS) was formed in 1795 by British
Congregationalists, Anglicans, Presbyterians and Methodists to promote Christian missions. Quakers were also involved. On Polynesians farther afield, S. Latukefu, R. Sinclair et
al., *Polynesian missions in Melanesia*, Suva, 1982. The term 'Melanesia' ('Black Islands') is
attributed to the French savant Charles de Brosses.
8 Garrett, *To Live*, pp.167, 172, 189–90.
9 On the Germans Ottow and Geissler, see *Die Biene auf dem Missionsfelde*, esp. No. 9, 1861,
pp.82ff., cf. F. C. Kamma, '*Dit wonderlijke werk*', Oegstgeest, 1977, vol. 1, pp.73ff; and on
Ambonese LMS workers, cf., e.g., *Atlas van der terreinen der Protestantsche Zending in*
Nederlandsch Oost- en West- Indie [Amsterdam?], 1937, p.17.
10 D. Hilliard, *God's gentleman; a history of the Melanesian Mission, 1849–1942*, Brisbane,
1978, chs 1–3; cf. H. Laracy, *Marists and Melanesians; a history of Catholic Missions to the*
Solomon Islands, Canberra, 1976, ch. 2.
11 See ibid., pp.22ff; cf. OT: D. Affleck, 1974.
12 e.g., OT: Jojoga Opeba 1973 (for the Orokaiva); M. Young, *Magicians of Manumanua*,
Berkeley, Los Angeles and London, 1983, p.93 (for the Massim).

13 cf., e.g., A. Valtierra, *Peter Claver: saint of the slaves* (trans. J. H. Petty and L. J. Woodward), London, 1960; W. L. Doughty, *John Wesley: preacher*, London, 1955, ch. 2. For methodological background on writing the history of missions, e.g., E. J. Sharpe, 'Reflections on Missionary Historiography', *International Bulletin of Missionary Research*, 13/2 (1989), pp.76–81.

14 See R. Lovett, *James Chalmers, his autobiography and letters*, London, 1912 edn, pp.21–22, 26–27, 29. Note also F. M. Hitchen, 'Training Tamate'; formation of the nineteenth century world view: the case of James Chalmers (doctoral dissert., University of Aberdeen 1984), chs 2–3.

15 See J. Flierl, *Forty-Five years in New Guinea*, Lightpass, 1931 edn, p.29 on the early missionaries (Schiedt and Boesch); and G. Fughmann, The history of the Lutheran Churches in New Guinea (roneoed, Melanesian Institute–Christian Institute of Missions, Alexishafen, 1972), p.1 on absconders. From 1884 the German New Guinea Company began its plantations in the region, first on the Gazelle Peninsula and then around Madang.

16 See D. G. Pilhofer, *Die Geschichte der Neuendettelsauer Mission in Neuguinea*, Neuendettelsau, 1961, vol. 1, pp.69–72; cf. Flierl, *Christ in New Guinea*, Tanunda, 1932, pp.7–9.

17 Flierl, *Forty-Five Years*, p.30.

18 John Kolia, Encounter at Gabuli Beach (mimeographed chapter for a forthcoming book on Encounters); cf. his *History of the Balawaia*, Port Moresby, 1976, ch. 5.

19 See A. K. Chignell, *An Outpost in Papua*, London, 1911, p.19.

20 For the death of the LMS South Sea missionary Tauraki and his son in similar circumstances (and he refused to use his rifle), see B. Jinks, P. Biskup and H. Nelson, *Readings in New Guinea history*, Sydney, 1973, pp.26–27.

21 All this was remembered by Bai Livana at Tauruba for John Kolia (OT: 1971).

22 See A. Dupeyrat, *Briseurs de lance chez les Papous*, Paris, 1964, pp.41–42.

23 See e.g., Burridge, *Mambu*, pp.122–23 on the Tangu people, near Bogia (Madang Province).

24 Fieldnotes 1974, regarding Verjus; see also R. P. A. Cadoux, *L'apôtre des Papous; Mgr Henri Verjus*, Paris, 1931, p.194; and see Dupeyrat, *Briseurs*, p.48 on de Boismenu.

25 See Chalmers in Lovett, *James Chalmers*, p.134.

26 ibid., p.135, on Ruatoka; N. E. Crutwell, 'A Bishop in "Shangri-la"', in *New Guinea Mission*, London, 1952, pp.3–6 (for an Anglican example of building on a sacred site in Daga country). Some conversions in Methodist country occurred after the missionary pointed out that yams could be grown in places where they were never planted before. e.g., among the Massim, D. Wetherell, *Reluctant mission*, Brisbane, 1977, p.168.

27 For many Papua New Guineans a hideous death is either a sign of punishment from the spirits or gods, or else a sign that one's spirit will be of the restless, haunting, dangerous kind. cf. chaps 2–3.

28 OT: Oa Aitsi of Waima village to Miria Ume, 1974.

29 See Lawrence, *Road*, pp.93ff., etc.

30 N. Oram, 'Towards a study of the London Missionary Society in Hula 1875–1968', in Trompf (ed.), *Mel. Judaeo-Christ. Relig. Trads*, p.123.

31 See esp. G. F. Vicedom, *Church and people in New Guinea*, London, 1961, pp.11ff., etc, and Keysser, *Eine Papuagemeinde*, Neuendettelsau, 1929, pp.68ff; cf. W. Fugmann (ed.), *Christian Keysser*, Stuttgart, 1985 (currently being translated into English, together with a selection of his other missiological works, by M. Wohlwill), and on the Rhenish Mission, 'Colonial movement and politics, business and Christian missionaries under colonial rule: the Rhenish Mission in New Guinea', in S. Latukefu (ed.), *Papua New Guinea: a century of colonial impact*, pp.203ff.

32 e.g., Oram, 'London Missionary Society', pp.125ff.

33 That is, Anglicans, Lutherans, Methodists and, of course, the LMS — combining Presbyterian, Independent and Quaker elements as well as Methodist and Anglican.

34 See British New Guinea, *Annual Report*, 1889–90, p.19.

35 See N. Lutton, 'Murray and the spheres of influence', in *Select topics in the history of Papua New Guinea* (ed. H. Nelson, N. Lutton and S. Robertson), Port Moresby, n.d. [1970?], pp.2–4.

36 A non-denominational 'faith mission' founded in London in 1931.

37 Most of the evidence for what follows derives from my own fieldwork in 1974, discussions with Fathers Gremaud and Barthes at Ononghe, and Bohn at Woitape, an examination of church records at Ononghe and patrol reports in the PNG Archives, as well as other writings, such as Dubuy's 'The Relations between Religion and Morality among the Ononghe Tribes of British New Guinea', *Primitive Mankind*, 4, (1931), pp.29ff. cf. also my '"Bilalaf"' in Trompf (ed.), *Prophets*, pp.30–35, 39, 41, 46, etc; Delbos, *Cent ans chez les Papous. Mission accomplie?*, Issoudun, 1984, pp.152–57 (now trans. by T. Aerts as *The mustard seed. From a French mission to a Papuan church*, Port Moresby, 1985).

38 cf. J. H. P. Murray, 'The *Utame* of Mafulu; interesting investigations by missionaries of the Sacred Heart', in *Papuan Annual Report*, 1937–38, pp.33–34, etc.

39 cf. esp. A. Dupeyrat, *Festive Papua* (trans. E. de Mauny), London, 1955, esp. chs 4–5.

40 '"Bilalaf"', pp.17ff, and cf. ch. 2 above.

41 Christian teachings about God as the creator of all things and the Father of all mankind are important considerations here.

42 Pre-war airstrips include Moresby, Lae, Salamaua, Rabaul and those in the Morobe Province goldfields (all built in the 1920s) and a few pioneering ones in the Highlands (1930s).

43 At the turn of the century the Anglican bishop, Newton, brought rice to famine-stricken Dogura by sailing to Cooktown, Queensland and back!

44 Photographs can be found in the de Boismenu Photographic Collection (ed. Trompf), New Guinea Collection, UPNG.

45 On Motu, T. Dutton, 'Language and trade in central south-east Papua', *Mankind* 11 (1978), pp.341ff; cf. Dutton (ed.), *The Hiri in history*. Note that some impressive linguistic works came out of the use of *lingae francae*; cf., e.g., O. Dempwolff, *Grammatik der Jabêm-Sprache auf Neuguinea* (Hansische Universität Abhandlungen aus dem Gebiet der Auslandkunde 50/2), Hamburg, 1939; H. Zahn, *Lehrbuch der Jabêmsprache* (Beihefte zur Zeitschrift Eingeborenen-Sprachen 21), Berlin, 1940.

46 Encouraged especially by Divine Word (SVD) Catholic Missionaries on the New Guinea side. cf. J. Lynch, *Church, State and language in Melanesia* (Inaugural Lecture), Port Moresby, 1979.

47 See esp. G. Saunders, *Bert Brown of Papua*, London, 1965, ch. 5 (on opening up the LMS mission to the Kunimaipa).

48 Quoted from C. Simpson, *Plumes and Arrows*, Brisbane, 1973 edn, p.159.

49 For the quotation, Chatterton, 'A History of Delena', in *The History of Melanesia* (ed. K. Inglis) (Waigani Seminar 1968), Canberra, 1971, p.288; cf. p.290 on the Polynesians' decline in influence at Delena and the phasing out of their role.

50 See, for example, A. K. Chignell, *Outpost*, p.117; D. Dickson, Government and Missions in education in Papua New Guinea with special reference to the New Guinea Mission, 1891–1970 (master's thesis, UPNG 1971), ch. 1.

51 cf. D. Whiteman, *Melanesians and missionaries*, Pasadena, 1983, esp. ch. 7 (on the Solomons).

52 See esp. M. K. Abel, *Charles W. Abel; Papuan pioneer*, London, 1957; R. Lacey, 'Abel, Charles William', in *Encyclopedia of Papua and New Guinea* (ed. P. Ryan), Melbourne, 1972, vol. 1, p.1.

53 cf. M. Buluna, 'The Milne Bay Development Company', in N. Lutton et al., *Select Topics*, pp.49–53.

54 See, e.g., Oram, 'The LMS Pastorate and the emergence of an educated elite in Papua', *Journal of Pacific history*, 6 (1971), pp.115ff.

55 Note that these terms can be, and have been, used pejoratively. cf. ch. 8 on cargo cultism. Some scholars, such as Harold Turner, prefer the term 'synthetism' to syncretism.

56 M. Mennis, *Hagen saga*, Port Moresby, 1982.

57 cf., e.g., Sisters of Our Lady of the Sacred Heart, *And red grew the harvest*, Sydney, 1947; G. H. Cranswick and I. W. A. Shevill, *A new deal for Papua*, Melbourne and London, 1949, chs 13–15; L. Scharmach, *This crowd beats us all*, Sydney, 1960; R. M. Wiltgen, *Aposteltod Neuguinea*, St Augustin, 1966; F. Walter, *Building Christ's Church at Manus*, Bad Liebenzell, 1981, pp.49ff.

58 e.g., C. G. ToVaninara, *The life of Peter Torot; catechist, church leader and martyr*,

Vunapope, [1975], chs 7–10 (Catholics); H. Linge, *An offering fit for a king*, Rabaul, 1978, chs 15–16; cf. N. Threlfall, *One hundred years in the islands*, Rabaul, 1975, pp.144ff. (Methodists).

59 See Trompf, 'Doesn't colonialism make you mad?' (cf. chap. 5, n. 59).

60 Trompf, Fieldnotes, esp. 1975–77 (in the southern and western highlands). Yabim workers were part of a westward movement of evangelization.

61 T. Bowden and H. Nelson, *Taim bilong Masta*, Sydney, 1982, p.159.

62 cf., e.g., H. Robin, The effects of mission presence and influence upon communities in the Southern Highlands Province (Classified Report to the Provincial Commissioner, Southern Highlands Province), Port Moresby, 1979; A Strathern, *A line of power*, London and New York, 1984, pp.33ff.

63 For a more complete list C. E. Loeliger, 'Further background information on the churches of Papua New Guinea', in Trompf, Loeliger and J. Kadiba (eds), *Religion in Melanesia*, Moresby, 1980, pt. B, pp.114ff. And for more complete details of the present Melanesian situation see David Barrett (ed.), *World Christian Encyclopaedia*, Nairobi, Oxford and New York, 1982 (s.v. 'Fiji', 'New Caledonia', etc.).

64 R. G. Williams, 'From mission to church: a study of the United Church', in M. Ward (ed.), *The politics of Melanesia* (Waigani Seminar 1970), Port Moresby and Canberra, 1970, p.668.

65 cf. S. Firth, 'The missions; from Chalmers to indigenisation', *Meanjin Quarterly*, Spring 1975, p.346.

66 See esp. J. O. Sanders, *Planting Men in Melanesia*, Mt Hagen, 1978.

67 cf., e.g., G. O. Reitz, 'The Contribution of the Evangelical Church of New Guinea to Development in Papua New Guinea', in Trompf (ed.) *Mel. and Judaeo-Christ. Relig. Trads*, bk. 1, pp.154ff.

T HE CATHOLIC MISSIONS: A CASE HISTORY

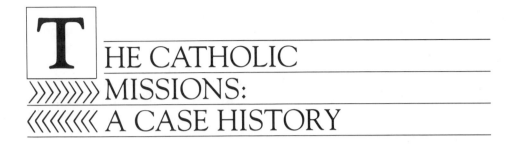

No part of the region, from Irian Jaya to Fiji, is without some Catholic presence. French colonial administrations in New Caledonia and the New Hebrides (now Vanuatu) have, of course, facilitated the work of French-originated (or -related) Catholic Orders, and in the centre of the Melanesian stage, Papua New Guinea and the Solomon Islands, the imperial pretensions of Germany had a comparable effect. The Catholic Church has had an immense influence on the history and development of Papua New Guinea and the Solomons: New Guinea's first two prime ministers, Michael Somare and Sir Julius Chan, for instance, are both Catholics; John Momis, a Catholic priest, and Ignatius Kilage, an ex-priest, served as deputy prime minister and governor-general respectively. Alexis (Holyweek) Sarei and Cherubim Dambui, both Catholics, were the first premiers of the North Solomons and East Sepik Provinces, respectively. And mention should be made, too, of the national roles played by such episcopal Tolais as To Paivu and To Varpin. Census statistics, moreover, whether or not they can be backed up by consistent allegiance or baptismal registration, suggest that approximately 31 per cent of Papua New Guineans and 13.5 per cent of Solomon Islanders currently claim to be Catholics.

Given that the influence and demographic impact are so great, many difficulties present themselves in providing an adequate account of Catholic mission history alone. One way of overcoming this is to represent a significant slice in great detail — a microanalysis to provide the distinct flavour of the Catholic tradition and its impact in a specific context in the hope of shedding light on the whole.[1] The other method is synoptic and more accepting of generalization, and enriched by a judicious selection of illustrative materials. It is this latter course which, for all its unsatisfactoriness, will be followed here.

There is no more helpful introduction for the student of missions than to outline or 'periodize' the basic stages of Christian expansion into the south-west Pacific. Periodization is, in any case, the very epitome of the synoptic approach. Chronological patterns may vary for different churches, but for Catholics, as with other 'mainline denominations', a simple order can be established: first, the 'prehistory', or preparation of mission, followed by the earliest, faltering attempts to establish footholds in the area; secondly, the period of genuine 'foundations', from the last decades of the nineteenth century up until the First World War; then, the inter-war period of 'consolidation', temporarily jeopardized by the Japanese invasion; and finally, the post-war stage of more remarkable 'expansion'.[2] It should be borne in mind, however, that Catholic mission history — which is complicated in any case, like that of others, by the involvement of personnel arriving in clusters from various countries (from Europe, America, and so on) — is all the more complex because of the deployment of different religious Orders, Societies or Congregations, which are distinct groupings of priests (and/or brothers) and nuns, such as: the Marists (members of the Society of Mary), founded in 1836 by a Frenchman, Father Jean C. Colin; or the members of the Missionary Congregation of the Sacred Heart (in French, *Sacré Coeur*), founded in Issoudun, France, by Father Jules Chevalier in 1854; or the members of the Society of the Divine Word (in Latin, *Societas Verbi Divini*), founded in Holland by the German, Father Arnold Janssen in 1875. All such Catholic Societies have a missionary orientation and each also has its own regulations of work and approach to spirituality, inspired by its pious founder, and its own headquarters; and all such groups have been commissioned into the field by Rome. In the various periods of mission history of Papua New Guinea and the Solomon Islands, so it shall be shown, some Societies and Orders have had a stronger and more continuous effect than others, a few have had but a temporary presence (for example, the Jesuits), and some have been comparative latecomers.

The first stage, the 'prehistory' and 'preparations' of the Catholic adventure in the south-west Pacific, has been covered elsewhere with painstaking care,[3] and there is little to report which concerns matters of socio-economic development. Attempts to establish missions by Marists and the Foreign Missions of Milan during 1835–55 were ill-fated. Sicknesses were followed by deaths, and this, together with local disinterest, led to withdrawal. Of permanent value, though, were ethnographic notes taken of the Muju (Woodlark) islanders by Father Carlo Salerio (of Foreign Missions of Milan). His researches were later publicized by the Italian savant Pier Ambrogio Curti (with little recognition) and constitute the earliest detailed European account of a traditional religion in Papua New Guinea (1885).[4]

During the second period, the 'foundation', the Sacred Heart Order stands out for its work in the Bismarck Archipelago in the New Guinea islands (from 1882) and in Papua (from 1885). Since Father Jaspers has written in great depth elsewhere about the achievements of Bishop Couppé and others under the German administration (1885–1914) — a very complex story — this account will concentrate more on Papua instead, while not forgetting Divine Word and Marist beginnings on the New Guinea mainland and in the northern Solomons respectively. It will focus, too, more on Catholic contributions to development and emergent nationhood than on the intricacies of hierarchical and organizational histories.

Foundations: mission priorities in Papua

The initial stage of Papuan evangelization was dominated by the figures of the stalwart Frenchman Louis-André Navarre (1836–1912) (archbishop from 1888) and his close companion, of mixed Italian and Savoyard extraction, called Henri Verjus (1860–92), a much younger man of intense dedication, whose new statue now overlooks the prominence on Yule Island (where he conducted the mission's first Mass on 4 July 1885). Both men shattered their health in the cause of the Gospel, Navarre such that he had to spend most of his time on Thursday Island in the Torres Strait, the base whence both he and Verjus had first voyaged to Papua on the *Gordon*. As for Verjus, this young Joshua in quest of 'the Promised Land', died of sheer exhaustion at 33 years of age. In his intimate diary (11 May 1885) he reveals his vocation to be a victim soul, expressing 'the conviction that the first missionary to New Guinea must be crushed and destroyed, to assure the success of the Mission'. Although receiving the role of auxiliary bishop because of Navarre's ill-health, Verjus was much more the evangelist than the administrator, and desperately desired to reach souls for Christ among the Roro (on the coast) and Mekeo (along the Angabunga or St Joseph's River). He spared himself nothing; when a village 'resisted grace', or when some catechumen preparing for baptism wavered, Verjus went to extremes to carry out self-mortification 'to supplement in his flesh the afflictions endured by Christ' (cf. Col. 1:24). In this spirit he composed a manual for 'The Victims of the Sacred Heart of New Guinea', upholding an ancient Christian paradigm that 'the blood of martyrs is the seed of Christians'.[5]

What of organizational style and method? There is little doubt that Bishop Navarre believed that the method of apostolate used in European parishes would work equally well in New Guinea. He therefore would have loved to establish strong centres along the coast, before reaching out to the mountains. The British policy of the 'spheres of influence' — which Navarre opposed in writing — was, however, partly responsible for the bishop's eventual approval of an expansion into the Kuni and Fuyughe hills, resulting in the foundations of Oba-Oba (by 1900) and Popole (1905). Experience was also to show him that he had to adapt to the special conditions of New Guinea. There were less pastors available than in Europe and many more people to cater for; in addition, the essential material needs in Melanesia were more demanding and time-consuming than back home, while the people pastors were preaching to could not be expected to have the receptivity of an already well-formed and age-old Christian society. The basic thrust of Navarre's guidelines for his missionaries (published in 1896) is important in understanding the values and priorities of the Sacred Heart missionaries in Papua, and shows he had come at least some way in unlearning less suitable Western moulds.

Nowadays, perhaps, we are offended to hear the people called '*mes chers sauvages*' as Navarre and Verjus did. We probably need reminding that at the time 'savages' often meant 'without education', or lacking the particular type of civilization familiar to the outsiders, and thus had less a pejorative than a benign meaning on the lips of 'paternalists'. This is indicated by the attitudes and actions called forth from those who worked in Papua as missionaries, and encouraged by Navarre. A first requirement was to respect the people and to make some attempt to become one of them; hence the need to learn the local language properly and to be wary about interfering with customs, social structures and the life style in general. Navarre believed that only through the vernacular, which revealed the people's soul, could the true faith penetrate and take roots. Such requirements led the fathers to specialize in linguistic and anthropological research.

As the Mission had its origins in another culture, Navarre emphasized the need to sift out very carefully what in the local customs needed conversion, while respecting at the same time the 'stepping stones' of the faith — such as the belief in spirits and in the immortality of the soul. Again, it was imperative to find substitutes for what was deemed to be harmful in the local culture: one means by which the bishop hoped to achieve this was to use local catechists to the full. So, in 1896 Navarre established a catechetical school in the vicinity of the Thursday Island headquarters. In its second year, however, it had to be given up because Lieutenant-Governor William McGregor did not agree to having Papuans trained outside their own country. Navarre tried again between 1899 and 1902 at Mea-Era, but this second attempt was not very successful, although several Filipino men recruited on Thursday Island gave valuable service at this early stage, one being Emmanuel Natera, who married a Roro woman and became the 'patriarch' of a well known Papuan family. In Navarre's view, catechists were to be like go-betweens for both the expatriate missionary and the local people. Their very presence contributed mightily to 'localize' the church and divest it of its foreign appearance. Catechists were also the men who assured the continuity of prayers and religious instructions in the villages. As a matter of fact these catechists had a definite role to play in the first mission schools. Besides the vernacular, they also imparted the rudiments of English — the language of the civil administration, and (according to the bishop) the future means to unify the country.[6]

Following Navarre's death, a different style emerged, that of the next bishop, Alain de Boismenu, a French aristocrat and more of a realist. 'It is a sad mistake', he wrote, 'to think that holiness is everything', and advised that 'an iron constitution' was just as fundamental a prerequisite for coming to Papua. Although he himself was first deterred from going to Papua, being told he was only heading for bad health and failure, things turned out quite differently. He arrived early in 1898, not even 28 years old, and in his second year became religious superior of the mission and a coadjutor to Archbishop Navarre with right of succession. From 1912 until 1945 he headed the Apostolic Vicariate of British New Guinea or Papua; after that, he lived for eight more years in retirement at Kubuna, finally dying in 1953, at the age of 83. Even though de Boismenu did not intend to make a drastic departure from the ideals held up to his time, the quotation above indicates a different spirit. Besides that, nobody doubted that the new bishop was not only 'a perfect gentleman' but a saint as well, and that he was not less convinced than others of the saving power of suffering and pain. The agonies undergone by the 'Papuan' mystic whom he guided, Mother Marie-Thérèse Noblet, AD (Hand-maids of Our Lord), were for him the surest sign that every so often the Devil had been defeated and that a rich harvest of souls had been won for Christ.

Seeing that de Boismenu's life and work takes us beyond the First World War and the 'foundations' period, we are bound to return to his inter-war dealings later on. At this point we consider only the first part of his term of office (c. 1900–26), commenting on his policies. To the outside world he made the claim for the Catholic Church that it should have 'its entire share of freedom (to preach and to teach) recognized in the whole Commonwealth, no more no less'. While following Navarre in combating the spheres of influence policy, de Boismenu also took steps to improve practical relations with other denominations. As for the internal apostolate, he insisted that the Catholic teaching had to be progressive, and should aim at the transformation of conduct.

De Boismenu gave much attention to the difficulties of his missionary companions (over seventy of whom were already working with him in 1900), and also the problems of catechetical work. To Father Fastré, who at the time had begun the evangelization of some mountain areas, he writes: 'Don't fear that I might reproach you for being too slow!' What the bishop wanted was that more time and effort should be spent on the assessment of catechumens' dispositions before they received baptism, in order to build up a solid Christianity. So as not to neglect his mission personnel, moreover, he restructured his vicariate into districts, each having a main centre where some type of community life could flower, and from which the missionaries could visit the surrounding villages. Finally, to deepen Christian life, he founded two local congregations — one in 1918 for Sisters, the 'Ancelles' or 'Hand-maids of Our Lord', and in 1920 a male society, the 'Little Brothers of Our Lord'. His pastoral letter of 1919, on the 'Apostolic Vocations', found its expression in his opening of the Minor Seminary of Yule (1920) and in sending candidates overseas, like Joseph Taurino from Pari village (died 1922) and a young Mekeo man, to be the first Papuan priest and bishop, Louis

Vangeke. In this whole course of action the bishop put into practice the stipulations of the 1917 Code of Canon Law, and he was endorsed by an important Apostolic Letter, *Maximum Illud*, issued by Pope Benedict XV in 1919.[7]

Foundations: New Guinea and the Solomons

Accompanying these developments before the war to the south, Catholic missions were established in the Bismarck Archipelago from 1882 (Sacred Heart missions), the north-western New Guinea mainland from 1896 (Divine Word missionaries), the north Solomons from 1898 (Marists), and the Admiralties or Manus group from 1913 (an extension of Sacred Heart work).

In 1895 the German government insisted that any more Catholic missionaries who came to New Guinea were to be from a 'religious institute having its mother house in Germany'. This political decision led, among other things, to the foundation at Hiltrup, Germany, of the 'Missionary Sisters of the Sacred Heart' by Father Hubert Linckens of the Sacred Heart Mission, to further staff the Rabaul mission. The arrival of Father Eberhard Limbrock and his five co-missionaries, all from the Society of the Divine Word, also satisfied this colonial requirement. But as soon as they landed near Madang in August 1896, the Rhenish Lutheran missionaries exerted pressure to have them move to another zone, and they had to start at Tumleo Island, opposite present-day Aitape. Thus, they began work on the Sepik coast before they were able to re-secure a main base in the Madang area, at Alexishafen (1905).

The pioneer missionary Limbrock, who laboured on until 1931, was a man of extraordinary energy and vision. Between 1901 and 1914 seventeen main mission stations were established between Madang and New Guinea's western border; sadly, though, a considerable number of missionaries (fathers, along with brothers and sisters who were supporting them) died from being in some of the most malaria-ridden country in the world. Despite terrible losses, Limbrock pressed on, protecting the remaining personnel with regular home leaves and securing a physician. Before the war some moves inland from the coastal stations had already begun, and it was the Divine Word Society's praiseworthy achievements in such difficult outposts which helped to convince the Australian government, whose forces took control of German New Guinea from 1914, not to expel all German missionaries once the League of Nations had decreed Australia's mandate in 1921. Their success in establishing schools was especially important. Already in 1898, for example, Tumleo Island school had 150 pupils, and by 1909 a sister at Bunumbo school (near Bogia) had charge of as many as 400 regular pupils. Eighty-six personnel were at work by 1914, and the number of baptized had already passed the 2000 mark.[8]

As for the Marists in the Solomons, the springboards for the second phase of their activity were: first, on Guadalcanal (from 1897), where they were heavily restricted by the pro-Protestant 'spheres of influence' policy of the British high commissioner (and thus had baptized only thirty-three adherents by 1913); secondly, in the Shortlands group of the North Solomons (from 1898), where they secured land from chief 'Ferguson' (a man who possessed at least 25 wives!). In view of their Samoan work, they had good relations with the German administration, which ceded land to them on Bougainville to set up their crucial station at Kieta by 1904. By the outbreak of war their progress in the North Solomons had been steady but not spectacular, their personnel being too small in number, and the local people being too strongly committed to the honouring of vengeance in tribal conflict. Although fourteen churches, twelve schools and some small hospitals had been erected by that time, and there was no competition from other denominations, the baptized and catechumens numbered only 480.[9]

Meanwhile, there was also the expansion of Sacred Heart work from Rabaul to New Ireland (then New Mecklenburg), especially through Lihir and the outlying islands (from 1902), and then to Manus (by 1913). Hopes for a mission to Manus arose when, as a result of a German punitive expedition to the island, Manus hostages were handed over to the care of the Sacred Heart Missionaries at Rabaul; yet the one who was groomed to go back home and spread the Gospel failed his mentors completely (1912). The mission on Manus operated in dreadful isolation and with even less success than the Evangelical Protestants (until the early 1920s, when local interest in both endeavours picked up).[10]

Inter-war consolidation: Papua

In all the zones we have mentioned, including the Bismarck Archipelago, there was notable progress between the wars. It is during this period of consolidation, moreover, that the significant contributions of Catholic missions to the development of Papua, New Guinea and the Solomon Islands become evident.

In Papua the second phase of de Boismenu's episcopacy (1926–45), was marked by the expansion of outreach or 'propagation' — to the west among the Toaripi by 1926, to the east up to Samarai (1932), and further into the mountains, to the Chirima Valley of the eastern Fuyughe (1926) and the Tauade (1937). De Boismenu set as the chief priority of the mission 'spiritual conquest', and he was constantly in correspondence and on the move to help make decisions about the best means of incorporating people into the church — restraining some of his confrères from baptizing too early, while prodding others for delaying the administration of the sacraments to catechumens too long. Along with helping others 'measure the speed', it was characteristic of him to discourage the cultivation of a special and 'meagre elite', maintaining 'it is a hundred times better to lead a lot of mediocre souls to heaven through their repeated falls' and thus gather into the fold as many as were at least willing to enter.[11]

On the other side, the big buildings and wide roads built under his direction are an index to material development as well. Since this account places special emphasis on Papua, the achievements can be divided into: food and agriculture; houses and buildings; roads and transport; the formal introduction of the cash economy; education; health services.

Food and agriculture

In the early days the missionaries had to resort to bartering to stay alive, and there were times of famine, penury and misery, which nearly led Navarre to wind up the whole enterprise. One early solution to such problems was the disposal of personnel over several villages on the mainland; another came with an initiative of the Italian brother 'Kala' (Salvatore Gasbarra), who obtained red rice seeds from the Philippines around the turn of the century. It is interesting to see how, as a result of the missionary experimentations, the Mekeo people of the Angabunga alluvial flood plain became interested in growing the new crop as a source of cash income — to pay head taxes imposed by the colonial government and to buy extra food and clothing.

Father van Goethem describes in vivid terms the earlier stages of this proto-commercial adventure:

> For many years only missionaries cultivated rice, and as a rule planted a couple of acres every year. The harvesting was a really pleasurable time, and every soul in the village would assist to get the crop in, and would help cutting and threshing and winnowing . . .

> One year Brother Salvatore succeeded in floating among the natives a rice growing company which he presided [over]. He directed the planting operations, the fencing in — for the wild pigs are very keen on rice — the weeding, and finally the reaping, when he divided the crop amongst the shareholders and gave them bags to store the rice in. The crop was so successful and the natives found themselves having such an amount of rice that they grew ambitious, and each native individually decided upon having his own field of rice and doing better next year. Banquets were held, to which natives from other clans were invited and were lavishly treated on the much-relished new food.

> Those that had regaled their neighbours on a sumptuous feast of rice, had the right to expect a rice-banquet in return, and made it incumbent on them to buy rice from the store of the trader, or to grow rice for themselves. Such was the origin of rice-growing in Papua.[12]

This initiative of the Catholic mission was subsequently taken up by the government with the Native Plantation Ordinance of 1918, which aimed at making the territory self-supporting through rice production. With some additional expertise, by 1931–32 as much as 94 tons (95 tonnes) of rice were processed through the government mill in Port Moresby, and the Mekeos found that working as families on growing and harvesting for only a few months yielded as much cash as one year of work on a faraway plantation. Production went up to 300–400 tons (304–406 tonnes) before the Second World War, and during the hostilities the Mission was able to counter the disorganization brought on with military hostilities by buying up excess rice stocks for their boarding schools.[13]

Houses and buildings

Initially, mission buildings were very makeshift, hardly matching the standard of traditional houses (let alone temples) or of traders' dwellings. During the inter-war period, though, buildings were erected by people who were skilled in particular trades (brothers and lay-people) and with first-class lumber (usually imported from Queensland) — for instance, the pro-Cathedral and some of St Patrick's school buildings on Yule Island itself, and also constructions at Mainohana and Inawi, which have stood the weather till the present day. A typical set-up of a mission station under de Boismenu's inter-war years comprised a church, with a fathers' house to one side and a convent (for sisters) on the other. A school and health centre also usually lay nearby. New materials used in these buildings included sheet metal and corrugated iron, later to be popular in village house designs.

Requirements for building such stations led to the establishment of sawmills. Trees were cut at Nabuapaka and floated across Hall Sound to Yule Island, where they were cut and dressed by a horse-powered mill (men often taking over when the horses became exhausted). Up in the mountains during the 1930s the ingenious Father Jules Dubuy was able to utilize the fast-flowing streams of Fuyughe country at places such as Ononghe and Woitape, to operate water-powered mills (one actually still running at Kerau). The Ononghe station, incidentally, is symbolic of the new architectural achievements, a continental-style church rising on a ridge 6000 feet (1830 m) above sea level, with a tall, elegant wooden framework, planked and sheet-metal walls, and a large Swiss clock up in its tower. This church was recently lined internally by Father Alfons Bohn — a man who, for over fifty years, coupled priesthood with carpentry in Papua, many of his early days being spent at Ononghe.[14]

Roads and transport

The Sacred Heart pioneer missionaries were early praised for their explorations,[15] and they developed a tradition of inland penetration into the unknown that lasted into the 1950s. We can quickly see that to limit the inter-war period to consolidation of previous footholds without reference to decisive steps in opening up new frontiers would be quite facile. Their entrances into untrekked areas also included brave acts of peacemaking — Verjus among the Mekeo in 1891 and de Boismenu among the western Fuyughe in 1904 — and, thus, a willingness to deal with dangerous places and people.[16] As mission bases were established, moreover, it was often necessary to open up tracks to facilitate the carrying of supplies. Even as early as 1890 Lieutenant-Governor McGregor saw that such routes would not only be of benefit to the mission-aries, but also 'an essential means of promoting civilization and peace'.[17]

The challenge of maintaining communications with outstations as the Mission penetrated inland was taken up during the inter-war years. Already by 1921 Lieutenant-Governor Hubert Murray could report that the French missionaries had supervised the construction of 110 miles (175 km) of road between Aropokina on the coast to Ononghe in the distant heights. The surveying and supervision was done by the missionaries without remunera-tion, while the administration assisted in providing tools and payment for the labourers. These mission roads were, as a rule, 8 feet (2.4 m) wide, and had an easy slope of about 5–8 per cent, which made them suitable for mules and horses, later for some 'prehistoric' tractors, and finally for motorbikes and four-wheel drives. The strict adherence to the principle of not exceeding a 10 per cent gradient made it necessary to have long stretches of switch-backs in the mountainous Goilala area. Thomas Crotty, an engineer with the Papua New Guinea Department of Public Works, judged that the location of these roads, 'in retrospect, has generally been superb'. Where needed, wooden bridges were added, usually covered by thatched roofs to protect their timbers (a practice recalling some Swiss examples, and again followed by government officials in later years), although the bigger span Dubuy built over the Vanapa near Ononghe has a steel frame.[18]

Several fathers and brothers became specialists in pegging out roads in a country they knew by heart, and their contribution to the development of the country has been repeatedly recognized by having their names given to particular features in the landscape. More than once they assisted patrol officers and surveying teams to draw up and correct the first maps of an area. This kind of work had its spiritual side too. It gave the missionaries the opportunity to mix freely with people, learn their languages, and prepare specific pastoral contacts for other occasions. For these reasons, Father Dubuy once said, 'If the work on the roads did not exist, one would have to invent it'.[19]

Cash income

If one means of benefiting the people was to bring roads and communications to them, another was to encourage Papuans to resettle in places where they would have greater access to the cash economy, to amalgamate hamlets into bigger villages for social cooperation and community building. The large Yule

Island village of Isiria resulted from this policy,[20] and other, later, interesting developments (such as the Kuni Bakoiudu, dealt with later in this chapter).

Certain special projects were related to such changes, including the Mekeo rice scheme. Plantations were involved here, but they have not been as important in Papua mission history as they were to the north, for at least two reasons: first, because the British administration prevented the acquisition of freehold land (from 1900), and secondly, because the French missionaries in Papua were disinclined to secure large properties. In 1918 they requested half a dozen leases measuring only 5 acres (2 ha) each (that is, five times less than the 25 acre (10 ha) properties applied for by Couppé on the New Guinea islands). Other bigger plantations came to the Papuan Sacred Heart Mission indirectly — those at Kivori and Obe, for instance, which formerly belonged to the settler J. Oberleuter. One property they were offered, from near Orokolo deep into Elema country in the Gulf, was accepted, interestingly enough, to secure some foothold in an area reserved for non-Catholic missions. These plantations, including one for rubber at Ukue in Kuni country built up by the brothers in the early 1940s, hardly paid nor made mission stations self-supporting, although they did help a limited number of able-bodied men enter the cash economy.[21]

Education

We have already seen how seriously Navarre, Verjus and de Boismenu viewed catechetical training. Not surprisingly, schools became an important part of the Mission, the first elementary school beginning on Yule Island in 1891 and subsequently in the other areas following sufficient contact. Filipino catechists and European sisters were the mainstay of these developments, and Yule Island became the centre for the best achievements. From there a press printed local legends in the 'native tongues' (Navarre, among his many directions to teachers, having stressed the importance of teaching local languages); by 1932 the official education report of the Territory of Papua acknowledged that Yule Island 'pupils read, write and speak English better than in other schools elsewhere', an accolade for the Australian sisters teaching there. As a matter of fact, some time in 1931 Lieutenant-Governor Murray had been greatly impressed when the pupils of Inawaia school had staged before him a play of Shakespeare, directed by Sisters James and Euphrasie of the order, Our Ladies of the Sacred Heart. The government had formally relinquished its responsibility for schools to the mission as far back as 1907, but the Queensland Education Department subsidized 'native children' according to their levels of attainment, and sent both syllabi and inspectors.

By 1926 a technical school was established, and during the 1920s Sacred Heart brothers were teaching carpentry, sheet-metal work and smithing in various centres. This same year, 1926, also saw the commencement of a Catechists' School at Kivori, first under Father Riegler and then, Father Paul

Sorin. Thus, the foundations for a seminary were laid, especially since the school, to be called St Paul's Teachers' Training College, was transferred in 1936 to Bomana, outside Port Moresby, very near what is now the Holy Spirit Seminary. The entrance level was set at Standard V, and the teaching was no longer done in Roro (as earlier at Mea-Era), but in English, which automatically limited the intake of pupils to the schools of Yule Island, Inawaia and, later, Terapo. The war, however, interfered with all this educational work, many boys being sent off to be carriers, and the Catechists' School was temporarily moved to Mekeo country (at Veipa'a, under Father Pinget).[22] Still, two of St Paul's ex-students, Guy Pioma and Ani Mange, were later to be called among the first permanent deacons in the diocese of Bereina.

Apart from their pedagogical role, many of the missionaries also engaged in more scholarly activities. Not a few excelled in this, moreover, as can be seen in the printed results of their efforts — in the range of prayerbooks, catechisms and scripture translations, in the articles for *Missions Catholiques*, *Annales d'Issoudun* (for example, by J. Guis) and certain scientific journals (for example, by V. Egidi), and also in the composition of dictionaries and grammars for various local languages. In addition, there were more systematic intellectual endeavours, most notably Father Paul Fastré's account of (western) Fuyughe manners and customs (Moeurs et coutumes Fouyoughèses), an unpublished ethnography which, only very recently translated, formed the basis of many popular books on Papua by his colleague, Father André Dupeyrat. Dupeyrat also published the first history of the mission in 1925.[23]

Health services

In 1912 the Sacred Heart Sister Gabriel (Marie Houdmont) arrived at Yule Island. Although not a trained nurse, she established a clinic at the Mekeo village of Inawaia by the end of this year, and for over thirty years the medical work of the Papuan mission in the Roro-Mekeo area had much to do with her labours — in treating hundreds of sick children, people with skin lesions, yaws, ulcers, snake bites, and so on.[24] She was joined by various sisters, mainly French, who received some training in nursing and midwifery before coming to Papua, and whose pioneering efforts first led Hubert Murray to secure government subsidization of Mission medical work.[25]

By 1935 a Foundling Hospital was erected at Kubuna (Kuni territory), babies being cared for by Reverend Mother Solange and a group of Papuan nuns (Handmaids of Our Lord, begun with Mother Thérèse Noblet).[26] Further inland at this time, among the western Fuyughe, one of the Papuan sisters was providing medical care, helping also to combat there the practice of infanticide, whereby a newborn child could be killed in favour of rearing piglets on women's breasts (so crucial for the people were the great pig kills and feasts, called *gabe*).[27]

From the missionaries' 'inside viewpoint', one must appreciate that neither education nor health were ever strictly divorced from spirituality, or in other words from the need both to study the Bible and spiritual writings to enrich the reflective life of the church and to pray for the total well-being of the Mission and the world. By 1934 the closed monastery of the Carmelite Sisters was built to fulfil some of these needs, after an appeal to France for a group of contemplative nuns had been launched by Bishop de Boismenu. (Later the monastery was moved, to Yule Island in 1946 and then to Bomana in 1973.)[28] The Carmelites have maintained the largest and longest standing of two Catholic contemplative monasteries in Melanesia (the other being that of the Poor Clare Nuns at Aitape in the West Sepik Province).

Inter-war consolidation: New Guinea and the Solomons

The histories of Catholic missions in places other than in Papua also reflect consolidation (and further exploration), although on the New Guinea side there were setbacks for German personnel in both Catholic and Lutheran stations during both wars. In 1915, following the Australian takeover of German New Guinea, it was officially required that missionaries of European extraction swear an oath of neutrality. Whether all the Germans did this in practice or not, we learn of only one Catholic missionary being deported for alleged pro-German sentiments.[29] There remained the possibility from 1921 on, however, that an Australian order to expel all German missionaries would be executed; however, owing to pressure from Australian churches (especially the Church of England) and the eventual entry of Germany into the League of Nations, the issue became a dead letter by 1928.[30]

As far as developments in the Bismarck Archipelago were concerned, work beyond the Gazelle area began in 1924. By 1929, there was a station at the far end of New Britain (Kilenge), and by 1931 there was a commencement of work in the Pomio (Mengen) area on the south-eastern side: fifteen stations, in all, being established on New Britain outside the Gazelle by the Second World War. Educational work even included a school for Chinese children.[31] Most of these developments occurred under the episcopacy of Bishop Vesters, Couppé's successor from 1923 on. Along the north coast of the mainland, progress continued (under Bishop Wolf, Divine Word Society, from 1922, with two vicariates, east and west of the Sepik River being formed in 1933). The most spectacular examples of Divine Word exploration during the period were along the great Sepik River, and then the penetration of Chimbu and Wahgi Valley areas of the central highlands, following the American Father William Ross's pioneer trek from Alexishafen. As for the Solomons, although Catholic workers faced new competition (the Methodists by 1916, the Adventists in 1924), the Marists on the North Solomons forged ahead — even breaking their own rule that Marists should not be deployed singly — by dividing their flock into smaller sections. The fathers worked from sixteen new stations with as many as 356 local catechists by 1935 and, thus, created a 'counter-offensive' against other denominations' intrusions. In the Solomons to the east, moreover, there was a leap in numbers of claimed adherents between the early 1920s and mid-1930s (for example, from 247 in 1923 on Guadalcanal, to 3317 in 1933; and from 357 in 1928 on San Cristobal, to 796 in 1936).[32] One must remember that in almost all the ambiences in which the Catholic missions operated there were denominational 'opponents', and there was no love lost between Catholics and Protestants. False rumours were spread between these two 'blocs' (that those in the wrong 'camp' could go to Hell, for example), and on many occasions local supporters of each side came to blows or damaged each others' properties. In hindsight, it can be seen that at least the conflict was limited, and administrators of Melanesian territories certainly preferred the 'diversions' and restrained outbursts associated with sectarian strife to the brutalities of tribal warfare and ambushing.[33]

Effective mission work was hampered through confusion and distortion during these inter-war years, so-called 'cargo cults' manifesting themselves in various Catholic zones of influence. These cults reflected both the clash of cultures and the expectation, on the part of local peoples, of dramatic material change resulting from the encounter with newcomers and their startling range of new goods. Better known cult episodes in this period include those surrounding Mambu near Bogia in 1937 (west of Madang), the popular espousals of Christianity to acquire the new wealth in the Madang area itself (1920s–1930s), and Pako on Buka (from 1932). These outbreaks had some counterparts in Papua, as well, for instance in the so-called 'Vailala Madness' around Orokolo, between 1919 and 1931 (before the Sacred Heart fathers entered the Elema area). Later the fathers themselves faced the 'Bilalaf' cult among the Fuyughe (from 1929), and the Filo cult among the Mekeo (1941). Leaders of all such movements were interested in the acquisition of special power, and in the setting up of alternative ways to the missions in order to bring back local self-determination and herald the arrival of 'the Cargo' (whether at the hands of a returning Jesus or the ancestors).[34]

Cargo constituted a nagging problem which was not to go away in the post-war years. The period of the Pacific War, however, marks a more definite time of serious setbacks, short but generally devastating. Virtually all Catholic mission personnel remained at their posts during the Japanese invasion, and not a few were killed. The Japanese did not take long to become suspicious of German missionaries (despite the Axis alliance), believing that the Australians or British had not extradited them at the beginning of hostilities because they were useful spies against the Japanese. In the course of the war there were some terrible atrocities: included among the sixty-two people executed by hanging and machine-gunning at the back of the Japanese destroyer *Akikaze*, for example, was Bishop Joseph Loerks of Wewak, as well as many Catholic priests, brothers and nuns (1943). And there were shocking tragedies, such as the American strafing of the Japanese ship, the *Dorish Maru* in 1944: forty-six Divine Word missionaries being killed because they were captives on this vessel, not counting the others, like Bishop Francis Wolf of Madang, who later died of their wounds. As for the Rabaul mission, the war saw the mission personnel interned for three years in the Ramale camp, and ended with an almost total destruction of the material property established or owned by the mission. Through famine, sickness, deportations and executions, one-third of the entire population lost their lives, reducing the number of Catholics by about 8000. Ten local Mary Immaculate sisters lost their lives, while the expatriate Sacred Heart staff lost twenty-six priests, twenty brothers and seven sisters, and four Dutch nuns.[35] The war yielded up its martyrs too, such as the Tolai catechist, Peter Torot (who symbolizes the work of local people to keep the church alive after expatriate missionaries were taken away). And the massive destruction of church buildings and property occurred not only under the Japanese (when the impressive stone cathedral at Rabaul was bombed to ruins) but also as a result of Allied airstrikes designed to root out the last remaining presence of Japanese soldiers (when, sadly, the great cathedral of Alexishafen was reduced to rubble). Yet despite the trauma, the church endured, and its endurance was a lesson in itself.

Inter-war years: contributions to development

Many of the themes singled out for Papua have parallels in New Guinea and the Solomons. Much could be written about the introduction of new foods and agricultural techniques: of experimentations with such imported vegetables as cabbages, beans, tomatoes and onions, and new timbers such as teak (under Divine Word Mission auspices, for instance, on New Guinea's north coast); or about the much more extensive coconut plantations under missionary supervision on the Gazelle and New Ireland (Sacred Heart), and near Madang (Divine Word). Over plantations, naturally, there had been a fair amount of jostling between mission and administration in German days. In the Bismarck Archipelago the secular authorities were embarrassed by the better and much more popular conditions of employment offered by the church. On the mainland, Father Limbrock found it hard to secure land and government cooperation to start coconut plantations, which, with considerable foresight, he thought would eventually 'bring about the most diverse advantages for the country itself', with the local people learning 'how to work and have order in their lives'. The missionary planters also knew very well that the coconut market could make their operations financially independent, and they were generally left maintaining their holdings after the Australian occupation — new settlers from the south being granted plantations expropriated from the previous administration and from German private companies. The church plantations have become increasingly controversial in recent years, with a concern about land alienation and about dissociating the church from profit-making; yet, in their continuity and improvement in earlier years they can be considered as 'groundwork for what was destined to become the backbone of the New Guinea economy'.[36]

Once again, one can emphasize the importance of new building styles, and the techniques used to achieve them. We have already mentioned Alexishafen Cathedral, probably the most impressive of all the buildings in New Guinea built between the wars. Significantly, it was close to a mission industrial workshop, where all sorts of new skills were imparted. During the 1920s and 1930s the 'higher' schools of Divine Word Society head stations included technical and practical subjects like carpentry in the curricula.[37] As far as encouragement of local participation in the cash economy was concerned, mission achievements were hardly outstanding at the time because of the very isolation of most areas; on the Gazelle, however, the mission encouragement of small village plantations and crop plots amounted to the initiation of 'the modern village economy'.[38]

As far as education was concerned, the Christians dominated the school system from 1914 to 1945. In 1927, for instance, there were 1320 mission-run schools in New Guinea (698 of them Catholic) and only 2 operated by the government. Even during the Australian military occupation (1914–21), what is more, all the Catholic educational institutions increased in number markedly (Sacred Heart schools increasing from 98 to 190; Divine Word from 19 to 58; and Marists, from 7 to 10).[39] As for health services, by 1928 the Sacred Heart Mission report of that year showed thirteen trained medical workers at large, about half posted to outlying points in the Baining and Sulka culture areas. Between 1931 and 1939 at least five trained nurses joined the Divine Word Mission to reinforce what was already a strong healing ministry among the sisters; while in 1935 Bishop Thomas Wade, the American Marist who arrived in Bougainville in 1923, inaugurated the Marist Medical Mission Society. All the dispensaries and clinics established had far-reaching consequences in regions plagued by long-standing diseases such as malaria and such introduced scourges as tuberculosis.[40]

Post-war period: expansion

The Pacific War put Papua and New Guinea 'on the map'. Many more people in Australia, Europe and North America perceived the needs of the romantically wild Melanesian islands; thus, many more people responded to the call to work there. The opening up of the central highlands of New Guinea also had much to do with this. If in 1934, for example, there were 564 expatriate missionaries recorded to be working in New Guinea, almost three times as many as this were to be found in the central highlands alone by the early 1960s, with considerable numbers moving into other unevangelized inland areas.[41] In terms of Catholic development in Papua New Guinea, new orders and mission societies began to have their impact, and more representation of American, Australian and Dutch missionaries was in evidence. In 1954 the inland mountain mission, extending to Mendi, Tari and Ialibu in the southern highlands, was given to the Capuchin order; while the Chimbu and both the eastern and western highlands were formally commissioned by Rome to the Divine Word missionaries by 1959 (since they had been in the central highlands since the 1930s). In the Western District a new Apostolic Prefecture of Daru was commissioned to the Montfort Fathers (1959). Australians came to assist at Aitape by 1946 (Franciscans) and in both Samarai and Port Moresby by 1951 (Sacred Heart Mission). Australians, Americans and Irish helped out in New Britain and especially New Ireland (Sacred Heart missionaries); the Australian Dominicans slipped into Gizo Island by 1957, while the Dutch Marianhill Fathers worked at Lae (formally commissioned in 1959). Among the orders of sisters, too, more Australian, New Zealand and North American nuns arrived after the war, and also (with the arrival of the Sisters of Charity from Calcutta in 1980) some Indians. The history of commissionings or Apostolic Vicariates thus reveals increasing complexity in the period of 'expansion' up until the present; in all the areas just mentioned, furthermore, Catholics were hardly the only presence in the field, the older Protestant denominations and various minor (often sectarian) missionary ventures also being involved in the post-war 'boom'.[42]

Papua

De Boismenu's successor was André Sorin, consecrated bishop in 1946. In his earlier years expansion continued into the Chirima Valley, reached as far as the Kunimaipa and the Kamea (or Kukukuku) areas, with various footholds in the coastal and hinterland Gulf. It was during Sorin's episcopacy that the developments in Mendi, Samarai and Daru all occurred. At his death, in 1959, the diocese centred on Yule Island was separated from Port Moresby (which was emerging as a fast-growing centre). The last separation came in 1976 with a new diocese of Kerema in the Gulf, under Sir Virgil Copas, one-time Archbishop of Port Moresby and administrator at Bereina. In 1970 the first Papua New Guinea-national priest, Louis Vangeke, was ordained bishop; he functioned initially as Auxiliary at Port Moresby and then — when Archbishop Copas administered the Bereina diocese (1973) — as the bishop's vicar-general, with residence at Bereina. There, Vangeke had full jurisdiction from 1976 to 1980, when he handed over the diocese to another Papua New Guinea-national, Bishop Benedict To Varpin. Meanwhile, in 1981, Port Moresby had received in turn its first Papua New Guinea-national archbishop, Peter Korungku. That these important posts were filled by locals was fitting now that Papua New Guinea had achieved independence (on 16 September 1975).

Among the new initiatives of Bishop Sorin one should note the employment in 1947 of the first lay missionaries (the *Mouvement Laïc Missionnaire*), the more professional organization of the health services (1948), and the upgrading of the school system to secondary level (1957). Being himself a fine musician and an artist, the bishop also fostered native Christian art and introduced it in the liturgy (1948). His successor in 1960 was Bishop Eugene Klein, who maintained Sorin's policy of expansion and a particular concern with education, especially important in a country heading for self-government and independence. Having been the business manager of Yule Island during the seven years prior to becoming a bishop, Klein was the right man to see the mission become economically and financially independent. From then on-wards, the stations had to support themselves, and several semi-commercial enterprises took shape, until the time came when these ventures, too, were left to non-mission agencies. The question of local leadership is also one of the points which received special attention in more recent years, some initiatives being: the establishment in 1974 of the Verius Catholic Council among the Roro people, from whom it spread to the Mekeo and Kuni as well; the opening of a new formation centre for catechists at Kubuna in the same year; the organization of training sessions for permanent deacons on Yule Island, between the years 1975 and 1978.[43] Again, better to assure the qualifications of the Handmaids of Our Lord, the sisters transferred in 1956 their head-quarters from Kubuna to Nazareth, near Port Moresby. This 'loss' was compensated in 1966 by the establishment on Yule Island of the Our Ladies of the Sacred Heart novitiate. Since both congregations became increasingly more nationally composed, the significance of these events is much wider than the one diocese of Bereina, and will therefore be left alone.

In the various periods of Papuan mission history the emphasis given in the apostolate has shifted more than once, but the constant factor seems to be the concern to introduce acceptance of Christian values, whereas other things were generally done in a less professional way — on a voluntary basis, out of necessity, or as subsidiary to the main objective. The motives behind these other activities were not the motives of government officers or businessmen, although the effects — 'respect for Western order', let us say, or 'receptivity to the domination and values of the whites, worship of the work ethic, and attention to hygiene' — were often the same.[44] Missionaries were not trained to be anthropologists and linguists, or builders and road engineers, or business managers and education officers; they became all this and a few things more out of necessity, and some of them — often the 'export quality' within the overseas missionary societies — did quite well in their new, secondary capacities. It would seem that their not too technical approach, and their preference for grassroots development — using, for instance, village technology and manual work instead of advanced machinery — was most laudable and smoothened in no small way the integration of new values and new approaches in the traditional societies of Papua New Guinea.

Many special developments occurred in the post-war years and, while reminding readers that Catholic work in Papua had expanded far beyond the original 'springboard', we can select one project of special interest — one designed to facilitate local peoples' involvement in the moneyed economy in hinterland Papua, west of Port Moresby. A quite spectacular achievement surrounds the new Kuni village of Bakoiudu. Its origins go back to the early 1960s when Father A. Boell was appointed to serve the Kuni people and to foster among them social and economic development. Before his time the Kuni had made some attempts to grow coffee. When Boell came to Oba-Oba in 1959, however, he soon noticed that, for this very scattered population, living on such a rugged terrain, there was not much hope for economic success except by a resettlement project, drawing people to Kubuna and Bakoiudu, set in a rather undulating landscape with better access to the existing roads and to some foreign-owned plantations. Under Boell's instigation, and with the help of a titular landholder, Faika Peto, and Assistant District Officer Ken Brown, the building up of a new station — Bakoiudu — began in 1961. The new centre held as may as 1300 Kuni by 1971, with about the same number living either elsewhere in Kuniland or outside their tribal territory. The allocation of land for resettlement was carried out on the principle of 'first come, first served', with the added injunction that claims to land thus obtained would be validated only by actual occupation and use. Through community efforts, the first houses were established, the first gardens planted and in 1963, with the help of a resident agricultural officer, a rubber plantation was started. In the venture during the 1960s labour time was initially equally divided between work in subsistence gardens, work on the rubber plantations (seen as a communal project), and voluntary road maintenance or service to a local aid post and school. Gradually the old structuring gave way to an interest in the more restrictive forms of cash cropping. Rubber tappings on the most advanced sections of the company block started in February 1968, and although only 8 tonnes of rubber were produced in the first year, prospects for the next ten years of production anticipated an estimated annual income of A$75 000 by 1978. This, however, was to prove too optimistic; yet, the involvement of the Department of Agriculture, Stock and Fisheries pushed the project further along, an expatriate project manager even arriving in 1970. The missionary now kept more in the background, but his help remained substantial. He had arranged for the purchase of a tractor in 1968, and tried to keep the collective effort going whenever it was threatened by disagreements and secessionist tendencies. Opinions may differ over the wisdom of some actions taken, but in this case an isolated, law-abiding but also neglected people certainly gained access to the modern cash economy, through a mission-sponsored project now largely in the people's own hands.[45]

New Guinea and the Solomons

Although administrative and episcopal histories in New Guinea and the Solomons are rather too complex to spell out in detail, some well known features can be pinpointed. There was the long episcopacy of the tough-minded, enterprising German Archbishop of Rabaul, Johannes Hoehne

(1963–78); the rampant expansion of the Catholic fold in the Western Highlands (and Enga) Districts under Bishop George Bernarding (1961–), with the number of adherents passing the 135 000 mark by 1981, and the appointment of Bernarding as Archbishop of Mount Hagen in 1983; there are the newer dioceses in the central highlands and west Sepik, with work in remote landlocked valleys over 7000 feet (2130 m) above sea level and in difficult terrain towards the northern end of the Papua New Guinea/Irian Jaya border (where the Passionist Fathers established themselves from 1963).

The amount of involvement in education, health services and development projects has increased into a multitude of separate diocesan histories. In 1948 the number of Catholic schools in New Guinea totalled 554, whereas in 1982 there were 743, and this despite the steady overtaking of the churches' role in education by the government. As in Australia and other parts of the world, the Catholics jealously guarded their right to maintain schools, and their strong emphasis on education has meant that their establishments serve many children from other denominational traditions (a policy further encouraged by the more ecumenical, post-Vatican II atmosphere) and receive state subsidies. Some of the most impressive high schools in Papua New Guinea are Catholic — such as Kondiu in the western highlands, Marianville at Bomana, and de la Salle at Bomana.[46] There are also the tertiary institutions. Before the Holy Spirit Seminary was inaugurated at Bomana in 1962, there were 'minor seminaries' for the priesthood at Ulapia (near Rabaul), at Kairuru Island (Wewak) and Alexishafen (Madang); but the new seminary came to take in students from the whole of western Melanesia (including the dioceses of Honiara, Malaita and Gizo) and even beyond. Colleges representing the various mission societies and orders, as well as a college for candidates of the diocesan priesthood, grew up in a cluster to form the 'Little Vatican' of Bomana and this, after the universities, is possibly the largest and best endowed of Melanesia's tertiary institutions.[47]

Responding to present-day needs, another tertiary institution has been started at Madang: the Divine Word Institute, which finally realizes Archbishop Noser's 1964 idea to open a Divine Word Society-run university. In just four years of operation the Institute already had a staff of just over twenty lecturers and an enrolment of nearly 200 students, from all the provinces of Papua New Guinea. Although a Catholic enterprise, students represented fifteen different denominations, and followed a programme leading to a diploma in either Business Studies, Communication Arts or Religious Studies. The Religious Studies Department is mainly concerned with giving 'the teaching and formation necessary for pastoral workers in Papua New Guinea, who will be able to sustain living and viable local churches'.

The general history of medical services in Papua New Guinea by Ellen Kettle testifies to the remarkable contribution of Catholic mission workers and their assistants in maintaining hospitals, nursing schools and aid posts, and in transporting medicines and sick persons to save lives.[48] Mention of transport calls our attention to the very great significance of air traffic in western Melanesia. Various diocesan air services have rendered signal services in this corner of the developing world, often at the cost of the lives of its faithful pilots in managing some of the most difficult air space anywhere to be found.

Catholic mission involvement in aviation has a history of its own, beginning in New Guinea, in 1937, to serve the Divine Word dioceses. In Papua, however, after some earlier yearnings by missionaries in the 1920s and 1930s, missionary aviation only developed in the post-war years; and it was in the 1960s that flying began to compete with sea transport and the use of muletracks. The beginning did not augur well. Two French Sacred Heart brothers trained to fly in 1965 but, because of a fatal accident, the purchase of a plane was delayed until 1967, when a VH-MYI was bought and flown by the lay missionary, Evan Duggan. In the early stages out-stations of the Papuan mission — such as Bema, Kanabea, Kainteba (in the Gulf), and Fane, Yongai, Kamulai (in the Papuan mountains) — were more than glad of regular airdrops. Then came the building of airstrips — first, at Kerau and then, over time, at Fane, Ononghe, Kosipe and Yonhai — there being few places with suitable spurs of approximately 500 metres. In New Guinea a certain amount of fame centred around Leo Arkfeld, the 'flying bishop' (of Madang) in the 1950s, who serviced many remote areas by his expertise both as a pilot and as a pastor. In recent years the Catholic contribution in the air has been no better illustrated than from the diocese of Daru, the government relying heavily on church aircraft to ferry foodstuffs and medical supplies to the thousands of refugees crossing the border from Irian Jaya, west of Kiunga.[49]

With all these developments, of course, including the use of the most modern technological advantages, there have arisen problems — and not only the difficulties of upkeep or defects: there are the cargo cults, as mentioned before; and there was white dominance, in the religious as well as other spheres, which continued after the Second World War. In fact, the astounding quality of machines, processed foodstuffs and money in evidence during the last stages of the war naturally contributed to the upsurge of cargo cults. Renowned movements affecting Catholic areas are Maasina (or Marching Rule), mainly on Malaita in the Solomons, 1943–50; the Yali movement spreading out from the Rai coast, Madang, 1945–55; the Paliau movement on Manus and outliers, from 1946 (Paliau's followers using a pidgin Catholic liturgy which excludes the consecration and distribution of the elements); the Pomio *Kivung* among the Mengen and their neighbours in the less developed region of East New Britain, from 1964; and the Peli Association in and around the Yangoru-Negrie sub-district of the East Sepik, from 1971.[50] All of the movements have attracted thousands of followers and have constituted no mean threat to the unity of parishes and the stability of communities.

If earlier missionary reactions to these 'growing pains of development' have been condemnatory, and repressive-looking,[51] more recent anthropological and missiological sensitivities have led to a more patient and conciliatory approach. With the foundation of the Melanesian Institute in Goroka (at first a Catholic organization in 1968, but ecumenical by 1971), there has appeared a remarkable number of crucial conferences and publications on new religious movements and the dialogue between traditionalists and Christians.[52] In the trials of confusion, and in the conflict of ideas and the struggle to articulate the message of salvation more relevant to Melanesians, the Catholic Church has played a vital developmentalist role in preparing a multitude of diffuse tribal cultures for the experience of nationhood. At one point in 1975, perhaps, the extraordinary unity brought to Buka and Bougainville Islands by Christianity, and especially Catholicism, could have produced a new nation of the North Solomons, which the national bishop, Gregory Singkai, admitted was the apparent wish of his flock.[53] But Christianity also had its part to play in the achievement of the wider unity of Papua New Guinea, when the pressure was on. As one young Catholic Bougainvillean student put it to a university tutorial in 1975: 'if it were not for the fact that you are my Christian brothers and sisters, I would not want to be here today'. That is a nice comment on the Catholic contribution to Papua New Guinean national unity, with which to conclude this survey of Catholic missions in the light of Bougainville developments.

NOTES

Chapter 7 has been written jointly with Father Theo Aerts and derives from material originally contributed to S. Latukefu (ed.), *The Christian Missions and Development in Papua New Guinea and the Solomon Islands.*

1 Thus, e.g., R. Jaspers, 'An historical investigation into the foundation of the Catholic Church in Papua New Guinea and the Solomon Islands', in S. Latukefu (ed.), *The Christian missions and development in Papua New Guinea and the Solomon Islands* (forthcoming).

2 For background, J. Garrett, 'A history of the Church in Oceania', in L. Vischer (ed.), *Towards a history of the Church in the Third World; the issue of periodisation*, Bern, 1985, pp.33–37; cf. Jaspers, 'A brief history of the Catholic Church in Papua New Guinea', in *Papers prepared for the visit of Pope John Paul II to Papua New Guinea, 7–10th May, 1984*, Port Moresby, 1984, pp.2–5.

3 R. M. Wiltgen, *The founding of the Roman Catholic Church in Oceania*, Canberra, 1981; R. Jaspers, *Die missionarische Erschliessung Ozeaniens* (Missionswissenschaftliche Abhandlungen und Texte 30), Münster, 1972.

4 See esp. D. Affleck, 'Notes and documents, Manuscript XVII', *Journal of Pacific History* 18/1 (1983), pp.57ff.

5 For primary materials, esp. Navarre, Notes et Journal, June 1888–July 1889; Verjus, Journal, 11 May, 1885 (MSC Archives, Issoudun), Verjus to Rev. J. Chevalier, July, 1885 in *The Australian annals of Our Lady of the Sacred Heart*, Randwick (Sydney), 4/10 (1983), pp.235–36. For secondary work, esp. G. Delbos, *Cents ans*, chs 4–6; cf. A. Dupeyrat, *Papouasie. Histoire de le mission 1885–1935*, Issoudun, 1935, chs 4–6; P. Seveau, *A life for a mission*, Port Moresby, 1985 (on H. Verjus); Garrett, *To live*, pp.237ff; Langmore, *Missionary Lives*, esp. pp.32ff.

6 See esp. A. Navarre, *Manuel des missionaires du Sacré Coeur parmi les sauvages*, Port Leon, 1896; and his *Letter to Lieutenant-Governor William McGregor, 31st July, 1897, from Randwick*, Sydney 1897 (published pamphlet). cf. also Delbos, *Cent ans*, chs 6–7;

Dupeyrat, *Papouasie*, chs 11–12, esp. p.435n; N. Lutton, 'Murray and the spheres', in H. Nelson et al., *Select Topics in the History of Papua New Guinea*, pp.1–13; Anon, 'Emmanuel Natera', *Yule Island News*, No.3 (1961), p.4, No.5 (1961), p.5.

7 Delbos, *Cent ans*, esp. pp.180, 186–88, 223–24, 241, 252–54, 271 (trans: 131, 135–37, 168–69, 184, 193–94, 208), for most of the specific points about de Boismenu. We await the editing of T. Cadoux's MS on de Boismenu's life. Meanwhile see also A. Dupeyrat and F. de la Noé, *Sainteté au naturel. Alain de Boismenu vu à travers ses lettres*, Paris, 1958.

8 See esp. T. M. Noss, A review of SVD and SSPS missionary activity in New Guinea (mimeograph, Madang, 1975); J. Tschauder, History of the Church on the north coast of New Guinea (mimeograph, MI-XI Orientation Course paper, Bomana, 1971–72), pp.8–12; cf. also Delbos, *Cent ans*, ch. 15 and G. Bus (ed.), *Divine Word Missionaries 1896–1971: 75 years in New Guinea*, Wewak, 1971.

9 See esp. H. Laracy, *Marists and Melanesians*, ch. 3; Tschauder, Church History in the Solomon Islands 1845–1945 (mimeograph, Bomana, 1972), pp.11–18; cf. J. Schmidlin, *Die Katholischen Missionen in den Deutschen Schutzgebieten*, Münster, 1913, p.190 (for the figures).

10 Tschauder, Church history of the Bismarck Archipelago (mimeograph, Bomana, 1972), pp.8–9; P. Kelly, Brief history of the Diocese of Kavieng (unpublished MS), Rabaul, 1978[?]; F. Walter, *Building Christ's Church at Manus*, pp.11–27.

11 See esp. Delbos, *Cent ans*, pp.254–55 (trans: 195); cf. de Boismenu, *Lettres pastorales 1ff*, Port Leon, 1908ff.

12 E. van Goethem, *Catholic Mission Papua*, Melbourne, 1923, pp.49–51.

13 See esp. F. J. Jeffreys, The Mekeo rice project (masters thesis, UPNG, Port Moresby 1974); M. Stephen, Continuity and change in Mekeo society 1890–1971 (doctoral dissert., ANU, Canberra 1974), p.xxiii, etc; cf. P. R. Hale, *Rice in Papua New Guinea*, Port Moresby, 1977 and Anon, History of the Mekeo rice project (typescript located at D.A.S.F. Central library, Port Moresby).

14 See Delbos, *Cent ans*, p.158 (trans: 113); cf. ch. 6. Trompf plans a small written memorial of Father Bohn's life.

15 e.g., by Lieut-Gov. John Douglas in 1887; cf. Dupeyrat, *Papouasie*, p.133, n.1.

16 cf. A. Dupeyrat, *Briseurs*.

17 P. Seveau, *Life for mission*, p.92.

18 T. M. Crotty, History of the Road Development in the Territory of Papua and New Guinea (Paper submitted to 42nd ANZAAS Congress, Engineering Section, Paper No.9), Port Moresby, 1970, p.9 (location: PNG Works and Supply Library); cf. also J. Specht and J. Fields, *Frank Hurley in Papua; photographs of the 1920–1923 expeditions*, p.80 (Murray's views); Trompf, '"Bilalaf"' in Trompf (ed.), *Prophets*, pp.30–35, 48–49 (roads, Vanapa bridge, etc.). According to Father Pierre Morant, MSC, of Kamulai Parish, the French and Swiss fathers built, over the years, easily 1240 miles (2000 km) of mule tracks (OT: July 1985).

19 Delbos, *Cent ans*, p.217 (trans: 162).

20 For background, see ibid., p.144 (trans: 102); cf. P. Chatterton, 'The story of a migration', *Journal of Papua and New Guinea Society* 2/2 (1968), pp.92ff.

21 cf. esp. Delbos, *Cent ans*, pp.352ff. (trans: 273ff.).

22 R. C. Wilkinson, Education in Papua and New Guinea: Mission and Administration policy (typescript, 1959); T. Aerts, '"The Little Vatican" . . . of Bomana', in *Papers prepared for the visit of Pope John Paul II*, p.69; also 'A short chronicle', in C. Braun et al., *The First 20 years of the de Boismenu College, Bomana 1962–1982*, Bomana, 1982, pp.i–xxviii (inserted page); P. Smith, 'Labouring with us in the Gospel' (unpublished working paper, UPNG, Port Moresby 1984); cf. de Boismenu, *Lettres Pastorales* 19 of 1916(23) (as important background).

23 See Fastré, Moeurs. The translator is the Carmelite nun, Sr Mary Flower.

24 E. Kettle, *That they might live*, Sydney, 1979, pp.20–21.

25 *Papuan Annual Report* (hereafter *PAR*), 1930–31, p.17.

26 ibid., 1934–35, p.22.

27 See A. Dupeyrat, *Mitsinari; Twenty-one years among the Papuans* (trans. E. and D. de Mauny), London, 1954, pp.13, 246–47; cf. Kettle, *That they might live*, pp.69–70. See also Dupeyrat, *Mother Marie Thérèse Noblet*, Yule Island, 1937.

28 See esp. Aerts, '"The Little Vatican"', p.70.
29 See esp. H. H. Rowley, *The Australians in German New Guinea, 1914–1921*, Melbourne, 1958, p.260, cf. pp.259ff. For Manus, not mentioned in this connection by Rowley, Walter, *Building*, p.13.
30 Jaspers, 'Brief history', p.3; Delbos, *Cent ans*, p.241 (trans: 184); OT: Archbishop David Hand, March, 1983.
31 Note Delbos' map, ibid. (English trans: 393). cf. D. Y. H. Wu, *The Chinese in Papua New Guinea 1850–1890*, Hong Kong, n.d., pp.117ff. on the Yang Ching school.
32 Jaspers, 'Brief history', pp.3–4; Tschauder, Church history of the Solomon Islands, pp.13–14, 19–21; cf. also M. Mennis, *Hagen Saga*; J. Ulbrich (ed.), *Pionier auf Neuguinea. Briefe von P. Alfons Schäfer SVD*, Steyl, 1960; F. Bornemann, *Missionar auf New-Guinea: P. Karl Morschheuser SVD, 1904–1934*, Mödling, 1938.
33 cf. Trompf, *Payback*, ch. 3A.
34 For general background, Lawrence, *Road*, pp.73–85; Worsley, *Trumpet shall sound*, pp.114–17, 121–22, 125–28. Lesser-known 'Papuan' cults occurred at Babiko-Nabuapaka (1969), in Roro-Mekeo-Waima (1929–30, 1937), at Inawaia and Mekeo (1940–47), at Keleipe and Goilala (1942, 1945–48), and among the Toaripi (1950s). Further details are given by F. Steinbauer, *Die Melanesische Cargo-Kulte*, Erlangen, 1971, pp.29–36, 84–85, 87–91, 99–100 (reproduced in the English trans.); Trompf (ed.), *Prophets*, chs 1 and 3; Delbos, *Cent ans*, p.310 (trans: 240).
35 For the most important references on the war years, see ch. 6, ns57–58 on the Sisters of Our Lady of the Sacred Heart, Scharmach, Wiltgen, and ToVaninara. Note also Kettle, *That they might live*, pp.vi, 84; Tschauder, History of the Church on the north coast, p.14; Walter, *Building*, pp.48ff.
36 cf. esp. R. M. Wiltgen, 'Catholic mission plantations in mainland New Guinea: their origin and purpose', in K. S. Inglis (ed.), *The history of Melanesia*, p.337 (first quotation), p.332 (second); P. H. Cahill, 'An Obsession of Coconut Planting'; expropriated plantations on the Gazelle Peninsula of the Mandated Territory of New Guinea 1914–1942 (doctoral thesis, University of Queensland, Brisbane 1987), ch. 3; Rowley, *Australians*, p.262; Noss, Review, p.6, etc.
37 For background, e.g., B. Hagspiel, *Along the mission trail: In New Guinea*, Techny, 1926, p.122 etc; P. Smith, 'Native Education policy in Australian New Guinea', in S. Latukefu (ed.), *Papua New Guinea: a century of colonial impact*, p.229.
38 Jaspers, 'Brief history', p.3.
39 *New Guinea Annual Report (NGAR)*, 1926–1927, p.38; Rowley, *Australians*, pp.266–67 (on 1914–21).
40 See esp. Kettle, *That they might live*, pp.42–46.
41 *NGAR*, 1933–34, p.101, sects 317–18, and recent extrapolations from the Papua New Guinea National Statistical Office; cf. *Papers prepared for visit of Pope*, pp.19–26.
42 See esp. Jaspers, 'Brief history' p.5, cf. also Trompf, *Payback*, ch. 3; Trompf, 'The expansion of the Christian missions after the War', in Loeliger and Trompf (eds), *Religion in Melanesia*, pt 2, pp.57ff; Aerts (ed.), *It all began on Yule Island 100 years ago*, Port Moresby, 1985, p.1.
43 For most of the information in the above two paragraphs, Delbos, *Cent ans*, chs 11–14; cf. also Aerts (ed.), *It all began*, p.10; Kettle, *That they might live*, pp.101–102, 133–36.
44 Phrases taken from R. Mortimer, 'The Colonial State: paternalism and mystification', in *Development and Dependency; the political economy of Papua New Guinea* (eds A. Amarshi, K. Good and R. Mortimer), Melbourne, 1979, p.170.
45 cf. also O. Gostin (née van Rijswijck), 'Ten years of resettlement, cash cropping and social change among the Kuni at Bakoiudu, 1961–1971' in *Change and development in rural Melanesia* (ed. M. W. Ward), Port Moresby, 1971, pp.449–88.
46 *NGAR*, 1947–48, p.xi; *PAR*, 1948–49, p.90; Catholic Directory, *Pipel bilong God*, Port Moresby, 1982, s.v. 'Diocesan summaries'.
47 T. Aerts, '"The Little Vatican"', pp.69–71.
48 Kettle, *That they might live*, pp.166–75, 188–94, 205–12, 278–80, 285–92, 298–99.
49 On Papua, e.g., A. Henkelman, *En bourlignant sur le Mer de Corail; souvenirs d'un Frère Coadjuteur, missionaire en Papaousie*, Issoudun, 1949, p.30; Delbos, *Cent ans*, p.403 (trans:

317), and on Daru/Kiunga, see A. Smith, G. W. Trompf and K. Clements, *Flight into Limbo; refugees in Papua New Guinea*, Canberra, 1985, pp.15–16.

50 For background, H. Laracy (ed.), *Pacific Protest; the Maasina Rule Movement*, Suva, 1983, esp. sect. C. (Solomons); Lawrence, *Road*, chs 5–9 (Yali); T. Schwartz, *The Paliau movement in the Admiralty Islands, 1946–54*, (American Museum of Natural History anthropological papers 49/2) New York, 1962 (Paliau); Trompf, *Payback*, ch. 2, pt B (Pomio); P. Gesch, *Initiative and Initiation* (Peli).

51 cf. Bishop Leo Scharmach, *Manuale Missionariorum*, Rabaul, 1953, p.1.

52 Note all those edited by Sr W. Flannery under the title of *Religious movements in Melanesia 1–3* (Point Ser. 2–4), Goroka, 1983–84; and *Religious movements in Melanesia, a selection*, Goroka, 1984.

53 See esp. J. Griffin, H. Nelson and S. Firth, *Papua New Guinea; a political history*, pp.216–17.

T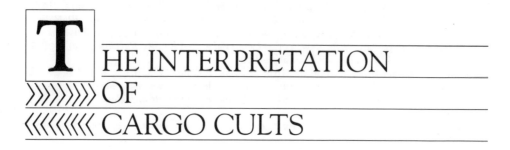HE INTERPRETATION OF CARGO CULTS

During the last two decades the dreams of the so-called 'civilizers' seemed to have been fulfilled in the granting of independence to Melanesian states: Fiji (popularly deemed the most cannibal of all islands, with its lack of pigs), from Great Britain in 1970; the Solomons (dreaded by early visitors for its headhunters), by 1978; and Vanuatu (formerly the New Hebrides), from both Britain and France in 1980. Until now the indigenous inhabitants in the western half of the great island of New Guinea (Irian Jaya) and in New Caledonia have missed out; participation for the blacks there, under neo-colonial Indonesia on the one hand, or a recently reformed yet French-dominated constitution on the other, remains highly problematic. Roads to independence have been fraught with difficulties, and the achievement itself brings upheavals, partly affected by the colonial inheritance. To the latter the anti-Indian Fijian coups under Colonel Rabuka (1987–88) are witness enough, let alone the struggle of the traditional landowners of Vanuatu's capital to seize special power (1988–89).

At the region's most populous centre lies the most impressive and politically formidable of all Melanesian powers. In September 1975, as was hoped by some and feared by a good many more, Papua New Guinea stood among the nations of the modern world. The country once deemed the earth's 'last known', once held in awe as the mysterious, impenetrable land of hostile savages, fever-ridden swamps and land-locked valleys, seemed to have come of age, tamed under the last throes of Western colonialism. And Albert Maori Kiki, the man who conceived himself to have lived '10 000 years in a lifetime' — from village childhood to urban politics — became the first minister for foreign affairs in the independent 'parliament of a thousand tribes'.[1] This newly acquired independence came as a surprise to many who still look on New Guinea as the most primitive, undeveloped place on the globe; for it has been renowned not so much as being the seat of a great self-conscious political force in Melanesia but rather as the scene of some of the most curious phenomena in human history — the cargo cults. On the road to independence and, somewhat surprisingly, even after it, a number of quite diverse groups of native New Guineans have been animated by the expectation that they will receive large quantities of European-style goods (or Cargo),[2] and have ordered their lives in the light of that expectation.

To these so-called cults we now direct our attention — not out of an insatiable appetite for oddities. No; it happens that in this case the unusual portends to be of more permanent human significance than even the impressive emergence of yet another black nation. For, cargo cults — both special in their Pacific context and strictly unprecedented in nature — vividly dramatize the confrontation between 'archaic' and 'modern' humanity (to use Mircea Eliade's distinction) — more particularly between the indigenous members of 'Stone Age' (or lithic) cultures and the intruding bearers of the highest technology known in history. Melanesia was being colonized and opened to the world between the time of the second industrial revolution (in the 1880s) and the age of the jet-plane and satellite communications. And from the time great steel-hulled German warships plied their way into Rabaul harbour at the turn of the century, up until the stage when geologists could still step out in a few remaining isolated places in the central highlands and appear like 'astronautic gods' to frightened villagers (in the early 1970s), Melanesians have had to make sense of a whole range of extraordinary new things. So much of interest in Melanesian religion, as we have already suggested, lies in the study of these Melanesian responses.

Terms of reference

Cargo cults are collective responses to the new order of life epitomized for Melanesians by 'the new goods'. They are typically ritualistic and agitated attempts by groups to prepare for the coming of these goods into the local people's hands, and have often been characterized by colonial authorities and expatriate settlers as unrealistic hopes to secure 'European' cargoes by bizarre and 'magical' means. Cargo cults are not, of course, unique to New Guinea and its outlying groups; but they are more numerous there (and, presumably, the actual number of cults which have crystallized there far exceeds the recorded estimates), even though such cults have been documented throughout Melanesia and from Polynesia as well. Papua New Guinea, too, is being very intensely 'studied' at present, and a good deal of very recent and exciting research has been devoted to the cults in question.

Not that this research, even when conducted by Papua New Guineans themselves,[3] has 'solved the riddle' of cargoism. But we are now in a better position to assess the usefulness of earlier interpretations, and to isolate those key issues and problems which require discussion and resolution before any more survey or generalist works can be justified.[4] So, from this ostensibly better position, a good start can be made by surveying general interpretations of cargo cultism and by asking what the social scientists (those 'sorcerers' as Stanislav Andreski describes them!)[5] have been up to.

First, certain anthropologists and sociologists have been busily fitting these so-called cults into their classifications and typologies. Even the word 'cult' itself reflects their enterprises. The word seems to stick to the phenomena like glue (and alternative expressions such as 'independent religious movement' or 'adjustment movement' seem doomed to inadequacy).[6] One wonders, in fact, whether 'cargo' and 'cult' could ever become unstuck because, with the persisting uncertainty as to how a cult should be defined, the power of alliteration is bound to prevail.[7] The term 'cult', though, is innocuous enough; for, at least it denotes a form of religious activity, even if the religious and the secular remained undifferentiated in traditional Melanesia. It is when one has to contend with the categorization of cargo cults as 'millenarian movements', however, that the real difficulties arise.

Despite tugs in contrary directions, it is by now almost a consensus view in textbooks that cargo cults are less profitably viewed as a species of 'nativism' or even 'revitalization' (that is, as movements seeking to perpetuate or improve select aspects of their culture)[8] than as group preparations for a dramatic external transformation. Stresses have fallen on the futurism of the cultists and on their expectation of a new order of plenty. As a result, they have been poured into the witches' brew of modern sociology, and conjured up as specimens of millenarism. 'Cargo cults', writes Professor Jarvie, in expressing a prevailing view, 'are apocalyptic millenarian movements, primarily of Melanesia, which promise a millennium in the form of material and spiritual *cargo*'.[9] We are thus asked to believe that, along with Qumranites and Anabaptists, Kimbanguists and Ghost Dancers, the Melanesian cults conform to a recognizable type of social phenomena. It has to be admitted that to manage such diffuse material under the heading of millenarism is not without usefulness, and certainly not without excitement for the comparative sociologist. The apparent validity of this recourse has been enhanced by the fact that in Melanesia itself 'so many specific items and patterns of behaviour . . . have their close equivalents in cult after cult', and these 'replications' cannot be easily accounted for by the diffusion of beliefs.[10] I myself have also acknowledged, at the outset, the importance of group anticipation of change. Yet Western scholars, I contend, have too often used broad categories like incantations of sorcery; it is now time to take stock, to reflect on our loaded vocabulary, and test our scientific frames of reference.

Before developing this particular quarrel, however, a second general observation should be made concerning the social scientific investigation of the cults. Characteristically, despite providing a variety of different theories about such enigmatic phenomena, most social scientists have also generally shown an unnerving propensity to avoid more complex, multiform lines of explanation or to avoid admitting that, in the final analysis, they are in the presence of a virtually unmanageable complexity.[11] They are not prone to being defeatist or concessive over individualities, divergences and exceptions; social science seems to invoke from them law-like generalizations. And where better to illustrate than from cargo cult studies? On the one hand, these cults have been deprecated as examples of irrational human behaviour — either because (as in the important case of the so-called 'Vailala Madness', described in chapter 5) they seem to bear witness to mass hysteria, or else because expectations of cargo in vast quantities are sometimes coupled with the hopes of Christian eschatology, which recalls to Western minds the 'lunatic fringe' or the 'heretical-sectarian' fanaticisms of their own tradition.[12] On the other hand, some social scientists have been eager to redeem the cultists in this respect. This has been done either by ascribing their apparent irrationality to the peculiar tensions which arose with the collision between traditional cultures and the colonial order,[13] or by coming to the conclusion that, given the magic-religious assumptions of the local peoples, it was quite rational for them to conclude that cargo derived from the ancestors and could be acquired by cultic procedures.[14]

This debate not only exemplifies the one-sidedness of scholarly explanations but also exposes the real problem of presenting a cargoist's view of the world that makes sense to a European or a learned audience. Theodore Schwartz is one who senses this difficulty more than most; yet, in his searching attempt to offer a necessarily complex solution, and to account for both the 'irrational' and the 'rational' in the one psychological explanation, even he was forced back on Festinger's theory of cognitive dissonance, a theory based on fieldwork in a Western setting.[15] Interestingly, too, Schwartz's good intentions are offset by another kind of misjudgement, a shortcoming he shares in common with the important writers, Peter Lawrence and Kenelm Burridge. These three men have all done exceptionally fine fieldwork on cults in selected parts of Papua New Guinea (on Manus, around Madang, and in the hinterland behind Borgia); yet, all three of them have tended to read the rest of highly variegated Melanesia from the confined areas they know so well.[16]

There are other bones to pick and more than one way of highlighting the pitfalls of social scientific interpretations. One might lament other 'one-track' explanations: cargo cults as stages on the road to political self-determination, for example (Worsley, Walters); as the result of missionization (Guiart); as revolutionist or thaumaturgic sectarian 'responses to the world' (Wilson); as the outcome of crises within traditional exchange systems (Brunton).[17] One might also express concern that scholars have rarely probed deeply to explore the intrinsically religious or spiritual nature of the cults but, instead, have tended to treat them more as instances of psycho-social adjustment or of social change.[18] Even when they have plunged below the superficial crust of structural-functionalism, they have either resorted to Eurocentric psychological categories, or else spun together a web of difficult quasi-theological abstractions, which lack clarity beside some of the more straightforward assessments of locally based missionary commentators.[19]

Key issues of interpretation

These critical comments arise from a growing awareness (as I myself continue to engage in and supervise fieldwork in a *variety* of Papua New Guinean contexts) that at least three fundamental demands should be placed on scholarship before we are ever going to replace *pre*mature conclusions about cargoism with mature ones. First, careful, sensitive and mainly oral historical work still needs to be done, not only on many cargo cults which have never been documented but also on most of those which already *have been* (even those which have been very intensely studied, though by one scholar).[20] Secondly, there are other religious cults and coteries of Melanesia (such as some of the 'independent' churches, for example), which are not readily placed in the pigeon-hole marked 'cargo cults'. These require attention, too, because they provide many intriguing points of contrast and comparison, indispensable for a well-balanced assessment of cargoism. In this connection, I would venture to suggest that the sensational aspect of cargo cultism has prevented scholars from doing justice to other related human activities, either trying to force phenomena under a rubric which is not appropriate for them or simply not recognizing the rich diversity of Melanesian responses to colonialism or social change.[21] Thirdly, an openness to particular historical contexts and to a variety of causal factors and explanations is required before an adequate general theory of cargo cults can become a real possibility. In this chapter, however, I shall confine myself to following up these brief introductory reflections by enquiring whether there is anything special that the discipline of Religious Studies (or Comparative Religion, or the History of Religions) might bring to bear on this subject, to make up for lack of depth and subtlety in the social scientific literature.

Who better to consider in this connection than the great doyen of postwar studies in comparative religion — Mircea Eliade, who took up the subject of cargo cultism in an intriguing 1962 essay?[22] Eliade's approach to the subject is characteristic. For him the cults furnish still another example of 'archaic man's' belief in the regeneration of time and the cosmos; thus, the cults 'become completely intelligible only in the perspective of the history of religions' as a whole.[23] This line has both significant advantages and disadvantages. Its main disadvantages lie in the fact that Eliade is committed to stating a general thesis about cargo cults because he holds to a general thesis about 'archaic man'. To note a main advantage, on the other hand, Eliade has raised what is probably the most fundamental of all questions which ought to be raised concerning these cults (and indeed concerning any chiliastic-looking movements in the Third World). It is a question about the understanding of time or, if we must say it, the religious understanding of time. In positing what is probably the most generalist of all cargo cult theories, susceptible as it is to the kinds of criticisms already outlined above, his sensitiveness towards the mythological mind has conducted him to what must come to the heart of the issue.

For Eliade the cults are syncretistic, combining both traditional and Christian elements. Since the supportive power of the ancestors had been considered necessary for the success of any 'economic' activity, it was not unnatural for Melanesians to believe that European goods derived from the dead, and really belonged to them rather than to the whites. Yet Melanesians were also exposed to mission teaching, to a very a compelling set of new beliefs which made their traditional values look questionable. Both in being deprived of Cargo and finding old patterns undermined, then, they faced a great 'reversal'. As Eliade has it, however, the cargo cults which arose within the tensions of this colonial situation were not tokens of despair or neurosis so much as positive expressions of spiritual renewal. They 'marked the resurgence of a truer religious life, infinitely more creative because nourished by a prophetic millenarist experience', and by the expectation of 'a new life, regenerated from the roots'.[24] Interestingly, the influence of Christian doctrine on these expectations of 'a Golden Age' or 'a new Heaven and a new Earth'[25] is not over-emphasized; Eliade is too interested in traditional mythology for that. His conclusions are striking:

> All these Melanesian minor religions share the same central myth; the coming of the dead is taken as the sign of cosmic renewal . . . The 'cargo-cults' have merely resumed, amplified, revalorized and charged with prophetic and millenary power the traditional religious theme that the Cosmos renews itself periodically, or . . . is symbolically re-created every year.[26]

In Christianity the native Melanesians simply rediscovered an 'old, traditional eschatological myth', which lay behind their collective, orgiastic feasts of the New Year.[27]

How are we to evaluate this thesis? I intend to do some dissolving first, and then engage in a work of reconstitution afterwards. For clarity's sake, I will draw the reader's attention to four kinds of variance useful in the assessment of Eliade's position — or any general interpretation of cargo cults for that matter. A critique of Eliade's approach, in fact, will provide the means to reflect more on the social scientific interpretations already mentioned.

Millenarian features

If one is interested in applying the category 'millenarian movements' to cargo cults (and Eliade himself is happy to do so),[28] one should at least be cautious about the varying degrees to which the cults reflect so-called millenarist features. Definitions of millenarism, or course, also vary. On the working assumption that definitions cannot be proved true or false, but only useful or useless, I shall choose a better known one for present purposes. The brilliant Israeli sociologist, Yonina Talmon, in what is probably the most helpful summation yet formulated, understood millenarism 'to designate religious movements that expect imminent, total, ultimate, this-worldly collective salvation'.[29] Talmon did not neglect to stress the Biblical roots of the chiliastic tradition and, thus, historical considerations have been a restraining factor in her typological application of millenarism to modern colonial situations. Most important, too, Talmon has reckoned with millennial views of time, earlier concluding that they are usually strongly linear (since a 'final future' is anticipated), although she later conceded that 'the cyclical paradigmatic time conception' can predominate in cases where the 'notion of time as duration and change' is vague.[30]

Adopting Talmon's definition, then, do cargo cults qualify as millenarian movements? In my considered estimate: some do, some do not, and there are matters of degree to be considered. Allow this answer to be fleshed out by isolating two issues: first, the notion of millenarism as content; second, the use of inappropriate categories of description.

The first issue can be introduced by concrete example: a comparison between phenomena from within the same well known area, the southern Madang district, New Guinea. Early in 1942 a certain Tagarab of Milguk led a new quasi-Christian revisionist cult, which set great store by the Japanese, whose coming would bring about the removal of Europeans. God, identified with a local deity named Kilibob, would initiate the great changes.

> He would leave Australia and return to Madang with his ships full of cargo: not only ordinary trade goods, but also rifles, ammunition and other military equipment.[31] These he would hand over to the spirits of the dead, who would appear in the guise of Japanese servicemen. They would bring the goods to the natives by aeroplane and help them drive out the Europeans, missionaries included. At the same time, God-Kilibob would change the colour of the natives' skins from black to white. These events would be heralded by the occurrence of storms and earthquakes of unprecedented severity and number.[32]

The people guided by Tagarab were also required to fulfil certain obligations. They sought to obey the Ten Commandments by eliminating sorcery feuds, love magic and adultery; they took special food offerings to the cemeteries as they awaited the spirits; and they honoured Tagarab himself by participating in his 'church services' and entrusting him with all European items, including money. War came — a war of armaments and aerial combat utterly staggering to the New Guineans who experienced it. Two years later the cult quickly disintegrated with the death of Tagarab, who was shot by Japanese soldiers while protesting about the ill-treatment of his followers to his new masters.[33]

By conventional standards, Tagarab's movement was clearly a cargo cult; European goods were expected to arrive in large quantities and people geared their lives in accordance with this expectation. It would be disingenuous, also, to pass over the movement's apparently millenarian characteristics: its members were to be saved and bountifully rewarded through a drastic reversal of events (and, at least, the prospective 'salvation' was 'imminent', 'collective', certainly 'this-worldly', even if any appeal to Talmon's adjectives 'total' and 'ultimate' would demand a careful justification).

In the same region a generation later, however, there were two cults which, although vitally concerned with Cargo, or more especially money, were not propelled by the motivating power of an eschatology. Both the famous Ngaing leader Yali Singina of the Rai coast (whose influence remains centred around Sor) and the lesser Yakob (operating near Sek), in contrast to Tagarab, encouraged periodic rounds of 'table ritual' to ensure that the ancestors would leave either goods or money in the bush and at sanctuaries. According to Yali, too, the acquisition of Cargo depended upon continuing the annual *Kabu*, a traditional ceremony through which youths had been initiated into the male cult. Rather than being animated by the prospect of cataclysmic change, these more recent movements — both ostensibly cargo cults — possessed institutions which actually maintain *day-to-day*, habitual activity (even though 'the element of suspense' had some part to play).[34] It is hardly feasible, then, to call them millenarian movements. One might protest that millennial hopes certainly contributed to the rise and sustenance of Yali's power, or contend that these two recent cults represent a stage of social change, which is attained to after earlier and wilder dreams fail to materialize (and which has also been capable of still more recent reactivation).[35] The most distinctive feature of Yali's movement, however, was its backward-looking appeal to the traditional means by which material well-being was procured; as a proselytizing organization, too, it took root in soil which had never experienced cargo millenarism.[36] In any case, the contrast is useful enough in introducing the less feverish, more institutionalized forms of cargoism,[37] and in showing that the category of millenarism will only suit these fascinating Melanesian movements to varying degrees.

With the second issue, we turn to conceptual and semantic problems. Such phrases as 'the millennium', 'the Golden Age', 'new Heaven, new Earth' or 'cosmic regeneration', which are often used to describe the hopes of Melanesian cargoists, call for circumspection. They are all familiar expressions from Western parlance, and yet that only goes to show how cautious we must be against foisting an ethnocentric mental baggage on people who cannot share it, or who are only able to accommodate it in part. When former missionaries reported 'myths of a Golden Age', for one example, they may well have amplified the content of prevalent expectations beyond justification.[38] When Melanesian 'prophets' foretell great natural catastrophes, for another, it is false to assume that they are extrapolating from Mark 13, since earthquakes, landslides and other fearful devastations remain an integral part of their environmental heritage. And when a pidgin-speaking informant tells of *taim bilong tumbuna em bai kam ap* (the ancestral time is coming), it is hazardous to draw the quick conclusion that he refers to some general resurrection, or to the ultimate, physical return of the ancestors in a large cargo ship. He may well be voicing a more traditional view that the spirits, as usual, will be present at the most significant incidences of group prosperity. In this important case, we have to assess whether any such return of the dead is understood to be an event of genuine finality, or whether it is taken more as a *continuation* of the ancestors' largesse in the (mythical) past, or as a spiritual renewal and adjustment that enables the people to cope with the new circumstances of colonialism.[39] However, this appeal for prudence simply underlines that it is a question of degree, without denying that some cargo cults satisfy Talmon's recipe for millenarism or Eliade's claims about the hope of 'cosmic' renewal. It is just that we ought to know the ingredients of any particular dish before we hurry down a misleading name on the social scientific menu.

Christian content

Most scholars (with Eliade among them) have rightly stressed the missionary impact on the formation of cargo cults. Yet there are clearly varying degrees of Christian content in cargoist views and behaviour: one might be tempted to draw a tentative spectrum between movements heavily imbued with mission language, liturgy and structure, and those that are not. To highlight the contrast between two extremes: first, picture the enormous Paliau church of Baluan Island in the Admiralty Island or Manus group, for instance, with the strains of its choir wafting through the tidy village; then, imagine a set of simple, bamboo, make-believe telegraph receivers, put up by scarcely contacted New Guinean highlanders in 1943–44 to welcome Jesus and the ancestors from the sky. And let it be clear that a small cluster of cargo cults bear next to no signs of Christian influence.[40] Thus, it is no longer feasible to interpret active cargoism as if, in each case, the Christian component stands at a relatively uniform level.

Although the range of potential is wider, however, one should never underestimate how difficult it is to fill out a broader spectrum with any real precision. Consider the problem. We are dealing with forms of 'syncretism', and *amounts* of syncretism are notoriously difficult to quantify.[41] We might like to think, for example, that cultist appeals to the Bible, or persisting church services, are reliable indicators as to the extent of Christian influences, but they can be quite deceptive — even the results of a conscious attempt to deceive 'outsiders'. We might like to gauge the relative degree to which the Christian message has been understood or misunderstood, but how slippery is the matter at hand, how easily affected by prejudice! Burning questions often call for answers: how consolidated is the cult group in its beliefs and aims? or does a noticeable gap exist between leaders and activists (who have status or knowledge) and the amorphous collection of hangers-on? Such queries could have everything to do with varying degrees of commitment to dogmas or aspirations; yet, only very exhaustive fieldwork will yield adequate answers. Most (or all) of the above problems are nicely illustrated by the Inawaia cult among the Mekeo of Papua (1940–41). When recently re-examined, it became obvious that there was not one cult but at least two, one surrounding the prophet Filo, whose filial devotion to Mary was self-avowedly bona fide (even despite her impressive vision of cargo and rifles descending on God's altar), and the other led by her uncle and other sorcerers, who evidently used Filo's small-scale Catholic revival as a cover for more traditionalist operations (and their temporary re-acquisition of power).[42] However perplexing the phenomena,[43] this stress on the varying degrees of Christian influence remains valuable; at least it may encourage us to be more open-minded when deciding on the ideological source of any 'millennial dream'.

The quantity of cargo

Most studies of cargo movements (including Eliade's) leave the impression that the cultists anticipated unlimited quantities of European items. To set the record straight, however, we know of clear-cut cases where cargo is only looked for in finite quantities and, although the available data is often problematic, there are good reasons for belief that it was *expected in varying amounts* across the board.

Even the wildest of imaginings, too, may bear some correspondence with 'reality', as with the members of the so-called 'first cargo cult' on Manus Island, for example. They put no limits upon quantity because their hopes were decidedly affected by the experience of seeing fighter planes, tanks, warships, one million Americans, and seemingly endless supplies of tinned food.[44] In other instances the quantum of goods may be vaguely defined in terms of a large ship or airplane, with the significance of the cargo lying in its *symbolic* value. So, when Pako of Buka prophesied 'the arrival of a cargo ship with iron, axes, food, tobacco, motor-cars, and significantly, firearms', he was projecting an important event which would equalize blacks and whites; when the leaders of the Vailala movement spoke of Cargo, they probably took its coming to signalize the corrected relationship between men and the spirit-world, a relationship which was primary for them.[45] Running down the tentative scale, we come to expectations of a 'limited happening' with an enduring pragmatic consequence, such as the miraculous appearance of a factory (immediate post-war Nimbora, north Irian Jaya), and then on to less spectacular hopes — the dream that one's everyday objects may change into items of European wealth, or that the cult leader will distribute large sums of multiplied money to his faithful lackeys.[46] The size of any cargo provision, then, is hardly fixed. We must hasten to add that the expected amount often relates to the anticipated nature of its distribution, and cult leaders are generally assumed to be less generous than either God or the spirits.[47]

This third variance throws light on the first two. By Talmon's standards, it is inappropriate to use the word 'millennium' of occurrences which do not bring total and ultimate salvation (as compared, let us say, to means of amelioration, or adjustment). One might well protest that the millennium will always be relative, that few Melanesian cultists have been in the position to visualize an eschaton like the macrocosmic world-collapse of the Western tradition. Yet one can protest too much. If a New Guinean highlander considers that the cargo-event is not that much more impressive than a great pig-killing, and that both transactions have everything to do with the continuing fertility of the cosmos, we ought to take this viewpoint seriously. If the arrival of cargo is conceived as but another, albeit very special, dispensation from the hands of the spirits, then we dare not read finality into the event without weighing other factors.[48] The more unbounded the hope of material abundance, though, or the more conclusive the process of salvation, or the more practised the language of Biblical eschatology, then the more we can write with confidence about millenarian movements, even shifts toward Christian sectarianism.

Colonial contexts

Several scholars (Eliade fairly included again) explain cargo cults in terms of native response to alien control. Whilst this approach is quite reasonable, one still has to account for the emergence of cults in differing colonial situations. Not only is it plain that they have arisen when contact with Europeans has been negligible,[49] but also, as Ronald Berndt has rightly stressed, 'they *do not* arise at any particular stage of contact with aliens, nor do they appear only in a society subjected to acute hardship, to war, epidemic and intense missionary evangelization'.[50]

If they are usually anti-white, too, it is obviously important to ask why. The posture may have more to do with the self-identity of the group than with a burning desire to eliminate outsiders. We also need to know the different causes of real aggravation: it might be a rice project foisted on the local people by the administration, an indentured labour programme, land alienation, an 'isolation complex', a spiritual crisis within the group, exasperation that the flow of the new goods to an area has been cut off, a simple suspicion that the whites are withholding the 'secret' of the Cargo, or an awareness that they are responsible for domestic troubles, sickness and death, and so on. Within each cult, of course, dissatisfaction can be expressed in quite divergent ways and its level of intensity can vary both across 'cult membership' and through time. All this confirms, then, that the nature of the interaction between locals and colonials requires careful historical investigation.

Interpretations of Mircea Eliade

I come to my last point of criticism, which is more specifically concerned with Eliade's thesis than with cargo cult scholarship as a whole. Professor Eliade has contended that all cargo cults 'share the same central myth' of cosmic regeneration, and that, although this myth gets 'revalorized' in millenarian terms, it derives from indigenous New Year festivals which celebrate the renewal of the known order, including the special return of the dead into the presence of the living.

This general view, Eliade admits, had already been expressed by Vittorio Lanternari, who certainly accepted 'the Feast of the New Year or the cult of the dead' as the 'myth and ritual' basis of cargo activities, yet who acknowledged Andreas Lommel as his predecessor.[51] Lommel argued that all traditional Melanesian life, as well as cargoism, sprang from the cult of the ancestors,[52] but it remained for Lanternari to link the belief in the returning presence of the dead to New Year festivals. This 'crypto-pan-Babylonian' view,[53] however, cannot bear the weight of the evidence both old and new. It is imperfect on two counts. First, it presupposes a uniformity of ritual pattern and belief structure among Melanesians. We are back to variances again. The annual turn of the 'seasons' (dry and wet) is very important in traditional life for a variety of reasons: for planting and harvesting, for gauging the 'ages' of people, pigs, trees, for good fishing, for recognizing the time to sail over long distances (as in the case of the famous *Hiri* expeditions). Among some peoples, it is true, the great feasts are also yearly affairs — the harvest and *Kabu* ceremonies of the Ngaing, for example, or the colourful dramas enacted by masked men in the secret societies of New Britain (such as the *Dukduk*) — and these events are said to be either initiated or witnessed by the ancestors.[54] Yet we also have to reckon with much larger cycles: a lapse of over seven years, for instance, can separate the great pig kills of the Wahgi peoples of the western highlands, or of the Chimbu and the Gururumba, moving east. Even then, the time for the festival will depend on a concurrence of factors, such as the position of the moon, the state of the animals, the absence of other ritual obligations.[55] For a grander cycle still, we have only to think again of the *Hevehe* cycle, that elaborate series of events among the Elema which used to reach its high-point about every 18–20 years.[56]

With many groups, though, there are no such ritual cycles; the major ceremonies may depend on times of death, of attainment of adulthood, even of birth and old age.[57] In these cases it is the life cycle and not the annual rotation of seasons which is determinative. Moreover, if prominent ceremonies in each culture betoken the concern or involvement of the ancestral company, it does not follow that they provide the occasion for a special 'return'. The belief that (benevolent) ancestral spirits dwell far from the villages but are still able to come to the feasts is not uncommon in Melanesia (especially on the smaller islands and along the coasts of New Guinea), but it is hardly standard. Myths about the eventual re-appearance of culture heroes or ancestors, too, as stated before, are few and far between. The spirits, whether favourable or easily displeased, may inhabit the bush or a known area not far from the group. Their freedom of movement and action may be recognized with awe, and their witness of ritual — whether splendid or insignificant, periodic or contingent — be simply taken for granted. Thus, a Gururumba informant was not commenting on the temporary homecoming of the dead when he declared: 'The ancestors see the "*iNgErEBe*" (pig festival) and they know we have not forgotten them. They look and their bellies are good.'[58] Certainly, he was revelling in the show of fertility — the 'cosmic renewal' if you like — but the dead were forever involving themselves in the lives of the clans, offering their powerful support or demanding to be pleased. Thus, in the light of such diversity, it is unwise to generalize about annual Melanesian ceremonies which signify the return of the dead, and more inadvisable still to found a theory of cargo cults on such shaky premisses.

In the second place, the combined theme of New Year festivals and the myth of the returning dead cannot serve to explain the cargo cult phenomenon in any adequate way if we are still left asking this crucial question: how is it that we find the cargo cult in some Melanesian societies and not in others?[59]

Despite weaknesses in his thesis, however, I must repeat that Eliade has still managed to put his finger on that crucial issue: time. He has an uncanny sensitiveness towards the assuring, enduring rhythmic order of archaic humanity's universe. And in view of our previous discussion no one will deny that Melanesian life is rhythmic: one can feel its pulse in the beat of a *kundu* (drum), the swayings of a mask or the chant of a dancing warrior. Traditional comprehensions of the known order, too, were authenticated by systems of logic which interpreted the relationships between the living and the dead, humankind and nature, the individual and the group, friend and enemy. However much we might like to wish it so, moreover, the phenomenon of the white (or red)[60] man was not really within the compass of traditional possibilities — as if the Melanesian could say with moving serenity, like Montezuma before Cortes, that he had long awaited the visitor. In encounter, admittedly, the whites were often confused with the ancestors, but this misapprehension rarely lasted long (and I know of no cargo cult which really perpetuates it).[61] The intruders, in the final analysis, threw the old rhythms into the balance and caused a sense of discontinuity. The feeling of disjunction was sharpened all the more by the utterly astounding material culture of the newcomers. 'The white man event', then, was too spectacular to evoke purely traditional explanations,[62] too astounding and curious to be recognized as a clear-cut threat, and it came to be so disruptive that intellectual and social adjustment was inevitable. Interaction with the sources of the disruption was a prolonged and disconcerting experience even if physical contact between black and white was historically intermittent.

Once the momentous event had become a quite unavoidable object of concern, however, it then marked the end of the 'older time', even if traditional patterns of life were carried on. The event, in fact, was as much *Endzeit* (End Time) as *neue Zeit* (New Time); for, it had the effect of displacing the older order and ripping it from its once stabilized locus in mythical time. Melanesian adjustment to mission evangelization, then, and to the new arrangements ordained by the administration and by business, has everything to do with modifying conceptions of time, myth and the cosmic rhythm. The cargo cult is one form of that adjustment; although, unlike other forms, it has been most unacceptable to the new masters, with their stringent prerequisites for normative acculturation. Almost always, however, spiritual and social 'negotiations' with the bearers of the new order meant that the old rhythmic cycles have given way to a more linear approach to time. If a new sense of time did not present itself through 'education' — through the message of a salvation history running from creation to eschaton, for example, or through talk of material and technological progress — then it was still driven into the indigenous consciousness by the visible facts of colonial rule and social change themselves. For those who believed that the soil they trod and handled belonged to their people and to black people, it was only fitting and true to expect that the great changes were for them and their kinsfolk. They could draw upon sacred lore both old and new to confirm their belief; they could be assured that the tangible embodiment of the new (perhaps final) order — the Cargo — was on its way.

There is no intention here to resort to any narrowing line of explanation, but to develop an argument from the best of Eliade's interpretation. Any attempt to understand how 'archaic man' comes to terms with modernity and temporal linearity ought to be related to other kinds of explanation, which in turn should be interrelated or at least tested. Eliade's work is nonetheless particularly inspiring for suggesting a reason (and it *could* be the most important reason) for the highly dramatic responses and expectations of cargoists. In the cases of those cultists influenced by Christianity, Eliade has argued that 'the prophetic and eschatological aspects of the Christian religion . . . woke the deepest echo in them';[63] but it was not because they wanted to appropriate eschatology as apocalypticists would, it was because the events of the encounter with the whites and their possessions were themselves 'eschato-logical'. They were 'eschatological' in the sense that they disrupted the long-standing primal rhythms of those men and women who, in all probability, had preserved their archaic consciousness of sacred time longer than any other people in the world.

New agenda for interpretation

How are these conclusions to be related back to what we have already singled out as the most significant themes in Melanesian traditional religions? And what bearing does this perception of a kind of 'hinge-point' eschatology have on the less earthier paradigms of social scientists already considered? In the first place, we must set a new agenda for the analysis of cargo cults in terms of the continuing influence of significant elements in traditional religions, el-ements which also have a strong bearing on the relative degree of response to Christianity in particular and colonial intervention in general. In the second place, social scientists are going to have to shift out of those mindsets which disallow religion any explanatory function in the analysis of social change, and also broaden their concept of religion to incorporate aspects of social life which Westerners too often compartmentalize into non-religious spheres.

In relation to the new agenda: if we return to the master themes in chapter 1, some of which were further developed in the subsequent chapters of the first part of this book, we can see how important it is *to test the relative resilience of various aspects of traditional religion* in a fine-toothed investigation of cargo movements.

One basic question to ask is *whether 'the old god or gods' have disappeared* from the culture (so that the cult concerned can have no other deity to focus on than the one widely accepted as the Christian one), or whether they are being revived through the cult. In one breathtaking moment during my fieldwork in the Yangoru area of the East Sepik, for instance, I asked a pointed question of Matias Yaliwan, the famous leader of the Peli Association, who had caused such a disruption in 1971 by inspiring a mass demonstration to begin removing the American concrete geodesic markers from the summit of Mount Hurun. 'You read about God in your copy of the *Nupela Testamen* [pidgin: New Testament]', I put it to him (after he had read Romans 13 and Revelation 20 in a small ceremony at his secluded headquarters), 'but would it be true that, for you, god is Huru[n], the god of the mountain?' The answer was a very quiet admission which drew our long conversation to a close. It was the disclosure of his most precious secret about his movement: that he wanted the wealth and total well-being formerly brought by the deity of the mountain to be reaccessible, and, in removing the markers causing the blockages, to allow the new wealth of the cargo to be released from the mountain as well.[64]

Another obvious question to answer concerns *the place of the departed or ancestors*, who could be the last crucial set of spirit-agencies to be left over in tradition once the old gods have been abandoned or redefined by missionaries as *satans* (pidgin for 'demons').[65] Is the hope of their grand *collective* return in many cargo movements — a hope that does not seem to be part of pre-contact beliefs — because the ancestors represent the only hope left in a highly problematic situation? Is it, alternatively, a way of swelling numbers in a final conflict or desired dénouement? Or else is their coming all this *and* a serious acceptance of the new message that, in the Last Times, the dead will be resurrected? In a time of general transformation, this cosmic event is a possible miracle alongside all the actualized ones perceived in 'the New Time' and concretized in the new goods. Among the members of the Pomio *Kivung* (organization), mainly among the Mengen of East New Britain, it has been assumed that, when the ancestors do come back as a group, they will bring into being the new material items by a mere wish. They will be able to create a whole city like New York, in fact, on the edges of Jacquinot Bay.[66]

In moving on to the subject of myth, there is another, related, question we could ask in passing: about the place of other spirit-beings, such as culture heroes, because whites or cult leaders have in various cases been identified with these beings brought back to life.[67] It is clear, though, that *many cargo movements appeal to a traditional myth*, and discovering the implications of such myths for cargoist activity is one of the crucial, often underdone, areas of scholarly investigation. It has been shown of the Biak Island region in Irian Jaya, for instance, that the myth of the culture-hero, Mansren, has been the basis for movements time and time again in the area, but the myth has experienced a variety of uses. When first documented (in 1857), it seemed only to have implications for cultural solidarity in the area; by the 1970s, however, it had inspired many protests and even given rise to novel theologies in which the suffering Mansren was made analogous to the despised Christ.[68] Plotting the continuities and deciphering the coded references back to basic myths in different cult outbreaks in a region is essential grist to a conscientious investigator's mill.

We are not to forget the *continuing reflections of negative and positive reciprocity* in cargo movements, and *upgraded logics of retribution*. What Henri Desroche has stated of all millenarian-type movements remains true of all cargo cults, whether millennially-focussed or not: they create *altercations* with those believed to have created an invidious social situation.[69] At one end of a working spectrum, cargo cults can erupt into violence — armies even being formed, as with A. B. Army among the Biakese, who were bent on rescuing their beloved prophet Angganita from the Japanese in 1943 — to a mere jousting with the colonial authorities by local exponents of a new experiment.[70] Hard indeed is it to find a cargo movement which does not have its butt of reprisal; but the real inequalities in weaponry being what they have been under colonial regimens, most protests have been sensibly 'psychological' and therefore non-violent.

As for positive reciprocity, cargo cultists have usually projected solutions which we can justifiably describe as the *perfection of reciprocal relations*, so that old problems will not return. Part of the confirmation that this perfection will unfold lies in the members' willingness to *sacrifice* all the current wealth they had — usually by killing their pigs and destroying their gardens, but sometimes by throwing out even the European items they have come to possess — so that the new order of wealth would be unleashed from a sympathetic spirit world.[71] The prospective perfection, it should be appreciated, is a total resolution of material, human and human–spirit relationships.

Accompanying these signs that the principles of recrimination and concessive exchange remain important, there are the constant adaptations of retributive logic. In cargoist talk the differences between the conditions of the local people and the outsiders always have to be explained, and it is common to find someone blamed: the blacks for their foolishness in not accepting the Cargo when it was first offered in 'primal time' (in various Madang stories), or the whites for not sharing their wealth or re-diverting it away from its true *kanaka* owners.[72] In verbal pictures of the coming scenario, moreover, retribution is conceived to lie in the hands of the greater-than-human powers in a projected imminent future. The bad (the white oppressors, for example) will be removed, while the good (the group's adherents) will be the recipients of total blessing. Traditional retributive logic has been steadily undermined by the assaults of new social realities and missionary teaching. The old rationale for payback killing and sorcery has been made to look like the inspiration of the Devil and the greatest threat to the newly proclaimed (would-be civilized) order. Even the great ceremonial exchanges which were highpoints in traditional religious life were bound to bear the brunt of missionary (especially of conservative Protestant) criticism.[73] In cargo cults, however, the general objectives implicit in traditional retributive logic have been preserved, yet with the sense of a justified requital and socio-economic balance, which is most often revalorized by touches of a wider, Christian world-view and by eschatological innuendo.[74]

There is much more to be said about the relationship between cargo activities and traditional religions. More work requires to be done on these *activities as akin to initiation ceremonies or rites of passage* (following in the wake of Patrick Gesch's fine, very recent study of the Yangoru cargo movement, *Initiative and Initiation*), and more on the place of revealed secret knowledge in the old and new cult.[75] Another area for further research concerns why these movements have *affected chiefly and non-chiefly societies*. A considered assessment will reveal that cult leaders have been either 'new men and women' — that is, individuals who have had a special and, to them, 'numinous' experience in the whites' world — or else persons without hereditary or 'managerial' status who have generated movements that side-step traditional social structures. (Concerning the circumventing of chiefly supremacy, one only has to think about 'Bilalaf' among the Fuyughe, or, further afield, about Irakau on Manam Island and John Teosin on Buka.)

In conclusion, what might be the implications of a more distinctly religious focus for social scientific revaluations? Bearing in mind what our critique of Eliade's interpretations have led us to affirm about 'the New Time' as pregnant with eschatological significance in post-contact Melanesian consciousness, I would suggest that such specialists as anthropologists, sociologists and political scientists develop a deeper and wider sense of religion in Melanesian affairs.

By deeper, I mean a greater sensitization to the awe and astonishment, nervousness and feeling of threat, which islanders have been experiencing in the face of intrusion. Instead of reducing this response to a set of psychological conditions — even psychosis[76] — or to mere epiphenomena beside the hard facts of socio-economic conditions, they ought to perceive it afresh as the religious coherence without which these movements would never come into being. This response, too, has everything to do with sacralized time: cargo cultists apprehend themselves to live in *the* time, in the Janus-faced position between an unsatisfactory, convulsed near past and present and the answer to all their hopes in the near future — with the material wonders of the present (the cars, the radios, the new tools, metal money) providing the visible confirmation that the Great (or greater) Transformation is at hand.[77] By the development of a wider sense of religion, I refer once more to that need for researchers to eschew old compartmentalizations that blinker approaches to religious issues.

As I have been continually suggesting, warfare and economic exchange can no longer be separated from traditional Melanesian religions because so much of life's vitality was gathered up in these activities, and they were enshrouded by so many ritualistic, ethical and existentially significant articulations.[78] Cargo cults will never be understood through hermeneutics made cock-eyed by 'secular' university disciplines. For, perhaps more arrestingly than any other social phenomena, they gather up physically-sublimated collective vindictiveness, the deep human desire for material security and community harmony, and the concerns for right relationships with the spiritual 'realm', into 'total visions' of the cosmos. In this they are new religious movements, picking up on the potentially all-embracing qualities of local traditional religions as well as on the proclaimed missionary message that a total vision and reorientation are what the transforming qualities of the Gospel are all about. In this, however, they have tried to recover what was lost and undermined of their past, and provide a lesson to Western purveyors of Christianity (and quasi-Christian ethics) bent on divaricating spiritual and material salvation.[79] As we shall see in the following chapter, moreover, some of them now do this in the guise of new churches.

NOTES

Chapter 8 is based on material originally published as an article in the journal *Religious Traditions*.

1 cf. G. Souter, *New Guinea; the last unknown*, Sydney, 1963; A. M. Kiki, *Kiki; ten thousand years in a lifetime*, and O. White, *Parliament of a thousand tribes; a study of New Guinea*, London, 1965.

2 Cargo will be capitalized in this chapter whenever it obviously refers to something *more than* mere European or internationally marketed goods — that is, when it refers to the coming of a 'totality' of material and spiritual 'blessing' (on this last usage, cf. ch. 3).

3 For references to work by Papua New Guineans, see ns1, 21, 35, 37, 55, 62 below. Almost all the writers mentioned are graduates of the University of Papua New Guinea.

4 Unfortunately, an overly-ambitious piece of generalism on this subject, and on the whole question of Third World 'sectarianism', made its appearance as recently as 1973. I refer to B. R. Wilson's *Magic and the Millennium; a sociological study of religious movements of protest among tribal and Third World peoples*, New York, 1973. In his brilliant and contemptuous review of this book, T. O. Ranger, in *African religious research* 3/2 (1973), pp.32–33, points out how Wilson has relied so heavily on older studies of African religious movements and shown no awareness of the ever multiplying number of recent critical analyses of particular groups and problems. In a parallel way, Wilson has not kept up with ongoing research into Melanesia.

5 cf., *The social sciences as sorcery*, London, 1972.

6 i.e., such movements animated by a concern for the coming of cargo. cf. L. P. Mair, 'Independent religious movements in three continents', in *Comparative studies in society and history*, 1 (1959), pp.113ff. (Mair, though, was evidently the first anthropologist to use the term cargo cult, in 1952); and see the journal *Point*, 1, 1974 on 'The Church and Adjustment Movements'. 'Nativistic' and 'Revitalization' movements are other possibilities — see n.8 below.

7 Concerning rhetoric, it should be noted that the phrase 'cargo cult' is now used in common parlance throughout Papua New Guinea (pidgin: *Kago Kalt*). On the history of the usage in scholarly literature, see esp. P. Christiansen, *The Melanesian cargo cult; millenarianism as a factor in cultural change*, Copenhagen, 1969, pp.15–21. On the debate over 'cult' as against 'social movement', see esp. M. W. Smith, 'Towards a classification of cult movements', *Man*, 59 (1959), pp.8–12; P. Brown, 'Social Change and Social Movements', in E. K. Fisk (ed.), *New Guinea on the threshold; aspects of social, political and economic development*, Canberra, 1968, esp. pp.163–65 (where Brown counters Margaret Mead's arguments that cults are not movements). I note here an appalling lack of communication between anthropologists and those historians of religion who have been at work on ancient cultism.

8 cf. R. Linton, 'Nativistic Movements', *American Anthropologist*, 45 (1943), pp.230ff; A. F. Wallace, 'Revitalization Movements', *American Anthropologist*, 57 (1956), pp.264ff.

9 So, 'Theories of Cargo Cults: a critical analysis', *Oceania*, 34 (1963), p.1, and see also his book *The revolution in anthropology* (International library of sociology and social reconstruction), London, 1964(7), pp.66–68. Not only Wilson (*Magic*, ch. 9), and Christiansen (*Cargo Cult*, pp.15–16) concur in calling cargo cults millenarian movements, but so too do other noted scholars in the field: H. Desroche, *Sociologie de l'espérance*, Paris, 1973, pt 2, ch. 12 (for Eng. trans. n.69 below); Peter Worsley, *Trumpet shall sound*, esp. pp.229–64; Peter Lawrence, *Road*, p.1; and Kenelm Burridge, esp. *New heaven, new earth; a study of millenarian activities*, Oxford, 1969, chs 5–6.

10 So Wilson, *Magic*, p.313.

11 The unmanageable complexity has led Judy Inglis to deny that any general theory of cargo cults is possible, cf. 'Cargo cults; the problem of explanation', *Oceania*, 27 (1957), pp.261–63. Her line of argument is different from mine, however, since she is emphasizing the uniqueness of every historical situation (an argument which, taken to its logical extreme, cuts at the roots of every social scientific generalization), whereas I am pleading at this point for polymorphic explanations. My position, then, does not preclude the *possibility* of a valid general theory. On some of the philosophical issues involved here, see (to begin with!) P. H. Nowell-Smith, 'Are historical events unique?', *Proceedings of the Aristotelian Society*, 57 (1956–57), pp.107ff.

12 On the so-called 'automaniacs' of the 'Vailala Madness' (I prefer the Vailala Movement), see esp. F. E. Williams, *The 'Vailala Madness'*, esp. pp.333ff; cf. also B. G. Burton-Bradley, 'The psychiatry of cargo cult', *Medical journal of Australia*, 4 (1974), pp.388ff., and note W. C. Clarke, 'Temporary madness as theatre: wild man behaviour in New Guinea', pp.198ff. On cargo cults as irrational see esp. R. Firth, *Elements of social organisation*, London, 1951, pp.111–14; cf. Mair, 'The pursuit of the Millennium in Melanesia', *British journal of sociology*, 9 (1958), pp.176–77. On millenarism associated with fanaticism, see esp. R. Zinsser, *Rats, lice and history*, London, 1937, pp.80–84, and, of course, the work of N. Cohn, e.g., *The pursuit of the Millennium*, London, 1970 edn, esp. pp.136–38, 176–77, 261–86.

13 See esp. Worsley, *Trumpet shall sound*, p.280, cf. pp.46, 85–102.

14 e.g., C. S. Belshaw, 'The Significance of Modern Cults in Melanesian Development', *Australian outlook*, 4 (1950), esp. p.124 and Jarvie, *Revolution*, esp. pp.146–49. On Eliade in this connection, see below.

15 See Schwartz, Cargo Cult; a Melanesian-type response to culture contact ([mimeographed] Paper written for the DeVos Conference on Psychological Adjustment and Adaptation to Culture Change, Hakone, 1968), esp. pp.68–80. cf., L. Festinger, H. W. Riecken and S. Schachter, *When prophecy fails*, Minneapolis, 1958; Festinger, *The theory of cognitive dissonance*, Stanford, 1957.

16 For Schwartz's fieldwork, cf. *The Paliau movement in the Admiralty Islands, 1946–1954*. On Lawrence, see *Road* (the result of very good fieldwork, though see ns20, 35 below), yet cf.

his over-generalizations in articles such as 'Cargo thinking as a future political force in Papua and New Guinea', *Journal of the Papua and New Guinea Society*, 1 (1966–67), pp.20ff., etc. On Burridge, see *Mambu* (a brilliant and insightful work on the whole), yet cf. his *New Heaven*, chs 5, 9. By contrast to these scholars note the apparent restraint of F. C. Kamma, who has done very important detailed work in the Biak region of Irian Jaya (see his *Koreri, Messianic movements in the Biak-Numfor culture area*).

17 See Worsley, *Trumpet shall sound*, esp. pp.235–64; M. A. H. B. Walter, 'Cargo Cults: forerunners of progress', in W. Flannery (ed.), *Religious movements in Melanesia today 1*, pp.190ff; cf. also T. Bodrogi, 'Colonization and religious movements in Melanesia', *Acta ethnographica*, 2 (1951), pp.259–92; J. Guiart, 'The millenarian aspect of conversion to Christianity in the South Pacific', in S. L. Thrupp (ed.), *Millennial dreams in action; essays in comparative study* (Comparative studies in society and history, supp. 2), The Hague, 1962, esp. pp.136–37; Wilson, *Magic*, pp.5–7, 309–47; R. Brunton, 'Cargo cults and systems of exchange in Melanesia', *Mankind*, 8 (1971), pp.115ff. Note also G. Cochrane's *Big men and cargo cults*, Oxford, 1970, an inadequate explanation of cults in terms of traditional leadership patterns. German overview studies of cargoism are not susceptible to precisely the same kind of criticism; they are less analytical and more a piecing together of case study materials — for instance, F. Steinbauer's *Melanesische Kargo-Kulte*; cf. also H. Uplegger, and W. E. Mühlmann, 'Die Cargo-Culte in Neuguinea und Insel-Melanesian', in W. E. Mühlmann (ed.), *Chiliasmus und Nativismus*, Berlin, 1961; H. Nevermann, in *Die Religionen der Südsee und Australiens* (with E. A. Worms and H. Petri) (Die Religionen der Menschheit 5[2]), Stuttgart, 1968, pp.106–13.

18 For a distinctly 'sociological' (as against 'anthropological') treatment of some cargo cults, cf. esp. L. Morauta, *Beyond the village* (LSE monographs in social anthropology 49), Canberra, 1974.

19 I must admit I stand in debt to such writers as Burridge and (much more recently) the Black American scholar C. H. Long, with his 'Cargo cults as cultural historical phenomena', *Journal of the American Academy of Religion*, 47 (1974), pp.403ff., who have attempted to bring spiritual or theological insights to bear on the study of cargoism. Yet perhaps *too much* of universal human significance can be read into these movements (for the benefit of a Western audience) (cf. esp. ibid., pp.412–14, Burridge, *New Heaven*, pp.4–14). In that Burridge, Long and others have awakened anthropologists' attention to the cargo cultist as *homo religiosus*, however, they have rendered a great service. Among missionary commentators, I include Kamma (n.16), Flannery (n.17), and J. Strelan, *Search for salvation*; and for the important case of missionary anthropologist Patrick Gesch, see below.

20 Regarding this last comment, it is interesting how Dr Morauta (n.18) (who was in a position to check on some of Peter Lawrence's sources of information in the villages around Madang township) encountered so much disorder in cargo cult oral tradition that she began to worry about the over-orderly and synoptic arrangement of Lawrence's fascinating work *Road belong Cargo* (unpublished Lecture to the undergraduate course, Millenarian Movements [16–236, UPNG], 24 July 1973).

21 The 'Taro Cults', incidentally, ought not to be treated as cargo cults (so, the Papuan writers John Waiko, 'Cargo cults: the Papuan New Guinean way', in *Niugini reader* (ed. H. Barnes), Melbourne, n.d., p.43, and Jojoga Opeba, 'Melanesian cult movements as traditional and ritual responses to change', in Trompf (ed.), *The Gospel is not Western*, pp.49ff., etc., against Worsley, *Trumpet shall sound*, pp.64–84). Other activities of interest include 'prophet cults', cf. Trompf, '"Bilalaf"', in Trompf (ed.), *Prophets*, ch. 1; or immediate pre-contact 'high deity' cults (such as the *Kor Nganar* cult described by R. N. H. Bulmer, 'The Kyaka of the western highlands', in Lawrence and Meggitt (eds), *Gods*, pp.148–51; cf. G. F. Vicedom and H. Tischner, *Die Mbowamb*, vol. 2 [1943–8], pp.423ff.), or certain 'charismatic' developments (among the Enga, for instance, cf. M. J. Meggitt, 'The sun and the shakers: a millenarian cult and its transformations in the New Guinea highlands', *Oceania*, 44 [1973], pp.1ff.); or more directly secular movements, such as those of Tommy Kabu in the Purari Delta area (1950s) and the Kabisawali organization on the Trobriand Islands (1970s); or 'Independent Churches', cf. ch. 9 below. For discussion of a range of phenomena, esp. C. E. Loeliger and Trompf, 'Introduction' to their edited *New religious movements in Melanesia*, Port Moresby and Suva, 1985, pp.xiff.

22 cf. esp. Eliade's *The two and the one* (trans. J. M. Cohen), New York, 1965, pp.125–40, 155–59 (ch. 3; 'Cosmic and eschatological renewal'), presented in a shorter form as 'Cargo-cults and cosmic regeneration', in S. Thrupp (ed.), *Millennial*, pp.139ff. cf. also Eliade (ed.), *Death, afterlife and eschatology (From primitives to Zen III)*, New York, 1967, pp.95ff. I have found only one critique of Eliade's interpretation of cargo cults, that of Christiansen (*Cargo cult*, pp.98–102), although Jarvie (*Revolution*, p.232) summarizes one of his main lines of argument, and M. Kilani has recently acknowledged the importance of his emphasis on time, in *Les cultes du cargo mélanésiens; mythe et rationalité en anthropologie*, Lausanne, 1983, pp.171–79.

23 *Two and the one*, p.132, cf. pp.133–36; *Cosmos and history; the myth of the eternal return*, (ET), New York, 1954, ch. 2; *The sacred and the profane; the nature of religion*, (ET), New York, 1957, esp. pp.77–95.

24 *Two and the one*, p.132, cf. pp.130–32.

25 ibid., esp. pp.133–37 for the use of these phrases.

26 ibid., p.137.

27 ibid., pp.138–39.

28 ibid., p.132 on 'these millenarist movements'.

29 'Millenarian Movements', *Archives Européennes de sociologie*, 7 (1966), p.159; cf. also her 'Pursuit of the Millennium: the relation between religious and social change', in ibid., 3 (1962), pp.130–34.

30 Esp. ibid. (1962), p.130 (for the first quotation) and cf. (1966), pp.173–74 (for the others). The concession, I find, drains her reference to *ultimate* salvation of its cogency.

31 According to one version of the Manup-Kilibob myth, Kilibob was responsible for giving men the techniques of warfare.

32 Lawrence, *Road*, p.102.

33 ibid., esp. pp.102–103, 110.

34 On Yali, esp. ibid., p.194; cf. also pp.203ff. For Yakob, esp. Morauta, *Beyond*, pp.37ff. and her lectures (see n.20). Eliade has written on Yali in *Two and the one*, pp.139–40.

35 Lawrence has not endowed the 'millenarian factor' in the Yali cult with much significance (*Road*, pp.138, 155, 192, 217 only), whereas T. Ahrens, makes much more of it by stressing the widespread belief in Yali as Messiah ('New buildings on old foundations; "Lo-bos" and Christian congregations in Astrolabe Bay', *Point*, 1 (1974), pp.31–37). In differing slightly with Ahrens, I think it is important to appreciate how Yali has managed to defuse intense millennial strains by a 'realized eschatology' (*pace* C. H. Dodd). In cautiously acceding to the idea of Messiahship, and in naming his adopted son Jesus, Yali continued to divert attention on to his own organizational programme, and thus away from a grand cargo millennium; cf. Kambau Namaleu, Yali after 1967 (unpublished lecture for Mill. Movts, UPNG, 16–236, 25/7/74 [cf. n.20], recorded for the New Guinea Collection, UPNG). Regarding stage theory, Worsley has placed Yali in the 'period of transition' between a very embryonic national consciousness and political self-determination, although only in Paliau's Manus Island movement does he find an 'example of a large-scale, successful independent native political organization' in New Guinea. Worsley does not wish to call either Paliau's or Yali's cults 'millenarian' (*Trumpet shall sound*, pp.204–14, 225–28). On recent Madang developments, Trompf, 'The theology of Beig Wen, the would-be successor to Yali', *Catalyst*, 6/3 (1976), pp.166ff.

36 Interestingly, a Yali missionary reached as far as the area around Goroka (Eastern Highlands). Lagitamo of Madang organized the Bena Bena village of Sigomi near Siokiei into a short-lived Yali cult in 1965. Sigomi had already experienced Lutheran, Seventh Day Adventist and New Life League Mission teachings about the End of the World, but Lagitamo did not bring any eschatological ideas. He convinced the villagers that regularly performed 'table ritual' would multiply their money, and that funds ought to be sent to Yali in Madang. They were also to cease from fighting, stealing and adultery; food was offered to the ancestors near the cemetery and a hut was erected to house four girls 'whose skin would be touched by Yali himself'. (Trompf, Fieldnotes, November 1973; cf. *Goroko Patrol Reports* (Connors), Nov.–Dec., 1965). For some further information on the spread of Yali's activities, e.g., Burridge, *Mambu*, pp.196–207, 233–37, A. Maburau, 'Irakau of Manam', in Loeliger and Trompf (eds), *New religious movements*, ch. 1.

37 If I may defend this general point with a pertinent example from my own field research: Kae Fo'o was a cult leader influential among the Toaripi in the Gulf District PNG during the 1960s. Trained as a London Missionary Society catechist, he was acquainted with Christian eschatological ideas; yet, he placed little stress on a prospective millennium. Although he taught that, at the end of Time, all the resurrected dead would possess Cargo, Kae Fo'o emphasized special rituals and routines as the preferred ways of increasing wealth (Trompf and V. Koroti, Fieldnotes, May 1974) (see also ch. 5 above at n.46).

38 See esp. Worsley, *Trumpet shall sound*, pp.108–109, 350. The use of the phrase 'Golden Age' is unfortunate since it assumes theories of world Ages which are foreign both to Melanesian thought and missionary Christianity. The terms 'golden' or 'perfect time' are more acceptable.

39 Interestingly, Maori Kiki re-interpreted the well known 'Vailala Madness' of 1917–19 (cf. ch. 5) by claiming that 'the main purpose' of the participants was 'to contact the dead' and so undergo 'some kind of cleansing process', which would make them adequate to the new situation (*Ten thousand years*, p.51). On the traditional beneficence of the spirits, see esp. ns54–58.

40 Schwartz, *Paliau movement*, plate 15 on Paliau's church; R. M. Berndt, 'Cargo movement', esp. pp.137–39, 231; cf. Eliade, *Two and the one*, p.136, on the highlands case, in which Jesus may have been confused with 'the Japanese'. In contrast, Berndt, 'Cargo movement', esp. pp.145–46 on the existence of 'secular' cargoism among the Omisuan-Arau villages, i.e., cultism without the syncretistic doctrines prevalent in other areas affected by the spreading movement. cf. also R. F. Salisbury, 'An "indigenous" New Guinea cult', *Kroeber Anthropological Society, papers*, 18 (1958), pp.67–78. Heavily nativistic cults, we should caution here, usually retain some Europeanisms, such as forms of organization or ethical teaching about cheating, stealing, fighting, adultery, etc. It often takes a discerning eye, though, to decide whether it is the missionaries as against the *kiaps* who are the source.

41 Some, like Harold Turner, might prefer the less pejorative-looking term 'synthetism' here. On the frequency of syncretisms, esp. F. Steinbauer, Die Cargo-Culte als religionsges-chichtliches und missionstheologisches Problem (doctoral dissert., University of Erlangen-Nürnberg, Nürnberg, 1971), rear chart; on problems of quantifying syncretism, e.g., B. M. Knauft, 'Cargo cults and relational separation', in *Behaviour science research* 13/3 (1978), p.200.

42 See esp. D. Fergie, 'Prophecy and leadership: Philo and the Inawai'a movement', in Trompf (ed.), *Prophets*, pp.100–104; M. Stephen, *Cargo Cult Hysteria*, researches which will make up for the inadequate accounts given by C. Belshaw ('Recent history of Mekeo society', *Oceania*, 22 (1951), pp.1ff.) and by Worsley (*Trumpet shall sound*, pp.120–22).

43 cf. also P. Lawrence, 'Statements about religion: the problem of reliability', in L. R. Hiatt and C. Jayawardena (eds), *Anthropology in Oceania* (Ian Hogbin Festschrift), Sydney, 1971, pp.139ff.

44 cf. Schwartz, *Paliau movement*, esp. pp.267–70, cf. 221–26.

45 Worsley, *Trumpet shall sound*, p.125 (for the quotation regarding Pako); R. Lacey, 'The "Vailala Madness" as a millenarian movement' (Comparative World History Seminar 'Millenarian Movements', University of Wisconsin, March 1971), p.14 (on the second example). cf. also n.39.

46 J. van Baal, 'The Nimboran development project', *South Pacific*, 6 (1952), esp. p.494 (on the factory); Berndt, 'Cargo movement', p.57; M. Reay, *The Kuma*, Melbourne, 1959, pp.197–99 (on metamorphosis); cf. A. Strathern, 'Cargo and inflation in Mount Hagen', *Oceania*, 41 (1971), pp.257–58; and the last point concerning gifts applies to such cases as the Yali and Yakob cults, see above ns36–37; cf. also Cochrane, *Big men*, p.156 on the Papuan Gulf (with caution).

47 Brunton ('Cargo cults', pp.113, 124) makes some comparable points.

48 cf. Trompf, 'Doesn't colonialism make you mad?', in S. Latukefu (ed.), *Papua New Guinea: a century of colonial impact* pp.247ff. I am also reminded here of a note by Bishop Navarre (Yule Island Catholic Mission) that certain Roro groups of Papua looked to the other side of the mountainous hinterland as the source from which their ancestors had brought great plenty and would bring it again in the future (Notes et Journal, 1888–89, p.90). Scholars have not generally been on the look-out for this kind of expectation. For

another case relevant to the comments here, see ch. 5 above on the Liorofa cult (eastern highlands, PNG) 1969–70.

49 As well as Salisbury ('Indigenous New Guinea cult', pp.67ff.) and Berndt ('Cargo movement', pp.40ff., 137ff., cf. his 'Reactions to contact in the Eastern Highlands of New Guinea', *Oceania*, 24 [1954], pp.190ff., 255ff.), note also J. M. van der Kroef, 'Patterns of cultural change in three primitive societies', *Social research*, 24 (1957), pp.428–33. J. V. de Bruijn, 'The Mansren cult of Biak', *South Pacific*, 5 (1951), pp.1–10, and G. W. L. Townsend, Letter of the Editor, *Oceania*, 24, 1953, p.77.

50 'Cargo Movement', p.155.

51 cf. Eliade in Thrupp (ed.), *Millennial*, p.139, n.1; V. Lanternari, 'Origine storiche dei culti profetici Melanesiani', *Studi e materiali di storia delle religione*, 27 (1956), esp. pp.77–84, and *The religions of the oppressed; a study of modern messianic cults* (trans. L. Sergio), New York, 1963, pp.184–86.

52 Lommel, 'Der Prophetismus in niederen Kulturen', *Zeitschrift für Ethnologie*, 75 (1950), esp. p.68; cf. 'Der "Cargo-Cult" in Melanesien; ein Beitrag zum Problem der "Europäisierung" der Primitiven', *Zeitschrift für Ethnologie*, 78 (1953), pp.17ff.

53 For Lanternari's universal synthesis placed more directly against a Near Eastern background, see 'Messianism: its historical origin and morphology', in *History of religions*, 1 (1961), esp. pp.55–56, 62.

54 See esp. P. Lawrence, 'The Ngaing of the Rai Coast', in Lawrence and Meggitt (eds), *Gods*, pp.205, 210–12; C. A. Valentine, 'The Lakalai of New Britain', in *Gods*, pp.176–77; Nevermann, *Religionen*, pp.95–98.

55 cf., e.g., L. J. Luzbetak, 'The socio-religious significance of a New Guinea pig festival', *Anthropological quarterly*, 27, 1954, pp.59ff., cf. T. Mambsu, G. Trompf, and M. Wandel, Fieldnotes, Nov. 1973; J. A. Gande, 'Chimbu pig-killing ceremony', *Oral history*, 2 (1974), pp.6ff; P. L. Newman, *Knowing the Gururumba* (Case studies in cultural anthropology), New York, 1965, pp.68–70. cf. also Bulmer, 'Kyaka', pp.148, 152; etc.

56 F. E. Williams, 'A cycle of ceremonies in Orokolo Bay', *Mankind*, 2 (1939), p.155; cf. *The Drama of Orokolo*.

57 The body of relevant literature is enormous. A culture with four major ceremonies connected with life stages, however, is worth singling out here; e.g. the eastern Fuyughe groups, yet cf. Fastré, Moeurs, esp. pp.19–23. Certain peoples, it should also be noted, act out their most important ceremony as a result of contingencies (cf. ch. 3).

58 So Newman, *Gururumba*, p.69. I have followed Newman's orthography in transcribing the name of the pig festival.

59 Quoting Christiansen's criticism of Eliade's interpretation (*Melanesian cargo cult*, p.99).

60 In the New Guinea Highlands whites were commonly described as red (cf. esp. M. Leahy and M. Crain, *The land that time forgot*, London, 1937).

61 Yet cf. n.48 on the Liorofa cult. Luliapo, though, made a clear-cut distinction between the $f^e re$ he encountered and other whites. For other possibilities, see below and n.67.

62 cf., however, C. Marjen, 'Cargo cult movement, Biak', *Journal of the Papua and New Guinea Society*, 1 (1967), pp.62–65.

63 *Two and the One*, p.135.

64 Trompf, Fieldnotes 1981. For background, H. Aufenanger, *The passing scene in north-east New-Guinea* (Collectanea Instituti Anthropos 2), St Augustin, 1972, ch. 7.

65 For background, Lawrence, *Road*, pp.79ff.

66 cf. Trompf, 'Keeping the *Lo* under a Melanesian Messiah', in J. Barker (ed.), *Christianity in Oceania; ethnography perspectives* (forthcoming).

67 See esp. Trompf, 'Macrohistory and acculturation', *Comparative studies in society and history*, 31/4 (1989), pp.624–27.

68 J. G. Geissler, 'Een Kort overzigt van het Land en Volk op de Noord-Oost-Kust van Nieuw Guinea'; Kamma, 'Messianic movements in western New Guinea', *International review of missions*, 41 (1952), pp.148–50; H. M. Thimme, 'Manarmakeri: theological evaluation of an old Biak myth', *Point* (special issue), 1 (1977), pp.21ff.

69 In his *The Sociology of hope* (trans. C. Martin-Sperry), London, 1979, esp. p.36.

70 Kamma, *Koreri*, pp.158ff.

71 Trompf, *Payback*, ch. 2, sect. B.

72 cf., e.g., Jojoga Opeba, 'Melanesian cult movements', pp.61–62.
73 Trompf, *Payback*, ch. 3, esp. sect. B.3.
74 Trompf, 'Introduction', in Trompf (ed.), *Cargo cults and millenarian movements*, pp.7–8.
75 Subtitled: *A cargo-type movement in the Sepik against its background in traditional religion.*
76 Against W. La Barre, *Ghost*, esp. pp.239ff.
77 We await M. Reay's monograph on *Transformation movements* regarding this point.
78 See ch. 3; cf. Trompf, *Payback*, ch. 1, sect. B.
79 cf. Trompf, 'Salvation in primal religion', pp.222–24.

INDEPENDENT CHURCHES

Despite popular impressions that the so-called cargo cults represent the only distinctive kind of indigenous response in post-contact Melanesia to colonialism and rapid social change, this, as has already been intimated, is a gross over-simplification. Even setting aside very recent developments, the history of Melanesia is dotted with a variety of protest movements — from the New Caledonian insurrection of 1878 to the formation of the Mataungan League in 1968 — which would be categorized as cargo cultist only in the most ill-conceived typologies. Forms of aggressive rebellion aside, there have also been milder efforts to preserve or reinstate traditional customs.[1] Much indigenous missionary activity in the history of Melanesian Christianity, moreover, though very rarely anti-white in impetus, has eventuated and secured its results quite independently of European supervision. Critical accounts of individual contributions (those of Fijian missionaries, Kota-speaking evangelists or Motuan pastors, for instance) and analyses of rapid church growth (through what Allan Tippett has termed 'people movements') are emerging as new subject areas for profitable research.

Although these movements are part of the general expansion of Christianity, there also remains a sprinkling of independent churches in Melanesia, as well as agitation bearing a so-called 'revivalist' or 'Pentecostal' stamp. With almost all these movements and social tendencies, even if 'cargo thinking' or 'cargoistic motifs' may often be detectable among them, the imminent or spectacular arrival of European goods has not been a prime preoccupation; thus, the phrase 'cargo cultism' seldom does justice to their aims or manifest characters. The previous chapter has already raised some of the problems associated with the term 'millenarian'. And, even if chiliasm (the excited expectation of the near return of Christ or a messiah) does appear in some of these activities, it does not appear in all. In any case, its intensity varies so markedly both diachronically and across the board that any attempt to classify these diverse responses as 'millenarian movements' would result in too many being excluded.

The category 'independent churches' has been bequeathed to us from seminal works by Bengt Sundkler on the multitude of Bantu splinter groups in South African Christianity, and by both a cluster of Africanists taking their cue from his earlier researches and others writing of non-African situations. Some authors prefer seeing these new religious developments placed within the broader classification 'messianic movements', or to consider them as 'sectarian responses' more or less paralleling the sects of western Christendom; I, however, believe Sundkler's approach stands the test of time. Messianism and even prophetism can be absent from some of the self-styled churches of colonized countries, and there is clearly point in distinguishing between deviating churches initiated by expatriate western sectaries and those created by indigenous people themselves.[2] The term 'church', further, though so antiquated a badge, does at least conjure up a fuller picture of buildings, worship services, (clerical) leadership and doctrinal stance, whereas other labels tend to over-play ideological factors. Independent churches are those indigenous movements with members who continue to understand themselves as adherents of a church body, and who want recognition and self-identity as such, while preferring a separatist or secessionist stance toward the older, introduced missions or sects, or even toward some pre-existing divergency already inspired by their own fellow countrymen.

Admittedly 'independent church' has been a tag used of virtually or fully indigenized churches which have stemmed from planted missions yet eventually attained autonomy, but these should be distinguished from independent churches proper for clarity's sake.[3] Defending 'independent church' as a category, however, does not blind us to significant differences in the size, age, background, discipline, social composition and status of their followers, nor to their varying appeal and influence. Cautious as one should be with every typology, this chapter will present examples of Melanesian independent churches — this time with room for a more exhaustive coverage of the whole region — documenting their characteristics and identifying those cases which have led to the adoption of the above definition. Each church will be placed in its appropriate historical context, with information about the predisposing effects of missionization and the derivation of some of these churches from cargo cult enclaves. There are at least three churches which are impressive enough to deserve prior treatment and proportionately more consideration; but fifteen other test cases are also of interest, to illustrate a spectrum which runs from groups strongly influenced by currents in traditional thought to those drawing more straightforwardly on Biblical or western Christian positions.[4]

The Christian Fellowship Church

Historical background

The Christian Fellowship Church (New Georgia, Western Province, Solomon Islands) is the largest independent church in Melanesia and, consequently, the best documented.[5] It was formed in 1960, separating from the Methodist mission. Its founder and prophetic leader, Silas Eto (otherwise known as Holy Mama), a Roviana from the Kolobagea area of west New Georgia, was trained as a pastor-teacher during 1927–32 at Kokeqolo station under the pioneer missionary, J. F. Goldie (1870–1954).[6] Between 1932 and Goldie's retirement in 1951, Eto fostered a distinct organizational, liturgical and theological style, especially among the Kusage lineages, his own people in western New Georgia. In 1956 the phenomenon of *taturu*, a form of mass enthusiasm which involved drumming, crying out, 'fainting' and collective involuntary movements in church services, led to a crisis between the Kusage and the white missionaries continuing Goldie's labours. Eto, believing the Holy Spirit to have visited his people, and understanding Goldie to have chosen him as his true successor, led his supporters out of Methodism to form a new church on 4 September, 1960.

Organization

By 1965 the church had its own constitution and was recognized by other missions and the government as a church in its own right. Milton Talasa was its first chairman,[7] Pastor Samuel Kuku (a member of the pre-independence parliament of the Solomons, 1972–75) being chairman/secretary in more recent years. Ultimate authority rested with Holy Mama until his recent death, and he usually sat aside at important meetings to ratify decisions (with the phrase '*Ai laik*', meaning 'I approve', and by leading ritual clapping). Many assume Holy Mama to have been the vehicle of the Holy Spirit, if not God himself.

The church has been well represented politically — the Holy Mama's son, Job Dudley, for instance, has been premier of the Western Solomons provincial government. At its start missionary records put the number of its followers at 3000 (in 1961), but by 1976 the census recorded 4800 followers. In 1980 there were twenty-two adherent villages with church buildings (mainly in the western New Georgia area), although four other groups met further west and as far as Honiara (Guadalcanal).

The church's headquarters lie at Menakasapa, a model village renamed 'Paradise'. Other villages, well planned and organized in keeping with Goldie's original industrial mission approach, have received second names from Biblical places and events (for example, Madou = 'Belitihema', Nusa Bagga = 'Pentecost'). Aside from five trade stores and involvement in the

North New Georgia Timber Co-operation, the church shows intense interest in business enterprises which offer long-term benefits to rural dwellers. The church also manages schools (five, in 1980), the staff of which have received government salaries since 1978.

Church services consist largely of hymn singing, some prayers, scripture readings and a sermon. Virtually all hymns are in Roviana and deviate in content from western hymnaries. As most of the tunes and words were not committed to paper,[8] Eto and Kuku commissioned Esau Tuzu (a Choiseul Islander) to arrange and edit them. Worship, which starts off to the accompaniment of a collection of brass instruments and sometimes continues through the night, may be said to climax with singing. It is the singing that provides the rhythmic and moving context in which *taturu* (now only occasionally) manifests itself. During services Holy Mama presided over, he used to sit on a 'throne' (or easy chair), often in the middle of the congregation. His wardrobe held a variety of garbs, including a special mitre and decorated white robes; it was in such robes that he met Queen Elizabeth II at Gizo in 1977 (see plate 9).

The Christian Fellowship Church has a number of its own pastors, who had originally been trained by the Methodist mission, and they conduct services in various villages. Holy communion (reminiscent, in form, of Methodist practice) is celebrated monthly and infant, rather than adult, baptism is the norm. In most villages services have become less regular, personal prayers and salutations being made in the form of special strings running between two posts and placed before houses or churches. There has recently been some concern for the effective education of pastors, both because the present ones were schooled by the Methodists and because of apprehension about the church's future now that Eto is dead. An indication of this problem was the church's difficulty in finding qualified people to staff a Bible training centre which was started at Paradise in 1975 and stocked with a small library financed by the World Council of Churches' Theological Education Fund.

Theology

Christian Fellowship Church beliefs centre around the role of the Holy Mama. A catechism is planned and will consist of his authoritative answers to a list of basic questions about doctrines. Various stances derive from Methodism: namely, the acceptance of two sacraments, baptism (including adult baptism) and the permission of lay leaders to administer communion when pastors are not present. On the Bible, Eto was accepted as the final interpreter because he had been able to counter the quotations of the missionaries by reading scripture in the light of the *taturu* phenomenon. Both leaders and followers hold that their ecstatic, 'heart-warming' services (note the connection with John Wesley's famous 1738 Aldersgate experience) marked the coming of the Holy Spirit to New Georgia, but there is a range of opinion as to where Holy

Mama fits into the supernatural order. A large minority consider him to be 'God'. The senior Christian Fellowship Church representative at Honiara went so far as to assert that 'hi winim Got' (he supersedes God), because sometimes he appears in visions alone, unaccompanied by the Father or the Son. Eto and the pastors have in the past acquiesced to these views but without, themselves, subscribing to them. Correctly, Tuza describes Eto's complex theology as Trinitarian; yet, although the Spirit is manifested through Father and Son, and mediated through symbols (for example, the crucifix, Wesley's portrait, just as *mana/minna* persisted through the skulls of the dead Roviana chiefs), Holy Mama is a fourth 'Man' or aspect of the Trinity. Over the last decade before his death, however, Eto's theology became increasingly practical; after interpreting his own dreams, he stressed in his talks what to do each day rather than what to believe, and encouraged the use of simple body actions to keep in contact with the divine.[9]

Eto, even if only disputedly a chief, saw himself in the role inherited by activist Goldie, and therefore among other things as the great chief (*ngati bangara*) of earlier slave- and head-hunting days. He welcomed participation of members of his church in Solomons politics and was committed both to the responsible payment of taxes and to realistic development.[10] Significantly, there is no apparent cargo cultism in this movement and no expectation of the imminent End of the World. Theological discourse among the leaders is sophisticated to the point that they refer to the church as 'charismatic' rather than 'pentecostal';[11] this despite the fact that pentecostalist groups sponsored Kuku's visits to Oregon and Oklahoma in 1979. The special position of Eto admits the description 'messianic', since he is comparable to a black African 'messiah' (such as Simon Kimbangu or Isaiah Shembe),[12] but neither Eto himself nor Kuku expressed satisfaction with such an epithet.

The Hehela Church

Historical background

The Hahalis Welfare Society, the organization from which Hehela emerged (in North Solomons Province, Papua New Guinea), has attracted the interest of various researchers.[13] The Society was founded publicly among the Tasi- or Halia-speaking people of Buka Island in January 1960 by John Teosin (born 1938), a Catholic catechist, who was earlier unable to withstand both the pressures of study at Kerevat (government) High School, New Britain, and of teaching back on Buka. The Society, first appearing as an anti-colonial, anti-taxation movement, and one with more punch and a fuller programme for island development than the East Coast Buka Society, was directed by Teosin so as to offer a completely alternative way of life, based on his own syncretistic philosophy of nature or natural feelings.[14] Soon after the Society was formally inaugurated with a public ritual mime of sexual intercourse, numbers at the Christian confessional dropped sharply and the Catholic Mission (based at Buka Straits, Gogohe and Gagan) moved to excommunicate its adherents. Relations between the Society and Mission worsened with the establishment of the so-called 'Baby Garden' early in 1961, when Teosin organized 'disinterested' sexual relations between young Hahalis supporters to shelve traditionally arranged marriages (and, thus, the use of ceremonial currency), and to weaken the chiefs' privileged access to women.[15]

It is virtually impossible to distinguish the origins of Hehela from the development of both the Society and Baby Garden; yet, the church side of affairs has been largely neglected in writings on the subject. Following outspoken rejection by the Catholic Mission, the Society began to build the first of its own special *haus lotu* (churches) in 1961 on Tabut Island near Hahalis. Francis Hagai, a former Marist-trained teacher and the Society's vice-president,[16] selected passages from Catholic prayer books and, supplementing them with ideas current among the Society's leaders, produced a set of liturgies in the Halia language. These liturgies, referred to in pidgin as *Sori Lotu*, were used in morning and late evening gatherings at cemeteries (where most believed ancestors would come to eat food offerings and bring items of European cargo), and also for more formal church worship (including marriage ceremonies).[17] Non-members were forbidden on pain of death to enter the Tabut *haus lotu*. It contained a large fire altar at one end, several infants being cast into the flames during services in the early 1960s. These sacrifices were connected with the Baby Garden in that they were accompanied by special Halia prayers for fertility and group prosperity, prayers which were now directed, not to *Deo* (the euphonic word for God often used by Catholics), but to a traditional deity, Sunahan ('the One who pinned the world'). Hahalis leaders began self-consciously reinterpreting Bible stories in terms of traditional custom and mythology. A special school was also built in 1962, as well as a 'convent' to prepare older girls for the Baby Garden.

From the safety of secluded headquarters in the jungle behind Hahalis, Teosin maintained supreme authority over the local chieftainships (*tsunono*), securing a strong following among the Tasi of eastern and northern Buka. With so little being known of the alternative church, it was the Society and Baby Garden which were more vulnerable to outside criticism. A series of issues all slowly undermined Teosin's credibility — clashes with police from December 1961 on, a variety of murders (mostly of defectors), the notoriety of the Garden 'prostibule', which attracted restless workers from the Bougainville Copper mine during the 1960s, and the apparent misappropriation of Society finances for the leaders' personal purposes. The effort by the famous Bougainvillean priest, Father John Momis, to involve Teosin in the Bougainville secession issue of 1975, when both took the legal brief to the United Nations, New York, had a quietening effect on the Hahalis movement. Although the Society continued to raise funds through a nightclub, it was 'Hehela' (Halia: 'Praying to God together') which became the most clear expression of their alternative way and which has remained the chief stabilizing factor.

Organization

The office bearers of Hehela are the same as in the original Society. Teosin is president and Hagai and Meksi, although both dead, remain vice-president and secretary, while Elijah Ragu (gaoled during 1979) is treasurer. In 1980 Teosin estimated that about 8000 people supported him (it was c. 4000 in 1970), but such figures, based on the paying membership of the Society, and in any case exaggerated, do not speak for Hehela. Pressures in the late 1970s by representatives of the Catholic, United and Seventh Day Adventist churches, as well as the Jehovah's Witnesses, have resulted in defections from his movement *qua* independent church, mainly in favour of the United Church, which is traditionally strong in north and east Buka. Nevertheless, in 1980 Teosin was claiming the strong involvement of thirty-two villages, including some well into Bougainville, and faithful groups on New Britain (Rabaul), New Ireland (Namatanai), Cataret Island, and at Madang (Iri), Samarai and Port Moresby.

Teosin, at that stage, denied that any church buildings were in current use by Hehela, but he preferred to call Hehela a 'church' — 'to avoid misunderstanding' — and to place it on a par with other forms of *lotu* around Buka. Ceremonies called *hats* (sacrifices) are usually held in the open air, often in close vicinity to a chief's club house. Gatherings are not regular but are called when the need or occasion arises (a marriage, for instance, or a family's intention to make new gardens), and can be led by any influential member. Naturally, most *hats* are celebrated in the open space before Teosin's own house, a large unfinished, two-storey sheet-metal construction begun in 1970 (see plate 10). Solemn hymns to Sunahan dominate worship, which finishes with a feast. In the past banana sliced into discs was used as the Host, but it is difficult to ascertain whether that practice persists.

Theology

In a nutshell, Hehela teaching 'traditionalizes' Christianity as completely as possible. God (= Sunahan) created the whole world and Buka — the order of Creation as recounted in Genesis and in the traditional cosmology of the Tasi culture being understood to correspond. The whites brought their beliefs, and Teosin is prepared to accept as true the divinity of Christ; the Buka, however, have their own traditional equivalents to God and Jesus. The Halia Christ-figure is Mattanachil who came in the middle (*namel*) of history just as Jesus did according to the missionaries. Many of Mattanachil's actions paralleled those of Christ: he brought law (*lo*) and good customs (*kastam*) to the people of

Buka and corrected them (*stretim manmeri*) so as to stop the frequent fighting among themselves;[18] he showed the road across the dangerous sea to Tulon (= Cataret Island); he performed certain miracles (*mirakel*) of healing and fertility through introducing the ritual *hats*; he eventually went up to the heights of Tehesi (the northernmost volcano of Bougainville, Mount Balbi), where he became a source of support and power (*paua*). The story of his final journey to Tehesi supposedly parallels the Christian passion narrative or the story of Christ's journey to his death at Jerusalem: Mattanachil's cousin-brother and disciple, Hanas, tried to prevent him from doing what he knew he had to do, by casting a net over him while he travelled on the sea, but Mattanachil broke the net and ascended to the heights. He shall return, but (as in Jesus's case) no one knows the hour or day.

A connection is made between the continual energy of Tehesi and the sacrificial *hats*, at which ceremony a small portion of every type of food laid out for the feast must be burnt by fire. In the days when the Hahalis movement was alleged to be 'the work of the Devil', Teosin's open acceptance that he and his followers were 'on the road to hell'[19] was evidently based on the belief that the missionaries had failed to reveal how all-consuming fire was the source of *paua*. More recently, however, Teosin has developed Hehela teaching on this point by distinguishing *heben bilon graun na heben ap antap* (heaven beneath the ground and heaven above). At death a person's spirit goes up (where it goes is left vague enough to accommodate the Christian heaven, the mountaintop places of the dead and the land of the sky people),[20] while the body, still in some sense a living thing, goes into the soil to enrich Buka. Cargo cultism is now renounced; for, with the prodigious growth of trees, vegetables, pig herds and human families brought about by *hats*, the Buka will obtain enough money to buy all the cargo they need at the trade stores.

The Kwato Church or Boda Kwato

Historical background

The Kwato Mission, founded in 1891 by Charles Abel (1863–1930) in Milne Bay Province, Papua New Guinea, has been the subject of various publications and considerable research.[21] When Charles Abel's attempt to establish an industrial mission failed to gain the support of the London Missionary Society, he returned from London to labour for twelve years as an independent missionary and the head of the Kwato Extension Association. Following his death in a car accident (England 1930), Kwato carried on under his sons, Russell and Cecil, who had both been influenced by the Oxford Movement (Moral Rearmament) while studying at Cambridge in the 1920s. Under these two the mission expanded its work well beyond the Suau-speaking area, into the unpacified mountain regions of the Doveraidi and Keveri.[22]

By 1963 Kwato was 'reunited' with the London Missionary Society[23] (and in 1968 they, together with the Methodists, formed the United Church of Papua New Guinea and the Solomon Islands). The special organizational and theological styles which had developed in relative isolation, however, produced dissatisfaction with the state of the union among the indigenous Suau leaders at Kwato and Alotau, and, despite opposition,[24] they worked to bring about formal separation by August 1977. Russell Abel having died in 1964, it was Cecil, the only surviving son of the great pioneer missionary, who was asked to draw up the constitution to give the Kwato Church its independence. Boda Kwato was incorporated by an act of the Papua New Guinea Parliament in June 1979.

Organization

The constitution provides for a president, an executive committee, central council and annual general meeting. It is important to recognize, however, that Kwato members dislike the 'undemocratic' and hierarchical nature of the United Church pastorate system, and prefer a more broadly based ministry. Leaders (Suau: *tangawa*), therefore, are more like Elders, an unpaid group of mature people who have proved their sincerity and dedication, but who may have had no formal training.[25] As Charles Abel was a Congregationalist, there has long been an emphasis on local congregations coming together to sort out their own problems — 'putting things right' (*hedudurai*) — and to send parties to neighbouring villages when trouble (such as fighting, divorce, 'pagan revivals') arises.

Large buildings one could readily describe as churches are absent, except on Kwato Island and in Alotau township. If both the council and general meeting are convened in these impressive structures, the norm at the village level is the gathering in a meeting house made of local materials. On Sundays worship parallels that of the United Church, with baptisms (adult as well as infant) and monthly communion being enacted by a *tanuwaga*.[26] Each morning, however, individuals are expected to spend a time of silence listening for directives from God, while towards sunset a circle is formed at the meeting house and those attending pray aloud (this session being called, from the English, *paua haus*). The majority of Kwato adherents use the Suau and Tavawa bibles with the Suau hymn book.[27]

The number of Kwato Church members is not yet known (perhaps 5000, at a conservative estimate, in 1980) because pressures to prevent division by the United Church keep matters in a state of flux. Within the Kwato District of the Milne Bay Province, there are eight church wards. Outside, people identifying with Boda Kwato can be found in most urban centres of Papua New Guinea (a consolidated group at Lae, for example, making up almost half the regular heavy transport drivers who negotiate the Highlands Highway). A distinctive characteristic is their advocacy of self-reliance and interest in small-scale industries and worker conditions.[28] Outside Milne Bay, however, it is not deemed necessary for members to erect distinctive churches or buildings. Although meeting together regularly, they are at liberty to attend any Sunday service of their choice — an indulgence in keeping with the Moral Rearmament view that its members should permeate throughout all branches of Christianity. In Port Moresby, incidentally, there are more opportunities for Kwato supporters to confer with Moral Rearmament followers who are from other Melanesian cultures and who do not consider themselves part of Boda Kwato.

Theology

The present theological stances derive from a running together of Charles Abel's democratic congregationalism and the teachings of the Moral Rearmament movement. The older generation, having felt threatened by the authoritarian power of the United Church bishops and pastors, hankered after the Abel heritage, while Moral Rearmament themes, hardly known before Charles Abel's death, have reinforced the emphasis on individual and local decision-making. New Testament Christianity, Kwato leaders maintain, was not hierarchically oriented; Jesus chose his followers from among the common folk, who were then able to present the Gospel in simple terms. Theological training is not considered essential for the spread and effective practice of the Christian faith, but a desire to be open to God's call and to lead others to listen for his directives is crucial. Confession, practising the Four Absolutes (of love, honesty, purity and unselfishness) and *hedudurai* are said to spring from such willingness.

Partly stemming from Charles Abel's stated aims to achieve a future national unity, Kwato leaders conceive their church's approach to self-determination to be important for the development of Papua New Guinea as a young state. The church is 'The Kwato Church of Papua New Guinea', and its second aim is 'to win people to believe in the Christian faith and commitment to the principle that God's will is supreme . . . as proclaimed in the Preamble to the Constitution' of that country.[29] Interestingly, the national Preamble mentioned here is not reckoned to be the achievement of the Constitutional Planning Committee, as is commonly supposed, but of Cecil Abel. While working for the prime minister's department, he believed he was 'inspired' to create its present form in a matter of a few hours. This kind of concern to serve the nation, presenting Kwato ideals and practice as an example for her peoples, is nicely illustrated by the recent autobiography of a well-known leader, Alice Wedega (1980), the first indigenous female member of the Papua New Guinea Parliament. Yet, with a European having written its constitution and Kwato itself being now financially too weak to finance various agencies, recent signs of disillusion at the grass-roots level presents a serious possibility of future divisiveness in this church.[30]

Other cases

There are fifteen comparable examples, which are no less interesting, although the present state of research means that some of these can be dealt with more fully than others. In certain of these cases membership is very small, and with others again it is difficult, as with Hehela, to differentiate the independent churches from movements which preceded and hatched them. The three examples we've just been looking at at least enable one to envisage a spectrum: the Christian Fellowship Church (or Etoism) standing as the *exemplum classicum* reminiscent of the better known independent churches of Africa, while Hehela illustrates a stronger nativistic thrust and Kwato a greater propensity to adopt imported styles. The remaining examples may be located along this hypothetical continuum in quite varied and not always stable positions.

The remaining examples can be divided into two groups: the first comprises eight more significant movements. Of these, the Paliau Church lies somewhere on the spectrum between Hehela and Etoism. Next, the Remnant Church fits more easily, by contrast, between Etoism and Boda Kwato; as do three other small independent churches — The Congregation of the Poor, NaGriamel Federation Independent United Royal Church, and the 'Friday Religion'. The Congregation of the Poor and NaGriamel are the most difficult to place because their messianic leadership is reminiscent of Etoism, while their doctrinal and institutional bases are more in keeping with imported beliefs or models, thus bringing them closer to Boda Kwato than the Remnant Church. 'Friday Religion', by comparison, fits nearer the Christian Fellowship Church in being less marginally affected by tradition than the Remant Church; poverty of information makes its positioning tentative, however, and some will prefer to parallel it with the Paliau movement. The three final cases in this grouping — the Peli Association, *Wok bilong Yali*, and the Moro Movement — each have a background of so-called cargo cult or nativistic movements. They, thus, reflect the influences of tradition even more noticeably than the Paliau Church or 'Friday Religion' and, hence, are closer to the position of Hehela.

The second grouping, comprising seven other possible candidates for the status of independent church, will be dealt with subsequently under a separate heading.

The Paliau (or Baluan Native Christian United) Church

This organization (in Manus Province, Papua New Guinea), which lays claim to being the first Melanesian independent or separatist church,[31] stands between Hehela's extensive traditionalization of missionary positions and

Eto's relatively sophisticated attempt to integrate inherited and introduced truths and to avoid patent syncretism. Paliau Church has been variously described as an independent religious movement, a cargo cult, a prophetic movement, a messianic sect, and an independent native political organization.[32]

We do not need to recount here the biography of Paliau Maloat (born c. 1918) — his creation of a community fund, his struggle to create the first local government council in New Guinea, and his terms in the pre-independence parliament (1964–72).[33] Suffice it to say that large meeting houses, soon to be accepted as churches, were being erected by Paliau's followers as early as 1946. The church on Mouk is among Papua New Guinea's most imposing church structures of local materials; also impressive is Mbunai, the long Paliau village which, with many newcomers, expanded so rapidly.[34]

Paliau's liturgy was not noticeably innovative — mainly Catholic prayers and hymns being used, yet with a cross or portrait of Jesus being central on the altar, no distribution of the elements, and services culminating in a talk by Paliau (or one of his associates) on the New Way (*nupela pasin*). The order of service followed a special pidgin liturgy, an incomplete version of the Catholic Mass, which combined previous missionary renderings with adjustments by Paliau supporters (who were thus engaged in New Guinea's earliest known autonomous indigenous literary activity).[35]

Paliau's followers were cut off from the Catholic church by the priests in 1947, following his insistence that the New Way — based upon 'right thinking' and his idiosyncratic interpretation of the Bible (or *long stori bilong God*)[36] — would enable the islanders both to abandon useless, unworkable customs of the past and to determine their lives independently of mission and administration. By 1980, however, because he devoted too much attention to the collection of taxes for the 1977 election and acquired too many 'wives' by apparently irresponsible means, Paliau's popularity had dropped sharply.[37] One of his former colleagues, Pita Tapo, who was dedicated to the church's continued existence, openly contended that Paliau had betrayed the church created in his name. Even though the number of pro-Tapo activists diminished to around 500 and were largely confined to the south-east coast of Manus Island in the mid-1970s, Tapo's staunchness was probably the main reason Paliau was ejected from Mbunai, even if in the long run it contributed to the former leader's comeback in 1978.

Paliau's new activity was centred around the old *Saarhut* (town council building) and also the house of Paliau Lukas (the son of one of Paliau's former 'lieutenants'), at the provincial capital, Lorengau, on the north coast. Attempts to revamp the church along lines now attractive to the new Manus intelligentsia await more up-to-date research.[38] It has, at least, become clear that the Lorengau meetings and services — focussing as they do on Paliau's newer theology of 'Wing/Wang/Wong'[39] (= me/God the Son/God the Holy Spirit)[40] — did succeed in recapturing interest, even among the 7000 or so on the south coast who had gone along with Tapo, as well as scattered supporters elsewhere (most numerous in Madang and Port Moresby). By 1980 followers had welcomed the production of a new White Book, a brief rewriting of the Bible in myth-historical terms, explaining the cosmic significance of Paliau's work, and introducing the church's symbol as the nautilus shell.[41] Preparations were also being made to erect a church building on a site secured at Lorengau, and Paliau formed an active political front called Makasol.

In spite of the relative fading of Paliau's (quasi-) messiahship, the organization bearing his name still seems to stand somewhere between the Christian Fellowship Church and Hehela. The Paliau Church teaches a Christology rather than adopting some traditional equivalent of Jesus, but Christianity has been tailored to suit indigenous needs much more obviously than with Etoism, and 'cargo cult' elements from the past linger on.

The Remnant Church

This independency nicely illustrates one possible intermediate position on the opposite side of the spectrum. It emerged in 1954 in Malaita Island, Malaita Province, Solomon Islands, as one of a series of defections from the South Sea Evangelical Mission, but the only one which could be said to have lasted. Its two most important founders were Christopher England (or Igalana) Kwaisulia and Sambilon Sisimia.[42] It is enough to comment on the decisive intrusion of Seventh Day Adventist theology, along with the labouring of certain purple passages in the Bible, to show that Western sectarian thought-moulds have had a stronger appeal in this church than in the Christian Fellowship Church.

The Old and New Testaments are given equal weight, and the Law — the Sabbath and various dietary, ceremonial regulations and sexual tabus — must be observed. It is argued, especially by Sambilon's partisans, that while members of the Seventh Day Adventist Mission might accept this position in principle, they generally do not practise it; as a result of unacceptable criticism Sambilon (who was educated at Betikama Seventh Day Adventist High School, 1947–49), was utterly disowned by the previously supportive Adventists in 1957. Counter-balancing the strict legalism, however, Remnant worship services are marked by 'charismatic' phenomena — 'speaking in tongues', 'prophesying' and 'ecstatic experiences' — which are characteristic of spiritistic tendencies in the South Sea Evangelical Mission.[43] The rationale behind the name 'Remnant' lies in Biblical verses (Isa. 10:21, Rev. 7:3–8).[44] Its leaders emphasize the need to preserve the purity of the faithful by disallowing outsiders to come into their villages,[45] and by condemning as false all the churches existing after Constantine for not insisting on complete separation of church and state.[46] The Remnant Church has its own flag — with twelve stars (for the twelve tribes of Israel) and an eagle (signifying God looking down on the world) — and have not only sought recognition from the Solomons government (1979) but also the right to refrain from paying taxes and to live separated from the world's evils.

On the other hand, these apparently non-Melanesian features are pressed into the service of Malaita tradition or *kastam*. It is claimed that the ancestor of all Malaitans was a son or descendant of Moses, whose name was Levi Moses Solomon. This man imparted the Ten Commandments but they were forgotten by later descendants until the missionaries came, although the whites only obscured the truth until it was disclosed by the Holy Spirit, even by a vision of Christ to Igalana revealing that the 'whole law' should be obeyed.[47] Thus, the teachers (*ticha*) of this church have conceded that one crucial person, equivalent in stature to a Biblical hero, is to be found in the indigenous tradition — an ancestral lawgiver. This concession, along with the curious mixture of charismatics and legalism, finds the Remnant Church sitting between Etoism, which is relatively freer of introduced form and content, and Boda Kwato, which is separatist while remaining highly informed by western orthodox and organizational styles. Interestingly, the Remnant Church has established itself less in the north, where it originated, than in five villages of western Malaita, an area occupied by pagans who have rejected Christianity in favour of tradition.[48] The Remnants do not adopt a strongly missionary stance; yet, for them the Millennium will only come when the Remnant is vast (Rev. 7:9), and thus is not *clos tu mas* (imminent). The members expect to have some time to expand their work, then, and also to secure the ownership of vessels big enough to ship in cargo for the community's needs.[49]

The Congregation of the Poor (Lotu ni Dravudravua)

Wanting in analysis, perhaps, Paula Rokutuiviwa's short study[50] provides a serviceable introduction to this small church in Suva, Fiji, which draws most of its followers from literate 'lower middle class' members of the civil service and business firms in Suva. On the one hand quite unlike the Christian Fellowship Church for being urban rather than rural,[51] the Congregation nevertheless possesses a leader comparable to Eto: Sekaia Loaniceva (born 1921), who occupies almost as central a place in the church he created as Eto does in the Christian Fellowship Church. He had been, variously, an armourer's assistant in wartime, a trade store manager and successful vegetable marketer before he was called into the ministry during the 1950s by visions and tests he believed were sent by Jehovah.

Although Loaniceva is not confused with God, his views on life and Biblical interpretation are considered by his followers to be final. He is acclaimed as 'Vuniwai' (the Physician anointed by Jehovah), and it is accepted that the Congregation, which is reckoned crucial for the future prominence of

Fiji in world affairs toward the end of this century, owes its existence to unique, miraculous experiences in the leader's life. Vuniwai acquires authority, moreover, as much from the results of his healing as from his teaching.[52] On the other hand, Vuniwai's message (which does not seem to have captured much more than a hundred indigenous adherents in a Fiji noted for the overwhelming and unifying sway of Methodism) is heavily oriented around the Bible. Scripture is quoted constantly; but it is used in such a way as to pinpoint, yet at the same time escape, compromises in prevailing Christianity.

The Congregation does not need church buildings, according to Vuniwai; for, true worship is 'in spirit and in truth' (John 4:23) and, thus, the houses where they meet and hold services (in the vernacular) suffice. The members share their wealth and choose simple living or 'poverty', in keeping both with the model of earliest Christianity (Acts 2:44–6, 4:34–5) and with their leader's warning that 'when man [sic] acquires great knowledge and wealth, he thinks himself powerful enough to leave God'.[53] New members are incorporated with a simple initiation ceremony, largely consisting of prayers (including Vuniwai's modified version of the Lord's Prayer), while baptism is of fire not water (cf. Matt. 3:11) and takes place for those worthy to receive it in an (indoor) session during a thunderstorm. Those members who develop spiritually are all expected to receive the same healing powers available to Christ's disciples and to Vuniwai himself (cf. John 14:12), and there are various grades in the Congregation: all initiates may don a white robe (which recalls Biblical dress), but there are various symbols — such as a white sword on a red vest for males nearest in rank to the founder — which indicate the degrees of mastery of the Bible and its application.[54]

Intriguingly, Vuniwai has made a number of impressive predictions, forecasting that Fiji would become 'head of the world' in 1991, with the Millennium actualizing in 2001. Such apocalypticism, however, is 'of secondary importance', and 'the year' of the eschaton 'is not something that is eagerly awaited'.[55] It is unjustified, then, to write of the Congregation as a somewhat agitated and therefore millenarian movement, and important to note that it is also self-consciously and unusually anti-cargoist in stance. The constraining influences clearly derive from scriptural sources introduced to Fiji by missionaries, but the particular interpretations have resulted from revelatory experiences which Vuniwai and his supporters believe God has sent to the peculiarly Fijian situation, and to a group specially set apart from other local churches.

The NaGriamel Federation Independent United Royal Church

In contrast to the Congregation, this church looks to be a mere offshoot from a political secessionist movement. Originating in March 1965 in Espiritu Santo, Vanuatu, from an association between Buluk, a chief of south-west Espiritu

Santo, and Jimmy Stevens, an islander of mixed ethnic background, NaGriamel (widely translated: Croton-Cycas Palm) began as a land reappropriation movement (in opposition to 80 per cent expatriate ownership of arable land). In search of a new identity, Buluk and Stevens sided with the Church of Christ Mission against Presbyterians, Anglicans and Catholics. Two indigenous Church of Christ pastors, Abel Bani and James Karai, worked vigorously to give NaGriamel their theological backing. As the emergent charismatic leader, however, Jimmy Stevens — with his syncretistic tendencies, his claim to be Moses leading his people to the Promised Land, and his freedom in sexual relations — greatly disappointed the previously elated expatriate Church of Christ missionaries, so that they had disowned NaGriamel by 1975.[56]

NaGriamel as a land reform organization has had a complex and dramatic history. With a *claimed* membership of 30 000 in 1971, Stevens tended to reduce his attention to Santo in the years following, developing a loose federation to secure Santo's regional autonomy.[57] As NaGriamel's only success in the 1979 national elections of the New Hebrides was to secure 50.59 per cent of the rural Santo vote,[58] Stevens organized partisans into two assaults on Luganville, the second being on the police barracks in late May 1980.[59] Lack of support in the 1979 elections probably reflected spreading disillusion with Stevens's political compromises, because he made outlandish concessions to the American Phoenix Foundation and other foreign (even sinister-looking) business interests. In being succoured by outside manipulators, then, who provided passports and equipment for an independent 'Vemarana', it was the eventual fate of Stevens's secessionist operations to meet armed resistance. This occurred when the prime minister of newly independent Vanuatu allowed, not British nor French, but Papua New Guinean troops to storm the secluded NaGriamel headquarters at Fanefo village.[60]

Although Karai was arrested along with Stevens on that occasion, it is evident that NaGriamel Royal Church has been distinct from, even if integrally related to, the land reform movement. Karai was pastor of the biggest church at Fanefo (with its hard core of 300), but supporters from western Aoba (where Bani supervised at least twelve bush-material churches), and from South Malekula, Epi, Pentecost and Maevo have been constantly visiting the Fanefo centre.

The pastors' appropriation of Biblical texts to justify traditional land rights (e.g. Prov. 22:28, Job 24:2) bears some resemblance to the selective use of scripture made by the Remnant Church, while the various displays of the two types of NaGriamel leaves — *ngria* and *mel* — in church services (as in a wedding witnessed by Michael Allen on Aoba), reveal a conscious attempt to hallow *kastam*, or customary land rights, through Christianity.[61] Allen also noticed that Royal Church elders feasted below the communion table after service, in a position equivalent to the one reserved for men of high status in the traditional club house. Even if most outward liturgical forms resemble Church of Christ practice, moreover, the high hopes placed in Jimmy Stevens (in spite of his extraordinary beytrayal of NaGriamel's original aims and his continuing imprisonment) may be paralleled to rank and file Christian Fellowship Church members' attitudes toward Eto.[62]

'Friday Religion'

Despite the extensive use of Christian motifs, this intriguing concern appears more to be on the Paliau Church 'side' of the Christian Fellowship Church than in a position close to either NaGriamel or the Remnants. The appellation 'Friday Religion' is one used by outsiders, not by the participants themselves. It originated as a separatist movement among the Nasioi in 1958 some 7 miles (12 km) inland from the Koromira Catholic Mission Station, eastern Bougainville, Western Solomons Province, Papua New Guinea, in relatively inaccessible mountain country. Half a dozen leaders came to the fore after collective spiritual experiences (the coming of 'strong wind', 'tongues of fire', and glossolalia), and four villages — Pontana most important among them — consequently sought a separate identity within the Catholic ambience.

According to Sipari,[63] the leaders set Friday rather than Sunday as the day of worship for three reasons. First, Jesus died on a Friday; secondly, three Nasioi seminarians were killed by a bomb blast on a certain Friday during the Second World War; thirdly, a Nasioi bigman and war veteran by the name of Barosi was beheaded by the Japanese on a Friday, a war memorial at Pontana now marking the place of execution. Followers attempt to keep six types of law (*lo*) written down by the leaders, the last type concerning marriage. Both the exchange of spouses and endogamy are permitted under careful supervision. Virgin births are expected to result from a ritual in which exchanged spouses can sit and walk around naked in front of each other — even touching — while refraining from sexual intercourse. The leaders, extolling the Blessed Virgin Mary as the centre of all Motherhood, as the spiritual mother of all human bodies and the mother of all the spiritual bodies of the departed, castigate those couples unable to contain themselves during the ritual encounters and limit their chances of further participation in them.

The separatists — who have no priests, say no Masses, work on Sundays, pray together on all days but with a special gathering on Fridays — wanted to stay within the Catholic fold. Gregory Singkai, Bishop of Bougainville, however, could not be persuaded (during 1976–77) to send priests to say Mass on Fridays and accommodate the demands of a few hundred persons who seemed to breach canonical regulations. For all their irregular Christianity, interestingly, they hold their *lo* to follow custom more closely than introduced practice.[64] As Laracy has pointed out, Catholic missionaries avoided making changes to Nasioi social life unless indigenous ways were explicitly contrary to

Catholic teaching, and the two traditions clearly proscribed for the baptized were polygamy and direct invocation of the spirits.[65] The exchanges of spouses in 'Friday Religion' revives polygamy but within a Christian community especially adjusted for the purpose, while the coming of the Spirit and the closeness of God's might and glory are seen to supersede, yet at the same time resemble, access to former sources of spiritual power. Unlike Paliau, the leaders do not denigrate the past, but the measure of their deviation from western beliefs and forms exceeds that of the Christian Fellowship Church. Like Teosin, they seek a Melanesian equivalent to Jesus and find it in Barosi, 'who died in the manner that Christ died to redeem the whole world' and who 'died for . . . Bougainville to redeem the island and its people from the devastation of the war'.[66]

The Peli Association (or Niu Apostolic)

The Peli Association ('peli' means 'hawk' in the Boiken language) is something of an anomaly, since it has passed so quickly from being a spectacular and flourishing prosperity/cargo cult[67] to being a disappointed, somewhat disoriented group seeking to regain lost prestige through the help of newcomer sectarian missionaries from Canada. The Peli Association of the Yangoru district (East Sepik Province, Papua New Guinea) was formed in 1971 by Daniel Hawina (born 1943) as the business arm to a protest movement generated by Matias Yaliwan (born c. 1929). It was Yaliwan who organized the mass demonstration to remove American geodesic survey markers from Mount Hurun in July 1971, in order to offset the decreased fertility of the Yangoru area. Many activities marked the following year: Peli members refused to pay taxes to the government; impressive rituals to produce Cargo were initiated at the focal-point village Marambanja; relations with the Catholic Mission reached their lowest ebb; and Yaliwan was elected to the parliament of Papua New Guinea on the ticket that he would bring independence as well as wealth to the country. During that year (1972), the Association's membership ranged between 100 000 and 200 000 people, huge sums of money being collected.

To follow the recent analyses of Gesch, the Association began to decline after large-scale disillusionment and Yaliwan's resignation of his parliamentary seat. Since then Hawina has attempted to divest Peli of its cargo cult atmosphere, and began by currying favour with the Canadian New Apostolic Church missionaries. In 1981 Hawina claimed that *Niu Apostolic* had over 30 000 members and listed for me forty-three villages which had erected church buildings. Peli has provided a basis for membership into the new organization, and many Peli committee representatives have become deacons in scattered villages throughout the Prince Alexander Mountains. Gesch estimates more than 500 adult baptisms had been performed by Hawina and his delegates independently of any mission; the Sepik Provincial Government's motions debarring the Canadian missionaries (passed twice, in June and November 1981) left Hawina with a free hand as organizer. Some 5000 people also remain interested in the next moves of the more mysterious, elusive Yaliwan, a Melanesian apocalyptist who broods over the Book of Revelation and continues to be politically aspiring (even if he articulated nothing during his short term in the Provincial Assembly in 1981).

Despite their attempts to re-establish themselves (including instituting the use of a pidgin worship Service Guide translated by a New Apostolic Church missionary), the Canadians have only been used by Hawina to provide some theological legitimacy for the Association but not to substitute for the old leadership. Yaliwan and Hawina probably want more theological justification for their separation from the Catholic Mission and, since the bitter pill of dashed cargo hopes has had to be swallowed, it makes sense for them to prove that something *has* happened following all the intense activities at Marambanja, rather than to admit misapprehension.[68] The precise relationship between tradition and introduced Christianity is difficult to ascertain at the moment, not so much because of syncretism but because of a split-level effect — two levels of discourse, the one more apparently Christian and the other more in keeping with Peli cargoist themes, manifesting themselves.

Wok bilong Yali (or the Yali Movement)

Yali's movement (in Madang Province, Papua New Guinea) is surely the most renowned cargo cult of all Melanesia. Collective anticipations of coming European cargo or hopes of unlocking the secret of the whites' superior technology have had a long history in the Madang area, going back at least to the German period (1885–1914), and a number of cults and prophets antedate the emergence of Yali's post-Second World War movement.[69] Yali of Sor (c. 1912–75), a Ngaing from the Rai coast and an (Allied) war hero, who organized a rehabilitation scheme to bring a significantly improved standard of living to war-torn Madangs, became the centre of cargo expectations after cessation of hostilities between the Allies and the Japanese. Eventually disillusioned with the Australian administrators and the Lutheran and Catholic missionaries, who distrusted his methods and motives, Yali succumbed to the view that only the correct practice of traditional (and semi-traditional) Madang rituals would bring the cargo and development long awaited by his people.[70] His influence and organization, of importance for over a hundred villages, spread along the New Guinea coast and hinterland from as far west as Manam Island to as far east as the Huon Peninsula.[71] Further inland, his impact was much weaker; some supporters, however, took his message as far as Kainantu and Goroka in the central highlands.

Without adumbrating the pressures inhibiting the progress of *wok bilong*

Yali until the 1970s, or the details of its beliefs, rituals and administration as a cargo cult,[72] it is important to note two things: Yali openly denounced cargo cultism in 1973;[73] on Yali's death, his former itinerant secretary, Beig Wen of Kauris, attempted to consolidate the declining movement from Madang township. As I have argued elsewhere,[74] Beig's efforts to purge *wok bilong Yali* of cargo cult associations, and his revisioning of 'macro-history'[75] mark 'an important shift in the history of Madang cultism'. According to Beig (who was once a Lutheran Church councillor), there are two plans of salvation: one for the whites and one for the native Madangs (the parallel with Teosin's position is obvious), and these two can be construed diagrammatically as shown in table 9.1 below.

TABLE 9.1   ONE SCHEME OF SALVATION IN THE YALI MOVEMENT

	Macro-history			
	Good Period	*Bad Period*	*Good Period*	*Expected*
for whites	Abraham to Moses	Angered Prophets	Jesus (revealing the right road)	Return of Jesus
for blacks	Ancestral time: ordered around the male cult	Competition between Christianity and tradition	Yali (revealing the right road)	Return of ancestors

Considering this systematic Melanesian theology(?), along with the new tendency to present leaders (*lo bos*) as ministers (*minista*) and to advocate Yali as a messiah equivalent to Jesus (with Yali's sayings actually being recorded in an exercise book), we now witness a self-conscious concern to develop a radical Melanesian alternative to the Christian churches. Yet, it is an attempt that seeks to earn respectability without declaring itself a *lotu* (as we know Hehela adherents have) or aligning itself with any Christian church or sect (as the Peli Association has), and roughly parallel developments may also be found in the recent history of the Moro movement.

The Moro Movement

Whether the Moro movement and the Yali movement should be described as independent churches is highly disputable. Despite their affinity to Hehela, they lie very much on the fringes of our spectrum if we are to allow them any foothold at all. Both *wok bilong Yali* and the Moro movement are decidedly nativistic: Yali espoused traditionalism to realize cargo, whereas Moro simply extolled the values and social structures of Guadalcanal *kastam* to counter the incursions of the whites. The Moro movement, however, right from the beginning of its history in 1957 on Guadalcanal Island, Central Province,

Solomon Islands, had features which enabled it to gain recognition as a pressure group by the Protectorate Government of the Solomons.[76] Moro's crucial vision of the creator being, Ironggali, the myths and shrines (*boko*) associated with it, and the use of this vision to reinforce the old chieftainship system, may well all amount to pagan revivalism, but his organization of piggeries, plantations and regional cooperation was to earn money for his people and secure them a place in the new social order.[77]

In recent years, possibly because people have still attended mission churches while identifying with Moro, the movement has developed a 'black theology' comparable to Beig's and Teosin's. Moro has lost some ground to the upstart Willi of Valebaibai (central Guadalcanal), who has trained within the South Sea Evangelical Church (formed from the Mission in 1964), and is more concerned to work out the traditional equivalents to Bible characters and truths than simply reiterate old stories and preserve customs. For Willi, whose support came from the strategic northern coastal villages of Lumata-popohu and Kekabona, close to Honiara, the Bible is for the whites and there is no reason to question its validity. Tradition, however, contains the same truths but for islanders only. Moses and Jesus, for instance, are paralleled by figures of Guadalcanal legend who have secret, undivulged names.

For Willi's supporters, the Bible properly understood confirms this understanding. From my efforts to decipher a diagram on their 'school' blackboard, I conclude that they recognize a distant genealogical connection between whites and blacks, who all have their source in God the Creator (as with the Remnant Church) but not even Willi's men use or read the Bible. Even if they consider the *boko* (or *haus memori* as it is called in pidgin) a place to wait upon God who created the Universe and not upon the old Ironggali ('maker of Isatabu' [= Guadalcanal]), and even if they seek God's will in these shrines before certain undertakings — such as going on a journey or planting a garden — we can only admit that the Moro movement edges toward a new stance and toward a statement of self-identity comparable to Hehela's. Since Willi is less anti-white than Beig, accepting the necessity of the islanders to pay taxes (unless they are clearly impoverished), his possible future succession to the ageing Moro's headship may bring to light the lineaments of an independent church much more rapidly than is likely with the more unsettled (and geographically dispersed) *wok bilong Yali*.

Other candidates for independency

Here, we can only take a cursory glance at other possible candidates for independent church status. Without going into the complex history of the so-called Jonfrum cargo cult, which forms their background, the Sulphur Bay and Lenakel movements (of Tanna Island, Vanuata) could be included as 'churches' akin to the Yali and Moro movements and to Hehela, with Jonfrum as the equivalent to Jesus. Under the leadership of Uwelas, the Sulphur Bay movement had its own government-supported schools (like the Christian Fellowship Church), its own 'chapels', along with outdoor shrines, and its own day of worship — Friday (as with 'Friday Religion').[78] Lenakel (now centred on Ionhanen, south of Lenakel village) is a schism from the Sulphur Bay movement and leans rather more 'towards the Presbyterian church, which, it declares, it will rejoin by degrees rather than be absorbed by the Sulphur Bay clique'.[79]

Then, only very recently brought to my attention, there are two small independent churches among the Enga, in Papua New Guinea, both separating from the Gutnius Lutheran Church in 1981. The first is styled *Namba Wan Brekawe Bilong Gutnius Sios*, the young, educated Engan, Chris Kopyoto, declaring himself its first bishop at Wabag; the second is named *Sios bilong Jisas Krais — Wok Apostel*, based at Warumanda. However, opportunity for research has not yet arisen.

While this survey was being completed, the beginnings of an independent church were in evidence in the Rigo sub-province of Papua, under the leadership of Bikana Veve, in this case, significantly, a woman in her thirties. At the new, modern design church of *Manana Kele*, she has taught about the visitation of angels and the dead, and claims to have become pregnant by the Holy Spirit.[80]

Of two movements I have been recently researching in the New Britain Provinces of Papua New Guinea, the one surrounding *Dakoa* on Unea (or Bali) Island can be classed as an independent church;[81] while the other, the Pomio *Kivung* on the north-eastern side of New Britain Island, is an expression of Melanesian Christianity without actually being a church (or pretending to be one).[82] Then, there remains the following of the elusive Demien Damen, who began a Nasioi (or central Bougainvillean) cult in the context of the Hahalis eruption in 1961. He advocates nominal Catholicism and a covert 'traditionalism'. As defender of 'Mekamui' (or, secession of the 'sacred island'), Demien Damen has been mentor of Francis Ona, leader of the Bougainville rebellion begun in 1988.

Other scholars may wish to add to the above listing, citing churches or closely related movements which are as yet unknown to me. I have, however, already excluded some other possible candidates; this is for a variety of technical reasons which I have given in another place.[83] These include groups which almost broke away from denominations, or were short-lived, or which quickly re-affiliated with established missions, or were expatriate-led despite strong indigenous participation, or were better described as cargo cultist. At the same time, however, the importance of spiritistic or pentecostal tendencies should not be overlooked; this is because, although the many so-called 'Holy Spirit Movements' currently erupting in the region can be taken as revitalizations of old denominational activity, they may well form the seed-bed from which various independent churches will spring.[84]

Furthermore, mutual understanding between various church leaders resulting from the perusal of this outline has been taken into account, since during the course of my fieldwork representatives from each church were eager to learn what I had discovered about the others. Their reactions to my reports indicate that these leaders quickly assess the differences between movements and, even if judging the organizations by criteria from their own church platforms, appreciate the polarity between tradition and the introduced. While listening to their viewpoints, I became convinced that certain categories applied to the African independent churches (such as 'syncretist', 'messianic', 'prophet-healing', 'Hebraist'[85]), do not usually suit the Melanesian scene.

Syncretism (or 'synthetism') has too many varied and subtle manifestations. All the Melanesian churches presented here have fused traditional and western Christian values, beliefs or practices to some extent, and it is thus preferable to visualize a continuum along which the impact of one basic tendency or the other can be tentatively plotted. Messianism, in spite of being quite obvious in the cases of Etoism and Beig's 'theological' re-evaluation of *wok bilong Yali*, appears in movements so markedly divergent in their general leanings that such a category loses hermeneutic power. The term 'prophet' has been used of Eto, Yaliwan and Yali,[86] but, of these, only Eto has emerged as a healer[87] (although there is also Loaniceva fairly begging to be called by both titles). As for Hebraistic or legalistic biases, it is fascinating how in two groups motivated by 'charismatic experiences' — the Remnant Church and the 'Friday Religion' — we find a strong insistence on *lo* (primarily for the ethical realm), mixed with the call to live 'in the Spirit' (primarily at worship). In both these churches *lo*, even if expressed in Christian terms, perpetuates the strict regulative style familiar in the traditional community of the past (as with Dakoa's church and the Pomio *Kivung*), and reveals that mainstream Christianity often appears too insipid and indefinite beside the rigid, precise formulae of primal rituals or rules. It is this very vulnerability within Christianity which has contributed to the reactions by Teosin and Yali in the name of tried and proven ancestral discipline.

Quite apart from the need for a suitable typology, however, there remains the problem of deciding when these movements pass their critical thresholds to become independent churches. It is far easier to establish their new identities when the passage has been 'from church to independent church', but usually difficult when it comes to new developments springing from cargo cults. Hehela, *wok bilong Yali* and Willi's arm of the Moro movement, furthermore, could be described as neo-pagan or neo-primal activities to be placed quite outside the Christian tradition. Certainly, although all three might accept Christianity as true for the whites, only Hehela has so far got to the point of seeking recognition as a *lotu*.

No one can now gainsay the importance, let alone existence, of independent churches in Melanesia, however, and it is clear that research into their doctrines and forms is long overdue. A comparison of these organizations reveals that more work is required to analyze the ways by which one kind of movement (usually dubbed with a European label!) transmutes into another. This survey is designed to open up the field of investigation, and is hopefully tantalizing enough to encourage further work on specific churches. It can only hint at a variety of issues, such as levels of literacy, relative deprivation, population mobility, the nature and stability of kinship structures — all of which await the assiduousness and expertise of others.

Suffice it to reiterate that Melanesian independent churches ought not to be generalized away as cargo cult or millenarian movements and, although some can be arguably placed in those categories, there is justification in grouping them together as a distinct class of social phenomena important for the overall assessment of Oceanic affairs. More of them are bound to emerge in the future as part of the ongoing, complex processes of indigenous response to change — including religious change — in Melanesia. Small as these independencies will doubtless remain, the sensitivities of the new national churches of Melanesia will be challenged in dealing with them.

NOTES

Chapter 9 is based on material originally published as an article in the journal *Oceania*.

1 See J. Guiart, 'Le cadre socio-traditional et la rébellion de 1878', *Journal de la Société des Océanistes*, 24 (1968), pp.97ff; W. Gammage, 'The Rabaul Strike, 1929', *Journal of Pacific history* 10/3–4 (1975), pp.1ff; R. Doussett-Leenhardt, *Colonialisme et contradictions: Nouvelle Calédonie, 1878–1978, les causes de l'insurrection de 1878*, Paris, 1978; R. M. Keesing, 'Politico-religious movements and anticolonialism on Malaita: Maasina Rule in historical perspective', *Oceania*, 48/4–49/1 (1978–79), pp.241ff., 46ff; A. Marmak and A. Ali (eds), *Race, class and rebellion in the South Pacific*, Sydney, 1979; P. Corris and Keesing, *Lightning meets the west wind: the Malaita massacre*, Melbourne, 1980; P. Hempenstall (ed.), H. Laracy, *Pacific protest*, Suva, 1983; *Protest and dissent in the colonial Pacific*, Suva, 1984 (for rebellions); W. Davenport and G. Çoker, 'The Moro movement of Guadalcanal, British Solomon Islands Protectorate', *Journal of Polynesian Society*, 76 (1967), pp.123ff. (traditionalist movement).

2 On Sundkler's work, esp. *Bantu prophets in South Africa*, London, 1961 edn; *Zulu Zion* (Oxford Studies in African Affairs), London, 1976. For other Africanists on independent churches, e.g., G. Balandier, *The sociology of black Africa* (trans. D. Garman), London, 1955, pt 3, ch. 3; K. Schlosser, *Eingeborenenkirchen in Süd und Südwest Afrika; Ihre Geschichte und Sozialstruktur*, Kiel, 1958; D. B. Barrett, *Schism and renewal in Africa*, Nairobi, 1968; H. Turner, *African independent church*, Oxford, 1967, 2 vols; and elsewhere, e.g. J. M. Henderson, *Ratana: the man, the church and the political movement*, Wellington, 1972 edn. On the other categorizations, e.g., V. Lanternari, 'Messianism: its historical origin and morphology', (messianism); J. Beckett, 'Mission, church and sect: three types of religious commitment in the Torres Strait Islands', in J. Boutilier et al., *Mission, church and sect in Oceania*, Ann Arbor, 1978, pp.209ff. (sectarianism).

3 On autonomy from Mission as church independence, P. Lawrence, 'Lutheran mission influence on Madang societies', *Oceania*, 27/2 (1956), p.76; R. G. Williams, 'From mission to church: a study of the United Church', in M. Ward (ed.), *The Politics of Melanesia*, pp.666ff; cf. the use of indigenous church instead in this connection, e.g., F. C. Horne, *The indigenous church*, Port Moresby, 1963; E. B. Idowu, *Towards an indigenous church*, London, 1965, etc.

4 Unless otherwise stated, the information in this chapter derives from fieldwork in Melanesia between 1972–80, including interviews with independent church leaders.

5 W. C. Groves, 'A model village, Menakasapa, New Guinea', *Open Door*, 19/1 (1940), pp.3–8; S. Eto, 'A native chief takes stock', *Open Door*, 29/3 (1949), p.3; Tippett, *Solomon Islands Christianity*, London, 1967, pp.219–64; F. Harwood, The Christian Fellowship Church (doctoral dissert., University of Chicago 1971); 'Intercultural Communication in the Western Solomons', in J. Boutilier et al., *Mission*, pp.231ff; E. Tuza, The Rise of Eto (master's qualifying thesis, UPNG, Port Moresby 1974); Tuza, The emergence of the Christian Fellowship Church (master's dissert., UPNG, Port Moresby, 1975); Tuza, 'Silas Eto', in Trompf (ed.), *Prophets*, ch. 2; Tuza, 'Paternal Acidity', *Pacific Islands Monthly*, 50/1 (1979), pp.8–9; Tuza, 'The Demolition of Church Buildings by the Ancestors', in Trompf (ed.), *The Gospel is not Western*, ch. 8; Chesher, 'Holy Mama, Solomon prophet, etc.' in *Pacific Islands Monthly*, 49/7 (1978), pp.18–20; G. Carter, 'Holy Mama', in ibid., 49/10 (1978), p.8; G. Bartlett, 'Holy Mama Again', in ibid., 50/1 (1979), p.8; J. Bennett, *Wealth of the Solomons* (Pacific Islands Monograph Series 3), Honolulu, 1987, pp.299–301.

6 Tuza, 'Silas Eto', pp.111, 123–32; D. Hilliard, 'Protestant missions in the Solomon Islands 1849–1942' (doctoral dissert., ANU, Canberra 1967), pp.346–47; Hilliard, *God's gentleman*, p.194.

7 Tuza, 'Silas Eto', p.143.

8 cf. Tippett, *Solomon Islands*, pp.254–61; Tuza, Rise of Eto, pp.107–10.

9 Tuza, pers. comm. 1977, and his writing, ibid., pp.90–91, 'Silas Eto', pp.136–38; 'The Demolition', esp. p.89; cf. Tippett, *Solomon Islands*, pp.257–59.

10 J. Dudley, 'The Politics of the Christian Fellowship Church' (forthcoming chapter for a book on *Politics in the Solomon Islands*).

11 i.e., they stress there are many gifts (= *charismata*) of the Holy Spirit, and thus the gift of speaking in tongues (as given at Pentecost, cf. Acts 2) is not to be over-emphasized nor considered the only mark of being truly Christian (as various Pentecostal groups teach). Note that money is acknowledged as a spiritual gift (Tuza, Seeking contexts within the new relationships, etc. [mimeograph, Melanesian Institute, Goroka, 1981] p.11).

12 cf. M.-L. Martin, *Kimbangu: an African prophet and his church* (trans. D. M. Moore), Oxford, 1975; Sundkler, *Bantu prophets*, pp.103ff., 159ff.

13 H. Willey, *Assignment New Guinea*, Brisbane, 1965; B. Bunting, Future changes in New Guinea (unpublished typescript, DPI Library, Port Moresby 1966); Tippett, *Solomon Islands*, pp.209–12; A. M. Kiki, *Ten thousand years*, pp.104–18; F. Hagai, 'Explaining Hahalis', *New Guinea and Australia, the Pacific and Southeast Asia*, 4 (1969), pp.8ff; T. Ryan, *The hot land*, Melbourne, 1969, pp.286–314; G. Fahey, Cargo cult movements in Bougainville (mimeograph, Melanesian Institute, Vunapope 1970); F. Steinbauer, *Melanesian cargo cults*, pp.79–82; M. Rimoldi, The Hahalis Welfare Society of Buka (doctoral dissert., ANU, Canberra 1971); H. Laracy, *Marists and Missionaries*, pp.135–143; H. Griffin, 'The Hahalis Welfare Society', in Trompf (ed.), *Mel. and Judaeo-Christ. Relig. Trads*, bk 4, pt D/3, pp.38ff; R. Tohiana, The Hahalis Welfare Society of Buka (honours sub-thesis, UPNG, Port Moresby, 1982).

14 Rimoldi, Hahalis, pp.280–97.

15 For background, B. Blackwood, *Both Sides of Buka Passage*, pp.97–99, 445–46.

16 Mathias Meksi was the first secretary but for a very short time, and was later beheaded in 1976 (Fahey, Cargo cult, p.3).

17 S. Bili, Hahalis Welfare Society (unpublished typescript, Holy Spirit Seminary, Bomana 1977), p.4.

18 Since Mattanachil is pictured as one concerned with internal affairs of all Buka, this theology obscures the fact that the Halia, Petats and Solos fought each other recurrently, and that the Halia were spirited raiders and cannibals until the turn of this century. Mattanachil is 'selected' for Teosin's purposes from among various 'culture heroes'.

19 Fahey, Cargo cult, p.4.

20 cf. H. McElhanon, *Legends from Papua New Guinea*, pp.104, 106.

21 e.g., C. W. Abel, *Kwato, New Guinea 1890–1900*, London, 1900; R. W. Abel, *Charles Abel of Kwato*, New York, 1934; N. Goodall, *A history of the London Missionary Society 1895–1945*, London, 1954, pp.431–32; M. K. Abel, *Charles W. Abel: Papuan pioneer*; R. Lacey,

'Abel, Charles William', in P. Ryan (ed.), *Encyclopedia of Papua New Guinea*, vol. 1, pp.1–2. P. Prendergast, A History of the London Missionary Society in British New Guinea 1871–1901 (doctoral dissert., University of Hawaii, Honolulu 1968), pp.212–29; C. Abel, 'The impact of Charles Abel', in K. Inglis (ed.), *The History of Melanesia*, pp.265ff; R. Williams, *The United Church*, Rabaul, 1972, pp.38–44, 64–65, 86–87; J. Parratt, 'A note on Kwato and the Oxford Group', in *Journal of the Papua and New Guinea Society*, 6/1 (1972), pp.91–96; N. Lutton, 'Larger Than Life' (masters dissert., UPNG, Port Moresby, 1979).

22 J. H. P. Murray, 'Kwato and the Oxford Group', in *Papuan Annual Report*, 1937–38, p.24; F. E, Williams, 'Mission influence among the Keveri of South-East Papua', *Oceania*, 15/2 (1944), pp.89–141, D. Wetherall, 'Monument to a missionary: C. W. Abel and the Keveri of Papua', *Journal of Pacific history*, 6 (1973), pp.40ff; cf. also Wetherall and C. Carr-Gregg, 'Moral Re-Armament in Papua, 1931–42', *Oceania*, 54/1 (1984), pp.177ff.

23 In fact a London Governing Committee of the LMS had continued to have interests in the Kwato Extension Association Incorporated, because the latter had leased the area of the Kwato Mission district from the LMS in 1919.

24 cf. Lebasi, 'Kwato is Dead', *PNG Post-Courier*, 22, 23 and 24 Nov. 1971 (p.5 each time).

25 A sprinkling of candidates for the ministry were taken from the Kwato area, however, and trained at the Raronga Theological Seminary during the period of union. At the present time only one Suau graduate has not reverted to the Kwato style of ministry, although (as minister to a congregation in Alotau) he is now in isolation from the United Church as well.

26 On the traditional *tanuwaga* (chief), see Seligmann, *The Melanesians of British New Guinea*, pp.454–58.

27 R. W. Abel, *Riba Hariharihuna* (Suau New Testament), London, 1962; J. Guilliam, *Buka Wane*, Stanmore, 1969 edn.

28 For background, M. Buluna, 'The Milne Bay Development Company', in H. N. Nelson et al., *Select topics in the history of Papua New Guinea*, pp.49ff; A. Austin, 'F. W. Walker and Papua Industries Limited', *Journal of the Papua and New Guinea Society*, 6/1 (1972), pp.39ff.

29 Boda Kwato Constitution, sect. 2A[b].

30 J. Kadiba, Unpublished Report on a Visit to Alotau, Oct. 1980 (handwritten MS, Melanesian Institute, Goroka, 1980). Note Wedega, *Listen my country*, Sydney 1980.

31 Thus, Tuza, 'Silas Eto', p.144; J. Strelan, *Searching for Salvation*, p.35; H. Turner, 'Old and New in Melanesian Religions', *Point*, 2 (1978), p.8.

32 For variations, L. P. Mair, 'Independent religious movements in three continents' (ch. 8, n.6), p.130; A. J. F. Köbben, 'Prophetic movements as an expression of social protest', *Internationales Archiv für Ethnographie*, 49 (1960), pp.117ff; M. Mead, *New Lives for old*, New York, 1961, p.170; Steinbauer, *Melanesian cargo cults*, pp.68–72; Worsley, *Trumpet shall sound*, p.204; cf. Schwartz, *Paliau Movement*, p.219.

33 Paliau, 'History bilong mi', in Ward (ed.), *Politics of Melanesia*, p.151; Trompf, 'The life and work of Paliau Maloat; an introduction', in Trompf (ed.), *Mel. and Judaeo-Christ. relig. trads*, bk. 2, p.53.

34 Esp. K. Kais, Paliau since 1957 (unpublished handwritten MS, UPNG, Port Moresby 1972); cf. Schwartz, *Paliau movement*, plate 15.

35 There is said to be three typescript copies of a 'Bible' in existence, but I now believe this is the same document referred to above which is now published, with hymns attached, by Kristen Press, Madang (1976). Note also that there were various diaries kept by Paliau supporters (Schwartz, *Paliau movement*, pp.230, 285).

36 cf. ibid., 'The long story of God', pp.252–57.

37 A. Kuluah, The Paliau movement (unpublished lecture, UPNG, Port Moresby 1977); cf. S. P. 'Pokawin, 'The elections in Manus', in *Prelude to self-government* (ed. D. Stone), Canberra, 1976, pp.400–14.

38 We await the doctoral thesis of S. P. Pokawin (currently premier of the Manus Province), for UPNG.

39 'Wing' means 'me' in Paliau's own language; 'Wang' and 'Wong' are totally new to Manus vocabularies.

40 See Pokawin, 'Developments in the Paliau movement', in W. Flannery (ed.), *New religious movements, etc.* (Point Ser. 2), pp.104ff.

41 It is entitled *Kalopeu; Makosal Kastam Kaunsel* [Lorengau, 1983]; cf. the more recent 'Papa Kastam Tumbuna Rul bolong Makasol Gavman' (mimeograph), Lorengau, 1985 (by kind permission of Pokawin and Manus Provincial Government).

42 Esp. M. Maeliau, The Remnant Church (A Separatist Church), (unpublished typescript, Banz 1976), pp.3–4; M. Maetoloa, 'The Remnant Church I–II', in C. E. Loeliger and Trompf (eds), *New religious movements in Melanesia*, ch. 9.

43 Maeliau, Remnant Church, p.4; cf. A. Griffiths, *Fire in the islands*, Wheaton, 1977, pp.3–4; J. Barr, 'A survey of ecstatic phenomena and "Holy Spirit movements"', *Oceania*, 54/2 (1983), pp.109ff.

44 cf. also the Seventh Day Adventist works E. G. White, *Testimonies for the Church*, Mountain View, 1948 edn, vol. 5, pp.475–76; vol. 6, p.19; cf. *The great controversy*, Mountain View, 1971 edn, pp.13–14, 276–78. cf. also D. L. Whiteman, *Melanesians and Missionaries*, ch. 6, and *Melanesian messenger*, Easter 1966, p.9. Members of the Seventh Day Adventist Church commonly refer to themselves as 'The Remnant'.

45 Maeliau, Remnant Church, p.4; cf. B. Burt, 'The Remnant Church: a Christian sect in the Solomon Islands', *Oceania*, 53/4 (1983), pp.334ff.

46 On background, esp. F. Littell, *The origins of sectarian Protestantism*, New York, 1964, pp.64–72.

47 Maeliau, Remnant Church, pp.3–4; Maetoloa, 'Remnant Church', pt 2; Burt, 'Remnant Church', p.344.

48 R. Keesing, *Kwaio religion*, Honiara, 1977, p.1.

49 Michael Maeliau and Meshak Maetoloa are continuing research into this church (with the support of the South Sea Evangelical Church).

50 P. S. Rokotuiviwa, *The Congregation of the Poor*, Suva, 1975.

51 Note, however, that other followers are found in the villages of Nadroga, Nairai (Is.), Taveuni (Is.), Makogai, and isolated families are as far flung as New Zealand, Australia, India, Canada and the USA.

52 Rokotuiviwa, *Congregation*, pp.2–17, 30–31, 52, 55 (general authority), pp.17–20, 35–44 (healing).

53 ibid, p.48, cf. 27–28, 45, 49.

54 ibid., pp.23–26.

55 ibid., p.51 (quotation), cf. p.53. The 1987 Rabuka coups, however, have heightened interest in the Last Days.

56 Steinbauer, Die Cargo-Kulte als religionsgeschtliches und missionstheologisches Problem, pp.345–46; D. Coulter, NaGriamel and the Churches of Christ (mimeograph, Church of Christ, Vila, 1972); W. Camden, The NaGriamel Church of Christ (tape-recorded interview by Trompf, University of Sydney, Sydney, 1979); Trompf, 'Jimmy Stevens as Betrayer of a Faith', *Pacific Islands monthly*, 51/11 (1980), pp.29–33.

57 A. L. Jackson, 'Towards political awareness in the New Hebrides', *Journal of Pacific history*, 7 (1972), pp.155ff; B. Hours, The NaGriamel movement: from Land Struggle to Secessionism (mimeograph, n.p., [Noumea] 1976); 'Leadership et cargo cult; l'irresistible ascension de J. T. P. S. Moïse', *Journal de la Société des Océanistes*, 32 (1976), pp.207ff; C. Plant, 'The Nagriamel federation: new country, old story', *Pacific perspectives*, 6 (1977), pp.49ff; J. Jupp and M. Sawer, 'New Hebrides 1978–79: Self Government by Whom and for Whom?', *Journal of Pacific history*, 14/3–4 (1979), pp.208ff; J. MacClancy, *To kill a bird with two stones; a short history of Vanuatu*, Vila, 1981; H. van Trease, *The Politics in Vanuatu: from colony to independence*, Suva, 1987.

58 *Nabanja* 21 Nov., 1979; Jupp and Sawer, 'The New Hebrides prepares for Independence', *Current affairs bulletin*, 56/11 (1980), pp.22ff.

59 *Seli Hoo*, No.11, 1980, p.2.

60 R. Shears, *The coconut war*, Sydney, 1980, pp.118–210. We await the article on Jimmy Stevens by Sione Latukefu for Trompf (ed.), *Islands and enclaves*, New York and Delhi (forthcoming).

61 For most of the above paragraph, OT: Michael Allen, Sept. 1980, cf. Allen, Roads, Cults
    and Authority (unpublished typescript, University of Sydney, Sydney, 1976), pp.28–37;
    Coulter, NaGriamel.
62 cf. also G. M. Douglas, NaGriamel: a cargo movement in the New Hebrides (honours sub-
    thesis, University of Otago, Dunedin 1976); Trompf, 'Melanesian "cargo cults" today',
    Pacific islands monthly, 51/11 (1981), pp.19–22 and Latukefu's forthcoming article (cf.
    n.60). The Constitution of the Confederation of Natakano (= NaGriamel's renamed New
    Hebrides), art. 1, sect. 3, and of NaGriamel, art. 2, sect. 3, mention the freedom of religion,
    but the phraseology is inspired, not by Church of Christ or Royal Church ecclesiology, but
    the American Constitution. The Phoenix Foundation, which secured provision for expatri-
    ate landholding under the former constitution, shows its hand here.
63 'Friday Religion', in Loeliger and Trompf (eds), *New religious movements*, p.30.
64 ibid., pp.31–32.
65 Laracy, *Marists*, pp.66–88; cf. E. Ogan, Dependence, Inferiority, Autonomy: a Bougain-
    ville Case Study in Colonialism (unpublished typescript, New Guinea Collection, UPNG,
    Port Moresby 1973), p.5; T. Bugoto, 'The impact of Western culture on Solomon Islands
    society', in Inglis (ed.), *History of Melanesia*, pp.459–60.
66 Sipari, 'Friday Religion', p.30.
67 L. I. Hwekmarin et al, 'Yangoru cargo cult, 1971', *Journal of the Papua and New Guinea
    Society*, 5/2 (1971), pp.3ff; M. Weinstock, 'Notes on the Sepik cargo cult', in H. Barnes
    (ed.), *Niugini reader*, Melbourne, 1972, pp.37–39; W. R. Stent, 'An interpretation of a
    cargo cult', *Oceania* 47/3 (1977), pp.187ff. (among various of his papers); B. Narokobi,
    'Who will take up Peli's challenge?', *Point* (1)(1974), pp.93ff; B. Allen, 'Pangu or Peli:
    Dreikikir open electorate', in D. Stone (ed.), *Prelude*, pp.133ff; Information flow and
    innovation diffusion in the East Sepik District (doctoral dissert., ANU, Canberra 1976),
    pp.267–87; R. May, *View from Hurun* (New Guinea Research Unit discussion paper 8) Port
    Moresby, 1975; cf. May (ed.), *Micronationalist movements*, ch. 1; M. Knight, 'The Peli
    ideal', *Catalyst* 5/4 (1975), pp.3ff; Steinbauer, 'Der Traum vom Glück', in H. Bürckle
    (ed.), *Theologische Beiträge*, pp.123ff. (among various of his papers); P. Gesch, *Initiative and
    Initiation*.
68 Gesch, 'Cargo-cults: the village-Christian dialogue', in W. Flannery (ed.), *Religious move-
    ments* (Point Ser. 4), pp.1ff; C. Camp, 'The Peli Association and the New Apostolic
    Church', in Point Ser. 2, pp.78ff. And more recently Gesch again, 'The cultivation of
    surprise and excess', in Trompf (ed.), *Cargo cults and millenarian movements*, ch. 5.
69 P. Lawrence, 'Lutheran Mission Influence on Madang Societies', pp.73ff; *Road*, pp.34–115.
70 ibid., pp.179–215.
71 cf. esp. A. Maburau, 'Irakau of Manam', in Loeliger and Trompf (eds), *New religious
    movements*, ch. 1; J. F. Wagner, The outgrowth and development of the cargo cult
    (mimeograph, Lutheran Mission, New Guinea, Ulap 1964), pp.15–25.
72 cf. L. Morauta, *Beyond*, pp.39–43, 107–21.
73 Lawrence, Tape-recorded interview with Yali (August, Old Sor Village) (University of
    Sydney, Sydney 1974).
74 'The theology of Beig Wen, the would-be successor to Yali', *Catalyst*, 6/3 (1976), pp.168–72.
75 cf. Trompf, 'The future of macro-historical ideas', *Soundings* 72(1977), p.73.
76 Davenport and Çoker, 'Moro movement', p.137.
77 ibid., pp.139–64.
78 For background G. S. Parsonson, The John Frum movement on Tanna (mimeograph,
    University of Otago, Dunedin 1975), p.4; K. Muller, 'Tanna awaits John Frum', *National
    geographic*, 145/5 (1974), p.706ff; L. Lindstrom, letter to Trompf, 5 Dec. 1983.
79 Parsonson, 'John Frum movement', pp.4–5, Lindstrom, letter (as in n.78), cf. also K.
    Calvert, 'Cargo cult mentality and development in the New Hebrides today', in A. Mamak
    and G. McCall (eds), *Paradise postponed*, Sydney, 1978, pp.209ff. for background.
80 A. Crossley, Research into the vision of Bikana Veve, Kapari village, Central Province, and
    the setting up of her church at Manana Kele village (unpublished report, with photographs,
    UPNG, Port Moresby 1985); John Guise, letter to Trompf, 2 April 1985; OT: Guise,
    August 1985.

81 Foreshadowing my study entitled *Minding your own business*, and some references in the book on *Islands and enclaves*.

82 'Keeping the *Lo* Under a Melanesian Messiah', in J. Barker (ed.), *Christianity in Oceania; ethnographic perspectives* (forthcoming).

83 i.e., in the article on which this chapter is based, in *Oceania*, 54/1 (1983), pp.69–70. Here to make up for my misapprehensions then, I should make it clear that New Caledonia's Église libre seceded (with its leader Charlemagne) from the Protestant Church.

84 See esp. the conclusion of J. Barr, 'Ecstatic phenomena', p.122.

85 cf. Turner, 'A typology of African religious movements', *Journal of religion in Africa*, 1 (1967), p.33; 'Old and new religions in Melanesia', *Point*, 2, 1978, pp.7–8.

86 Tuza, 'Silas Eto'; Steinbauer, 'Der Traum', pp.130–34; Lawrence, *Road*, pp.251–52; Burridge, *New Heaven*, pp.157–58, 161.

87 Chesher, 'Holy Mama', p.19.

SECULARIZATION FOR MELANESIA?

Despite the religious phenomena and developments covered thus far, the question may fairly be asked: are there also emerging signs of secularization in modern Melanesia? If so, how does one go about assessing its effects — even its relative value?

First, what actually is 'secularization', or the process whereby things become secular? In tackling this question, thinkers have converged on much the same phenomena, yet their answers have varied — being affected, above all, by their own value judgements and the expected nature of their audience. Some people may find 'secularization' too vague a term, but I am going to bear with it, accepting it as a general designation for complex, related phenomena such as the decline of religion, or the tendencies to disengage religion from society and to convert religious symbols into desacralized terrestrial realities.[1] While noting different approaches along the way, however, the first of my discussions will centre around two important and digestible interpretations of secularization, which I consider to be most relevant to the Melanesian scene — my early comments thereby setting the stage for what I say about Melanesian issues in particular.

Two theologians on secularization

For Harvey Cox, author of that influential book *The Secular City*, 'secularization marks a change in the way men [*sic*] grasp and understand their life together'; they turn their attention away from 'supernatural myths', 'sacred symbols' and 'world beyond' (in heaven) to 'this world and this time', which are now left in human hands alone.[2] According to Cox, mankind has been passing through three stages, those of the tribe, the town, and the modern city (or *technopolis*). The effect of urbanization is to detribalize society; kinship ties tend to lose their importance, for instance, and the writing used in towns undercuts dependence on time-inured oral traditions or oracles. Above all, the emergence of towns in humanity's history entails that the belief in ghosts and demons are left behind for a belief in God or gods; spells and incantations are replaced by the use of prayers; priests and teachers are sought instead of witch-doctors and sorcerers, while myth and magic give way to religion and theology. The town culture which supplanted most tribal societies, however, has prepared the way for the complex, highly mechanized technopolis, for an irreversible course of change in which religion and metaphysics are disappearing forever as we 'immerse ourselves in the new world of the secular city'.[3] Secularity, thus, becomes the end of a process, when we no longer think about higher, other-worldly beings and what they do with us; instead, we relate only to those things encountered directly around us, to realities which function as pragmatic humans perceive and dictate.[4]

Cox's bold global perspective bears comparison with an interesting chapter on the 'Process of Secularization' by Lesslie Newbigin.[5] Writing from south India, Bishop Newbigin argued that mankind was being unified, not on the basis of 'a common religious faith or even a common ideology', but on the basis of 'a shared secular hope' in socio-economic development. The relatively recent preoccupation with modern developmentalism — with technical improvement, industrialization, economic planning, productivity — eats away at 'the cyclical pattern of human thinking which has been characteristic of many ancient societies', and replaces it 'by a linear pattern, a way of thinking about human life which takes change for granted, and which looks for satisfaction in an earthly future'.[6] The innocent-sounding word 'development', Newbigin contends, involves a 'far-reaching shift of allegiance' on the part of non-Western peoples; for, they are now required to abandon 'standards or judgment' which have been 'venerated for centuries' in the hope that their material conditions of life might be radically bettered.[7] According to this line of argument, secularization amounts to an absorbing pursuit of this-worldly goals, with traditional religious quests losing their former attraction.

The generalizations of these two thinkers are sufficiently broad, fortunately, as to encompass changes occurring in Melanesia. Other writers on this subject have been rather more concerned with Western people's flight from a Christianity which has become burdened by mythological and hackneyed language,[8] or else concerned with the way religious beliefs in the West have been increasingly irrelevant to people's daily, mundane, 'secular life'.[9] Cox and Newbigin, as well, hardly limit secularization to the constitutional procedures through which the church (or other religious institutions) become separated from the state. Disestablishing a state religion could certainly be one impressive signal of the secularizing process, but it is neither necessarily nor often the crucial factor. A people may remain profoundly religious even though it is their nation's policy to disallow an advantage to any one particular faith;[10] besides, it does not follow that the existence of a state-supported religion is the most effective way of forestalling secularization in modern society.[11] So it is that Cox and Newbigin have rightly perceived, first, that the secularizing process cannot be identified with fashionable currents of anti-religious thought (such as atheistical existentialism and linguistic analysis in the West); and second, that this process, far from having merely superstructural implications, has been realizing itself along with the very basic transformations of human history, with changes in social organization, in the means of production and in the way peoples have controlled their environments.

Most interestingly, moreover, both these writers have declined to treat secularization as a form of cultural *rigor mortis*. Instead of lamenting the moral bankruptcy evident in the last hundred years of war and imperialism,[12] instead of deploring history's decline into the 'secular abyss', where humankind is dispossessed of old comforts provided by close-knit societies and by feelings of supernatural support,[13] these two thinkers announce the positive benefits of modern secularizing tendencies. For both, secularization can bring liberation to those enslaved by traditional religions; men and women come to realize that nature is no longer enchanted by spiritual (and therefore often dangerous) forces, and that earthly political rule ought not to be identified with the will of the divine.[14] In so desacralizing nature and demythologizing politics, each argues, secularization is both the inheritor and fulfilment of the Biblical understanding of reality.[15] Admittedly, neither Cox nor Newbigin fail to toll their bells of warning: Cox distinguishes 'secularization' from 'secularism', classing the latter as a potentially dangerous ideology or tool for power-seeking social engineers; while Newbigin, the more worried of the two, fears the terror and meaninglessness which will befall humanity if it dispenses with religion altogether.[16] Both writers, it would appear, dislike political messianism or the rush for economic development inspired by a purely secular ideology of hope.[17] Both, I suspect, would concur with the judgement that secularization becomes 'sin' when it produces crass materialism, or when men and women begin to 'settle down in the dull conviction that the world and history, and ourselves in them, are at the end of the day self-explanatory, self-based, self-sufficient and — given time to know enough — self-evident.'[18]

But Cox and Newbigin reject the ideal of a total war against secularization, and encourage Christian communities — for it is above all to those touched by Christianity they speak — to welcome the dissolution of diehard myths or closed systems of thought, of institutions encrusted by out-dated, introspective, or unjust traditions.[19] The two of them recognize the possibility of 'secular man's' enslavement, but they choose to be positive and optimistic.

These perspectives have obvious relevance for Melanesia. Harvey Cox, in giving us a sense of macro-historical change and of time depth, has grappled with primal, tribal societies, which are still maintaining their own in Melanesia, even within a few miles from such a sprawling, turbulent, and up-and-coming technopolis as Port Moresby. And Newbigin, though mainly reflecting on Asia, reminds us that, after all, Melanesia's transformations and troubles are hardly in every respect unique, and that they are now beginning to be viewed as by-products of an international impetus towards secular development, and one arising on the prior foundations of colonialism and Christianization. In turning to Melanesia, however, and to the extraordinary melting-pot of Papua New Guinea in particular, I should stress that it is not easy to present a tidy picture of what is actually going on in this part of the globe, and still more difficult to foresee what will happen. Further, I shall have to be generalist and provocative here, rather than exhaustive and measured; that, nevertheless, will be in the spirit of the two theologians who have served to introduce the topic at hand.

Melanesia — how secular?

Papua New Guinea, the largest Melanesian nation, is an independent, secular state. While its constitution speaks of God's guiding hand, Christian principles and our noble traditions (Preamble), it does not provide for an established religion, nor does it debar proselytism by any religion which is neither Christian nor Melanesian.[20] Although some ordained churchmen have taken official political positions, the churches have tacitly accepted the separation of church and state (Lutheran leaders being publicly emphatic about it), and the coalition governments since independence in 1975 have governed in an openly secular style, heavily influenced by Australian expatriates who feared sectarian rivalry or who dismissed religion as wrongheaded.[21] Work to set up a viable government department of religious affairs was short-lived; a state system of education has fast outstripped the combined educational facilities of the various denominations and missions; while initiative in national health care has steadily been placed into the hands of the public service.[22] All of these shifts, to a greater or lesser degree, can be paralleled from other Melanesian contexts. But, being superstructural, and having no really vital effect on the majority of people and their consciousness as yet, none of these shifts are reliable indicators of the extent or pace of secularization in this country. We are required to probe much further.

First, these developments should be assessed along with transformations in Melanesian societies which are more fundamental. The various agencies of the region's governments have been bent on a policy of urbanization, rural development, technological advance, and, above all, the 'monetarization of the economy'.[23] Both the policies and their results up to this point obviously represent very severe pressures on ancient tradition. The changes brought by urban life or access to towns, or by the introduction of new agricultural methods, stock, crops and machines, and above all by the availability of money, are so basic that they disturb old symbioses or life patterns, forcing people to question not only their former techniques but their traditional values, explanatory models and world-views as well. To the extent that these newly introduced items and methods are left unendowed with any neo-traditional or deeper significance, they become the devices of secularization — the non-magical, value-diluted tools of a mixed capitalistic economy.[24] Their potential for setting in motion an apparently irreversible process of modernization, which undercuts the archaic order of Melanesia at almost every point, cannot be underestimated — even though there is a long way to go yet!

Second, though, the superstructural developments, as well as the phenomenon of national or regional progress, ought to be assessed along with counter-impressions, viewed against the enormous amount of evidence revealing that the people of Melanesia are decidedly religious, or consciously preoccupied with the spiritual dimension to human life. Most Melanesians still remain deeply affected by the traditional religion of their *ples* (home location). Cox has miscalculated when he conceives 'tribal man' to be in a *pre-religious* world of spells, sorcery, myth and magic; with such premature conclusions, actually, he would find he had some unlikely allies in those conservatives who speak of pre-Christian superstitions in Melanesia. It is incumbent on us to face the fact that there are over a thousand living traditional religions in Papua New Guinea alone, and only in very isolated instances have such religions been completely obliterated by missionization or drastic change.[25] Not only do there remain thousands of traditional religious functionaries and committed practitioners in the region, but traditional beliefs and rituals have very much influenced the attitudes, behaviour patterns and worship of Christian (and syncretic sub-Christian) communities, or else have constituted the 'older partner' in forms of 'split-level Christianity', thus continuing to exert a residual influence on Christian converts without being effectively interrelated with the new faith.[26]

Urbanization and modernization, moreover, as destructive of ancient preconceptions as they have been, have not annihilated traditional ways of viewing and doing things. If town and city dwellers find it hard to accept that their old gods are still with them, for instance, it is a different matter with the spirits of dead relatives. If one prominent black Zimbabwean intellectual could doubt there were 'more than half a dozen' of his fellow countrymen who disbelieved in the spirits, members of the new elite can claim something similar of Papua New Guinea.[27] No Melanesian has yet dared to donate a corpse for medical research; the bodies of those who die far from their own *ples* are carefully shipped home to be received by their kin for burial; students have no compunction in abandoning study at the most inopportune times to do their duty by a recently departed close relative. And the dead are disposed of properly not only because they are loved but because they are 'feared' (at the very least in the sense of stern requirement).[28] To go on, towns and cities may bring release from age-old, cramping obligations, but one must not underrate the (often covert) role of traditional religious beliefs in the process of migration to these centres. It is not just a matter of cargoist expectations. Thousands of Gulf immigrants to Port Moresby have come over the years through terror of sorcery; more than once I have heard that very few Tolais make the move to live at Lae or the capital without first having a dream to vouchsafe it.[29] Deeply felt intuitions — *long bel bilong ol* ('in the gut') — stir Melanesians powerfully: even in the urban situation their sense of sacred kinship ties persist (though often within the broader ambit of 'the *wantok* system'),[30] and these feelings not only foster a wariness of 'outsiders' but may drive someone to physical payback. Above all, urban Melanesians usually find themselves searching to recapture, in an artificial environment, the lineaments of the socio-spiritual unity which they experienced in the village community they left behind.

Christianity and secularization in Melanesia

It has to be conceded that Christianity, which is enormously influential in Melanesia, has seriously modified most traditional religions and has occasionally driven them underground. Thus, has not Christianity had a secularizing effect? Is not the missionary an 'agent of secularization'?[31] We can surely answer this in the affirmative, although only with caution. Along with the administration, the missions and churches have laboured to remove barriers that separate clans and cultures. Pacification is a work of secularization, because it involves the attempted suppression of war magic, or of sorcery directed towards enemy groups, or life-for-life payback principles. The intermingling of people within the great family of God (and the nation), furthermore, means that the old sense of one confined, secure territory tends to be dissolved: a Fuyughe man, for instance, can now find confidence to leave the hamlets so well guarded by familiar protector spirits, and thus live happily elsewhere.[32] And the missionaries have certainly been busy desacralizing nature; for them, sacred flutes are flutes and sacred stones, just stones. They openly lament the way traditional preconceptions hinder the dangerously sick from reaching the hospital in time; armed with stalwart disbelief and the malaria pill, they have walked in places where evil forces supposedly killed trespassers instantly.

Those who observe the missionaries acting in this way take note. So it is that, as each dose of penicillin eases the swelling, as each new adventure in the mission workshops reveals the laws of mechanics, and as each sermon batters against fear of the vengeful departed or the demoniacal forces of the universe, secularization is bound to be on its onward march. Many people actually come to believe the missionary when that missionary insists on being no more than an ordinary mortal after all, without supernatural power in the traditionally conceived (immanent) sense. And many nationals have deprecated ancient custom even though it can isolate them from their former contexts, and have abetted the missionary and others in the modern work for 'social betterment';[33] they complete exercises behind school desks, find jobs in town or technopolis, sing the anthems of their new secular nation. And the churches are there in the towns, too — a quite impressive set of fixtures, placed where the ancestral religions are weakest and where the forces of secularization are at their strongest. The members of urban congregations (and others who do not want the ministrations or the constraints of the Christian community) find themselves in a world of natural cause and effect, of committee- (and back-) room politics, class struggle, ethnic-intermarriage, the nuclearization of the family, and a host of other forces, all of which wage 'war against village conservatism and traditional separatism in the Third World'.[34] Christianity, then, has been an agent of secularization in Melanesia, both because it is anti-animistic and because it eases the transition from village to urban patterns of life. To reiterate, however, we must be cautious in our assessments.

It would be foolish to conclude, for a start, that the process of Christianization (which involves the general permeation of Christian influences, not just conversions and church growth) should be *identified* with the processes of secularization. An earlier school of evolutionists (and Cox seems to be one of their legatees) has tried to show that Christianity stands as a bridge-head between primitive (or less-developed) religions and the religionlessness of the future, so that Christianity contains within itself the seeds of an emergent world-view which has no need of worship, supernaturalistic explanation, or of unseen divinity.[35] According to this view, though, which is not unhelpful, secularization plods further along the road of demystification than Christians usually like. Thus, although the world holds those Christians who are struggling to divest themselves of religious and mythological trappings to be men and women open to this (secular) world alone and not to one enshrouded by 'worlds beyond', they represent a daring, highly reflective, minority. In Melanesia, indeed, such people would be very avant garde. One simply has to acknowledge that, whether they have thought through the theoretical issues or not, most Melanesian church leaders and members fear and oppose secularization as a tendency towards a way of thinking and acting in which God becomes redundant and humanity self-sufficient.

Neither of the two currently prevailing (and apparently conflicting) strategies of Christian mission in the region, moreover, seem to welcome secularization as a healthy and inevitable side to youthful nationhood. The first and older of the two strategies is marked by the conservatives' attempt to replace 'old pseudo-religions' by the new 'true religion', to train new converts in the practice of Christian piety, prayer and doctrinal purity, and to destroy the artifices by which Satan has kept the Melanesian in bondage to sin for thousands of years. The second, generally more recent approach, by contrast, sets far greater store by traditional belief and custom, accepting them positively as the 'Old Testament' of Melanesian peoples, even nurturing them so long as they do not compromise the essence of the Christian faith, or as long as they are capable of being slowly Christianized in their significance.[36] Yet, whether the sacred dance, art and ritual of tradition are condemned in order to make room for the (too often rather colourless?) Gospel, or are left to continue side by side with emergent church life until they come to acquire new associations, it was not the intention of missionaries and evangelists to bring secularization, but rather to bring a new spiritual awareness. They are, perforce, agents of secularization because they usually manage in their environment in a modern scientific way, and because they must introduce those in their charge to the unsettling facts to be met in the big town or in future rural development.

It is to promote the Kingdom of God, however, which has been the prime concern of missionaries, and there are times when one wonders whether they can be rather more religious and less secular than certain Melanesians they are trying to reach. Some traditional belief systems, let it be noted, are already more open to secularity than others, either insofar as some do not pay very serious attention to ritual, or else because some tend to leave a good deal to people's 'purely human intellectual resource'.[37] It has even been contended to me, further, by a Papuan political activist, that the mythological Christian idea of Heaven has been 'disrupted by trips to the moon', whereas the essence of the Melanesians' own beliefs, that the ancestral spirits are with them, accords much more with common sense.[38]

The anti-secular front of mission and church cannot be afforded too much space when there is so much to say about Melanesians in general. Yet here again there is too much worth commentary, and arbitrary selectiveness will be inevitable. So, to round off this assessment of the relative impact of secularization on Melanesian societies and the all too sketchy analysis of current trends, we shall now focus on three key issues, which are suggested by the social and mental life of Melanesia when it is envisaged as a whole. These issues concern: first, ideas about history; second, explanations of significant events occurring in the life of an individual and a society; and third, the sense of community. Each will facilitate concluding discussion as to directions Melanesia might preferably take.

Select issues concerning secularization in Melanesia

The understanding of history

In the Western tradition, it may be justifiably argued, history became secularized when it ceased to be represented as a theatre of divine action and was understood as the province of humans alone. In our day there are very few professional historians who even toy with the supernaturalistic interpretations of human affairs so prevalent in mediaeval chronicles. When, as a prelude to current attitudes, humanist historians of the Renaissance wrote less of God and Providence in the interest of mankind and *fortuna*, when the Protestant reformer Melanchthon doubted that history was neatly divisible into seven Great Days between the Creation and Eschaton, and declared that even church history ought to be narrated as part of the history of temporal affairs, then were the forces of secularization being unleashed.[39] So it is that, today, Westerners are often just left with the trite model of successive centuries (or *saecula*), as if there are no 'true periods' of history.[40]

Melanesia has inherited these forces at the level of professional history-writing as it is presented to the literate (and especially to English speakers)[41] on the shelves of bookshops and libraries. But these pressures have barely touched the great majority. The shifts in thinking which affect most people belong to the level of popular macro-history, of 'folk' impressions as well as to the very sweeping, broad changes of past, present and future. As the momentous transformations which have produced a modern Fiji or an independent Papua New Guinea continue to take their course, it is virtually inevitable that Melanesians will be at work trying to make sense of what is going on around them. Yet, for those who care to discover what macro-historical pictures are shared among the villagers and the non-literate, it will be plain that the voice of secularization has barely been heeded. The notion of a secular progress contingent on national unity and prosperity, for example, is not yet the distinctive feature of the 'average' Melanesian's historical consciousness — despite the efforts of governments. However vaguely and mythologically it may be conceived, history is most commonly defined by the quasi-eschatological events which brought the age-old, cyclically-oriented order of things to a close; it is defined, that is, by 'the Whiteman phenomenon'.[42]

Depending on the culture concerned, a group may trace its past back some seven or eight generations, or to some striking pre-contact event, but the crucial reference-point will almost invariably lie in the first interactions with the newcomers (especially the missionaries), and from these interactions at the least, it seems, history must begin. As for the past of 'world culture', it will be very commonly represented by the sacred history of the Bible, reaching back to Adam and including the great figures of the Biblical panorama. Even though it may often get laden with Melanesian mythology, this sacred history, together with the memory of a culture's particular past, comes to express a linearity, so that Melanesians now perceive the new changes as a movement towards a goal; by looking at matters in this way, they are enabled to find meaning and context in the turbulence of modernization. A national, secular goal does not come easy to them, though; it makes more sense to reflect on the 'New Time' as one of spiritual significance — one which reaches towards the point when God will take control, for instance — or a finale manifested by *paua tru* ('real Power'), by a reunion between the living and the dead.[43] It is small wonder, therefore, that Biblical material is often fused with traditional mythology to produce forward-looking macro-historical ideologies for cargo cults and other independent religious movements.[44] As the accumulation of wealth and prestige has always been bound up with socio-spiritual relationships, moreover, equipping oneself to participate in the new world of cargo demands attention to the supernatural realm as much as to the pragmatic. So, the person who can by-pass ritual, magic and pressing moral obligations to become a modern secular businessman or successful 'man of this world', is as yet an exception.[45] So too, indeed, is the Melanesian with a secularized vision of history.

Explanations of significant events

As we have already observed, men and women in any society learn to recognize 'significant events' in their own (and their own group's) lives. Such events usually include noticeable success or failure, along with sickness and death, or salvation from either scourge. We may feasibly argue that secularization has occurred if people no longer reflect on these special events in religious or supernaturalistic terms. In the West, for example, one cog in the wheel of secularization was set in motion when certain people declined to interpret such events in terms of God's rewards and punishments (or Satanic afflictions). The Florentine Renaissance humanist, Niccolò Machiavelli, for instance, considered that favourable and adverse situations experienced by humans were the results of their skill or stupidity rather than of divine requitals — the by-products of fortune and circumstance, not of a higher Design. If a cruel prince died a most painful death, it was not because God punished him, but because he had not calculated his odds cunningly enough.[46] With this kind of approach to human affairs, then, sickness, trouble and death (or their discernible opposites) are never explained supernaturalistically — if it can be possibly helped.

This aspect of secularization is encountered by Pacific islanders when they listen to 'neutral' commentaries on human affairs over the radio, and read the *Fiji Times*, the *Papua New Guinea Post-Courier* or even the Christian newspaper *Wantok*! But they will not be satisfied with mere superficialities when they are personally affected. Of such a momentous event as death, or of sickness and social trouble, we have already seen that the Melanesian has long since been asking questions about non-empirical (apparently non-scientific) causes — about the hurt feelings of a dead relative who may want attention, companionship or revenge, about the anger of deities or place spirits, the schemes of a sorcerer, or about a personal failure to perform rituals correctly. It is the same with the African: imported science and technology 'are unable satisfactorily to explain why snakes bite, why lorries have accidents, why some people are childless', and so on; thus, secular explanations do not automatically obliterate traditional or religious ones.[47]

Significant events, then, situations of great prestige and real despair, of prosperity and hardship, fecundity and infertility, well-being and malady, will all continue to be connected with the likes and dislikes of spirit-beings, or the appropriation of spiritual power whether for good or ill. And the Melanesian varieties of 'retributive logic', as set out earlier, are hardly confined to the traditionalists. They are being carried over into Christianity, so that more and more frequently God is referred to as a bringer of rewards for righteousness and of punishments against sin. There is a complex transfer from one species of retributive logic to another. The shift is often from more ritually-oriented to more morally-oriented notions about the consequence of one's actions, and it is further complicated by the influences of modern secular attitudes towards commonsense realism, expediency and politics, some of which attitudes have their natural antecedent in the age-old pragmatism of the Melanesians themselves. Although such a transfer may be considered as partial secularization, it is probably more accurate to speak of it as religious change, change which bears comparison with the ideological adjustments of the Mediterranean world during the early Christian centuries, and change which takes place at a point where 'the traditional' and 'the introduced' intersect happily (though I am reluctant to say fruitfully).[48]

The sense of community

Secularization manifests itself in a society when its members lose their sense of social cohesiveness in religious terms. As Marx and Engels quite rightly observed, and the sociologist Tönnies after them, the decreased importance of blood ties, the increased division of labour, the monetarization of the economy, the creation of a wage-earning proletariat, industrialization, and the alienation of humans from the fruits of their own work, are all salient features of a society which has left the primitive community (*Gemeinschaft*) behind.[49]

To take off from this almost exclusively socio-economic analysis, we may affirm that, for Western people, their present-day spiritual dilemma is in large measure due to their loss of a sense of community gathered around a sacred space or under God. In consequence, nationalist and secular ideologies have had unnerving success during this century in filling the vacuum. For almost all Melanesians, however, the village community whence they came — enshrouded as it remains by super-human and mysterious forces — is still accessible, and offers a homely alternative if one's experiment with urban living palls. Besides, it is still the *locus* for the majority of people in the islands of the south-west Pacific. Most villages of today, too, although their size and position have been affected by the requirements of mission and administration, are very rarely centres of defence and plain survivalism. Admittedly, they are susceptible to the tiffs and bickerings of all small-scale communities, and to intra-village sorcery, but they remain cohesive, comforting unities, nevertheless. The village can readily be comprehended as one's secure, deep roots. Its inheritor will always have a part to play in it, and can quickly grasp its principles of reciprocity. Despite its weaknesses, it endows one's life with spiritual significance, a sense of wholeness which the hurly-burly of urban life usually fragments. And a rural community is more often than not held together by the wielding of religious authority; church office-holding produces a new power structure at the local level, while men (and it is usually men) often utilize traditional spiritual power to bolster their non-church (some would call it secular!) pursuit of clan leadership.[50]

There are other important issues hinted at — changes in political organization, in technology and the human manipulation of the environment, for example — which have not been covered here. But, however selective this summary has been, one important general point being made is this: secularization is evident in Melanesia most distinctly in urban areas and in the work of government, and less distinctly in the work of the churches. Today one can find a variety of Papua New Guineans who are by-passing the rituals, old and new, to obtain the material comforts of life, and some will tell you that they have had their fill of religion. On the other hand, there are very many forces working against secularization in Melanesia, very many attitudes and phenomena which, once we are sensitized to them, will persuade us that the heart-beat of Melanesia is a religious heart-beat, one which continues to pulsate as it copes with the corpuscles of 'creeping secularization' in its system.

How welcoming should Melanesians be?

Thus far descriptions of 'what is' have been presented; the question now remains, 'what ought to be'? Instead of proffering an answer some might prefer just to 'wait and see'. Believing secularization to be inevitable and irreversible, they may contend that the south-west Pacific is experiencing it as a creeping, evolutionary process, not as something imposed by social engineers. To live in ostensibly liberal democracies like those found in Papua New Guinea, the Solomons and Vanuatu, however, only means that there are more potential social engineers free to have their say, and a diversity of strategists rather than a consolidated party machine. And among those who have power to influence most Melanesian nations are people — still mainly expatriate advisors to governments, and also intellectuals at the universities — who are positively abetting the secularizing process. They often welcome it because, among other things, they have rejected religion in their original cultural contexts and dislike the idea of organized Christianity having too bright a future. Such people will criticize the church's involvement in politics as a dangerous tendency towards theocracy, for example; they may even seek to keep Religious Studies (let alone Religious Instruction) out of school curricula. Where European expatriates dominate in continuing colonial situations, furthermore, as on New Caledonia, suspicion of church influence in *kanak* affairs arises for fear it might incur political trouble, not just competition against the widespread French secularist *mentalité* in Nouméa.[51]

Among expatriate intellectuals there are various brands of secularism. An academic at the University of Papua New Guinea once expressed surprise that there were so many fundamentalist students in his classes and added 'after all, I thought we were supposed to be trying to get people to grow out of religion'. Marxist intellectuals, moreover, tend to conceive religion as a barrier to 'development', or as a signal of inequalities in society. Thus, we will find new cultural imperialists at work in Melanesia and, paradoxically, many of them leave the old-style missionaries for dead. Some are ready to attack the churches for their destruction of indigenous cultures and for not giving a choice over cultural direction; yet, it is patently obvious that the only culture they can really handle is not religious at all — whether traditional or Christian — but the 'white mask' secularity of such artists as Kauage or Valaosi.[52] Other persons of influence view Melanesia's hope almost exclusively in economic terms, emphasizing the need for the locals to be productive, to save, to be business-like and economically successful (or, more euphemistically, to be self-reliant). The administration, and the elite being trained for its ranks, have already felt pressures from these stances; even though these are not the only approaches being contended with, they are attractive through being (unnervingly) reminiscent of temperaments and styles prevalent in the 'big brother' Western power-broker nations of the Pacific. The trouble is, though, the more distinctly secular world-views are having their impact on a small minority who are in danger of being desensitized to the real heart-beat of their countries.

We must be realistic. Secularization is a process of change which will go on gathering momentum. However, it is probably not sensible to push secularity as a goal for any young South Pacific nation. In the long run, perhaps, primal traditionals will concede more and more to the claims of Christianity and to the facts of modern science; yet, why sell secularization as a kind of 'naked lunch', in the hope that the pickles will be devoured for their own sake when what the eater really wants is a tastier, healthier combination of victuals? Melanesian spirituality and morality are age-old, and are both durable and valuable. Even where they have been transformed by Christianity, the old devotion, the commitment, the faith, the sense of obligation — all have generally been reinforced, and have reappeared in the life of the churches and the nation. There is a nice symbol of this in the 96-year-old Sere Bodibo, many times *helaga tauna* or holy man on the *Hiri* voyages from eastern Motuan territory to the Gulf. This dedicated man was so indispensable to expeditionaries that he was among the last in the village of Porebada to become Christian; upon his conversion, however, he became as outstanding a Christian as he had been a traditionalist.[53]

Melanesians share many profound and intriguing insights which have much to teach modern humankind — insights about the nature of community, for example, people's relationship to the environment and to the unseen world, or about the wholeness of reality. To hold up before them a model of a purely secular development, then (as against what young Utula Samana has called 'total development'),[54] or to push national economic growth with little else but crass materialism and purely terrestrial success as ends in view, is to short-change these people, to lead them by the nose towards disillusionment, disorientation and shallowness. Already, perceptive young Papua New Guinean authors have hinted at the emergence of the Melanesian 'hollow men', exemplified by the person who cannot face the disciplines of the village and who ends up as an over-contented *haus boi* (house boy) in town, with cinemas and a range of women at his disposal, or as a soldier who is waiting for the day he can die.[55] Is it the disenchantment of rootlessness we are working for? — a kind of 'over-secularization', a resignation before the sheer fragmentedness and banality of life — 'a sweet and poisonous disenchantment which makes their faces extraordinarily definite, as though they had been struck out of stone'.[56] And it will not suffice to assess social malaise solely in terms of individual clinical cases who are deemed paranoid or depressed by Eurocentric standards of psychiatry, we must come to grips with the crises, breakdowns and shifts in the ever-moving, dynamic relationships between social beings and groups.[57]

For all their shortcomings — and they have in numerous instances brought prolonged disorientation themselves — the churches are the buffers between the primal consciousness of Melanesians and the 'brave new world' of secularity. From the time of blatant immoralities by blackbirder and trader to the more surreptitious (insidious even) machinations of today's big business and big politics, the churches have almost always played a commendable role as protector; for, after all, they have been intensely interested in the people's welfare and in the same spiritual issues which preoccupied Melanesians for centuries. In the final analysis, moreover, it is the churches which have provided the basis for national unity in Papua New Guinea (and in wider Melanesia).[58] However, the task of the churches is not only to cushion people from dislocation and anxiety brought by powerful modernizing and secularizing pressures, but to nurture the spiritual vitality which is the proud possession of Melanesian peoples, and to channel it positively to serve the people's needs with carefulness, and to provide a broad integrated vision of human betterment.

Already the villagers are becoming restless. Most of them are not so much waiting on either achievements or even changes of governments as on the young ones who have left home to become educated, and from whom they expect great things. Over recent years, though, if my assessment is correct, more and more parents and elders have been disappointed to find their hopes unfulfilled. Education is a crucial area. The educated ones are too often like 'foreigners', schooled-up like Europeans, very self-confident, yet unable to cope with their own people for too long, unsympathetic with 'strange' village beliefs, and less willing to share because of their new individualistic ways. If the churches have engaged in educational programmes which have been rather too narrow, at least they have been deep and morally-oriented; yet, now the churches are becoming irritated with the failure of the upgraded state educational system to transmit ethical principles and religious insights — let alone desirable results at the topmost levels of political power.[59] Furthermore, the almost unavoidable assumption that nations come of age when they acquire a fully-fledged state educational system, only reinforces 'attitudes of inferiority and dependence' among those never introduced to such a system.[60] At least the churches have attempted to act as 'schools' to all ages, but state education systems have placed a top-heavy priority on the young and are generating awkward side-problems — drop-outs, unrealistic school-leaver goals, as well as spiritual anaemia — with which Melanesian societies cannot cope.[61]

Various images related to this and to the whole problem of uncontrollable secularization float before one's eyes at this point. Think of Hanuabada, Port Moresby (the largest village in Papua New Guinea), whose crowded residents give their love gift to God and his church, each year trying to beat previous records with huge offerings over and above Sunday collections. Yet deep in its heart are the groups of restless young, who, in highly organized and ritualized gang activity, work out their frustrations and failures by paying back the system and harassing the successful.[62] Imagine, too, the quiet Papua New Guinean villages a hundred miles (160 km) away on either side of the capital, whose inhabitants lament the passing of former days. They sit down to make the point that, whereas Christians and traditionalists manage to work together (they have an understanding with each other), the young 'bigheads' are quarrelsome and demanding, shallow people who neglect their obligations and pursue worldly, self-centred goals — people who have not lived up to village expectations, however cargoist such hopes may have been.[63] Another picture coming to mind is of the debasement of the game called *karim lek* ('carry leg') in the Chimbu and western highlands. In the old days, a man would bring great fame to himself when he lay beside a woman between her parents after this game, and when he disciplined himself to avoid sexual contact. Now the game has become progressively secularized, and adolescents, if they can get away with it, prefer to indulge themselves in the bush for fun during school holidays, flouting both the annoying ecclesiastical condemnation of sin and the demands of their noble tradition.[64] Then there are the massive numbers of those who try to discover their lost identity at the bottom of a beer bottle. One can now witness them tippling at Madang, crouching over table and bar in imitative poses, the black replicas of their big-bellied, ruddy-nosed white prototypes. Even in Papua New Guinea's university students of recent years, one easily detects worrying changes which throw light on the whole question; the once impressive soul-searching qualities of an earlier generation of candidates have been replaced by a noticeably higher degree of complacency, by the feeling that they have got it all before them, and with very little effort.

We have been ranging far and wide, but deliberately so, for the lineaments of secularization are manifold. Let a conclusion be made by contending that, while being open to the potential of a secular outlook for liberating the human spirit from hidebound religiosity or a religious system,[65] and while welcoming the positive benefits of a world without fear of the vengeful departed or a world redeemed from cramping ethnocentricity, the churches (and government) ought to protect the interest of their peoples. They ought to protect it against a shallow secularization, against pressures which leave Melanesians without roots, without self-identity and a mature sense of self-confidence, against forces which do not guide men and women towards a higher perfection but direct them to some second-rate, deficient anchorage which cannot hope to satisfy their complex requirements.[66] Jesus said the Kingdom of God is like discovering a pearl of great price; John Steinbeck, in that small masterpiece of his, *The Pearl*, reminds us that finding the pearl without the Kingdom can lead to great sorrow.

NOTES

Chapter 10 is based on material originally published as an article in the journal *Point*.

1 See esp. L. Shiner, 'The meaning of secularization', *Internationales Jahrbuch für Religions-soziologie*, 3 (1967), pp.52–59.
2 H. Cox, *The secular city*, New York, 1965, pp.1–2.
3 ibid., pp.3–13.
4 ibid., esp. p.65; cf. C. A. van Peursen, 'Man and reality — the history of human thought', *The student world*, 56, (1963), esp. p.16. For important nineteenth century background, see K. Löwith, *From Hegel to Nietzsche* (trans. D. E. Green), New York, 1967, pt. I, II, 2 and III, 2.
5 L. Newbigin, *Honest religion for secular man*, Philadelphia, 1966, ch. 1.
6 ibid., pp.13–14; cf. also M. Eliade, *Cosmos and history*, pp.159–162.
7 Newbigin, *Honest religion*, p.26. For other, related issues, see Trompf, 'The ethics of development — an overview', in S. Stratigos and P. Hughes (eds), *The ethics of development*, (Waigani Seminar 1986), Port Moresby, 1987, ch. 7.
8 e.g., O. van Buren, *The secular meaning of the Gospel*, Harmondsworth, 1968, esp. pp.192–98; cf. P. Tillich, *The courage to be*, London, 1962, pp.66–67, 123, 138; J. A. T. Robinson, *Honest to God*, London, 1963, esp. pp.29ff.
9 e.g., E. Raab, 'The nature of the conflict; an introduction', in *Religious conflict in America*, (ed. E. Raab), Garden City, 1964, esp. p.15; cf. W. Herberg, 'The religion of Americans and American religion', in ibid., pp.101ff; P. Tillich, *Systematic theology*, Welwyn, 1964, vol. 3, pp.167–72 on the divorce between morality and religion in the narrow sense.
10 See esp. D. E. Smith (ed.), *Religion, politics and social change in the Third World; a sourcebook*, New York, 1971, esp. pp.2–3, pt I, 2–3. cf., also, Kamal Jumblatt's proposal for a secular Lebanon, 'The New Lebanon', the *Economist*, 3 April, 1976, pp.13–14; and note the secular provisions in the 1957 constitution of the 'primal religious' society of Haiti, D. Healey, Religion and Poverty (mimeograph, University of California, Santa Cruz 1973), p.27 on art. 27.
11 I think especially of Great Britain; see esp. J. R. H. Moorman, *A history of the Church of England*, London, 1953, pp.413–419; cf. B. Wilson, *Religion in secular society*, Harmondsworth, 1966; but also consider Catholic-dominated Italy, D. A. Martin, *A general theory of secularization*, London, 1978, ch. 2.
12 cf. esp. E. H. Carr, *The twenty years' crisis*, London, 1939, p.80; (Bishop) G. K. A. Bell, *Christianity and world order*, Harmondsworth, 1940, ch. 2 (on 'modern secularism').
13 Note G. S. Graham and J. Alexander, *The secular abyss*, Wheaton, 1968 edn, esp. pp.10, 243. cf. also Pope Paul VI, encyc. *Populorum progressio*, art. 10 ('Conflicts of civilizations').
14 Cox, *Secular city*, pp.21–36; Newbigin, *Honest religion*, pp.22–30; cf. esp. A. T. van Leeuwen, *Christianity in world history* (trans. H. H. Hoskins), London, 1964.

15 cf. also D. Bonhoeffer, *Letters and papers from prison* (trans. E. Bethge), London, 1953, pp.124–25 (21 July, 1944).

16 See Cox, *Secular city*, pp.18–21 (and on the foundations of the philosophy of secularism, G. J. Holyoake, *The Origin and Nature of Secularism*, London, 1896); Newbigin, *Honest religion*, esp. pp.31–32.

17 cf. also J. L. Talmon et al., in *Die industrielle Gesellschaft und die drei Welten* (Rhenfelden Seminar), Zurich, 1961, pp.199ff.

18 So, C. F. Evans, 'The search for wholeness', *Woroni*, 11 March, 1970, p.10.

19 Cox, *Secular city*, esp. chs 7, 10; Newbigin, *Honest religion*, esp. pp.36, 41–42, cf. ch. 4.

20 See art. 45. By contrast, cf. the Greek Constitution (1952), art. 1. (*Publications de l'Institut Hellenique de Droit International et Etranger* 5); and the 1887 concordat between the Vatican and the Republic of Columbia, esp. art. 13 (Smith, *Religion, politics*, p.18).

21 An impressive group of Catholic priests having held government positions, including Fathers Ignatius Kilage, Cherubim Dambui and John Momis. On Lutheran views, see esp. *Tok bilip bilong yumi* (Lutheran Churches and Missions), Lae, 1972, pp.214–17; cf., however, Bishop Zurewe in *Papua New Guinea Post-Courier*, 8 Oct., 1976, p.3. On the typical style of politics, see M. Somare, *Sana*, Port Moresby, 1975 pp.83–148.

22 Note a fairly recently proposed composition of the Health Commission and Provincial Health Boards by C. Smith, Medical care symposium September, 1976; Church and Government Relationship in Health Care, (mimeograph, Port Moresby 1976), pp.10–12. It should be conceded here that the government has tentatively legitimized practitioners of traditional medicine (*Hansard*, National Parliament PNG, 18 March, 1976, pp.241–61) in moves which are to the favour of religiously oriented as against secular medicine; cf. ch. 4.

23 See esp. A. P. Power, A Study of Development in Niugini from 1880 to 1940, (master's dissert., UPNG 1974), pp.35ff. on the Papua New Guinea case.

24 cf. A. Clunies Ross and J. V. Langmore (eds), *Alternative strategies for Papua New Guinea*, Melbourne, 1973, esp. chs 7 and 9.

25 As, for example, the Seragi, through the colonial government policy of relocation (Northern Province, Papua New Guinea). cf. also R. Weymouth, The Gogodala Society and the Unevangelized Fields Mission in Papua New Guinea 1890–1977 (doctoral thesis, Flinders University, Adelaide), pp.269ff.

26 cf. J. Butalao et al., *Split-level Christianity*, Quezon City, 1966; L. Luzbetak, *The church and cultures*, Maryknoll 1988 edn, pp.368ff; T. Ahrens, 'Christian syncretism', *Catalyst*, 4/1 (1974), pp.3ff; B. Blowers, Religious Syncretism (mimeograph, Kudjip, 1971).

27 See A. C. Fisher, 'Rhodesia, a house divided', *National geographic*, 147 (1975), p.662; and I also rely here on student comments at UPNG. cf., however, the odd case of atheism (which does not exclude concern for the dead), as in M. F. Smith, 'From heathen to atheist: changing views of Catholicism in a Papua New Guinea village', *Oceania*, 51/1 (1980), pp.40ff.

28 See W. Ferea, Fear in Melanesian Religion (honours sub-thesis, UPNG, Port Moresby, 1984).

29 For background, e.g., Siaoa, Gods, spirit and religion among the Eastern Toaripi, pp.6ff; cf. also on another case, J. F. Koroma, 'Tribal cohesion and cultural change', *Point*, 1 (1975), p.2 (on sorcery); OT: Francis Mamia; Celia Tirpaia, 1975 (on dreams) (cf. also ch. 5).

30 cf. especially M. Stevenson, *The Wantok Connection* (Institute of Papua New Guinea Studies Discussion Paper 42), Port Moresby, 1942.

31 cf. E. S. Millar, 'The Christian missionary; agent of secularization', *Missiology*, 1 (1973), esp. pp.102ff.

32 For background, Trompf, '"Bilalaf"' in Trompf (ed.), *Prophets*, ch. 1.

33 Note J. J. Considine, *The missionary's role in socio-economic betterment*, New York, 1960; for Papua New Guinea, cf. esp. G. O. Reitz, The contribution of the Evangelical Lutheran Church New Guinea to development in Papua New Guinea (mimeograph, Lae, 1975).

34 Trompf, 'Macro-Historical Ideas of the Future', p.73.

35 Note esp. A. Comte, *Positive philosophy* (trans. H. Martineau), London, 1853, esp. vol. 2; H. Spencer, *First principles*, London, 1900 edn, sects 30–34; M. Guyau, *The non-religion of the future* (trans. Guyau), London, 1897; cf. E. Fisher and F. Marek, *Marx in his own words*, London, 1970, pp.20–21.

36 cf. Trompf, 'The religious history of a Melanesian people from the last century to the present, the Middle Wahgi, New Guinea highlands', in Trompf (ed.), *Mel. and Judaeo-Christ. Relig. Trads*, bk. 3, pt C/III, p.46.

37 So Lawrence and Meggitt, 'Introduction', in *Gods*, p.19; cf. also B. Finney, *Big men and business*, Canberra, 1973, esp. pp.144–45, and for a criticism of the Lawrence and Meggitt distinction between 'highlands-secular' and 'seaboard-religious' phenomena, see A. Chowning, 'Lakalai religion and world-view'.

38 So, James Mopio, MP and executive of Papua Besena, a separatist movement for Papua, 1973.

39 See Trompf, *The idea of historical recurrence in Western thought*, vol. 1, ch. 5, sect. B(4); A. Klempt, *Die Sakularisierung der universal-historischen Auffassung* (Göttingen Bausteine zum Geschichtswissenschaft 31), Göttingen, 1960, pt. 1.

40 See E. Rosenstock-Huessy, *The Christian future*, New York, 1966 edn, p.87 for the quotation. Cox is wrong to translate *saeculum* as 'this age'; it is 'an age', 'a generation', 'a hundred years'.

41 I know of only one general history of Papua New Guinea written in a non-European language: A. Klein, *Histori bilong Papua Niugini*, Goroka, 1974 (a decidedly Eurocentric work!), cf. also P. Lawrence, *Road bilong Kago* (trans. W. Tomasetti), Melbourne, 1987.

42 See Trompf, 'Macrohistory and acculturation'.

43 cf. esp. F. Tomasetti, *Traditionen und Christentum im Chimbu-Gebiet Neuguineas*, Wiesbaden, 1976, pt D(a), pp.14–15, 91–93, 148, 211–16, etc. esp. on 'The New Time'.

44 See esp. Lawrence, *Road*, pp.75–76, 93–94, 100–101, etc., and his 'European cultism; the skeleton in the scientific cupboard', *Point*, No. 2, 1974, pp.81ff.

45 Note H. Janssen, 'Religion and secularization', *Catalyst*, No. 2, 1972, esp. pp.61–65; cf. Finney, *Big men*, pp.84ff.

46 On the secularization of retributive logic in Machiavelli and Guicciardini (16th century), see Trompf, *Historical recurrence*, ch. 5, pt B(2). cf. also T. Hobbes, *Leviathan*, (1651), esp. I, xiii.

47 See P. Sarpong, 'The search for meaning; the religious impact of technology in Africa', in *Selected papers from the West Africa Conference on science, technology and the future of Man and society* (from the *Ecumenical review*, 34 [1972], p.21). Recourse to two or three levels of explanation, of course, is not uncommon in *Western* societies.

48 I discuss the relationship between Graeco-Roman and Judaeo-Christian retributive ideas (1st–5th centuries AD), and the (justifiable) opposition of St Augustine to both pagan and certain Christian interpretations of history in terms of rewards and punishments, in *Historical recurrence*, ch. 4, pt. G.

49 See K. Marx and F. Engels, *Selected works*, Moscow, 1951 edn, esp. vol. 1, p.33 and vol. 2, pp.200–201, 322–27; cf. E. Terray, *Marxism and primitive societies* (trans. M. Klopper), New York, 1972, ch. 1, and on Tönnies, see Trompf, *In search of origins*, ch. 4.

50 Important work is being done in this connection on the Gari of Guadalcanal, Solomon Islands, by Father Kerry Prenderville, who has allowed me to anticipate his Masters Thesis, UPNG. Also see esp., E. Hau'Ofa, *Mekeo*, chs 7–8, and cf. N. Oram., 'The London Missionary Society pastorate and the emergence of an educated elite in Papua', pp.115ff.

51 In other situations again, as in Indonesia's neo-colonial control over West Papua (= Irian Jaya) or Fiji's 'lapsed democracy' (after the 1987 coups) it is just as much a matter of tensions between particular religions as between religion in general and secularizing tendencies.

52 I worry about the writings of P. Kros, *'A certain foreign cult called Christianity.' Do we need it?* (Institute of Papua New Guinea Studies discussion paper 3), Port Moresby, 1975, and U. Beier, The Position of the artist in a changing society, and The artist's struggle for integration in modern society, Lectures to Humanities Foundation Year, UPNG, 3 June and 5 August, 1976 in this connection. The whole problem of secularization in art is more complex than they seem to realize. For background, see esp. G. Barraclough, *An introduction to contemporary history*, Harmondsworth, 1967, ch. 8.

53 OTs: John Guilliam and Sere Bodibo, 1976.

54 Pers. comm., and cf. 'Considering alternative directions for the Evangelical Lutheran Church of Papua New Guinea', in M. O'Collins (ed.), *Introduction to social welfare* (External Studies course booklet, 21.111, UPNG, Port Moresby, 1976), bk. 3, pp.45–46.

55 See A. Kituai, 'The flight of a villager', and J. Baital, 'Tali', in M. Greicus (ed.), *Three short novels of Papua New Guinea*, pp.37ff., 87ff.

56 A few lines by James Baldwin about Harlem in *Another country*, London, 1963, p.116, but why not about Port Moresby?

57 So, against the approach of B. B. Bradley, esp. in *Longlong: transcultural psychiatry in Papua New Guinea*, Port Moresby, 1973, and *Stone Age crisis*.

58 cf. also E. Olewale (then minister for education), in The impact of the missions (typescript, National Broadcasting Commission, Port Moresby, n.d.), p.13.

59 This irritation was already being expressed in Port Moresby, for example, in the United Church Refresher Course for Ministers and Lay Persons by Sept. 1976, but there have been many similar expressions of concern around the region since the mid-1970s.

60 See S. G. Weeks, *If Education is the answer, what is the question?* (Inaugural Lecture, UPNG, Port Moresby 1976), p.10.

61 cf. J. Conroy, 'Dilemmas of educational policy', in Clunies-Ross and Langmore, (eds), *Strategies*, pp.139ff; Br. Leo, School dropouts in villages and towns (mimeograph, Melanesian Institute–Xavier Institute of Missiology, Alexishafen 1972), etc., on the Papua New Guinea situation at least.

62 Vasi Gadiki, 'Offering; an approach to practical theology', p.16, together with OTs: Gadiki (Pastor of Hanuabada) and Dick Avi. cf. also B. Narokobi, in *PNG Post-Courier*, 7 Oct., 1976, p.3.

63 I rely on my own fieldnotes, especially along the Papuan coast and in the central highlands, 1972.

64 OTs: Amin Opai (Community Welfare Officer, Mount Hagen), his father and family (Kuma, Wahgi), 1974.

65 On this 'religious emancipation from religion', see esp. T. Rentorff, 'Zur Säkularisierungsproblematik', in *Internationales Jahrbuch für Religionssoziologie*, 2 (1966), pp.66–67.

66 cf. F. L. Mordaunt, A role of the Church in community development (master's qualifying dissert., UPNG, Port Moresby 1975), pp.7, 11 (together with Vatican documents cited there).

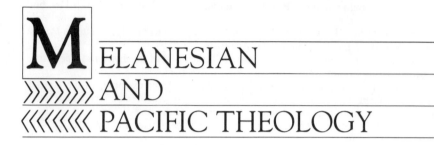

CHAPTER 11

MELANESIAN AND PACIFIC THEOLOGY

At the end of the last chapter we had the temerity to make recommendations concerning Melanesia's religious condition. But what about theology as such? Should this study include formulations for a contextual theology for the south-west Pacific? Actually the burning religious issue of the moment for Melanesian thinkers does not so much concern straightening anthropological perspectives or rendering accurate mission histories — the previous business of this book — as it does the working out of fruitful relationships between their locally conditioned traditions and Christianity, the most welcomed of the introduced religions. Other introduced religions are in the region, of course: Islam to the west, Hinduism (with some Muslims again) to the far east, and a sprinkling of Bahais across the board. But the reception of these religions among Melanesians has been minimal. Even the building of mosques in rural areas of Irian Jaya with Saudi Arabian money, around Jayapura for example, has hardly drawn any local response. The really pressing need is to develop a dialogical agenda between indigenous world-views or village religion and the various denominational expressions of the Christian faith.

That does not make for an easy conclusion to this book. I find myself hesitant to wax theological and project what should be the spiritual and community life of Melanesia's future. Certainly, it is out of place for an expatriate or foreigner to engage at this point in some full-blown theological enterprise. The least one can do, along with expatriates who have been trained in theology elsewhere and who are teaching in tertiary institutions in the Pacific, is to suggest guidelines as to how an agenda for indigenous theology might be conceived. In keeping with the rest of the book, moreover, the approach will be to acknowledge what is already going on, and contemplate what seems to arise from contemporary changes in society for the black theologian's workshop. From seminaries to village Sunday schools, there is a massive and complex process of acculturation currently in train. Some may want to call it the 'Melanesianization' of Christianity, others the 'Christianization' of Melanesia; but, all would concur, it involves the working out of Melanesians' relative commitment to persuasive truths and claims upon their lives both old and new. Academic research falters badly if it cannot grasp some of the 'theological nettles' burgeoning from this momentous religious transformation.

In universities as distinct from seminaries, perhaps, we do not expect modes of theological discourse to be aired much, let alone predominate; it is no longer the appropriate role of university teachers either to profess their religious commitments as quasi-evangelists or to openly build up the faith of their students. A university which makes no provision for theological reflection, however, cannot even be said to be a *universitas* (and in this respect could even become less adequate a custodian of 'knowledge as a whole' than seminary institutions).[1] Theology, after all, is a holistic discipline through which all compartmentalizing world-views and relative values can be put to the test (and usually found wanting!).

Since the majority of students in existing Melanesian universities consider themselves Christian or open to Christianity, one can expect indigenous theological exploration to keep arising spontaneously; besides, with different denominational backgrounds represented, students will not want any teacher to adopt a dogmatic stance in favour of one church's position as against others. That being likely, historically-oriented undergraduate courses on religion are certainly to be preferred,[2] with encouragement to engage in theological matters more frontally left for a few postgraduates.[3] But it does not follow that concern for theological questions should be written out of the average academic teacher's purview. Training in a subject, certainly, is necessary for presenting an adequate course, but all researchers in Melanesian social affairs should try to apprise themselves of theological issues, because they are going to become central to an understanding of changing Melanesian *mentalités* as the years proceed.

Theology, in any case, is not the exclusive province of Christians, let alone clerics, because any non-Christian can reason through his or her own beliefs about 'the divine or supernatural', and certain non-theistic Western philosophers, such as Ronald Hepburn, have even been acclaimed as very good at this.[4] By the same token it would be utterly facile to maintain that personal religious commitments can only make illegitimate intrusions into the world of learning, or only reflect particular interests rather than general principles,[5] when these commitments actually coincide with the emergent outlook of whole nations. The national or proto-national importance of these commitments in Melanesia is simply immense, so much so that avoiding them is sheer myopia and embracing a study of them, however difficult, is fast becoming a basic necessity for understanding the region's culture and politics.

To theological matters we turn, then, in conclusion.

Melanesian theology: basic issues for an agenda

What follows are some fundamental background points we consider useful for the development of Melanesian theology. They are partly in response to black theological insights formulated in Melanesia up to this point, and partly informed by the author's own explorations into comparative missiology, Third World and contextual theologies, as well as Biblical Studies.

Role of Christian influences

First, Christianity is a world phenomenon; it is not confined to the 'white givers' and the 'black receivers' in the Melanesian part of the universe. The founder of the Christian faith was not a white man; he almost certainly had light brown skin and was born a Jew and an inhabitant of western Asia. As for the various European peoples, they once lived with belief-systems and world-views quite comparable to those held by Melanesians during pre-contact times, and it took years of missionary work to establish the church in Europe. And Christianity not only spread to Europe (and eventually America), but also to Asia and Africa very early on. The Egyptian, Ethiopian, Syrian, Armenian and Indian churches are among the oldest in the world, and Melanesians need to break down their image of Christianity being white and European, and to realize its tremendous impact on world cultures as a whole. Most readers will have heard some of these things before; but most rural dwellers have not or else continue to live under false or blurred impressions.

Second, it is useful to draw a rough distinction between the spread of Christianity and modern Western imperialism. To generalize about the more distant past, Christianity was in no position to obliterate the pre-existing culture when it entered into the cultural life of a people. In most instances the bearers of the Christian message began as a small minority without any material or military power to impose its will. In their work of proclamation, these earliest Christians were not bent on replacing one culture by another but on endowing pre-existing traditions and norms with a new Christological meaning. They sought to show, for instance, that Jesus was the fulfilment of a group's longings or aspirations, that old ceremonies (such as the once pagan Romano-Hellenistic Spring and New Year festivals) can be performed with a transformed significance (as Easter and Christmas), and that churches could be built over old sacred places as a fulfilment rather than a disruptive replacement. Although ways of looking at the divine and of doing good or performing sacred actions underwent radical change upon the impact of missionization, people still carried their past with them into a new stage — their ethnic character, their language and conceptualizations, their common tasks, social attitudes and so many other things which were modified and reappraised, but not destroyed. In many modern instances this same general picture still applies, but the difference is that hundreds of missionaries working among primal-traditional religious groups in Africa, the Pacific and south-east Asia, have become associated with colonialism, or the expansion of European powers among the undeveloped countries of the globe.

It remains true that many missionaries came to such places with the blessing of colonial powers and with a material and military order to reinforce their work. In the case of Melanesia, moreover, missionaries came from societies which, to them, appeared infinitely more superior than the essential, disease-ridden, warring, survivalist societies they met in Papua New Guinea and the other islands. Many of them tended to be condescending and paternalistic, and often strove more for a replacement of primitive ways by 'civilization' than a grafting on of the essential Christian message to the pre-existing cultures. The role of missionaries in the 'pacification' process has already been mentioned. It is difficult to generalize, and not as easy as some might think to decide whether the early missionaries were right or wrong in their approaches. Yet, one thing stands out as obvious, and it presents a problematic for Melanesia's future — that the indigenous peoples have found it very difficult not to feel inferior before the whites and their new ideas, and have not found it easy to sense the free responsibility of developing Christianity in their own terms, without slavish dependence on white, 'apparently superior', models. One crucial task of Melanesian theology is to conscientize people about their peculiar circumstances, and to assert that now, especially in a post-colonial (for some, post-independence) age, it is free for them to think out their Christian faith in a more decidedly, authentically indigenous manner.

The Biblical tradition

It is sensible to make good use of the Biblical material (as well as pertinent materials from church and mission history in general) to guide theological thinking about a healthier Christian faith in Melanesia. The New Testament, for a start, is the very distillation of the new message of spiritual change. Now, it is important to realize that the early Christian writings were geared to the cultural and indigenous intellectual predispositions of those peoples meant to read them. Paul's epistles are outstanding cases in point; his letters cannot be fully understood unless we learn — both from the letters themselves and other sources — what the beliefs and world-views of the recipients were like. In the life of the modern church such matters are easily forgotten, but we ought to recapture something of the original situations if only to throw critical light on what is currently happening in Melanesia.

When Paul, just to take a few examples, wrote to the Romans about dying and rising in Christ at baptism (Rom. 6:1–11), and to the Colossians about how Christ was the fullness of all things (Col. 2:9 and see Col. 1–2 as a whole), he was speaking the language and using the terminology of the people with whom he was corresponding. The Romans, for instance, were used to the idea of baptism symbolizing rebirth; in the cult of Cybele, increasingly popular in the first century AD, initiates would descend into a pit of ritual death and, after a bull had been slaughtered on a platform above the pit so that its blood spilled over those below, they would rise up out of the depth to 'new life'. The Colossians, for their part, had believed that the whole universe in its fullness (*plēroma*) contained divinities — each planet was a god — and Paul challenges them to think about Jesus or God filling up the universe instead and, thus, to transform their own world-view (rather than obliterating it or devaluing it altogether).[6] A careful reappraisal of Paul's letters (and other New Testament material) reveals how the early Christian theologians set out to graft 'the new vine' on to old well established roots and stumps. The reasons for theological variation in Paul's letters, for different emphases and themes, is that each letter is written to a distinct cultural setting. Paul, as he put it, strove 'to be all things to all humans' (I Cor. 9:22, cf. 10:33),[7] and this stance provides a helpful basis on which to evaluate the work of Christian missions in Melanesia and develop a Christian orientation more responsible to cultural diversity.

Since there are many 'correspondences' between the Christian and what is the (ever-developing) 'traditional', it will always be healthy to permit constructive interaction between the two pressures, so that the members of any one culture can be given the freedom to justify their cultural expressions, and test their strengths and possible validity against the claims of the new message, whether as preached or interpreted from the scriptural text. Only then will come an authentic revalorization of old local traditions into a universal orientation, and the most fruitful incorporation of the Melanesian heritage into the life of the church. There will be mistakes made in the process, and there have already been strange fits and starts, but discussion must be between equals, and integrity granted to both (or various) parties. It is time for more and more Melanesians to state their minds; for those trained in Religious Studies or Theology, it is time to frame theologies which are culturally contextualized to their part of the world (and perhaps to imagine what it would be like if Paul wrote an epistle to the inhabitants of the south-west Pacific). A number of principles to avoid pejorative assessments of pre-contact belief and custom will be of value for a better dialogue. Both Christian and traditionalist will do well to work on the presumption that there were indeed 'noble traditions' in primal Melanesia (as the secular Constitution of Papua New Guinea puts it), and so give a healthy honouring to each individual society's worthier achievements. Theology engenders an appropriate respect for cultural pluralism, moreover, when acknowledging that God was 'never without a witness' on any part of the globe, and provided a 'General Revelation' (Acts 14:17, cf. Rom. 1:20–21, Acts 17), or basic social laws long before Moses (for example, Gen. 9:6), by which all societies could be left open to His stirrings.[8]

Pinpointing theological aims

It should be conceded that no-one can formulate a theology which will be entirely satisfactory for one culture, let alone for the more than a thousand distinct cultures of Melanesia. At this point, it is useful to see how theology can operate on at least two distinct levels in the region — at the local, *tok ples* (or vernacular) level, and at the national and lingua franca level. At the grass-roots, lack of literacy will mean concentration on practical and social as against more intellectual and dogmatic concerns, and the development of a good ear for 'folk Christianity' (or for simplifying, experimental attempts to compre-hend the Christian message).[9] Here, the collection of prior village impressions about the first whites or outsiders will be important, or the local adaptation of folktales, both Western and Melanesian to serve the preaching of the Gospel, and so forth. Here, too, one of the biggest issues to be explored is one already touched upon much earlier, concerning the extent to which veneration of the ancestors can be accepted as compatible with Christian views about the role of the dead (cf. for example, Heb. 12:1).[10]

Work at the national level, in comparison, will naturally take into account political independence, and the need in such new states as Fiji, Papua New Guinea, the Solomon Islands and Vanuatu for sets of values and ideals to cement nationhood. This will for long remain a virtually mandatory task, considering the rapidity with which independence has been gained in a country like Papua New Guinea after centuries of separated (and so-called 'stateless') societies. In those situations in which independence has not been secured (in French-dominated New Caledonia, and under the neo-colonial Indonesian rule in Irian Jaya), theology can provide the inspiration for nationalism, or for the accommodation of difference and the spirit of coopera-tion where ethnic divisiveness is pronounced (as also on Fiji).[11] In all Melanesian countries, moreover, when theology is carried out beyond the village context, it is forced to wrestle with social change, especially urbani-zation, the growing inequality between rich and poor, between powerful and powerless, and the social destructiveness arising from corruption, ethnic favouritism, gang mentality and the breakdown of *communitas*.[12]

Remember, of course, that theologies aimed at national (and typically elite and literate) audiences, will be in competition with other introduced world-views. In a 1976 symposium on the uses of the university, for example, Michael Somare, the then prime minister of Papua New Guinea claimed that he was looking to the intellectuals of the country for useful criticism and for national ideologies.[13] Apart from whether Mr Somare was looking for the right kind of ideology, or not, one should not fail to notice how intellectuals (too many of them expatriates) have been trying to make up the Melanesians' minds for them on general questions of national development and values.

Some of these intellectuals are far from being advocates for Melanesian theology. Not long ago, an expatriate, posing under the Melanesian pseudonym of Peter Kros, published a diatribe against Christianity in Papua New Guinea as 'a certain foreign cult', admittedly with a minimum of 'homework' into these matters and a maximum of glib generalization.[14] Yet it is publications like these which could well give certain potential leaders of independent spirit the kind of counter-ideology they need to build up an urban-oriented state which could pay little heed to the most influential grass-roots institutions in this country, namely the churches. And those less sensitive 'Marxist' thinkers at the universities who teach that the churches of Melanesia represent vestiges of colonialism, as I've suggested before, do so without having pursued careful studies of the multiformity of the Melanesian scene, and without conceding that their own dream of a world with no need of religion at all might also be deemed colonial. And then there are those protagonists, one might even say 'missionaries', for education, who treat school and university learning as Salvation, preferring it to be separate from religion.

Melanesian theologians are surely called to respond to such alternatives, then, to the challenge of competing ideologies as well as confront the problems of fragmentation, 'unequal development' and disunity throughout the region. Already thinkers such as Fathers John Momis and Walter Lini, Alexis Sarei, Bernard Narokobi, Utula Samana, and a sprinkling of other Christian thinkers who approached Melanesian problems with the prophetic concern for social justice, were beating drums in the 1970s.[15] More such people are steadily emerging, and their nations and churches are advised to facilitate their contributions.[16]

Fifth, we should note that, even before Melanesians who were well educated in religious matters had put pen to paper or delivered their sermons, there were many Melanesians propounding their own versions of the Christian message, their own syncretisms or re-expressions of tradition. While it is easy for some to pour scorn on the theologies of Yali or Beig Wen, Paliau or Eto, and to say 'they got it wrong', there is much to learn from their explorations, their daring attempts to Melanesianize Christianity or propose a counter-religion. In the earliest days of the church there were similar efforts — and we still have documents left over from Docetic and Gnostic Christians, whose so-called syncretisms came to be rejected by the orthodox. These reflectors' efforts were finally not acceptable, but certain strains of their thinking have informed the New Testament and the formation of Christian doctrine — early as they were in their expressions — and have, thus, added to the richness of Christianity's foundation period. Similarly, Melanesian theologians would do well to ponder on what is useful and vital in cargo cult and separatist theologies, as well as in traditional belief-patterns, in order to build a Melanesian theology on principles which relate to the hopes and fears, conceptual frames and behaviour patterns of Melanesians.[17] Cargo cults, as was observed before, are usually about the Melanesian struggle for self-identity and for equality with the whites; a Melanesian theology worth its salt must strive to fulfil the same needs even more constructively.

Lastly, since we have come to the matter, a primary occupation for Melanesian theologians is to establish what actually are the main hopes and fears, conceptual frames and behaviour patterns of Melanesians, both in particular settings and more generally. They join with social scientists or analysts in the task of understanding cultures, beliefs and social relations, yet with the additional business of constructively relating Christian faith and praxis to social morphologies, consolidating a society's strengths and healing its ills. That is no easy job in so complex a place. Even Melanesian intellectuals generally get bogged down with their own culture, as if it is *the* Melanesian culture or the only one worth considering, and they balk at saying anything about a *range* of other Melanesian cultures, with effective use of available ethnographic knowledge. The region badly needs minds that stretch beyond such 'ethnocentricity' and combine learning about both Melanesian religious variation and the Christian faith, with a wisdom to interrelate the two in a way which does justice to Christian and traditional beliefs, to leave men and women less confused, more able to secure human dignity in the exercise of responsible choices.

Pacific theology: finding the common ground

Can the theological agenda be widened to include other indigenous Christians of the Pacific? Are there other issues to be adumbrated which incorporate a wider range of social developments surrounding the Melanesian region? At this point one naturally stops to acknowledge that the Melanesians are not the only black peoples in the south-west Pacific. In connection with these questions, then, it is appropriate to begin by reflecting on 'black theology', especially considering the recent publication of *The Gospel is Not Western*, a book in which Australian Aboriginal, Torres Strait and various Melanesian thinkers reflect together for the first time on the relationship between Christianity and their cultures.[18] The interchange between these people, as one might expect, did not produce a perfect consensus — regional differences made for divergent emphases. Yet, the very experience of dialogue exposed a host of common concerns and the crying need to pool theological insights in Australasia and beyond.

Admittedly, even the premises of the black theologies seem incompatible at first glance. The Aboriginal contributors chose to make no hard-and-fast line between their tradition and the Christian outlook — as if Christianity was eternally integral to their Dreamtime. That makes psychological, let alone polemical sense, when the enormous encroachment of White Australia is taken into consideration.[19] Most of the Melanesians, by comparison, at least the members of independent black nations, operated much more readily and cerebrally with Western theological categories (although they had some difficulty relating introduced modes of thought and action to tradition), and some had no compunction about emphasizing the gulf between the worst of pre-Christian life (with sorcery and headhunting) and the best under the new order of the churches.

At the conference from which *The Gospel is Not Western* arose, however, some of these same Melanesians sensed very keenly how important it was that the Aboriginal participants stood closer to their age-old traditions (which appeared very resilient) and explored the relationship between pre-contact ways and the introduced patterns at a deeply spiritual and not so much intellectual level. The Melanesians thus came to see the need to dig deeper into seams of wisdom which had often been set aside, and to avoid estimating ancestral cultures as inferior beside the achievements of the whites.

But there is no reason to stop short at black theology, and less of a reason in this part of the world to labour any point about *'négritude'*.[20] Since there have been historic links between diverse Pacific territories (through traditional trade, for instance, as between Fiji and Samoa, or through Polynesian missionary contributions in Papua New Guinea), let alone many contemporary interconnections (with the South Pacific Development Fund, the University of the South Pacific, the migration of central Pacific islanders to Australia, New Zealand and Hawaii, and the like), it makes sense to attempt Pacific-wide theologies. The presence of strong Christian communities scattered through all Oceania, most of whom are experiencing basic shifts toward moneyed, consumer-oriented economies, even urbanization, actually makes it imperative to share mutually supporting insights and programmes. Since 1961, in fact, colloquia sponsored by the Pacific Council of Churches have been designed to do just that.[21]

But can a Pacific theology work? Are there not too many geographical, socio-economic, cultural and attitudinal complications to handle? There appear to be such great gaps between (let us say) the suburbanites of Honolulu and the hamlet-dwellers who work their confined sweet-potato patches in the landlocked valleys of the New Guinea highlands; or between *kanaks* who want to secure autonomy from the French, and Tongans who have long since achieved independence (1970) yet are ruled by a monarch! What have villagers on Micronesian coral atolls, who even become fearful when they visit land masses which go on and on, to do with inhabitants of an enormous continent, some of whose indigenous peoples used to go walkabout over trackless wastes often never seeing the sea? At first sight here, there seem so many obstacles to effective cross-cultural theological endeavour.

On the other hand, the pressures to uncover common ground, the yearning for ties of common consciousness and spirituality, have already been felt. The very reality of a shared humanity, as well as the uncanny property of the Christian message to cross seemingly impenetrable barriers and to unify estranged peoples, makes for renewed confidence in the effort; and, if they are prepared for differences from the start, theologies can be framed to account for contextual variations.

Some of the 'whiteman's burdens' have already been identified in this book: the weight of ecclesiastical structures, liturgical forms and theological moulds implanted by missionaries or representatives of the Old World over the last two centuries — all this is still being felt right across the Pacific. A typical danger that exists is that what has been introduced becomes hallowed by the past or (as far as indigenous peoples are concerned) untouchable as the rituals and tabus brought by the 'superior, all-knowledgeable' whites. Ideally, theologians will do well to cultivate a wider Pacific perspective. Working at the interface between two or more cultures, interpreting the constraints and freedoms of the Christian tradition with a sound knowledge of the colourful variances within Christendom, possessing some grasp of anthropological issues, and educating people for a broader range of choices than they first thought they possessed, all are roles to be welcomed across the whole island world of the Pacific, as well as among black Australians. Those with traditional backgrounds, who have been taught their old ways were 'Satanic', for instance, might relearn from such work the values of the pre-contact past within a more flexible framework. Already there have been creative attempts to portray Jesus as the Great Ancestor of a new dispensation (John Strelan, for the Melanesians), or Aboriginal rites as analogous to sacraments or church worship (following Martin Wilson and David Thompson).[22] Despite conservatism in these matters, modes of church iconography, liturgy and celebration have nonetheless undergone impressive changes throughout the Pacific since the Second World War.[23]

It is a priority for the indigenous and contextualizing theologians to counteract the deadening forces of diehard paternalism and develop those lines of thought and action which root Christianity much more deeply in the socio-spiritual soil of the different regions. Only a species of social ill-health results if Christianity is left as a veneer, a magical sugar-coating which does little to transform everyday lives, or which only gives vague hope and no room for initiative to the average member of the *populus fidelium* (or congregation of the faithful). One suspects the charismatic and Holy Spirit movements of the Pacific, which have attracted not just white Australians and New Zealanders but urban Aborigines and many groups in Melanesia as well, are symptomatic of the churches' prior failure to have touched the depths, to reach beyond the personal ego to the spiritual being, as Thomas Merton would have put it.[24] The movement of the Spirit, however, should not be left as sufficient unto itself, psychologically satisfying; it should be carried through — with the help of theologians — in works of justice and love, the conveying of sound knowledge, and in providing a balance between intellectualism and enthusiasm.

Furthermore, whereas some Pacific societies undergoing rather turbulent change would welcome theological signposts to cope and pass into a new era (one thinks especially of Papua New Guinea), others, substantially Christianized, betray an unfortunate complacency which requires a strong prophetic stance from theology (as in the Samoas, Tonga, and even in recently jolted Fiji). Wherever people are found to have lost sight of the Gospel's challenge or to rate among the 'world's spoilt brats', as the *Maui News* (Hawaii) aptly describes the [white] Australians, the role of prophetic theology is to invoke a 'returning' to a fulfilment of the divine Demand; it is to proclaim that, without the shake-up of justice, there come ruptures and stupor of a sick society — as an unassailable retribution.

On mentioning retribution it appears fitting to approach the closure of this work by contemplating two themes which have made Melanesia (as part of the Pacific) so important for the world as a whole — expectations about Cargo (and money), and so-called payback. These must surely be placed high on the theological agenda, and for the Pacific in general as much as for Melanesia in particular. Money and the consumer items it has brought in this century constitute a central problem for Pacific societies and for any contextual theology to address. Significantly, the Pacific is ringed by power-houses of international consumerism: reflection on the roles of Tokyo, Seoul, Hong Kong, Taiwan, Singapore, Sydney and Los Angeles in the world economy will quickly convince one so. Thus, there is the usual ever-present danger that Money will settle or emerge as the new God because it is so much more effective, so much more capable of getting tangible, material things done over vast oceanic distances, than the old God (who seems sometimes to have just thundered on Sinai and performed a number of miracles in Galilee).

Theology has to deal with money, then, and not just with it as mere dross dragging down humans to superficiality and crass materialism (which is, admittedly, the appropriate paradigm for most Australians, let us say, or for most inhabitants of once phosphate-rich Nauru, which has the highest per capita income of any nation in the Pacific). Theology must also attempt to account for the remarkable theophanic properties of both the modern money system and the new wealth in the consciousness of Pacific peoples. Melanesian cargo cults, in which the new items of European riches are expected to arrive miraculously, often with the returning Ancestors or with Jesus' Second Coming, teach us much about how Cargo and money can come to symbolize a total salvation. Cargoism, the thinking which incorporates the dream of modern wealth into religion, is highly prevalent in the Pacific. It drives Tongans from their peaceful islands to touristized Hawaii; rural highlanders to bustling Lae and Port Moresby; it expresses itself in the alliances between Western churches and Western business life in countless different forms; it can have devastating consequences for environments and fragile ecological systems. In confronting these issues, a traditional function of theology has been to discriminate between the true and false divinity.[25]

Finally, but not least, violence is a fundamental problem to be faced by theologians. 'Pacific' may mean 'peaceful', but the ocean has never been without its storms, and bigger ones are brewing. There is a broad spectrum of conflict-theatres: sporadic tribal warfare persisting in the New Guinea highlands (for instance at Porgera, where, were it not for inter-tribal conflict, one might have anticipated a gold rush); violent sabotage on Bougainville; a double coup in Fiji; attempts at armed anti-colonial resistance in French and Indonesian Melanesia; on top of these, bad omens of a nuclear showdown, with France's nuclear bomb tests at Mururoa Atoll and the United States' use of Micronesia, Hawaii and other outposts as points of strategy in a frightening game with the Soviet Union. No Pacific theology will retain credibility if it fails to provide constructive yet non-violent solutions to zones of tension. Pacific theology should work for peace, never forgetting, however, the many faces of payback nor using peace as a way of diverting the oppressed from achieving the victory they deserve over colonization and exploitation. The best payback, surely, is to be found in reciprocity, not reprisal. Pacific societies possess many forms of mutual aid, provided by extended families and kin connections, let alone church and state welfare programmes. Theologians will be constantly pressed to seek out the worthiest institutions in this extraordinary trans-cultural, international mix, and build bridges of communication and caring support, as expressions of the Gospel of love.

While raising all these issues, of course, there can be no question of policing the theological styles chosen to handle them. These styles will, we can assume, continue to appear in their diversity — whether evangelical or liberal, formalist or charismatic, politically conservative or liberationist, quietist or millenarian, and, for that matter, systematic or more story- and issue-oriented (as found in Melanesian theologies thus far). And we can hardly dictate here how theology will be used. Some, like Anthony Trollope's devious Mr Slope, will manipulate it to enhance personal power,[26] and in the sociology of knowledge academic ambition will always be a factor to consider. The perennial debate will also go on between those appealing to theology to secure social stability and those deploying it as a subversive tool against morally bankrupt regimes. We can only affirm in closing that, when prescriptions are imposed on theology, whether by governments or churches, religious freedom will surely be threatened. By the same token, however, the guidelines for an agenda outlined above remind one that the religious freedom of those belonging to smaller, vulnerable indigenous traditions has to be respected as well, and that theological endeavour will court the charge of irresponsibility (and accompanying political censure) if it is not related to context and fails to address the central issues of the day in context.

Moreover, theology that does not allow itself to be judged by such criteria as truth, integrity, justice and unconquerable goodwill, as reflected in the foundation documents of the Christian tradition, will always be susceptible to the charge of insensitivity and dogmatism. While preparing to embrace their futures in the next millennium, all the countries of the vast Pacific region have much to teach, and learn from, each other to ensure their psychic and social health. Unexpectedly for those in more secularist quarters and mindsets, theology will go much further than it has already in providing a significant forum of understanding and inter-group cooperation in this process. In laying a groundwork for the better framing of ideals and policies, too, the critical study of religion, which has governed most of the pages of this book, will not be without its useful part to play.

NOTES

The first part of chapter 11 is based on material originally contributed to University of Papua New Guinea Extension Studies booklets and the second part, on material originally published as an article in the journal *Mission Review*.

1 Needs at the various universities differ. At UPNG exploring the relationship between traditions and Christian denominations has been fundamental (though sadly neglected in courses since 1987). At the University of the South Pacific (USP) members of other world faiths, from among the Indian population, present an element of diversity not experienced at UPNG. At Cendrawasih University in Jayapura, Irian Jaya, there is roughly equal pressure to propagate the Christian and Islamic orders, and unfortunately less concern to understand traditional world-views.

2 Most big seminaries in Papua New Guinea also provide historically-oriented courses, but they are interlocked with theology courses suitable for training in the ministry.

3 Trompf, *The condition of Religious Studies at the University of Papua New Guinea* (UPNG Report), Port Moresby, 1985, pp.1ff.

4 cf. R. W. Hepburn, *Christianity and paradox*, London, 1964.

5 For the background to this distinction in Enlightenment theology and history, esp. P. Riley, *The general will before Rousseau* (Studies in moral, political and legal philosophy), Princeton, 1986.

6 For background, e.g., J. Ferguson, *The religions of the Roman empire*, London, 1970, pp.29–31 (on the *taurobilium* in the Cybele cult); C. F. D. Moule, *The Epistles of Paul the Apostle to the Colossians and to Philemon*, Cambridge, 1957, introd. (Colossians).

7 See esp. H. Chadwick, 'All Things to All Men', in *New Testament studies* I (1955), pp.261ff.

8 For background from various theological viewpoints on general revelation, esp. *Seminar in missionary theology*, Bangalore, 1975; B. Demarist, *General revelation; historical views and contemporary issues*, Grand Rapids, 1982. On older views on the seven divine precepts to the world's nations via Noah, see J. Spencer, *De legibus Hebraeorum*, London, 1685, vol.1, pp.594ff., and for Isaac Newton's unpublished views on this subject, Trompf, 'Newtonian history', in *The uses of Antiquity in the Scientific Revolution* (ed. S. Gaukroger) (Australasian Studies in the history and philosophy of science ser.), Dordrecht (forthcoming).

9 cf., e.g., T. Ahrens and W. Hollenweger *Volks-Christentum und Volksreligion im Pazifik; Wiederentdeckung des Mythos für den christlichen Glauben* (Perspektiven der Weltmission 4), Frankfurt, 1977.

10 See, e.g., Trompf, J. Gough and E. Otto, 'Western folktales in changing Melanesia', *Folklore*, 99/2 (1988), pp.204ff. (on folktale adaptations), and H. Janssen, 'Dilemma over the departed', *Catalyst*, 4/4 1974, pp.3ff; cf. L. Luzbetak, *The Church and cultures*, pp.249ff. (on veneration of the dead).

11 See esp. Trompf (ed.), *The Gospel is not Western*, pt V, chs 16–20; cf. also pt IV, ch. 15.

12 Thus ibid., ch. 16; cf. J. P. Chao, *Life in a squatter settlement: an Epistle to the Christians of PNG*, Goroka, 1986.

13 At the Seminar on the 10th Anniversary of the University of Papua New Guinea, August 1976; cf. the 1977 *Yagl-Ambu* 3/3 (1976), esp. pp.145ff. (Gris), 188ff (Momis).

14 P. Kros, '*A certain foreign cult called Christianity.' Do we need it?* For a solid criticism, see esp. I. Stuart 'Christianity — Do we need it?', in *PNG Post-Courier*, 21 Feb., 1975, p.25.

15 Note J. Momis, 'Values for involvement', *Catalyst* 5/3 (1975), pp.1ff; cf. P. Murphy, 'Momis' theology of politics interpreted', *Catalyst* 5/3 (1975), pp.19ff; W. Lini, *Beyond pandaemonium*, Wellington, 1980 (partly bringing together Lini's pieces from the 1970s); A. M. Sarei, *Traditional marriage and the impact of Christianity on the Solos of Buka Island*, (New Guinea research bulletin 57), Port Moresby, 1974, esp. see p.57; B. Narokobi, *Foundations for nationhood*, Port Moresby, 1975; U. Samana, 'Considering alternative directions for the Evangelical Lutheran Church of Papua New Guinea', in M. O'Collins (ed.), *Introduction to social welfare*, bk 3, pp.38ff. For general background, Trompf, 'Competing value orientations in Papua New Guinea', in *Ethics and Development* (ed. G. Fugmann) (Point ser. 9), Goroka, 1986, pp.17ff. (also in German as 'Konkurrierende Wertevorstellungen' in H. Wagner et al., *Papua-Neuguinea: Gesellschaft und Kirche* (Erlanger Taschenbücher 93), Erlangen, 1989, pp.314ff.

16 I think especially of Melanesian writers' contributions to the Melanesian Institute's *Catalyst, Point series* and *Melanesian journal of theology*, to J. D'A. May (ed.), *Living theology in Melanesia: a reader* (Point ser. 8), Goroka, 1985, and my edited collection *The Gospel is not Western*.

17 As in Strelan's *Search for salvation*, and by the Sepik writer Narokobi, 'Who will take up Peli's Challenge?' (cf. ch. 9, n.67). cf. also Trompf, 'Missiology, methodology and the study of new religious movements', pp.102–103.

18 Funding for the conference behind *The Gospel is not Western* was provided by the Australian Board of Missions (Anglican), publication by the Maryknoll Fathers and Brothers, New York State (Catholic), and contributions by black writers from a whole range of denominations.

19 ibid., esp. chs 9–10 (Guboo Ted Thomas, Mick Fazeldean). cf. also H. Petri and G. Petri-Odermann, 'Stability and change', in R. Berndt (ed.), *Australian Aboriginal anthropology*, Perth, 1970, p.258 and various pieces in T. Swain and D. B. Rose (eds), *Aboriginal Australians and Christian missions*, Adelaide, 1988.

20 As in F. Fanon's *The wretched of the Earth*, New York, 1968 (North Africa).

21 See esp. J. Kadiba, 'In search of a Melanesian theology', in Trompf (ed.), *Gospel not Western*, pp.139–41 (s.v. 'Pacific Theology'); cf. also [World Vision], *South Pacific Theology: Papers from the consultation on Pacific Theology, Papua New Guinea, January 1986*, Oxford, 1987.

22 Strelan, *Search for salvation*, esp. chs 3–4; Wilson, esp. *New, old and timeless* (Nelen Yubu missiological ser. 1), Canberra, 1979; Thompson, *'Bora is like church'*, Sydney, 1985.

23 cf., e.g., T. Aerts, 'Christian art in Melanesia', *Bikmaus*, 5/1 (1984), pp.47ff.

24 cf. esp. *The seven storey mountain*, New York, 1948.

25 See Trompf, 'God as the source of wealth', *Melanesian journal of theology*, 3/1 (1987), pp.74ff; cf. S. McDonagh, *To Care for the Earth*, Quezon City, 1986.

26 *Barchester towers*, London, 1857, ch. 4.

SELECT
BIBLIOGRAPHY

Traditional religions

ALLEN, M. *Male Cults and Secret Initiations*. Melbourne, Melbourne University Press, 1967.

HABEL, N. C. (ed.). *Powers, Plumes and Piglets: phenomena of Melanesian religion*. Adelaide, Australian Association for the Study of Religions, 1979.

JACHMANN, F. *Seelen- und Totenvorstellungen bei drei Bevölkerungsgruppen in Neuguinea* (Arbeiten aus dem Seminar für Völkerkunde der J. W. Goethe-Universität Frankfurt am Main 1). Wiesbaden, Franz Steiner, 1969.

LAWRENCE, P. and MEGGITT, M. J. (eds). *Gods, Ghosts and Men in Melanesia*. Melbourne, Oxford University Press, 1965.

McELHANON, K. A. (ed.). *Legends from Papua New Guinea*. Ukarumpa, Summer Institute of Linguistics, 1974.

NEVERMANN, H., WORMS, E. A. and PETRI, H. *Die Religionen der Südsee und Australiens* (Die Religionen der Menschheit 5[2]). Stuttgart, Kohlhammer, 1968.

PARRATT, J. *Papuan Belief and Ritual*. New York and Washington, Vantage, 1976.

SCHMITZ, C. A. *Oceanic Art: myth, men and image in the South Seas*. New York, Abrams [1969].

STEPHEN, M. (ed.). *Sorcerer and Witch in Melanesia*. Melbourne, Melbourne University Press, 1987.

TROMPF, G. W. (ed.). *Prophets of Melanesia: six essays*. Port Moresby and Suva, Institute of Papua New Guinea Studies and Institute of Pacific Studies, 1986 edn.

New religious movements

CHRISTIANSEN, P. *The Melanesian Cargo Cult: millenarianism as a factor in cultural change*. Copenhagen, Akademisk Forlag, 1969.

FLANNERY, W. (ed.). *Religious Movements in Melanesia Today 1–3* (Point Series 2–4). Goroka, Melanesian Institute, 1983–84 (3 vols).

GESCH, P. *Initiative and Initiation: a cargo-type movement in the Sepik against its background in traditional village religion* (Studia Instituti Anthropos 33). St Augustin, Anthropos Institute, 1985.

KILANI, M. *Les cultes du cargo mélanesians: mythe et rationalité en anthropologie*. Lausanne, Den Bas, 1983.

LAWRENCE, P. *Road belong Cargo: a study of the Cargo Movement in the Southern Madang District, New Guinea*. Manchester, Manchester University Press, 1964.

LOELIGER, C. E. L. and TROMPF, G. W. (eds). *New Religious Movements in Melanesia*. Port Moresby and Suva, University of Papua New Guinea Press and Institute of Pacific Studies, 1985.

STEINBAUER, F. *Melanesian Cargo Cults* (trans. M. Wohlwill). Brisbane, University of Queensland Press, 1979.

STRELAN, J. G. *Search for Salvation: studies in the history and theology of cargo cults.* Adelaide, Lutheran Publishing House, 1977.

WILLIAMS, F. E. *'The Vailala Madness' and Other Essays* (edited by E. Schwimmer). Brisbane, University of Queensland Press, 1976.

WORSLEY, P. *The Trumpet Shall Sound: a study of 'cargo' cults in Melanesia.* London, Paladin, 1970 edn.

Mission history

BOUTILIER, J. A., HUGHES, D. T. and TIFFANY, S. (eds). *Mission, Church and Sect in Oceania* (Association for Social Anthropology in Oceania Monograph 36). Ann Arbor, University of Michigan Press, 1978.

DELBOS, G. *The Mustard Seed: from a French Mission to a Papuan Church* (trans. T. Aerts). Port Moresby, Institute of Papua New Guinea Studies, 1985.

GARRETT, J. *To Live Among the Stars: Christian origins in Oceania.* Geneva and Suva, World Council of Churches and Institute of the South Pacific, 1982.

GUNSON, W. N. *Messengers of Grace: Evangelical missionaries in the South Seas 1797–1860.* Melbourne, Oxford University Press, 1978.

HILLIARD, D. *God's Gentleman: a history of the Melanesian Mission 1849–1942.* Brisbane, University of Queensland Press, 1978.

JASPERS, R. *Die missionarische Erschliessung Ozeaniens* (Missions-Wissengeschaftliche Abhandlungen und Texte 30). Münster, Aschendorff, 1972.

KAMMA, F. *'Dit wonderlijke Werk'. Het problem van der communicatie tussen oost en west gebasserd op de ervaringen in het zendingswerk op Nieuw-Guinea (Irian Jaya) 1855–1972: een socio-missiologische benadering.* Oegstgeest, Raad voor Zendin der Nederlandse Hervormde Kerk, 1977 (2 vols).

LANGMORE, D. *Missionary Lives: Papua 1874–1914* (Pacific Islands Monograph Series 6). Honolulu, University of Hawaii Press, 1989.

PILHOFER, D. G. *Die Geschichte der Neuendettelsau, Mission in Neuguinea.* Neuendettelsau, Freimund, 1961–63 (2 vols).

WETHERELL, D. *Reluctant Mission: the Anglican Church in Papua New Guinea 1891–1942.* Brisbane, University of Queensland Press, 1977.

Neo-tradition, indigenous Christianity and black theology

AHRENS, T. and HOLLENWEGER, W. *Volks-Christentum und Volksreligion im Pazifik: Wiederentdeckung des Mythos für den christlichen Glauben* (Perspektiven der Weltmission 4). Frankfurt am Main, Lambeck, 1977.

BARKER, J. (ed.). *Christianity in Oceania: ethnographic perspectives* (Association for Social Anthropology in Oceania Monograph N.S.12). Lanham, University Press of America, 1990.

FORMAN, C. W. *The Island Churches of the South Pacific: emergence in the twentieth century.* Maryknoll, N.Y., Orbis, 1982.

MAY, R. (ed.). *Micronationalist Movements in Papua New Guinea* (Political and Social Change Monographs 1). Canberra, Australian National University, 1982.

NAROKOBI, B. *The Melanesian Way.* Port Moresby, Institute of Papua New Guinea Studies, 1983 edn.

SIWATIBAU, S. and WILLIAMS, D. B. *A Call to a New Exodus: an anti-nuclear primer for Pacific people.* Suva, Pacific Conference of Churches, 1982.

STRATHERN, A. *A Line of Power.* London and New York, Tavistock, 1984.

TOMASETTI, F. *Traditionen und Christentum im Chimbu-Gebiet Neuguineas: Beo-bachtungen in der 'utheranischen Gemeinde Pare* (Arbeiten aus dem Seminar für Völkerkunde der J. W. Goethe-Universität Frankfurt am Main 6). Wiesbaden, Franz Steiner, 1976.

TROMPF, G. W. (ed.). *The Gospel is Not Western: black theologies from the Southwest Pacific*. Maryknoll, N.Y., Orbis, 1987.

[WORLD VISION] (edited collection). *South Pacific Theology: Papers from the consultation on Pacific Theology, Papua New Guinea, January 1986*. Oxford, World Vision, 1987.

INDEX

Abel, C. W., 155, 219–21
Abel, M. K., 161, 219–20, 231
Abel, R. W., 219–20, 231
Abelam, 33
Aborigines, Australian, 9, 64, 98–9, 267–9
accident, notions of, 67–8, 122–3
Admiralty Islands, *see* Manus
Africa: regions of, 20, 148, 213; religions in, 79, 99, 102, 205, 216, 222, 234, 245, 250, 262
after-life: notions of, 17, 34–50, 53–4, 71–3, 125, 219; reincarnation, 46; *see also* resurrection
agnosticism, 8–9
Aitape, 179
Aitsi, L., 135
Alexishafen, 168, 175, 182
Allen, B. L., 49 n.24
Allen, M., 227
Alotau, 220
altered states of consciousness, 102–32; *see also* glossolalia; prophets; shamanism; spirit movements
Ambonese 142–3
America: regions of, 144, 202; religions in, 148, 164, 175, 216, 229–30, 239
amok, 132, 136
ancestors, 9, 13–16, 30, 36, 39, 43–9, 53–5, 57, 64–5, 68–70, 84, 108–9, 117, 119–20, 194–5, 199–200, 209–10, 219, 225, 231, 248, 270; as ghosts, 14–16, 39, 41, 43–4, 125, 127, 146, 210; return of, 46–8, 194–6, 199, 202; *see also* spirits
Andreski, S., 190
Anglican missions, 129, 143, 145, 153–4, 160, 175, 227, 273
Angoram, 27, 33
apotropaism, 15, 81

Arapesh groups, 27, 33
architecture: Christian, 269; traditional, 22, 26–8
Arkfeld, L., 183
Aroma, *see* Hula-Aroma-Velerupu
art: Christian, 232, 269; neo-traditional, 253, 259; traditional, 26–8, 33
Asaro-Gururumba, 63, 72, 76, 199–200
Asmat, 27, 33
Assemblies of God, *see* Pentecostalism
atheism, 257
Atzera, 21, 65
Augustine, Saint, 258 n.48
Avatip, 31 n.24

Baal, van J., 23, 31, 73, 209
Bahaism, 260
Baigona cults, 111–12
Baining-Sulka, 11, 100, 132, 136, 178
Baitel, J., 59
Baktaman, 23, 32, 55, 59, 85, 87, 101
Bali Vitu, *see* Unea
Baluan Island, 196, 222–3
Bani, A., 227
Banks Islands, 13, 31
Bantu, 213
baptism, Christian, 169–70, 215, 220
Baptists, 157, 190
Barr, J., 132
Barth, F., 59, 61, 85
Baruya, 32
Bastide, R., 107
Begesin, 109, 112, 122–3
Bena Bena, 46, 52–5, 57, 63, 68, 70, 76, 93, 124, 127, 208–10
Benedict XV, Pope, 168
Berndt, R. M., 31 n.28, 128
Biak Island, 17, 31, 42, 124, 127, 142, 203, 207
Binandere, *see under* Orokaiva
'blackbirding', 12
blame, *see* retribution

body: adornment of, 27–8, 33, 43, 60; and life-cycle, 34–41, 199; notions of, 23, 60, 94, 106–8; *see also* ordeals; retribution, as punishment
Boell, A., 181
Bogia, 176, 191
Bohn, A., 152, 171
Boismenu, A. de, 166–7, 169, 171–2, 175, 179
Bonarua (Brumer) Islands, 7–9
Bougainville Island, 163, 165, 169, 175, 178, 184, 216–17, 228–9; and rebellion 233, 271; and secessionism, 184, 217
Brazil, 107
Brennan, P., 94
Brethren missions, 157
Brown, G., 143
Brown, H., 154
Brown, N. O., 12
Brunton, R., 191
Buddhism, 100
Buka Island, 176, 184, 197, 204, 216–19; *see also* Halia, Solos
bull-roarer, 28
Bulmer, R. N. H., 12
Buluk, chief, 226
Buna, 60
Bundi, 154
Burridge, K., 191, 207 n.19

cannibalism, 23, 41, 55, 150, 188
cargo cultism, 46–7, 62, 67, 74, 111–12, 125–6, 128–30, 132, 155–6, 161, 176, 189–205, 208–9, 217, 219, 223, 227, 229–31, 233, 266–70
Carmelites, 175
Catholicism, 81–2, 126, 141–54, 156, 163–84, 217–18, 223, 227, 228–230
ceremonies: cargo cultist, 189, 195–7, 208–9, 217; Christian, 165, 224,

DATE DUE
